British Diplomacy and US Hegemony in Cuba,
1898–1964

British Diplomacy and US Hegemony in Cuba, 1898–1964

Christopher Hull

Lecturer, Department of Spanish, Portuguese and Latin American Studies, University of Nottingham

First published 2013 by
PALGRAVE MACMILLAN

Palgrave Macmillan in the UK is an imprint of Macmillan Publishers Limited, registered in England, company number 785998, of Houndmills, Basingstoke, Hampshire RG21 6XS.

Palgrave Macmillan in the US is a division of St Martin's Press LLC, 175 Fifth Avenue, New York, NY 10010.

Palgrave Macmillan is the global academic imprint of the above companies and has companies and representatives throughout the world.

Palgrave® and Macmillan® are registered trademarks in the United States, the United Kingdom, Europe and other countries.

ISBN 978–0–230–29544–5

This book is printed on paper suitable for recycling and made from fully managed and sustained forest sources. Logging, pulping and manufacturing processes are expected to conform to the environmental regulations of the country of origin.

A catalogue record for this book is available from the British Library.

A catalog record for this book is available from the Library of Congress.

10   9   8   7   6   5   4   3   2   1
22   21   20   19   18   17   16   15   14   13

Printed and bound in Great Britain by
CPI Antony Rowe, Chippenham and Eastbourne

Contents

List of Tables and Illustration

Tables

Illustration

Acknowledgements

A bursary from the School of Cultures, Languages and Area Studies at the University of Nottingham enabled me to undertake the research on which this book is based. I am also grateful to the Society of Latin American Studies (UK) for funding a six-week research trip to Cuba. Membership of the Centre for Research on Cuba at Nottingham provided me with various opportunities to disseminate my work and receive the feedback and support of others working in the field of Cuban studies.

The expert guidance and encouragement I received from Antoni Kapcia in the Department of Spanish, Portuguese and Latin American Studies at the University of Nottingham helped me greatly in completing this book. I am also grateful to John W. Young and Gareth Stockey at Nottingham for their valuable advice and to the late Jerry Hagelberg for reading Chapter 5 and giving me his expert feedback on the Cuban sugar industry and economy. I remain most thankful for the valuable research guidance I received in Cuba from Jorge Ibarra Guitart, Francisca López Civeira and Sonia Enjamio.

Without the generous hospitality of family and friends in London I would not have been able to carry out research for extended periods at the National Archives in Kew Gardens. I therefore owe thanks to my brother Robert and his partner Jane, Anthony and Anjli Carlucci, and Iona Keen.

I gratefully acknowledge two publishers for allowing me to reproduce extracts from the following articles: Taylor & Francis – 'Our Arms in Havana: British Military Sales to Batista and Castro, 1958–59', *Diplomacy & Statecraft*, 18.3 (2007), and 'Parallel Spheres: Anglo–American Cooperation over Cuba, 1959–61', *Cold War History*, 12.1 (2012); John Wiley and Sons – ' "Going to War in Buses": The Anglo–American Clash over Leyland Sales to Cuba, 1963–64', *Diplomatic History*, 34.5 (2010).

I am grateful to René de la Nuez for his kind permission to reproduce his political cartoon 'El León y Androcles' from October 1962. I thank both the Trustees of the Harold Macmillan Book Trust for their kind permission to quote from the prime minister's diaries, and the Selwyn Lloyd

Trustees for their kind permission to quote from the Foreign Secretary's diaries. I also thank David Higham literary agents for their kind permission to cite from Graham Greene's screenplay for *Our Man in Havana* (Columbia Pictures, 1959), based on his novel of the same title.

My last words of gratitude go to my late father Oswald Hull. His life-long interest in history and research evidently rubbed off on me, and I dedicate this book to his memory.

List of Abbreviations

BT	Board of Trade
CAB	Cabinet Office
CoCom	Coordinating Committee on Export Controls
CO	Colonial Office
ECGD	Export Credits Guarantee Department
EEC	European Economic Community
FO	Foreign Office
HMG	Her/His Majesty's Government
m-fn	Most-favoured nation
PRO	Public Record Office
RAF	Royal Air Force
SIS	Secret Intelligence Service
T	Treasury
TNA	The National Archives of the UK

Introduction

In February 1898, a mysterious explosion in Havana's harbour killed 266 sailors on board the USS *Maine*, a battleship undertaking a peaceful mission to Cuba. In the United States much newspaper and public opinion held Spain responsible for the large loss of life. Three years after the start of a second war of independence between Cuba and Spain, the alleged act of treachery contributed to Washington's decision to intervene militarily in the island. Within weeks both the conflict and Spanish colonial rule in Cuba were over.

In late October 1964, an inbound Japanese boat collided with a chartered East German freighter on the River Thames, just minutes into its voyage from London to Havana. The outgoing vessel partially capsized, ruining its cargo of 42 British-built Leyland buses. But was the collision accidental or an act of sabotage, sanctioned by the US Central Intelligence Agency (CIA)? The British government's decision to provide credit-backing for the bus exports, breaching Washington's economic blockade of the communist-ruled island, had already provoked a serious rift between the transatlantic allies.

The years 1898 and 1964 demarcate the following historical narrative. It investigates the relations of two insular countries, dependent on trade for their economic prosperity. The mysterious sinking of two ships in Havana and London, in very different circumstances, provides the start and end point for this study of British diplomacy and US hegemony in Cuba. The *Maine* disaster hastened the end of Spanish rule in Cuba and the beginning of close US–Cuban relations, and the later incident, whatever its causes, was emblematic of the Cold War.

Renowned twentieth-century figure Winston Churchill (1874–1965) exemplifies British contacts with Cuba. He was born into an aristocratic family, the son of a prominent Tory politician father and an American-born mother. At 20 years old he first visited the island in 1895 as a war correspondent, contracted by the *Daily Graphic* in London to report from the battlefront of a renewed insurrection in Cuba against Spanish rule. He ended his final despatch by lamenting Cuba's predicament, and imagining how the island might have been had the British not exchanged Havana for Florida in 1763 following their 11-month occupation:

> It may be that as the pages of history are turned brighter fortunes and better times will come to Cuba. It may be that future years will see the island as it would be now, had England never lost it – a Cuba free and prosperous, under just laws and a patriotic administration, throwing open her ports to the commerce of the world, sending her ponies to Hurlingham and her Cricketers to Lords, exchanging the cigars of Havana for the cottons of Lancashire, and the sugars of Matanzas for the cutlery of Sheffield. At least let us hope so.[1]

Churchill's correspondence highlighted the unrealized commercial potential of Cuba under Spanish rule and its possible development in the future.

Eight months before Churchill's first visit to Cuba, founder of the Cuban Revolutionary Party José Martí had written to the British Foreign Secretary from Guantánamo in April 1895. He explained to him the circumstances in which a British subject had died during the landing of independence rebels in eastern Cuba. In a similar vein to Churchill, Martí appealed to Britain's commercial outlook and implored its government not to intervene in a renewed rebellion against Spanish rule in the island. His letter concentrated not on lost opportunities in the past, but on new commercial openings in the future, if only Britain would stay out of the conflict:

> The Cuban nation, fully prepared, from well seasoned culture and habits of creative work, to take its natural place in the labors of modern development and due harmony between the powers of the Earth, has reentered the path of sacrifice and war to give birth, at the very entrance of the fast opening new ways of commerce and human intercourse, to an independent, self-suffering and impartial Republic ready to open its abundant opportunities to the energy and industry of the world.[2]

Three weeks after writing this letter, 42-year-old Martí, a literary man and the apostle of Cuban independence, died in his first-ever armed conflict. His description of 'fast opening new ways of commerce' reflected the Cuban dream of independence from Spanish colonial rule, and complete freedom to trade abroad without metropolis-imposed restrictions.

In a similar vein, the young Churchill visualized Cuba 'throwing open her ports'. His statement reflected the success of his country's industrial revolution, and the pervasive – but not uncontested – Victorian conviction that international trade should be free of protectionist tariffs. The issue of 'free trade' versus 'tariff reform' split British opinion in the early 1900s. 'Tariff reformers' argued for duties to be levied on foreign imports, alongside a system of Imperial Preference for goods traded between Britain and its colonies. Strict adherence to 'free trade', they argued, was leading to the dumping of foreign goods in Britain, a weakening of its industrial base and a subsequent loss of jobs. The issue divided Churchill's own Conservative Party. The young politician, a vociferous supporter of 'free trade', crossed the floor of the House of Commons in May 1904 to sit as an opposition Liberal MP, only returning to the Conservative fold 20 years later.

Following US military intervention the Spanish empire lost its Cuban colony in 1898, three years after Martí's and Churchill's correspondence. After nearly four years of US military occupation the island finally achieved its independence, at least nominally. The increasingly assertive United States exerted indirect political and economic control over the island during the first three decades of the Cuban republic, making it a virtual US protectorate.

Half a century after first visiting Cuba as a war correspondent, Churchill travelled there again following the Allied victory against the Axis powers in the Second World War and his shock general election defeat in 1945. The ex-prime minister returned to the island on holiday in February 1946, to swim and to paint. Locals showered him with gifts of the Cuban cigars he so habitually smoked, and he judiciously batted away questions on political matters.[3] Churchill then toured the United States, where at Fulton in Missouri he made a speech that described an 'iron curtain' descending across Eastern Europe.[4] His comments presaged the impending Cold War between the capitalist Western world and the nascent communist camp in the east. In the same speech, he celebrated his country's close cooperation with the United States in the Second World War by coining the phrase the 'special relationship'.[5]

Anglo–American affinity derived from a shared language, joint military endeavours and a similar outlook on the world. Britain and the United States continued to exchange vital military intelligence during the ensuing Cold War.

One of Britain's strongest cultural connections with Cuba is the spy-fiction novel *Our Man in Havana*, written by peripatetic British author Graham Greene, and published just 12 weeks before the triumph of the Cuban Revolution on 1 January 1959.[6] The novel's main protagonist is Jim Wormold, an expatriate vacuum cleaner salesman. The Caribbean network of the Secret Intelligence Service (SIS) recruits him as its British agent in Havana, but he invents his sub-agents and intelligence in order to finance his daughter's expensive tastes. Production of a film version commenced within five months of the novel's publication. Released later in 1959, it starts with the disclaimer, 'This film is set in Cuba before the recent revolution'. In an early scene, SIS Caribbean station chief Henry Hawthorne, played in the film's outstanding performance by Noël Coward, first encounters Wormold (Alec Guinness) in his shop and enquires about his business:

> *HAWTHORNE* Do you do pretty well?
> *WORMOLD* Yes, but there's not much electric power since the troubles began.
> *HAWTHORNE* When was that?
> *WORMOLD* Oh, about the time Queen Victoria died.[7]

The last is a throwaway line, but replete with historical significance. Considering the two Castro-led rebel actions in July 1953 at Moncada and the *Granma* landing in December 1956, a common link between recent Cuban and British history would have been Elizabeth II's Coronation (June 1953) or the Suez Crisis (July to November 1956) respectively; but instead, the historically and politically astute Greene refers us back to 1901, to the period of US military intervention and occupation (1898 to 1902).

Cuba's 'Republic'

It is the period in Cuba's history from 1898, when 'the troubles began', that is the main focus of this study. Throughout the years 1898 to 1964, covering the whole life of what many Cubans define as their 'república mediatizada' (US-supervised republic: 1902–58), the most important factor in British policy towards Cuba was the US dimension. The closeness of the US–Cuban and Anglo–American relationships compromised the operation of Anglo–Cuban relations, as both Cuba and Britain prioritized their overriding diplomatic and economic contacts with the United States. Within this triangular set of relations, the nexus between London and Havana suffered markedly.

The various ministers, ambassadors and other diplomats posted to His/Her Majesty's Government's mission in Havana fully appreciated this fact. In 1921 the British chargé d'affaires in Havana described the composition of a forthcoming Cuban mission to London, headed by the recently deposed president Mario Menocal (1913–21). The long-delayed visit reciprocated a British mission to Cuba three years earlier. Godfrey Haggard emphasized that the Cuban government had made a real effort to include personnel 'de lo mejor'.[8] Met with heavy fog on its arrival in London, the mission's short stay included a banquet at the House of Commons where the Conservative leader of the House and former Chancellor of the Exchequer Austen Chamberlain made light of his decision to impose a war-time duty on Cuban cigar imports.[9] Luncheons were taken with King George V at Buckingham Palace and the Lord Mayor of London at Mansion House. They visited the Cenotaph, the Tower of London, a chocolate factory in Bristol, an arms factory in Birmingham and the city's Chamber of Commerce. From Windsor Castle they paid a visit to Eton College, described as 'one of the most venerable curiosities of England. Through the corridors of this college the young men who later were to form the British Empire have played [sic]'. Their last call was upon foreign secretary the Marquis Curzon of Kedleston, for tea.[10]

Ahead of the mission, Haggard qualified his advice to colleagues in London that they explore rich openings for British exports in the island: 'Our interests in Cuba are purely commercial. On the other hand, politically, the country is an annex of the United States.'[11] Two years later, chargé d'affaires Donald St Clair Gainer wrote that Cuba was 'too important economically to the United States of America to be allowed full freedom of action, and Cuban politicians must either entirely acquiesce in American domination or face direct action from their northern neighbour'.[12] In his 1931 annual report, British minister Joyce Broderick, an Irishman, described the predicament of both the island and British interests: 'The aspirations of the Cubans to complete independence are doomed to permanent disappointment, and the representatives in Havana of European countries must make the best of the situation as it stands.'[13] In the security-conscious era of the Cold War, and just weeks before the 1956 *Granma* landing of Castro's rebels from Mexico, an official British overview stated, 'Both because of her geographical position and because of the part played by the United States in her struggle for independence, Cuba must be regarded as lying almost entirely within the United States zone of influence.'[14]

In this way US preponderance constricted not only the Cuban goal of true independence, but also Britain's willingness to defend its interests in the island. From the point that the United States intervened in Cuba's drawn-out struggle for independence in 1898, Britain's long-standing commercial and financial interest in the island became practically its sole focus, as Washington assumed strategic responsibility for the Caribbean.

The principal aim of this book is to judge the extent to which British policy in Cuba acted within the margins of US acquiescence. With one notable exception, during the final period under study, Britain pragmatically yielded to US wishes. But US supremacy, even before 1959, did not always prejudice British freedom of action. In an exceptional case in the mid- to late 1930s, for example, a change in Washington's hemispheric policy inadvertently aided Britain's efforts to defend its interests in Cuba.

Diplomats and Diplomacy

For many years the Foreign Office was an elitist department of government overseen by aristocrats. The long list of Old Etonians who have held important positions within its hierarchical structure went a long way to confirming this impression.[15] In the case of His/Her Majesty's mission in Havana, several British diplomats posted there had also attended Eton School (see Table 1). The Foreign Office had a reputation as a very conservative policymaking institution, one prominent official in 1900 referring to it as a 'very slumberous lion [...] so very deferential and polite to all the other lions'.[16] Generations later, Conservative politician Edward du Cann, economic secretary to the Treasury (1962–63) during the Leyland bus sales controversy, levelled similar criticisms against the department: 'Many Conservatives have a low opinion of the FO in general. They regard it as a rather woolly-minded organisation, too self-contained, too often self-satisfied, and not as zealous as it should be in promoting Britain's interests.'[17]

The American Department of the Foreign Office was responsible for most decisions concerning Cuba, its head generally acting as the arbiter of British foreign policy towards the island.[18] For important decisions touching on Anglo–American relations such as the Anglo–Cuban Treaty

Table 1 British diplomats in Havana, 1898–1964[a]

Name	Service in Havana	Diplomatic rank	University/School (and/or military service)	Previous two postings
Adam Watson	1963–(66)	Ambassador	King's College, Cambridge Rugby	Nuffield College, Oxford Dakar
Herbert Marchant	1960–63	Ambassador	St John's College, Cambridge Perse	Düsseldorf San Francisco
Stanley Fordham	1956–60	Ambassador	Trinity College, Cambridge Eton	Buenos Aires Stockholm
Wilfred Gallienne	1954–56	Ambassador	Royal Field Artillery, First World War[b]	Guatemala City Chicago
Adrian Holman	1950–54 1949–50	Ambassador Minister	New College, Oxford[c] Harrow	Bucharest Paris
James Dodds	1944–49	Minister	Wadham College, Oxford[d] Marlborough	La Paz Tokyo
Sir George Ogilvie-Forbes	1940–44	Minister	New College, Oxford[e] Beaumont	Berlin[f] Madrid > Valencia
Herbert Grant Watson	1937–40	Minister	*see below*	Helsingfors (Helsinki) Havana
Thomas Snow	1935–37	Minister	New College, Oxford Winchester	Madrid Tokyo
Herbert Grant Watson	1933–35	Minister	Trinity College, Cambridge Eton	Guatemala City Lisbon
Sir John Joyce Broderick	1931–33	Minister/consul general	Royal University of Ireland Blackrock College, Dublin	Washington DC New York

Table 1 (Continued)

Name	Service in Havana	Diplomatic rank	University/School (and/or military service)	Previous two postings
Thomas Morris	1925–31 1924–25	Minister Chargé d'affaires/consul general	Imperial Yeomanry, Boer War	Caracas Canary Islands
Godfrey Haggard[g]	1921–24	Chargé d'affaires/consul general	Honiton Grammar School	La Paz Guatemala City
William Erskine	1919–21	Minister	Magdalen College, Oxford Eton	Rome Athens
Stephen Leech	1909–19	Minister[h]	Magdalen College, Oxford Eton	Peking Christiana
Arthur Grant-Duff	1906–09	Minister	Balliol College, Oxford Clifton	Darmstadt and Carlsruhe[i] Mexico City
Lionel Carden	1902–06 1899–	Minister Consul general	Eton	Guatemala City Mexico City

[a] Most information taken from *Who Was Who*: www.ukwhoswho.com.
[b] Served from 1915. Seriously wounded in 1917. Seconded for service with Royal Engineers at War Office, 1918.
[c] Served in First World War (1915–18). Awarded Military Cross, mentioned in despatches. Two brothers died in same war.
[d] Served in First World War (1915–19).
[e] Served in First World War: Gallipoli (1915), Egypt and Mesopotamia (twice mentioned in despatches). War Office General Staff, 1918.
[f] Discounting short period in Norway (1939–40).
[g] Information found in Christopher Hassall, *The Timeless Quest: Stephen Haggard* (London: Arthur Barker, 1946), pp. 24–33.
[h] Also accredited to Hayti and Santo Domingo from 1913.
[i] Ignoring subsequent temporary postings.

(1901–06), recognition of a radical government (1933–34), British arms sales (1958–59) and the Leyland bus deal (1963–64), files containing incoming and outgoing letters and telegrams, internal memoranda and so forth filtered their way through the Foreign Office hierarchy accumulating written minutes and marginalia. A few privileged documents even acquired the scratchy red annotations of a hurried foreign secretary or a laconic prime minister.

Havana proved a difficult posting for foreign diplomats. British minister Joyce Broderick (1931–33) pointed to the seasonal character of political and social disturbances in the island. Winter months, he wrote, saw a fall in the atmospheric and political temperature, a season when the rural population devoted their energies to cutting and grinding the sugar crop. The hot summer months, meanwhile, witnessed a minimum of manual work in the sugar industry, leading to idleness and discontent.[19] The weather often mimicked political and social turbulence, with tropical cyclones of dangerously high winds and heavy rains regularly afflicting the island. Soon after his arrival, Broderick made light of Cuba's extremes when inviting an ex-colleague from the Department of Overseas Trade and his wife to Havana: 'Lady Crowe and you should come out and pay us a visit. We shall insure you against cyclones and revolutions.'[20]

Havana, like other diplomatic postings in Latin America, was not considered a destination for high-fliers. And Cuba proved a challenging environment in which to practise diplomacy, not least because foreign envoys outside the US diplomatic circle were considered, or considered themselves, as minor actors in a much larger drama. Ahead of his 1935 posting on promotion as His Majesty's minister to Havana, Tom Snow wrote to the head of the American Department to ask for 'guidance [...] in connection with the degree of liaison advisable with the U.S. Ambassador'. Robert Craigie replied:

Both in practice and in theory we like to keep in close touch with the Americans in dealing with South and Central American countries [...] [However,] there is undoubtedly a tendency on the part of the American Embassy in Havana to regard themselves as being in a category quite distinct from the other representatives and, consequently, to play a lone hand. In so far as this tendency is displayed we must, of course, avoid the appearance of being a suppliant for American advice and must play an independent part, or rather try to act in cooperation with the representatives of the other principal powers.[21]

During a period of heightened political unrest in the mid-1930s, Herbert Grant Watson pointed to the skewed view of foreign representatives held by some elements in the island:

> There is, unfortunately, among the people of Cuba a false notion of the position of the Diplomatic Corps. Whether it is on account of the Platt Amendment or from some other reason, the Cubans feel that they can involve foreign representatives in their internal quarrels and intrigues and attempt to do so.[22]

From its inception in 1902, the most notorious of the Platt Amendment's seven articles had given the United States the right to intervene 'for the preservation of Cuban independence', and led to three US military interventions between 1906 and 1921. This extraterritorial power, encoded in the island's constitution, led Cuban opposition politicians to create conditions for US intervention in order to oust an incumbent government from power.

Of course, diplomats themselves were not infallible. In July 1959, British Ambassador (1956–60) Stanley Fordham lamented both his misreading of the insurgency that had led to Fulgencio Batista's rapid demise months earlier, and his backing for sales of British tanks and fighter aircraft to the dictator. Evidently crestfallen by the turn of events, he wrote, 'Members of Her Majesty's Foreign Service are expected to be right when all around them are wrong. I have been greatly concerned that I have failed in this respect and that in consequence I led you and others astray.'[23] He was perhaps suffering the existential despair common to ambassadors from time to time, vulnerably exposed at the end of a long and often encrypted line of communication when fluid events conspire to overturn their considered predictions.

Cuban 'Independence'

Cuba, a 'new nation', has defined its national identity in contrast to aggressors who acted against its independence aspirations. Since 1959, for example, many Cubans have viewed their country in polar opposition to the United States of America, which, from a nationalist perspective, intervened at the eleventh hour in 1898 to restrict ambitions for full independence. Cubans of a nationalist bent have viewed their 'patria' ('homeland') as a victim of imperialism, initially engaged in a drawn-out nineteenth-century struggle to free itself from Spanish colonial rule, only to achieve a nominal independence constrained ignominiously by Washington from 1902 to 1958. Cubans belonging to the economic and political elite, however, benefitted from this period of close collaboration with the United States, and have been viewed as traitors to the cause of true independence.

Britain's historic involvement with Cuba has also led to negative views. In past centuries Britain was seen as an untrustworthy nation of pirates and enslavers, referring to the actions of various sea-going adventurers, both state-sponsored and unofficial, during the sixteenth century and beyond; corsairs and buccaneers, figures such as John Hawkins and Francis Drake, who sacked and plundered in Caribbean waters.[24] Britain's alleged duplicity in abolishing slavery and the slave trade, institutions it had upheld for centuries, led to severe censure from Spanish colonial authorities and Creole sugar planters alike in the nineteenth century. In this light, its opponents portrayed Great Britain as 'perfidious Albion', a term invented by the French for their cross-channel rivals in the eighteenth century, referring 'to their alleged treacherous policy towards foreigners'.[25]

On the other hand, various prominent Cubans held a certain respect for British institutions and authority, and experience derived from control of the world's largest empire. At the end of the nineteenth century the island's elite were well informed about the industrial revolution, the influence of British capital, democracy and traditions. When Spain lost Cuba, the Caribbean island seemed ripe for financial investment and commercial exploitation. Britain and its empire, along with the United States, appeared well positioned to partake in the potential bonanza, although geographic proximity naturally gave US interests a great permanent advantage over British competitors.

When the United States defeated Spain in 1898, it had no precedents of its own on which to model its military occupation of Cuba. Naturally, new Secretary of War Elihu Root (1899–1904) consulted British models for instruction. In December 1899 he wrote,

> The first thing I did after my appointment was to make out a list of a great number of books which cover in detail both the practice and the principles of many forms of colonial government under the English law, and I am giving to them all the time I can take from my active duties.

Root's archive contains a list of 15 such works, dealing with English colonial policy and practice.[26] Of course, US administrators appropriated and rejected those parts of the British model that did not, in their view, accord either with their own principles or with conditions on the ground. India and Egypt were a long way geographically and culturally from Cuba, with different native experiences and aspirations. And given the history of their own colonial subjection by the British, US officials were at pains to show that they were not acting imperialistically.[27]

There was, however, a notable symmetry between British control in Egypt, initially a 'veiled protectorate' from 1882 and then a formal protectorate from 1914 to 1922, and US ties with Cuba from 1898 until the early 1930s. British proconsul Lord Cromer famously asserted, 'We do not govern Egypt, we only govern the governors of Egypt'. The statement might equally have been applied to US influence over Cuban politicians during the first three decades of their republic.[28] There were analogies between Egypt and Cuba in military occupation, strategic control of shipping lanes (and access to the Suez and Panama canals), protection for the export of essential commodities (cotton and sugar) and periodic readjustments in formal and informal control through revised treaties: the 1936 Anglo–Egyptian defence treaty (ending British occupation, but maintaining a garrison and canal zone control); the 1954 Anglo–Egyptian defence agreement (relinquishing canal zone control); the Platt Amendment, 1902–34; and two US–Cuban reciprocity treaties in 1903 and 1934. The proconsular roles of colonial/diplomatic representatives and their overbearing interference in the internal affairs of Egypt and Cuba provoked virulent nationalist reactions, as did an ongoing foreign military presence, at Guantanamo Bay for example. Furthermore, there is a remarkable symmetry in the unravelling of Anglo–Egyptian and US–Cuban relations, notably the nationalization of the Suez Canal and the Eden government's doomed military invasion in 1956, and Cuba's nationalization and expropriation of US companies and properties from 1959 followed by the Bay of Pigs debacle in 1961. Nationalist leaders of these small nations, namely Gamal Abdel Nasser and Fidel Castro, both revelled in the ignominious defeats of their alleged imperialistic oppressors.

Three decades earlier in 1931, in the midst of a severe economic crisis, Cuban nationalist elements railed against US support for President Gerardo Machado's increasingly dictatorial rule. In temporary charge of the British legation, Clarence Ezard described how Cubans could not bring themselves to believe that Americans were neutral in their disputes. Ezard shared their point of view that the US ambassador need only express open disapproval of Machado's government for it to fall. In his opinion, they therefore drew the erroneous conclusion that the US government was supporting the president. Local feeling, he wrote, aped what had been reported from Egypt the previous year. By doctoring a recent diplomatic despatch from Egypt and replacing Prime Minister Ismail 'Sidky' with 'Machado', British 'residency' with the US 'Embassy', and inserting 'Cuban' instead of 'Egyptian', his view of the political scene in Havana now imitated that in Cairo:

> The rough conclusion drawn is that 'Machado' continues in power on a sort of monthly renewable licence from the [United States] 'Embassy', and the conclusion is not very far from the reality, as viewed through 'Cuban' spectacles. The possibility of a force remaining really neutral when it had the power to intervene, and may at any moment have the will, simply does not exist in their philosophy.

Absorbing their colleague's reflection, David Kelly in London annotated, 'The comparison with the situation in Egypt is original & suggestive.' Permanent Under Secretary Robert Vansittart added, 'The Egyptian parallel is apt.'[29]

Cuba's Foreign Relations

Until the 1959 Cuban Revolution, the United States appeared in full control of its neighbour's political destiny. But by early 1960, Washington had received a rude shock to its accustomed primacy with the sudden emergence of a rapidly radicalizing communistic regime in the island. After a series of incendiary incidents early that year, British Prime Minister Harold Macmillan commented that the Americans were 'pained and uncertain'. 'What a pity they never understood "colonialism" and "imperialism" till too late', he lamented in his personal diary.[30] This acerbic private observation, written just four months after his 'wind of change' speech concerning African decolonization, highlighted an apparent gulf between the allies in their experience and handling of unruly domains.

This study of Anglo–Cuban relations adds a new point of view to the considerable historiography on Cuba. In one sense its findings confirm why studies of the island's foreign relations have been so fixated on the Havana–Washington axis. Nations like Britain acted as passive bystanders to a struggle largely peripheral to their essential interests. Cuba faced experimental and evolving US foreign policy in the early post-1898 period. One scholar accurately defined the early US approach as 'a mixture of policies and actions characterized by paradox and ambiguity; a kind of ambivalent imperialism continually modified by guilt, domestic policies and the lack of a true colonial drive'.[31]

The period of study, from 1898 to 1964, also witnessed a transformation in the status of Britain and the United States. From the end of the nineteenth century, Britain was an imperial power in decline, while the United States was an ascendant economic and political power. Financially and militarily, the United States assured British victory in two world wars, although the conflicts decimated Britain's economy and global trading position. Massive US loans to its wartime ally meant Britain was in financial debt to the United States for the rest of the twentieth century.

Only occasionally did the transatlantic allies fall out. The 1956 Suez Crisis was the prime example, although the two allies soon resolved their differences, agreeing to share nuclear weaponry from the 1960s. Harmonious Anglo–American relations were the cornerstone of British foreign policy during the twentieth century, and particularly after 1945. In this sense, the following analysis of Anglo–Cuban relations constitutes an original case study of London–Washington relations in the twentieth century. But while the United States was increasingly powerful and dominant for much of the century, the 1959 Cuban Revolution indicated the limits of US power. Cuba soon shifted from US tutelage to Soviet influence, commencing a key stage in Washington's superpower rivalry with its Cold War adversary, the Soviet Union.

It is therefore time to dilute the narrow US–Cuban focus adopted by many studies of the island's history. While Cuban diplomatic records are closed to all but the most trusted foreign scholars, and US records from 1898 to 1958 contain only occasional mentions of British involvement in Cuba, the British governmental records are uninterrupted and revealing. The British views they contain were not neutral or disinterested, but neither were they uninformed, at least most of the time. Professional diplomats and the institution they worked for had long-standing experience in the administration of empire, making them experts in the control of foreign possessions. Their views on Anglo–Cuban relations and the island's trajectory from the juncture of the US military intervention in 1898 add a new dimension to the existing historiography.

1
Perfidious Albion?
Britain and Cuba before 1898

English involvement in the Caribbean was longstanding. As long ago as 1586, for example, pirate Francis Drake headed a large fleet that threatened Cuba's long coastline, but he neglected the island for more easily attainable mainland treasures. Following this scare the Spanish strengthened their colony's defences.[1] At great expense they erected impressive fortifications to guard the entrance to Havana's natural harbour, an essential port of rendezvous for galleons returning from Central and South America laden with gold and silver treasure, and continuing in convoy to Spain. The Spanish considered Havana impregnable to foreign invasion, but from 1748 to 1815 the British prioritized the Caribbean – strategically and economically – as never before.[2]

Spain's entry into the Seven Years War between Britain and a French-led coalition of countries turned the Caribbean into a theatre of conflict. Havana, a vital military outpost and conduit of the Spanish Empire's riches, was a key strategic target. A hastily assembled British fleet departed from Spithead near Portsmouth on 5 March 1762. After joining up with other forces off French-controlled St Domingue in the Caribbean, the British took Havana by surprise. With amphibious landings of 16,000 men, they undertook a diversionary attack west of the city and covert main assaults east of Havana. Columns attacked Spanish rearguard defences and laid siege for two months. Reinforced by a contingent from its New England colony in North America, sappers finally breached the seaward wall of the Morro Castle and stormed inside.[3]

But a lengthy mid-summer siege, amidst the ravages of mosquitoes and tropical diseases, decimated the British. As was the case with Cuba's nineteenth-century independence wars, far more foreigner combatants died from sickness than in battle. Between 7 June and 9 October nearly 800 seamen and 500 marines of the Royal Navy perished, only 86 from

15

enemy action. Of the 2673 seamen and 601 marines sick in October, only a few were expected to recover. Meanwhile, the army's losses were even greater: 5366 dead between 7 June and 18 October, 4708 of them through disease.[4]

The British had seized the Spanish power base in the West Indies in a single action. Spain's most important link between the Old and New Worlds was in foreign hands, a shattering blow to Spanish prestige. There were celebrations with bonfires and gun firing at the Tower of London. The Duke of Cumberland wrote to campaign Commander Lord Albermarle:

> Upon the whole no joy can equal mine, and I strut and plume myself as if it was I that had taken the Havanah. In short you have done your King and Country the most material service that any military man has ever done since we were a nation.

With this trump card now in British hands, prominent personages implored their government to drive a hard bargain with the Spanish.[5]

British Occupation and the Slave Trade

Cuba was an excellent bargaining counter, and not for the last time, foreign powers negotiated possession or control of this strategic entrepôt. Planters in the neighbouring British colony of Jamaica worried about a lengthy occupation of Havana, fearful for their wealth should Britain become responsible for other Caribbean islands. In London, parliamentary members with West Indian interests lobbied on their behalf against such action.[6] In Paris peace negotiations, the Spanish gave up East Florida and recovered Havana from the British, returning it to Bourbon rule. But in less than a year, British merchants and commercial practices had given the island's producers a taste of Cuba's economic potential when opened to free trade with Britain, the British West Indies and North America. Spain's trade monopoly ended at a stroke and more than 1000 vessels called at Havana's port during the occupation, compared to a previous annual average of around 15.[7] The short occupation also left a linguistic legacy. Havana's inhabitants likened the British Redcoats to a local tropical fruit, the black-seeded and red-fleshed *mamey*. For the occupying soldiery they invented the expression *a la hora de los mameyes*, a pertinent equivalent in Spanish to 'when push comes to shove'.[8]

Cuba's increased trade included the importation of slaves, during and following occupation. British merchants such as Cornelius Coppinger delivered increased numbers of African slaves to Cuba from Jamaica and Barbados. But the American Revolution and subsequent war (1776–83) interrupted British trade. The loss of its 13 North American colonies obviously lessened Britain's power in the continent, but commerce was not slow to recover, including trade in slaves.[9]

Britain, for so long heavily involved in the slave trade, was paradox-ically instrumental in the long campaign to abolish this practice in its colonies and throughout the Atlantic. A reform movement finally achieved its aim of outlawing the slave trade in 1807. By 1833 the prac-tice of slavery had ceased to exist in British colonial possessions, and the vociferous campaigners targeted instead the suppression of flourish-ing slave traffic in other parts of the Atlantic; for example, from Africa to Brazil and Cuba. Much of the stimulus for British abolitionists came from religious conviction and newfound humanitarianism, but there was also an economic imperative. By the 1820s it was difficult to justify British taxpayers' subsidies to West Indian planters, which supported the importation of slaves. Or, as one strong Latin American critic of foreign exploitation in the continent asserts, 'The English were the champions in buying and selling human flesh until it ceased to be convenient for them.'[10]

With the abolition of the slave trade in British island possessions, Cuba became its principal centre in the Caribbean. Britain's determina-tion to suppress the trade attracted the corresponding odium of those in the island who depended on slave labour for their lucrative agricultural production. Through the course of the nineteenth century this princi-pally and increasingly involved sugar cultivation. British government pressure on Spain's government impelled it to sign two treaties in 1817 and 1835, prohibiting the slave trade in the Spanish Empire, but nei-ther agreement achieved its objective. Creole planters and merchants feared economic ruin if the Spanish authorities implemented such a policy. Meanwhile, British West Indian planters pointed to their com-petitive disadvantage, having to pay workers on their estates while rival producers exploited slave labour.[11]

Spanish officials themselves were up in arms when the British gov-ernment appointed to Havana a declared and assertive abolitionist, David Turnbull, to replace Consul David Tolmé – a merchant accused of involvement with slave-trading interests. Tolmé's case highlighted a very real conflict between British commercial and humanitarian interests. Criticism by abolitionists contributed to his recall and replacement by Turnbull, a former *Times* correspondent in Europe, who had travelled in and written about the West Indies (including Cuba).[12]

Turnbull's abolitionist activities on the island soon led to vociferous demands from the Spanish authorities for his recall. Even those few Creoles that supported his efforts suspected sinister motives.[13] Britain had the power to enforce the treaties made with Spain, so why did it allow the trade to flourish? Did it have annexationist designs on the island?[14] Cuban historians have concluded that Britain was playing a double game in the island; Rodolfo Sarracino, for example, argues that behind the facade of an abolition campaign the inconsistent British were actually contributing to the strengthening of slavery as an institution in Cuba.[15]

Even British interests in Cuba reacted negatively to the campaign, but support at home from the abolition movement was decisive, at least initially. Turnbull's critics included Tolmé. David Murray, author of *Odious Commerce*, writes, 'The rivalry between commerce and humanitarianism in British foreign policy which had, in part, been responsible for Turnbull's appointment surfaced again to bring him down.' With a commonality of interests, British merchants on the island along with London merchants and shipowners lobbied the Foreign Office to remove the root of their discontent. In fear for his life, Turnbull sought refuge on a British vessel at anchor in Havana, and his wife eventually persuaded him their future lay elsewhere.[16] In this way ended the representation of one of Britain's first men in Havana, who had stridently defended Britain's controversial position on abolition. Owing partly to the slowness in communications in a period before the telegraph, he had enjoyed considerable autonomy during his posting. His activities, however, left many Cubans with the impression that Britain's policy in the island could be duplicitous and certainly not altruistic, as sponsors of the abolition movement claimed.

Cuba's classic nineteenth-century novel *Cecilia Valdés* voiced such sentiments. Its author Cirilo Villaverde had escaped from a Cuban prison in 1849 a year after participating in an anti-colonial conspiracy. He settled in the United States and continued his political activism against the colonial regime, first publishing his lengthy novel in 1882. Set in 1830s Havana, its main character is a beautiful fair-skinned mulatta who is pursued by the son of a slave owner, but both are unaware they share the same father. Reflecting contemporary society and the Spanish colony's troubled political and economic affairs, the novel is replete with references to the treacherous English. Citing the

1817 treaty between Britain and Spain that stipulated the complete cessation of the slave trade within three years, Cecilia's male suitor asserts,

> That's where the evil lies. For £500,000 sterling the unwise counsellors of the best of monarchs granted perfidious Albion the right to inspect our merchant ships on the high seas and to insult, as it still insults with impunity day after day, the sacred flag of the nation that not long ago was mistress of the seas and owner of two worlds.[17]

Britain's projection of power in the Caribbean was keenly felt at this point in the colony's development, while Spain's star appeared to be waning.

British and US Interest in Cuba

British commercial interests in Cuba fluctuated during the course of the nineteenth century. From 1829, the Anglo-Cuban company *La Consolidada* started to extract newly discovered copper in Cuba, soon becoming Britain's chief source of the commodity with annual exports of 10,000 tons. But from the outbreak of the ten-year independence war in 1868, Chilean and South African mines began to out-compete their rivals and the Cuban copper industry collapsed.[18] British capital was heavily involved in the financing of a private railway system. Preceding its mother country by 11 years, the island's first line from Havana to Bejucal opened in 1837, only 12 years after the inauguration of the first public railway in North-East England.[19] British Minister in Madrid George Villiers had put the proposers of Spanish America's first railway in contact with London bankers, and Alexander Robertson provided a loan.[20]

One of London's oldest merchant banks, J. Henry Schroder & Company (with origins in Hamburg, Germany), was the principal source of British capital for railway construction in the island. In the mid-nineteenth century, Cuba held the largest concentration of Schroder's clients outside Hamburg, owing to their longstanding interest in sugar and its export to Europe and the United States. Starting with the company's first ever bond issue for the Matanzas & Sabanilla Railroad Company in 1853, Schroder & Company continued to invest in railway infrastructure that considerably reduced the freight costs for transporting sugar and its derivatives from the island's interior to its coastal ports.[21]

Indeed, Britain's chief interest in Cuba, as with the rest of Latin America, lay in the economic field. For most of the nineteenth century, Britain was pre-eminent in international trade, manufacturing and finance.[22] Due in great part to technological advances in communications that linked the world by railway, steamship and telegraph, world trade grew tenfold between 1850 and 1914, after doubling between 1800 and 1850.[23] The security offered by the solid and conservative institutions of British commercial banking and insurance gave Britain an advantage in Latin America, where easy access to cheap capital was in much demand.[24] For decades, the stability of new import–export elite regimes in Latin America depended to a significant degree on their financial connections with capital-rich London, in mutually profitable economic dependence.[25]

For Latin America, Britain was the most important trading partner, as well as being its pre-eminent foreign investor from the 1820s until the start of the First World War. From the mid-nineteenth century until the war, British holdings in railways and government loans constituted the largest areas of investment in private industry.[26] In pursuance of new commerce or simply to maintain that existing, Britain rarely asserted itself politically, instead allowing its supremacy in these fields to function mostly unaided, carried out by merchants in the field.

Foreign trade brought Britain huge economic benefits. Liverpool, which like Bristol had profited enormously from the slave trade during the eighteenth century, was Britain's premier Atlantic trading port. Through its enlarged and improved system of docks, sailing and steam ships imported sugar, tobacco and raw cotton for households and mills in the north of England. A new canal network connected the northwest port with inland manufacturing centres like Manchester. From Liverpool, outbound ships exported cotton and other manufactured textiles and goods from outlets such as Manchester mills and Sheffield foundries, reaching consumers around the globe who demanded the cachet of British products. Merchant shipping also re-exported British Empire produce such as Indian and Burmese rice to foreign markets.[27] Havana was one of the closest Latin American ports to Liverpool. It was also conveniently located for the lucrative triangular trade between Britain and the Atlantic and Gulf ports of the industrially booming United States.

The political outlook changed with the increasing continental assertiveness of the United States. Mutual distrust between British Foreign Secretary George Canning and John Quincy Adams resulted in the US Secretary of State's sponsorship of a new doctrine, applicable to the whole continent. On Adams's advice, President James Monroe declared the Americas closed to further colonization. The 1823 edict gave notice that the United States would not interfere with Europe or with existing European colonies in the Americas, but would oppose further colonization or transfer of colonies between European powers.[28] The Monroe Doctrine unilaterally set the parameters for European action. But US expansion itself continued; settlement of Texas began in 1824 followed by annexation in 1845. Growing conflict between North and South checked southward expansion of the United States, and eyes turned westwards instead, towards the Mississippi Valley and beyond.

With Britain and the United States contemplating the advantages of a trans-isthmian canal, Anglo-American negotiations led to the Clayton–Bulwer treaty in 1850. The two nations provisionally agreed the joint construction of a canal across Central America, linking the Pacific and Atlantic oceans. Despite its apparent bipartisan approach, it was in fact an early manifestation of British retreat from the region. Despite enduring distrust and the risk that either party would denounce the treaty, its terms endured until the early 1900s. Prime Minister Lord Palmerston signalled the inevitability of creeping US hegemony and British acquiescence some years later, remarking on the benefits to Britain of a 'whole American continent occupied by an active enterprising race like the Anglo-Saxons instead of the sleepy Spaniards'. He also recognized the security danger to the empire's West Indian possessions.[29]

A Prize Caribbean Possession

Foreign powers coveted Cuba. For much of the century Britain was keen to see the island maintain its status quo, not wishing to see either its transfer to the United States or to another European rival. The question of Cuba's sovereignty arose in 1825, during a period when the United States and Britain deliberated over recognition of various newly independent states in Spanish America. George Canning wrote to the US minister in London, 'You cannot allow that we should have Cuba; we cannot allow that you should have it; and we can neither of us allow that it should fall into the hands of France.'[30] Decades later the island's increasingly assertive and dominant northern neighbour hesitated in swallowing it whole. President James Polk offered $100 m to buy the Spanish colony outright in 1848, and six years later President Franklin Pierce proposed a $130 m purchase, both without success.[31]

Hamilton Fish (secretary of state, 1869–77) visited Cuba in 1855 and recommended caution. Like others who preceded and followed him, he baulked over the issue of race: 'I can see no means of getting rid of a population of some 450,000 called whites but really of every shade and mixture of color, who own *all* the land on the island.' The first Cuban–Spanish War of Independence broke out in 1868, launched by Creoles in opposition to the overbearing colonial regime. It lasted ten years, but Cuban insurgents were unable to spread war to the western provinces. The US Congress urged an amenable President Ulysses Grant to recognize Cuban belligerency, but Fish countered the pressure. He argued that such a move would relieve Spain of responsibility for payment of war reparations.[32] It would also permit Spain to search US vessels on the high seas and provoke a US–Spanish war, an outcome to avoid at all costs. The secretary of state was less fearful of Spain's continued rule than that of black and mulatto revolutionaries.

Britain showed no desire to become embroiled in the Ten Years' War (1868–78). However, mindful of its commercial interests in Cuba and the wider region, it mediated in the troubled diplomacy between Spain and the United States. Of course, the British government was not enamoured with Spanish rule in Cuba. Corruption in Spain's colonial administration, delays in settling British claims, the continuation of slavery and a protectionist commercial policy were serious impediments. But British fear of both a naval war in West Indian and North American waters, and regional dislocation to commerce and shipping, overrode these reservations.[33] In London, *The Times* lamented the atrocities perpetrated by the Spanish and wondered whether a 'perpetual curse' lay on Cuba. An editorial asked,

> Will the Spaniards pause before they accomplish their own ruin in their eagerness to bring about the annihilation of their disaffected colonists? The possession of Cuba can no longer have any other object for Spain than either the gratification of a silly pride, or subserviency to selfish considerations no longer in harmony with sound liberal principles.[34]

In 1872 a maritime incident involving a US-registered steamer, the *Virginius*, threatened to spark a US–Spanish conflict. Flying a US flag but in the service of filibusterers, it was laden with contraband arms. Following a long chase, a Spanish cruiser captured the vessel off Jamaica and towed it to eastern Cuba. At Santiago de Cuba the Spanish military commander ordered the execution of suspected insurgents among the crew and passengers. Acting on his own initiative, Captain Sir Lambton Loraine of the Royal Navy's HMS *Niobe* sailed his sloop from Kingston to Santiago.[35] He demanded an end to the butchery and trained his boat's guns on the port. Frantic and fraught diplomacy ensued between Madrid, Washington and London. There was a popular clamour in the US press to avenge alleged Spanish cruelty. Loraine's prompt action and the resulting diplomacy halted further executions of British and US subjects, as well as Cuban insurgents. During the crisis the major objective of British diplomacy was to prevent a US–Spanish war. In this and other actions British diplomats helped maintain peace between the two powers.[36]

After 1885, increased economic competition in Latin America modified Britain's attitude and it was not uncommon for economic interests to be sacrificed to safeguard political and strategic goals. London frequently vetoed initiatives recommended by consuls on the ground. Even when supported, action was often more defensive than aggressive. From the mid-nineteenth century there was a gradual marginalization of the British position in Latin America in the face of increasing US assertiveness. In order to avoid complications, and expediently pleading adherence to the age-old doctrine of laissez-faire, the Foreign Office often found it less quarrelsome to do nothing and leave the protection of economic interests to the commercial world. Official government intervention went no further than the negotiation of bilateral commercial agreements, these being non-discriminatory most-favoured nation treaties agreed with republics such as Argentina, Guatemala and Mexico.

In the same period, Washington exercised its newfound economic strength through negotiation of a number of reciprocal trade agreements, most significantly with Spain and including its trade with Cuba and Puerto Rico. However, while the US executive had the power to negotiate treaties, it deferred to the Senate in the matter of ratification, this body often influenced by powerful domestic lobby groups in favour of protection, including such sectional interests as sugar.[37] John W. Foster, the US diplomat in charge of the drawn-out negotiations with the Spanish in 1884, described the treaty signed in Madrid as 'the most perfect reciprocity treaty our Government has ever made [...] I am quite confident it will result in giving us the almost complete commercial monopoly of the commerce of Cuba [...] It will be annexing Cuba in the most desirable way.'[38]

From the first Cuban–Spanish war of independence, Cuba's society and economy were transformed by growing integration of US capital with the island's rich sugar plantations.[39] But in 1894 the Wilson–Gorman Tariff Act imposed a new duty of 40 per cent *ad valorem* on all US sugar imports, undoing the existing reciprocal trade arrangement between Washington and Madrid. In the process, Cuba lost its preferential access to the one sizeable market capable of absorbing its sugar exports and insulating it from the vagaries of world competition. Cuba's sugar exports fell through the floor, plunging from $64 m in 1893 to $45 m in 1895 and just $13 m the following year. Cubans felt impotent, decisions affecting their political and economic future imposed by metropolises in Madrid and Washington respectively.[40]

Spheres of Influence

Important clashes with the United States in the 1890s caused Britain to acquiesce and recognize US hegemony in the Caribbean. London was more preoccupied with other global concerns involving its formal empire and the rising power of Germany, and did not wish to risk antagonizing its improved relationship with Washington. Chief amongst the disagreements at the end of the century was the Venezuelan–British Guiana boundary dispute from 1895 to 1896, when, despite Prime Minister Lord Salisbury's initial reluctance, the British Cabinet agreed to US demands to submit the question to arbitration.[41]

The primary aim of British foreign policy was to avoid conflict with any Great Power; war with the United States was unthinkable. Decisions also reflected the reality that US commercial and geopolitical objectives were in this period concentrated in the Caribbean, while Britain's main interests lay further south, particularly in Argentina and Brazil.[42] The British government accepted the 'natural hegemony' of the United States in its own sphere.[43] In relation to the boundary dispute, Prime Minister and Foreign Secretary the Marquess of Salisbury stated in February 1896, 'Considering the position of Venezuela in the Caribbean Sea, it was not more unnatural that the United States should take an interest in it than that we should feel an interest in Holland and Belgium.'[44]

The father of US naval doctrine, Captain Alfred Thayer Mahan, was adamant about the Caribbean: 'One thing is sure. In the Caribbean Sea is the strategical [sic] key of two great oceans, the Atlantic and Pacific; our own maritime frontiers.'[45] In his 1890 essay *The United States Looking Outward*, he proclaimed, 'It should be an inviolable resolution of our national policy that no foreign state should henceforth acquire a coaling position within three thousand miles of San Francisco'.[46] In order to pre-empt European ambitions in the Caribbean, Mahan prescribed a vigorous policy that included acquisition of US naval bases and coaling stations. He was also mindful of the economic opportunities pertaining to his nation in its hemisphere. Along with figures such as Senator Henry Cabot Lodge, it had not passed their notice that other nations' wealth equated with possession of an empire, as evidenced by a glance at any contemporary world map. Furthermore, the fact that several positions of great strategic importance in the Caribbean sphere were in the hands of weak and unstable governments appeared to Mahan a security danger. Britain's eventual deference to Washington's protestations over the 1895 Venezuela border dispute marked a watershed.

Insurrection in Cuba, 1895–98

As well as being a source of wealth, Cuba gave Spain status, long after the loss of its other American colonies (excepting Puerto Rico). Internationally, Spain was too weak – both economically and militarily – to participate in the main scramble for Africa alongside more powerful imperial powers. In the north of the continent it held two enclaves on the northern coast of Morocco and a weak grip on Atlantic-facing territories opposite the Canary Islands.[47] In the realm of domestic politics, Spain's Restoration monarchy was vulnerable. Any sign of weakness, such as the inclination to relinquish control of *la isla fiel*, threatened to unbalance the fragile established order and hasten the overthrow of Spain's constitutional monarchy under the reign of María Cristina, an Austrian Hapsburg.[48]

Insurrection broke out again in Cuba in 1895. On the face of it, Britain might have been expected to support Spain. The sympathies of confirmed aristocrats belonging to Britain's ruling class – such as Prime Minister Salisbury – were predisposed towards traditional monarchical regimes rather than the brash anti-establishment outlook of the United States. Furthermore, the Queen Regent was Queen Victoria's niece.[49] She wrote to her aunt in May 1896, beseeching the monarch's advice and her 'powerful friendship'. Her letter complained about US duplicity, promising Spain 'neutrality and friendship' but sending money and arms to the Cuban insurgents instead. Salisbury advised the Queen to offer only her deep sympathy in reply. He acknowledged their country's 'great goodwill' towards Spain, but his government would maintain its policy of 'neutrality'. The prime minister also predicted that the United States would commit 'mischief' without going to war.[50]

A month later the US embassy in London requested Salisbury's views on the Cuban conflict. Britain's interest was purely commercial, the prime minister replied, adding, 'It is no affair of ours, we are friendly to Spain and should be sorry to see her humiliated, but we do not consider that we have anything to say in the matter whatever may be the course the United States may decide to pursue.'[51] The British were over-extended internationally and preoccupied by other issues. They faced opposition in the wake of the scramble for Africa, most notably from the Boers in the south. And rivalry from Germany, Japan and Russia threatened in central Asia and the Far East.[52]

Churchill in Cuba, 1895

Winston Churchill arrived in Cuba on 20 November 1895, ten days before his twenty-first birthday. He had recently graduated from the Royal Military College at Sandhurst where he was commissioned as a Second Lieutenant in the 4th Hussars cavalry regiment. Enjoying ten weeks' leave in anticipation of military service in India, he had read about an insurrection of rebels in Cuba against their Spanish colonial masters. Demonstrating precocious enterprise he wrote to Sir Henry Drummond Wolff, Her Majesty's ambassador in Madrid and a friend of Churchill's recently deceased father, who furnished a letter of introduction from Spain's minister for foreign affairs to the Captain General of Cuba Arsenio Martínez de Campos. Additionally, Churchill secured an arrangement with London's *Daily Graphic* to send dispatches from the front in Cuba at a payment of five guineas per letter.[53]

On arriving in Havana the young English aristocrat was struck by the island's beauty, its temperate yet ardent climate and luxuriant vegetation, and by the absence of news about the rebellion. Writing years later he recalled feelings of regret about the 'absent-minded morning when our ancestors let so delectable a possession slip through their fingers'.[54] Along with a regimental travelling companion he resided at the capital's Hotel Inglaterra and consumed oranges and cigars. In search of action, they travelled by armoured train to Santa Clara, and thence by rail to Cienfuegos. After catching a steamer they joined a Spanish regiment in Sancti Spíritus. From here he wrote his second dispatch, contrasting the island's providence with Spanish rule: 'One cannot fail to be struck by the irony of a fate which offers so bounteously with one hand and prohibits so harshly with the other.'[55]

Churchill was impressed by the marching prowess of the Spanish infantry regulars, rising early to cover some eight miles by nine o'clock. Officers would then consume a hearty breakfast consisting of coffee and stew, and the general's *aide-de-camp* served rum cocktail from a long metal bottle. An early siesta followed, the men retiring to hammocks in the shade for some four hours until around two o'clock. From three o'clock they marched for a further four hours or so, reaching the camping ground at around dusk. All this the young Winston found most agreeable. He blamed a restricted education for his surprise that his Spanish hosts felt about Cuba, just as the British did about a possession like Ireland. Until then he confessed to having sympathized with the rebels or at least the rebellion, but now he began to feel for his hosts, so unhappy at contemplating the loss of their cherished 'pearl of the Antilles'.[56]

It was his first encounter with a popular revolt. On his twenty-first birthday, while bathing in a stream, for the first time in his life he heard bullets fired in anger. For a figure later revered as a wartime leader and statesman, this experience was in itself significant. The Cuban insurrection and the subsequent wars he encountered 'deeply coloured his military outlook and strategic thinking'. From personal experience he gained 'profound respect for the rebellious and an acute awareness of the damage they could inflict on imperial rule'.[57] Unlike Spanish officers, young Churchill did not anticipate a speedy end to the conflict, just months into the renewed insurrection. With the Cuban insurgents employing hit-and-run tactics, he judged that 'they can neither be caught nor defeated'.[58]

British 'Neutrality'

Britain remained ostensibly 'neutral' in the Spanish–American War and during the short US military intervention in Cuba that brought Spanish colonial rule to an end. However, the British supplied coal to US ships, and leaned on the Egyptian government to refuse refuelling facilities to the Spanish navy, effectively denying it a shorter routing (via the Suez Canal) to the Philippines, another Spanish–American theatre of war.[59]

British Ambassador in Madrid Sir Henry Drummond Wolff was sympathetic to the Queen Regent and an advocate in Spain's defence.[60] But Salisbury repeatedly rebuffed Spanish attempts to influence his government through the ambassador's persistent pleas. He also rejected Wolff's requests to intercede with Washington in favour of Spain, and then studiously ignored his later messages.[61] Future prime minister Arthur Balfour wrote to Wolff in March 1896: 'We are not on good terms with the United States just now as a consequence of Venezuela and any interference of ours would be worse than useless.'[62]

Consul General Alex Gollan represented Her Majesty's Government in Havana. But with the seat of insurrection in Oriente province, Consul Frederick Ramsden held a more important posting in Santiago de

Cuba. An English firm of exporters had first sent Ramsden to Cuba as its representative. Within two years he was appointed secretary to the consul at Santiago and then rose to full consulship, a post he held from the 1860s.[63] Like many of the British consuls dotted around the ports of the island, he maintained commercial interests in Cuba to supplement his meagre consular allowance. For example, he co-owned various sugar plantations in Guantánamo with Consul Thomas Brook.

The second major insurrection from 1895 settled into a war of attrition, with Spanish Captain General Valeriano Weyler practising a brutal *reconcentrado* policy towards the civilian population by herding them into concentration camps. Meanwhile, pro-independence insurgents laid waste to the island's agricultural production and infrastructure. Ramsden wrote in mid-1897, 'In consequence of no crops having been made, and also as a result of the concentration of the people in the towns, great misery and want prevail.'[64]

By the year's end the war had reached a stalemate. Wolff described the dilemma of the new Spanish government under Práxedes Mateo Sagasta, now committed to granting autonomy to solve the Cuban problem:

> If the army at present in Cuba has not been sufficient to reduce the island to obedience, it is difficult to perceive how this can be done now when no further troops can be sent out, and no further funds can be found.[65]

Wolff also reported a meeting with his US counterpart in Madrid. US Minister General Stewart Woodford informed him that a scheme was afoot to exploit 'the richest slice of earth' with US and hopefully British capital. Cuba possessed vast swathes of untapped land for increased cultivation of fine tobacco and sugar. Its mines were mere 'scratches' in comparison to what could be developed to extract 'the best iron in the world' and other 'great mineral wealth'. From Spain, it appeared to Wolff 'that the United States' Government are bound in one way or another to become masters of Cuba'.[66] Meanwhile, insurgent leaders feared a repetition of the Pact of Zanjón some two decades earlier, when the ten-year insurrection had petered out in a series of divisions and defections within rebel ranks.[67]

The strategic and economic importance of the island to the United States was beyond doubt, as highlighted by Captain Mahan's main arguments in an 1897 essay: (1) Cuba's domination of three of the four main communication routes in the Caribbean; (2) its short interior lines between ports, long coastline and many harbours that made blockade nearly impossible; and (3), $50 m of US investments in the rich sugar and mining industries.[68]

Two events in early 1898 deepened the crisis for Spain's colonial regime and precipitated US intervention. Firstly, the Cuban junta in the United States purloined an 'insulting' letter from the Spanish ambassador in Washington and published it in the US sensationalist press, stirring a clamour of injured pride. Just as soon as this crisis had dissipated the USS *Maine* exploded at anchor off Havana with dreadful loss of life, a disaster quickly blamed on Spanish treachery.

Unlike their US counterparts, opinion in British newspapers did not immediately condemn the Spanish for the *Maine* disaster on 15 February 1898. But Britain instinctively empathized with its Anglo-Saxon cousins across the Atlantic. London's *Daily Chronicle* affirmed that

> Whatever our disagreements with the United States may be from time to time, and however apt we are on both sides of the Atlantic to use sharp words about each other's shortcomings, at bottom we all regard America as – to use the phraseology of sport – 'our side' in the great game of the world. It is no exaggeration, therefore, to say that the sorrow and sympathy felt by us on this occasion is but little less vivid than if the appalling calamity had overtaken one of our own ships.[69]

External events and domestic pressures in Spain and the United States drove the two nations to war. Britain's chargé d'affaires in Madrid laid out the predicament of Sagasta's government:

> It seems to be regarded as a truism in Spain that the Sovereign who gave up Cuba while there was any strength of resistance left in the Peninsula would have to fight for his throne. Spain may therefore be forced into a hopeless war in order to preserve peace at home.[70]

The Spanish press fully supported Sagasta's rejection of an ultimatum by US President William McKinley for an armistice. *El Correo de Madrid* denounced 'outside intervention' that would impinge 'on Spain's national honour and affect the integrity of the nation'. It was preferable 'to succumb with glory than to live with a stigma of humiliation and cowardice'. In the opinion of *El Heraldo de Madrid*, 'To abandon Cuba in the midst of a rebellion offended the nation's dignity; to give it to the Yankees [...] would be even more humiliating.' *El Imparcial* implored, 'It is better to weep over lost loved ones than to live in shame and dishonour.'[71] The Cuban insurgent leaders, meanwhile, were insistent that their struggle for emancipation continued, especially during the rainy season, when the rebels held a military advantage. Their position had been unchanged since 1895: insistence on full independence and recognition of their Republic.[72]

European powers made tentative joint representations in Washington in an effort to prevent war and respond to last-minute Spanish moves to seek their mediation.[73] Wolff was still eager to assist his Spanish hosts and beseeched Salisbury's assistance in making Spain and the United States negotiate. Again the prime minister rebuffed him.[74] Britain's strictly neutral policy throughout favoured the United States at the expense of Spain. Just three years after the Venezuela border dispute, it was important to avoid complications with Washington. The British government also favoured US annexation of the Philippine archipelago from Spain over its possession by a European rival. US actions thus suited Britain's wider objectives, and explain London's general acquiescence regarding the military intervention and ongoing policy in Cuba.

President McKinley could no longer resist the persistent calls for his government to intervene militarily, declaring war in order – at least ostensibly – to put an end to Spanish cruelty and misrule in the island. In the event it was a short intervention, starting on 22 June and ending 12 August. The US army was only 28,000 strong in its entirety, with no experience of overseas service.[75] Some 5400 of its troops died in the war, only 379 of them in combat; most of the rest were victims of malaria and yellow fever.[76] They fought Spanish forces also decimated more by disease than enemy fire, amounting to around 80,000 troops 'fit for duty' at the time of intervention.[77] A superior US navy annihilated the Spanish fleet off Santiago de Cuba in less than four hours on 3 July.[78] The Spanish considered their honour intact because their army and navy had fought and lost with dignity.[79]

Like other British consular officials, Ramsden represented US interests in Cuba once Washington had declared war on Spain. He was indefatigable in his efforts to assist US navy personnel imprisoned at Santiago, possibly influenced by his commercial interests in Oriente province. Ramsden was a planter, albeit a foreign planter. Many of the island's planter class shifted their allegiances during the insurrection from support for Spain to support for independence, then for autonomy, and finally for US intervention in the latter stages of the war.[80]

Ramsden witnessed the Spanish fleet's suicidal departure from Santiago harbour on 3 July 1898 and counted 2545 shots during the following 65 minutes. The next day he joined the mass exodus of civilians to El Caney, ordered by a Spanish proclamation to leave the city. There, alongside 18,000–20,000 people in a settlement of 300 houses, he became one of an epidemic's many victims.[81] He delayed his own evacuation to Kingston, Jamaica, where he died on 10 August.

Captain Arthur Lee served as a British military attaché to the US army during its intervention. Similar to many US commentators, he disparaged the contribution of the Cuban insurgents, but he also condemned the management of the whole US intervention, judging that there were 'few, if any, lessons for the British Army to learn from the conduct of this campaign'. British views of US actions in Cuba were often laden with censure. A sense of racial superiority still shone through in Lee's report, however, and the British officer noted with 'pride and satisfaction' the 'unimpaired survival of the old fighting spirit in the other great division of the Anglo-Saxon race'.[82] Future president Theodore Roosevelt led a cavalry brigade during the US campaign and made Lee an honorary 'rough rider'. They henceforth maintained a 'constant and intimate' correspondence.[83]

Other British witnesses were less quick to condemn the native insurgents. On his first sight of the *mambises*, John Black Atkins of the *Manchester Guardian* described 'men incredibly tattered and peaked and forlorn. On many of them a few ribbons of clothing suggest the outline of a jacket or trousers. They are lean as men might be who have been living in the mountains on cocoa-nuts [*sic*].' Atkins believed that the US army judged the Cubans too harshly, making 'the very old mistake' of judging their allies by their 'own standards'. The strategy of the ill-equipped Cubans was to 'make quick concentrations and wolf-like disappearances'. They were 'not in the habit of taking part in the pitched battles of drilled armies'.[84] Three years later, Atkins reported from the Boer War in South Africa alongside Winston Churchill. Here the future prime minister first became a household name following his capture by Boer troops and escape from a prisoner-of-war camp.[85] Like the Spanish army in Cuba, British officers struggled to combat guerrilla tactics. They similarly concentrated the local populace into camps, where neglect also left many thousands (mostly women and children) to perish from disease and starvation.[86]

Severe economic dislocation provoked by war in Cuba interrupted mortgage bond repayments to Schroder & Company and negotiations in London for the complete transfer of the United Railways of the Havana and Regla Warehouses Company to British ownership and control. A £2 m debenture issue financed the acquisition of United Railways as an English registered company under an identical name. On 26 March

1898, in the midst of insurrection and international diplomacy that would decide the island's political future, United Railways transferred to British ownership.[87] But monopolistic control of railways in the western half of Cuba would prove a mixed blessing. The British company only remained profitable until the 1920s, a decade when it suffered from the advent of road competition, a surge of nationalism and a prolonged economic depression.

Conclusion

The respective victorious and defeated forces of the United States and Spain mingled freely in the island following Spanish capitulation.[88] Just weeks before the formal commencement of US military occupation on 1 January 1899, President McKinley's second annual message set conditions for his country's withdrawal. Several British newspapers excused themselves before questioning the president's commitment. They likened his words to those of previous British governments with regard to the continuing occupation of Egypt. The attributes which the free and independent Cuba must possess, the *London Standard* argued, were 'defined on such a Utopian model, that the day of emancipation from military tutelage may be indefinitely postponed'. On the subject of McKinley's timetable and stated precondition of 'complete tranquillity' in order to end the military occupation, a *London Chronicle* editorial remarked that this was 'precisely the language that successive British Governments have maintained about Egypt, with a result known to the world, and an omen which is certainly not inapplicable'.[89] The *Daily News* pointed to the president's 'language of somewhat ominous ambiguity upon the commercial part of the subject' and 'the conspicuous absence in his remarks of any allusion to free trade'.[90]

British shipping and export interests wanted the United States to maintain an 'open door' to trade in Cuba, replicating what they hoped to achieve with regard to China and its vast market. While Britain held a far greater commercial presence in the East, it needed US support there in the face of other great power rivalries, particularly from Germany and Russia. In a spirit of turn-of-the-century rapprochement, the two Anglo-Saxon powers agreed – albeit informally – to adopt a common approach towards an 'open door' in China. This arrangement was discussed just as Washington declared war against Spain in Cuba and the Philippines.[91]

Following McKinley's annual message in late 1898, a leading article in Britain's most authoritative newspaper sounded a note of warning:

In this country no jealousy has been provoked by the natural desire of the United States, an advancing and expanding Power, to acquire points of vantage, outside the limits of the American continent, as naval stations and as openings for trade. At the same time we have hoped that in taking up such a position the Washington Government would be actuated by the principles which are laid down, in relation to the spheres of European influence in China by President McKinley in his Message to Congress. The absence of 'exclusive treatment' is the foundation of our own commercial policy in the colonies and dependencies of the British Crown, and we have a right to look for reciprocity of conditions from the United States as a colonial Power.[92]

These remarks reflected jockeying between the dominant imperial powers – such as Britain, France and Russia – as they sought to control colonial territories relinquished by weaker powers – for example Spain, Portugal and Italy.[93] The United States, meanwhile, was an expanding power, hitherto untested in the administration of foreign acquisitions. Cuba would thus serve as a testing ground for US foreign control.

2
Uncle Sam versus the British Lion

Following centuries of Spanish colonial rule from 1511 to 1898, prominent Cubans at last looked forward to determining their country's political and commercial trajectory. But the US military intervention that definitively ended Spanish rule merely shifted the locus of external control from Madrid to Washington. US officials proclaimed their military occupation was temporary and that Cuba would soon achieve independence. The United States fulfilled its promise, but only partially. It withdrew its military forces but continued to supervise the island's export economy. This seriously impinged upon Britain's commercial position and its attempts to agree a commercial treaty with the new republic.

Cuba achieved nominal independence on 20 May 1902, but the United States still exerted indirect control. An amendment to a bill appended to the republic's new constitution, the infamous Platt Amendment, formalized political control. Mimicking British rule in Egypt, US ministers in Havana operated in a proconsular type role, supervising the government and political elite as if Cuba was a formal US protectorate. The United States and Cuba then bound their export economies though the 1903 Reciprocity Treaty. Commercial and financial groups in the United States, with substantial and growing interests in the island, continued to lobby the US executive and Congress.[1]

Spanish Colony to US Protectorate

Britain's acting consul general in Cuba, an Irishman, described the ceremony at noon on New Year's Day 1899 when tearful Spanish officers and officials handed authority over to their US counterparts.[2] Lucien Jerome identified the early distaste of Cubans – 'these amiable but very unruly sons of the south'– toward the 'somewhat Puritanical' US supervision of public morals, including restrictions on liquor sales. With the political future of the island still uncertain, he noted that temporary Cabinet Council members, instilled with a French education and sympathies, favoured a constitutional model based on the French republic.[3]

New British Consul General Lionel Carden had spent his whole consular career in Latin America, previously serving as vice consul in Havana from 1877 to 1883.[4] An old Etonian and son of a Church of England priest, he then served in various consular roles and diplomatic assignments in Mexico during the second presidential term of Porfirio Díaz (1884–1911). At the end of 1899, Carden reported the unexpected replacement of General John Brooke by General Leonard Wood as military governor of Cuba, and noted the impatience of islanders who were 'quite determined to have their complete independence' and prepared, if pushed, to fight for it again. Wages were high and opportunities for making money numerous.[5]

One of his early concerns was the 'simply atrocious' cost of living, and his 'quite inadequate' consular salary.[6] On the political front, the new consul general continued to report mounting Cuban frustration at the continued impasse over independence. If the US authorities showed any sign of annexing the island or prolonging occupation indefinitely, he warned, they would 'sooner or later have a revolution on their hands'.[7] During a visit to the island, the US secretary of war advised Carden to discount annexation. Elihu Root explained that even if his government desired it, 'strong opposition' by US sugar and tobacco planting interests would obstruct the policy.[8] Britain's representative focused on the economic potential of the island, which following 'Spain's loss of sovereignty over Cuba [...] was now thrown open to the competition of the world'. It was a new market for foreign goods worth close to £9 m per year. Now unburdened with foreign debt, the island's purchasing power would soon rank amongst the richest markets of the continent, comparable even to Argentina and Brazil, he wrote. Other European countries, particularly Germany, did not appear alive to this unique opportunity.[9]

Furthermore, Carden deemed the 'majority of thinking men in Cuba' to be in favour of the 'freest commercial relations with the rest of the world'. Only some members of the planter class desired a reciprocity treaty, he explained, under the illusory expectation of higher sugar prices. A treaty could only be passed under the strongest US government pressure, and would be a 'death blow' to British trade with Cuba.[10]

Results of municipal and constituent assembly elections, despite manipulation of the franchise by General Wood, did not prove favourable to Root's plan for the island. Cubans of an *independentista* persuasion, most of them war veterans, dominated leadership positions. In a change of tack, Root devised a scheme to unilaterally impose conditions by which his government would maintain control over Cuba as a condition for granting the island its independence.[11] The strategy resulted in the Platt Amendment and it owed something to Britain's model of direct control in Egypt. Root eulogized a system – in a letter to Secretary of State John Hay (1898–1905) – that allowed Britain 'to retire and still maintain her moral control'. He instructed the State Department to make a study of the subject.[12]

A Cuban constituent assembly commission visited Washington in April 1901 to discuss political ties between the two countries. US officials refused to accede to Cuban requests for a direct quid pro quo in the form of favourable commercial relations, but Root did offer to negotiate a reciprocity treaty after the government had formed. By June, a majority of constituent members had been persuaded to accept the terms. One of them, Manuel Sanguily, concluded that limited sovereignty was preferable to no sovereignty at all. The convention accepted the Platt Amendment – an amendment to the Army Appropriations Bill appended to the island's new constitution – through a vote of 16 to 11, with four abstentions.[13] Its third article conceded to Washington 'the right to intervene for the preservation of Cuban independence', and proved a severe external restriction to the island's freedom to rule itself. This burdensome concession enabled US military forces to intervene legally in 1906, 1912 and 1917, before the abrogation of its terms in 1934.

Aware of 'agitation' by Cuban sugar planters in favour of US–Cuban trade reciprocity, Carden warned in January 1901 that the 'very existence' of British trade to Cuba was threatened if tariff advantages were added to the United States' natural geographic advantages and lower freight rates. The only hope of averting such a serious blow, he argued, lay with the actions of the Cubans themselves. In fact, Carden had expressed his arguments to leading delegates in the hope of 'neutralizing' the efforts of planters and their sympathizers. Foreign Office officials in London reacted negatively when they read of his actions. Under Secretary of State Sir Thomas Sanderson wrote,

> I think Mr. Carden ought to be very careful how he puts his fingers into this pie. The U.S. Auth[orities] might feel very angry if they thought he was intriguing against their policy. He might perhaps have a private hint to be cautious.

Foreign Secretary Lord Lansdowne concurred that a warning should be given, and Carden received instructions to 'avoid any appearances of putting forward views on political subjects which might not be acceptable to the U.S. authorities'.[14] This was early evidence that Britain's defence of its interests was going to be less than robust.

In March, Carden explained to London how domestic opposition by sugar and tobacco interests in the United States was bound to oppose vigorously a reciprocity treaty with Cuba. At the same time, he argued, the 'thinking part' of the Cuban population was hardly likely to want to close its market to European exports. For the first time Carden suggested that a Cuban government, when formed, would be willing to negotiate a commercial treaty with His Majesty's Government.[15] A month later he reported strong local reaction to US press reports about a 'protectorate' in the island, confirming some delegates' suspicions that the proposed Platt Amendment was not compatible with independence. He wrote ominously, 'The hot-headed spirits commenced to talk about taking to the woods again'.[16]

British Chambers of Commerce

From the industrial, manufacturing and shipping centres of Great Britain, letters started to rain on Foreign Office desks from British Chambers of Commerce, fearful of damage to their members' lucrative trade with Cuba. In Liverpool there was substantial interest in the carrying trade, principally in the shipping of rice and jute sugar bags from India and Rangoon, via England and Hamburg, to Cuba. Vessels under the British flag also carried sugar from Cuba to the United States, with inbound freight completing this triangular trade from US ports on the return leg to Liverpool. Textiles – particularly cottons and linens from the Manchester area – sold well in the Cuban market. Glasgow-manufactured machinery and tools enjoyed a good reputation and were in demand from the island's recovering sugar industry. Some Chambers of Commerce were unimpressed by official replies to their complaints about the US imposition of a tariff on third-country imports. British Ambassador to Washington Lord Pauncefote countered that preferential advantages meant no such thing.[17]

In Birmingham, one chamber member with an interest in cutlery exports recalled receiving a similar assurance over British trade to Puerto Rico, only later to find an 80 per cent duty imposed on British as opposed to US goods. He wrote, 'My opinion is that we shall close the stable door when the steed is stolen.'[18] Unfortunately for British merchants, protective tariffs did gradually close markets in the former Spanish colonies of Cuba, Puerto Rico and the Philippines.[19]

Queen Victoria's death in January 1901 commenced an eventful year. An anarchist shot William McKinley in September, and the president succumbed to his wounds eight days later. Theodore R. Roosevelt, veteran of the Spanish–American War in Cuba, became the new president of the United States. The Foreign Office continued to be preoccupied by larger foreign policy questions. Britain's fortunes had improved in South Africa, but the Boer War dragged on. Russia threatened in the Far East, and Japan requested British assistance. More widely, increasing concern about German ambitions and an overstretched Royal Navy overshadowed the whole tenure of Foreign Secretary Lord Lansdowne (1900–05).[20]

Drawn-out Anglo–American discussions in Washington finally resulted in the abrogation of the Clayton–Bulwer accord half a century after its inception, superseded by the Hay–Pauncefote Treaty. Britain thus renounced its right to jointly construct a trans-isthmian canal, leaving the project a sole US ambition. This British concession recognized US supremacy in the Caribbean and Central America, and transformed the strategic balance in the region.[21]

By August 1901, the most senior Foreign Office officials in London appeared more amenable to Carden's suggestion to undertake exploratory discussions with leading Cubans over a possible commercial treaty. Under Secretary Lord Cranborne, Prime Minister Lord Salisbury's eldest son, wrote,

> On the one hand it is important to be early in the field, on the other the US might be annoyed if they heard of us negotiating. On the whole I am inclined to think that if Mr Carden is a good man he should be trusted to act confidentially.

Lansdowne concurred and Carden received instructions to enquire 'unofficially and in the most tactful manner possible, in order to avoid all danger of giving offence to the United States Government'.[22] Encouraged, Carden tentatively asked about the British position on future recognition of the new government in Havana. His professed knowledge of the 'Spanish American character' convinced him that timely recognition after the United States would win 'genuine and lasting goodwill', and benefit British trade. Additionally, the accreditation of a diplomatic representative of 'suitable' rank in advance of other powers, would go a long way to gratifying the Cubans' *amour propre*.[23] Such a change in status would also, it must be added, advance Carden's career.

After consultation with the Board of Trade, and Pauncefote in Washington, Carden received a model 'most-favoured nation' commercial treaty in October.[24] Britain's consul general voiced concern over Root's statements that Cuba's imports from third countries would transfer to the United States under reciprocal arrangements. Carden expressed his horror: 'The gravity of this threatened blow to British Commercial and Shipping interests in Cuba can scarcely be exaggerated'. He also pointed to difficulties in getting these measures through the US Congress. In the short term, as with the US–Spanish treaty of 1891, direct experience of reduced sugar duties might well serve to 'disabuse the minds of the Cubans' away from the illusory benefits of permanent reciprocity.[25]

A 'Thorny' Issue

Competing domestic interests in Cuba, the United States and Britain sought precedence in settling the US–Cuban reciprocity negotiations in their favour in 1902. Within Britain, the Chambers of Commerce made repeated and strenuous efforts to galvanize the Foreign Office into taking a harder line with the United States. But in the face of their own timidity and US unresponsiveness, British diplomats in Washington and London offered little to pacify these vocal protests. Carden continued to fight his lone battle in Havana at close proximity to the intrigues at work in favour of US interests.

It was not only Carden and Britain's merchants who warned of the dangers posed to British trade. The Board of Customs published 'striking' figures for 1899 to 1900, demonstrating the rise of US merchandise exports to first rank in Cuba. More worryingly, while Britain had maintained third position, other nations had far surpassed her in capturing Spain's lost trade. France had increased her share by 150 per cent, Germany by 122 per cent and Britain in comparison by a meagre 5.2 per cent.[26]

Carden was now more wary than ever of US commercial avarice in Cuba. He advised that recent proclamations by Roosevelt and the military governor demonstrated how the United States was not satisfied with 'considerable preponderance' in Cuban trade, but 'wants it all'. The island's population had been 'quite taken in' by US newspaper reports of their neighbour's 'disinterested professions', convincing them they were on the 'brink of ruin'. Without opposition, reciprocity would be rushed through 'with the avowed object of excluding European trade'. Referring to earlier Foreign Office instructions not to engage leading Cubans on 'political subjects', Carden asked if he could approach them about reciprocity. US authorities would be alerted by such deliberations, but he argued that 'the political and commercial sides of the Cuban question are so interwoven that it is impossible to say where one ends and the other begins'.[27]

Superintendent of the Foreign Office's commercial department Sir Henry Bergne considered the question 'a thorny one to touch'. Carden's argument persuaded Lord Cranborne, who counselled tact and caution. But Lansdowne's wariness continued; for Carden to succeed he would have to embark on a 'propaganda' effort and thus alert US officials. The foreign secretary wrote, 'It will be safer to tell him that we are not prepared to relax our instructions.'[28]

Carden continued to highlight the mendacity of US reports that described an island threatened with 'misery and starvation', and instead he pointed to a rosy future for its sugar exports and purchasing power. He was prepared to defend the accuracy of his own figures, already quoted in the US Congress, and suggested their wider dissemination in Britain. Such action, he argued, could deal a *coup de grâce* to reciprocity.[29]

Supporters of reciprocity did receive a further blow in March when European powers ended their system of support for sugar beet production through export bounties. Although not to take effect until September 1903, the removal of this artificial stimulus to European sugar producers promised to lessen world over-production. All indications showed that Cuba would be wise to await the effects of the Brussels Convention in anticipation of more demand, better prices and alternative buyers (especially Britain) for its principal product. At the very least, it had much enhanced the island's bargaining power vis-à-vis the United States.[30]

With Carden's pleas from Havana falling largely on deaf ears, the fearful Chambers of Commerce increased their pressure on the Foreign Office to defend British trade in the face of an impending disaster. With its substantial interest in the 'carrying trade', Liverpool coordinated strategy with other Chambers of Commerce in Manchester, Birmingham and Belfast. A resolution by Mr J.E. Hawkes of 'Messrs. Hawkes, Somerville, and Co.' referred to their country's treaty with Japan and the benefits now enjoyed in the United States through an 'open door' in China. It accused Washington of acting in bad faith, by undertaking in 1898 not to control Cuba, and now negotiating a reciprocity treaty to 'entirely exclude' British trade.[31] A local newspaper reported his arguments:

> The United States having approved our opening the door to them in the East, how can they consistently justify closing the door against us in the West? Gratitude alone ought to deter them from proposing such a thing. President Roosevelt has publicly said that the United States owe us a debt of gratitude they can never pay. Let us ask for an instalment now. [...] On the grounds of justice, equity, and fairplay, besides that of conscience, I claim we have a right to object to the proposed treaty of reciprocity.[32]

Austen Taylor MP, attending a Liverpool Chamber of Commerce committee meeting, suggested a joint deputation to the foreign secretary including other Chambers and members of parliament with an interest in Cuban trade.[33] Lansdowne was reluctant to accept, arguing that British action was unlikely 'to produce favourable results'.[34] The Chambers persisted and gained an audience at the Foreign Office. On 11 March 1902, they complained that the 'philanthropic purpose' of intervention had been replaced by a US wish to 'monopolize the island'. While the foreign secretary 'quite entered into their feelings', he could offer little practical help beyond communicating their views to Ambassador Pauncefote in Washington.[35] The US State Department took a considerable time to make a substantive reply.

'Open Door' in Cuba?

Ahead of Cuban independence celebrations on 20 May 1902, Carden made a less than subtle bid to remind the Foreign Office about elevating the status of British representation in Havana. It was to Cuba's advantage to 'encourage European trade and enterprise' and Britain had 'every reason to expect favourable treatment from them'.[36] Five weeks later, Lansdowne authorized Carden to open commercial treaty negotiations with the new government. His telegram included the following warning:

> It is necessary that you should exercise caution in dealing with this question, and you will be careful to avoid committing H[is] M[ajesty's] Govt., without previous instructions, to any course of action which might lead to friction with the U.S. Govt.[37]

In the following days His Majesty approved the appointment of a diplomatic representative at Havana, and Carden rose to the rank of minister.[38] In the summer months following independence the project for reciprocity stalled in a Washington committee, but its powerful supporters were not about to concede defeat.

Carden attempted to impress his arguments against reciprocity on Estrada Palma, the republic's first president (1902–06). According to Britain's minister, the Cuban leader now saw the whole subject in a 'totally new light', but was too 'deeply committed' to reciprocity to turn back. He argued that Palma may be amenable to a compromise that let him meet British wishes 'without giving offence' to the United States.[39] But no amount of potion could magic this solution from the bottle.

In late summer the British minister sensed a change of mood. A rise in the sugar price had encouraged Cuban planters and increased opposition to reciprocity in both Houses of the republic's new Congress. He wrote, 'There is no doubt that the opportunity the United States unquestionably had at one moment of obtaining a commercial control over Cuba with the fullest acquiescence on the part of the immense majority of its people has passed by, never to return.'[40] For a brief period the Foreign Office was assertive and appeared willing to defend British commercial interests, instructing Carden to draw Palma's attention to the 'far-reaching nature' of reciprocity's provisions.[41] At the same time, the minister identified a critical tone in US newspapers, lambasting the 'ingratitude' of Cubans who now dared to question reciprocity.[42]

Almost inevitably, US representatives caught wind of Carden's efforts to dissuade leading Cubans. In London, US Ambassador Joseph Choate approached the Foreign Office and accused its minister in Havana of offering Cuba the "moral & material support" of Great Britain, alongside Germany.[43] Carden's superiors in London requested an explanation, reminding him that such action ran contrary to his instructions. He should be 'especially careful' to avoid suspicion that Britain wished to thwart US policy in Cuba.[44] The minister denied ever mentioning Germany in negotiations, but confirmed his repeated counsel to Cubans to conclude a 'most-favoured nation' treaty with Britain. He added, 'In so far as this might conflict with the U.S. policy which is directed towards exclusion of British trade there is some truth in the report.'[45]

To make matters worse, US authorities then accused Carden of leaving Palma a note that offered Britain's 'moral support, if not their material support'. The Foreign Office and the US ambassador in London accepted Carden's defence that it was an 'absolute fabrication'.[46] But the whole episode highlighted his exposed position in Havana.[47] His superiors had relaxed his strict instructions ever so slightly, only to urge caution when Washington reacted. No reprimand followed, but the margins for his freedom of action had narrowed further still.

As the two-year reciprocity struggle between the US government's executive and Congress reached resolution, Carden's report on general Cuban trade described conditions far more favourable than anything published in the United States since 1898.[48] Signing of the Reciprocity Treaty took place in December 1902, but it still required ratification in Washington. Its terms extended a 20 per cent tariff preference to Cuban sugar producers, and stipulated that all imports from the island (not already on the free list) should enter the United States at a reduction of 20 per cent in the ordinary tariff rates. Dutiable US goods entering Cuba would be reciprocally divided into four classes, entering at rates of 20, 25, 30 and 40 per cent below the rates applied to other foreign imports.[49]

Foreign Office officials in Washington and London examined the new treaty. Senior Clerk Algernon Law considered that remonstrance would be 'useless' and only give rise to 'unnecessary irritation', writing that Cuba's position vis-à-vis the United States was to all practical purposes similar to that of Australia and Canada to Britain, and that Washington's aim was 'quasi Imperial Conversion'. Eldon Gorst agreed, but emphasized the 'irritation' of the Chambers of Commerce and Parliament and the potential loss of £2.5 m trade a year, in addition to the ruin of the rice trade in India and Burmah. Their previous representations remained unanswered and they required a reply 'for Parliamentary purposes'. London instructed its ambassador in Washington to inform his host government that the new Bill appeared to be 'destructive' to all non-US trade with Cuba and 'quite contrary to the policy of "open door" so strenuously advocated' by the United States. To this communication Lansdowne added in red ink that it would create 'much irritation' and a 'considerately worded reply' was therefore 'most desirable'.[50]

The Anglo–American entente in China thus loomed large in Foreign Office thinking. It needed to temper domestic pressure, particularly from parliament, but felt little impulse to insist on the protection of British trade in Cuba. However, it required a form of words from Washington in order to placate these vociferous interests. In response to Lansdowne's request for a 'considerately worded reply', US Secretary of State John Hay responded anaemically:

> The conclusion of the treaty in question, as in the case of the numerous like international arrangements which have been entered into by

this and other governments, is based solely upon the prerogative of independent nations to enter into such compacts for their mutual benefit.[51]

This statement did little to assuage the demands of British merchants for maintenance of an 'open door' in Cuba.

Indefatigability: Carden and the Chambers

While Chambers of Commerce pondered their strategy for combating US domination of Cuban trade,[52] the British government became involved in a further imbroglio in December 1902 when Royal Navy and German ships blockaded and bombarded Venezuelan ports in pursuance of unpaid debt claims. Under pressure from President Roosevelt's administration, the three powers involved agreed to settle the dispute through arbitration. The 'precarious' state of the Anglo–American relationship and the prioritization of 'cordial relations' with Washington dominated British policy.[53]

Reluctant to accept another deputation from the Chambers of Commerce, Lansdowne initially referred them to Hay's reply, but then bowed to pressure and granted a meeting on 22 January 1903. Ahead of their journey to London, Liverpool members complained about the 'manifest injustice' of the reciprocity treaty that had 'practically shut out the rest of the world'. They argued that Britain's colonies had been open for 200 years with no preferential tariff for their mother country. One discordant voice gave lie to this assertion by mentioning the case of Canada.[54]

Representatives from Liverpool again underlined the threat to their members' interests, to inbound and outbound shipping freight and to the city's rice trade – 'the backbone of the whole rice trade' – that had supported Burmah's development. The foreign secretary agreed with their assessment of reciprocity's 'objectionable' nature. But, as a memorandum of the meeting reported, Cuba had 'started with a clean slate', and had every right to make its own arrangements. Lansdowne rejected a suggestion to retaliate, tantamount to 'a new departure in International Law'. He had little to reassure the gentlemen from Liverpool, who offered no 'practical proposal' in return.[55]

The reciprocity project continued its passage through the US Senate. Through the course of 1902 and 1903 the American Sugar Refining Company, popularly known as the 'Sugar Trust', bought up the country's sugar beet interests in order to solidify support behind reciprocity, thus eradicating much remaining opposition. It finally became law in December 1903, definitively cementing US–Cuban economic ties.

The passage of reciprocity delayed Anglo–Cuban treaty negotiations, first started by Cuban Secretary of State Carlos de Zaldo in January 1903. Carden remained optimistic, despite US–Cuban reciprocity. In 1904 he again highlighted the richness and 'brilliant possibilities' of Cuba's market, pointing to the recent rise in the price of sugar and the island's purchasing power.[56] He urged and urged again the securing of a treaty with Cuba.

Reciprocity did not spell immediate doom for British exports to Cuba. *The Economist* carried news of Carden's commercial report and his 'optimistic view' in December. Exports of British cotton exports amounted to £709,972, an increase of £169,683 over the previous year, and representing 55 per cent of the island's total imports of this manufactured product.[57]

British Chambers of Commerce continued their efforts to pressure the Foreign Office into a more robust defence of their interests. The Liverpool Chamber cited ten representatives of rice firms anxious to be included in a further deputation to London in January 1905. Acting on instructions from London, Carden protested to the Cuban government on their behalf, pointing out that 90 per cent Cuba's rice originated from British India, and constituted half of Liverpool's cargo shipments to Havana.[58] A proposed increase on import duties, first passed in Cuba's House of Representatives in July, was defeated in the Senate in August.[59]

Following more machinations and efforts from Carden, the Anglo–Cuban Treaty of Commerce was signed on 4 May 1905, but it required ratification to enact its terms. Discussion of the treaty moved to Congress, where a drawn-out battle would take place. How free was Cuba – senators asked – to agree treaties with foreign powers other than the United States? The debate went to the heart of the fledging republic's 'independent' status. In the summer of 1905, discussions about ratification in the island's Senate Committee on Foreign Relations became bogged down. The treaty was the object of forceful opposition from a certain Antonio Sánchez de Bustamante, a non-party senator for Pinar del Río and chair of the committee.[60]

British Positions on the Treaty

Lionel Carden had meanwhile exchanged the palm trees of Havana for those of Torquay on the English Riviera, and described the disappointment of US interests with reciprocity. They now desired a new

'Convention' of a 'more sweeping character', and as a means to this end, interested parties such as the American Shipping Association were keen to emasculate or strangle the proposed Anglo–Cuban treaty. He emphasized the danger posed to the totality of Britain's Spanish American trade by the 'exceptional' case of Cuba, 'an outpost of the position' which the United States was attempting to capture.[61]

Lansdowne's final opportunity to assertively defend British interests came when he again received a deputation of shipping interests. Mr Pembroke of the North of England Steamship Owners' Association explained how two-fifths of Cuban sugar exports were carried to the United States in 'British bottoms' (compared to one seventh in US ships), making the difference 'between a profit and a loss' in their triangular carrying trade. Lansdowne's response did not intimate forceful action. He told them he supported the treaty's ratification, but exerting 'pressure' at Washington was a 'somewhat delicate operation'.[62] He wrote privately to the British ambassador in Washington, leaving the matter of pressurizing the US government to his judgment. The foreign secretary added: 'Our Liverpool people are considerably excited over the question, and most anxious that something should be said to the Americans.'[63]

Two weeks later, Sir Edward Grey replaced Lansdowne as foreign secretary under new Liberal Prime Minister Henry Campbell-Bannerman, following the resignation of Arthur Balfour's Conservative administration. Arguments over tariff reform had divided his Cabinet and led to defections of prominent 'free-traders' like Churchill to the Liberals, contributing to the Conservatives' crushing election defeat in January 1906. There were also announcements to change British and US diplomatic representation in Havana. Carden would soon transfer to Central America after seven years on the island.[64] Meanwhile, Root pressured Herbert Squiers to resign from his post as US minister in Havana, after expressing a favourable attitude towards annexation and invoking the anger of Cuban politicians by his over-zealous opposition to the Anglo–Cuban treaty.[65] Continuity reigned in the island's politics, at least in the short term, with the presidential re-election of Estrada Palma at the end of the year, albeit the beneficiary of a fraudulent election process.

1906: Final Efforts at Ratification

Unsurprisingly, discussion of the treaty in the Senate's Foreign Relations Committee suffered delay in early 1906. Despite earlier reassurances to Carden over ratification, committee members' inability to form a quorum deferred the matter. Aside from the opposition of three detractors (including Chairman Bustamante) in the five-member Committee, Carden pointed to support from the influential Agrarian League. But when the new Congress met in April, with Bustamante re-elected as chairman, four of its five-member committee were now hostile to the treaty.[66] By the middle of May, even Carden sounded fatalistic, facing continued delays and his own definitive departure for Guatemala.[67]

In his permanent absence the final battles for ratification took place: one inside Cuba's Senate chamber, the other involving a final Liverpool deputation to the Foreign Office. On 23 May the Foreign Relations Committee recommended ratification, but only after imposing several key amendments to the treaty, including the removal of m-fn treatment for British shipping. Opinion in London was unanimous that the agreement was now so emasculated as to be 'useless', and one that would set 'a very bad precedent'.[68] Independent Senator for the Province of Matanzas and President of the Senate Manuel Sanguily was the principal defender of the treaty in the face of Bustamante's unbending opposition. Veteran of Cuba's Ten-Year War of Independence, Sanguily staunchly defended his republic's freedom to agree a treaty with a third foreign power.

He rebuked the members of the Liberal Party and the Moderate Party for discrediting Cuba in the eyes of Britain and the world. The republic was just starting its international career, he argued, but was so fearful of the United States that it would lose its independence. With the insertion of so many modifications the Committee had practically annulled the treaty. In the most impassioned section of his speech, he proclaimed that Cuba's independence would prove 'fictitious' if it failed to agree a treaty with a third power. Cubans would start to imagine they were incapable of resisting US will, and their island would be nothing but an enslaved trading post of its powerful neighbour. In response, Bustamente, a recognized expert in international relations, argued against using Britain and the treaty as a counterweight to US power, of which there was no need to be suspicious or distrustful. Sanguily, meanwhile, questioned his colleague's submission to the United States and the republic's surrender to 'the fate of history'. Bustamante declared that Cubans should have 'full trust in the United States'. But Sanguily retorted: 'Faith in the United States! This is the problem! Nobody has it'.[69]

The senate adopted the committee's report with a vote of eleven to four, and ratified the treaty with its two emasculating amendments.[70] Apparently unaware of Carden's departure, Sir Edward Grey pondered whether he could bring 'pressure to bear on the Cubans', and commented, 'Th[ough] Cuba is in theory independent of the U.S.; In practice it is probably not so.'[71] Unsurprisingly, the Liverpool Chamber of Commerce requested another meeting. Its chairman wrote to the foreign secretary, 'If the Americans are allowed to get their own way the result will be the total annihilation of British trade with Cuba.'[72]

A memorandum for Grey detailed the previous four deputations in March 1902, January 1903, January 1904 and November 1905.[73] On this occasion a member of Liverpool's deputation attempted to enlighten Grey after he declared that 'the hand of the United States Government' had not figured in the amendment annulling m-fn treatment to Britain's shipping trade. 'United States Senators?', riposted Mr Scholefield (vice-chairman, West India Section). Displaying continuity in Lansdowne's policy towards Washington, Grey developed his argument:

> Yes. But American Senators do not form part of that Executive on which we should have to bring pressure. Bringing commercial pressure to bear on the United States is a very large and difficult question. Further, it would be very undesirable to open up, in connection with Cuba, the question of commercial relations with the United States.[74]

Within Grey's explanation was the suggestion of larger and more important issues at stake in Anglo–American relations. Cuba was but a peripheral consideration in the eyes of the Foreign Office. For the Chambers of Commerce, however, trade with the island was their lifeblood.

The assertiveness of the mercantile and manufacturing classes, many from England's North West, had fallen on deaf ears in the Foreign Office. The department had dominated negotiations for the conclusion of the treaty, but its officials, many with close links to the aristocracy, viewed commerce – and the men who practised it – with indifference.[75] The Board of Trade, meanwhile, had minimal interest in outposts such as Cuba, lying outside the British Empire. It only introduced an effective and widespread system of commercial intelligence abroad near the end of the First World War.[76] Although newspapers reported news of the treaty's progress and London meetings between the Chambers of Commerce and the Foreign Office, it barely aroused public and parliamentary opinion. The decisive issue was the prioritization of Anglo–American harmony over commercial advantage in Cuba, with continuity between Foreign Secretaries Lansdowne and Grey.

Cuba's nascent economic and political elite, meanwhile, prioritized a collaborative relationship with the United States and not Great Britain. The case of the frustrated Anglo–Cuban Treaty bode poorly for the new republic's independence of action from Washington, and signified an inauspicious start for commercial relations between the two island countries.

The Second US Intervention and World War

Periodic political and social unrest in Cuba during the republic's first two decades led the United States to intervene militarily on three occasions in order to restore stability and protect its interests, all the while anxious to deny any imperialist design. Great Britain, meanwhile, enjoyed the not inconsiderable benefit of commercial opportunities in an expanding and prosperous market, protected by a dominant and friendly ally at no direct cost to His Majesty's Government.

In 1906 the United States felt compelled to invoke Article III of the Platt Amendment for the first time and 'exercise the right to intervene for the preservation of Cuban independence'. President Tomás Estrada Palma won a second four-year term in 1905, but the main coalition opposition party did not contest the disputed election. Armed rebellion ensued, forcing Washington's hand. Roosevelt could not countenance permanent 'misrule and anarchy' in the island, but neither could he contemplate direct control. He also dreaded accusations from other countries that this was his government's ambition.[77]

Reluctantly, Roosevelt sent marines to quell the revolt and occupy the island. While the 1906 intervention put paid to any lingering possibility of US annexation, it set an instructive precedent to those Cubans outside government. As an alternative to defeating a serving administration through purely democratic means, opponents could provoke Washington's intervention instead. The second intervention was a shattering psychological blow to the republic's self-esteem and its legacy was pessimism, disillusionment and a 'Plattist' state of mind: one of leaving important political decisions to Washington.[78]

Disturbances delayed the outward journey of newly appointed British Minister to Cuba Arthur Grant-Duff, and postponed his meeting with Manchester merchants, eager to highlight their valuable cotton export trade.[79] Once established in Havana, he commented on the island's lack of domestic manufactures and its large import requirements. The lack of grain production made Indian rice – especially Rangoon and Patna classes – a principal import, although Louisiana and Texas producers had tried to displace this empire trade by pressing for higher import duties. British cottons and linen articles continued to dominate the Cuban market, accounting respectively for one-third and four-fifths of the import market.[80]

Secretary of State Elihu Root supervised the second US military occupation (1906–09) from Washington, directed within the island by Provisional US Governor Charles E. Magoon. The dynamics of the US–Cuban relationship and Washington's emasculation of the island's self-determination were evident to British diplomats. In each annual report they highlighted Cuba's limited freedom of action. There was therefore a substantive difference between British and US judgements on the US–Cuban relationship. The British tended to highlight overbearing US control, while US commentators viewed a guiding and benevolent hand.[81] Britain's longest-ever serving representative in Havana, Stephen Leech (1909–19), described the island as a 'lap dog', kept on a tight leash by her powerful northern owner. A regular and informed visitor, the English journalist Sydney Brooks, described a 'half-autonomous, half-vassal state'. Following termination of US provisional control, Leech poured scorn on Cuba's political culture, on politicians' self-interest and 'selfish and unpatriotic frame of mind' and their 'get rich as quickly as possible' approach. Brooks highlighted the island's factional politics, a violent fight between those in and out of power desperate to plunder the considerable spoils of office.[82]

In the period leading up to the First World War there was 'intense Anglo–American commercial and financial rivalry' for the abundant economic opportunities available in the island.[83] Britain and its empire were able to excel in some economic areas. For example, capital invested in railways was predominantly British, with dividends going to Britain. And banking was a success story for Canada, a dominion of the British Empire from 1867. Two banks, the Royal Bank of Canada and the Nova Scotia, held capital of £2,200,000 and £300,000 respectively.[84] Legislation in the United States prohibited US banks from establishing operations abroad until 1913, and Canadian rivals took full advantage of the lack of competition. After opening its first branch in 1899, the Royal Bank of Canada had expanded to 11 branches in 1908 and 27 by 1918, with an impressive 65 dotted around the island by the mid-1920s.[85]

But US hegemony, imposed rapidly on Cuba, did not augur well for diplomats' negotiations with government officials, and for many other British commercial interests. The rigidly exclusive structure of the US–Cuban relationship only left them limited areas of the economy in which to operate. Third countries trod carefully in Cuba, in the face of US dominance and 'evasions and prevarications' from the island's politicians.[86]

Leech and his colleagues repeatedly complained at the inertia of Cuban ministers, their 'evasion' in dealing with complaints and making decisions. While Secretary of State Manuel Sanguily was a man of 'unimpeachable honesty' who might often 'favour foreign interests [...] as a counterpoise to the influence of the United States', this rarely translated into positive action on his part.[87]

A case in point related to the joint representations made by Britain, France and Germany over claims for property damage during Cuba's Second War of Independence (1895–98). British claims relating to the later 1906 rebellion were settled satisfactorily in 1908. But the Cubans were naturally reluctant to assume responsibility for damage caused by insurgents during their earlier independence struggle. Though these claims were revived on several occasions over two decades, the European powers never obtained Cuba's consent to take them to arbitration. Secretary of State Sanguily was left forlorn when US President Taft first agreed to arbitrate in the matter and later withdrew his offer.[88] The Cuban government pleaded with Washington for support in the face of joint European pressure. Tellingly, Sanguily reasoned with the US minister that the Platt Amendment gave his government the right to intervene, but also 'the obligation to defend' Cuba from stronger nations.[89]

But despite the US refusal to get involved, the European countries struggled to maintain a united front. At one point, the British minister recommended delay to the Foreign Office in order to retain Cuba's goodwill for the negotiation of more important issues.[90] The French had the largest interest in the matter, with claims amounting to approximately £1.2 m, while the British (£0.3 m) and Germans (£0.25 m) sought lesser amounts. The matter dragged on until the early 1920s, but the Europeans never received compensation.[91]

In 1911, Cuba's Congress hastily approved a 30-year concession for running the principal ports of Havana and Santiago. US ships would pay lower tonnage rates than other foreign vessels. Protests from other countries were to no avail, but Britain, at least initially, took solace in the fact that London was the source of the original £1.2 m loan that financed the project.[92] There were further machinations concerning this and other concession controversies during the José Miguel Gómez presidency (1909–13), over what US economic historian Leland Jenks described as 'the most grandiose attempt at plunder in the history of Cuba'.[93]

Cornell University-educated Mario Menocal replaced Gómez (*el Tiburón*, 'the Shark') as president in 1913. Promising a more honest administration, he annulled the ports concession, a decision later upheld by the courts. In defence of British stock and bond investors in the ports company, His Majesty's Government told the Cuban government it was considering a warning to British depositors to desist from further investments. By the year's end, Cuba was practically excluded from the European money market owing to this action and the lack of progress over the 'war claims' issue.[94]

Like other commercial interests, Britain's main capital interest in Cuba, its ownership and management of the railways, suffered protracted problems. The relocation of Havana's central station terminus from its inconvenient site in Villanueva to the Arsenal property near the capital's harbour, led to a dispute for rights to use the new terminus between two British railway companies: the Western Railway of Havana and United Railways of Havana. The quarrel was only resolved when the two companies amalgamated. Meanwhile, another British company, Cuban Central Railways, was involved in a fight with the island's Railway Commission over rates. The next year the same British company found itself in a dispute with the Cuban-American North Coast Railway Company for a concession to build a new line. The US State Department, after initially acceding to British pressure to 'exert its influence' and secure justice in the matter, later withdrew its offer. After lengthy negotiations, United Railways again stepped into the breach by buying out its British rival and coming to an arrangement with the Cuban-American company.[95]

In 1899, three British-owned railways in Cuba had a combined capital of £8.34 m and total track mileage of 569 miles: Western Railway of Havana (registered in 1892) with 110 miles; United Railways of Havana (registered in 1898) with 245 miles; and Cuban Central Railways (registered in 1899) with 214 miles.[96] United Railways steadily came to dominate all rail transport in the western portion of the island through amalgamation and acquisition of other companies, as well as new track construction.[97] By 1911 it had expanded to become Cuba's largest railway, extending its network to 684 miles.[98] By 1913 its rail lines converged under one roof at a new Central Station terminus close to water frontage on the Bay of Havana, where the company owned extensive warehousing facilities. It also came to own termini and facilities at the important ports of Matanzas and Cienfuegos. In an apparent division of spoils, the British railway held a practical monopoly of western Cuba, while the tracks of the multinational Cuban Railroad covered the central and eastern segments of the island.[99]

The integration of railways, warehousing and dock facilities during a bonanza period for the Cuban sugar industry did reap large rewards for British companies. In this early period of the republic the expanding United Railways of Havana and Regla Warehouses Company, established with substantial British capital investment, made large profits as Cubans – to cannibalize a familiar expression – cut cane while the sun shone. The sun shines often and long in Cuba, and it shone on this British company as the sugar industry expanded greatly. United Railways charged high freight and warehouse rates to convey and store sugar, and paid large dividends to stockholders and investors as a result.[100]

The cusp of disruption to world markets provoked by the First World War is a good juncture at which to take stock of Britain's stake and interests in Cuba. There would be periods of resurgence, but Britain would never again attain the same proportion of capital investment and exports to the island compared to the United States. In 1913, British Vice Consul Denys Cowan reported that the United Kingdom exported twice the amount (40 per cent) of cotton goods to Cuba as the United States (20 per cent). For woollen goods the figures were even more positive for the United Kingdom: 40 per cent as opposed to 17 per cent. In rice exports Germany dominated, with 42.6 per cent of the trade, but combining India's exports (22 per cent) with those from the United Kingdom (30.7 per cent) gave the British Empire the lion's share of this commerce.[101]

Although they differed in type, British and US investments in Cuba are listed in several sources as more or less equal in 1913.[102] North American investment was typically direct, to US enterprises and subsidiaries. Britain tended to hold passive portfolio investment of minority stockholdings and government and private bonds.[103] But a significant problem lies in categorizing the nationality of investments. With regard to the ownership of sugar mills, Leland Jenks sets out the difficulty of defining and disaggregating the domicile of a corporation from the nationality (rarely single) of stockholders and/or directors, not to mention the nationality of a mill's proprietors.[104]

Conclusion

The reluctance of the Cuban Congress in 1906 to ratify the commercial treaty without emasculation set the tone for Anglo–Cuban relations in the first three decades of the republic. At almost every turn the predominant position of the United States in Cuba impinged upon British interests there. Britain espoused free trade and pleaded for an 'open door', but the weight of US trade and financial interests pressured Washington to control Cuba's abundant market and leave its door only slightly ajar. Successive British governments were supine in defence of their private economic interests, leaving them to fight their battles alone with minimal official assistance.[105]

The British government's general submission to US supremacy partly responded to the need to reduce naval commitments in the Americas as part of a global strategy of political realignments. Stark economic realities and the ascendancy of a friendly power in the hemisphere facilitated a reduction in imperial garrisons and naval squadrons in Canada and the West Indies between 1904 and 1906. As a result of these economies the Royal Navy would only maintain a cruiser squadron (with a landing party) at Bermuda to perform policing and ceremonial duties in the Caribbean.[106] In such a way, the United States could be left to supervise the region alone and Britain could redeploy its stretched resources elsewhere.[107] British eyes and military resources were concentrated against an increasingly powerful and aggressive imperial Germany. The first of two world wars against this European adversary began in 1914, shattering Britain's global economic supremacy and costing it more than 700,000 men in uniform.

3
The First World War to Boom and Bust

The opening of the Panama Canal before the First World War further reduced the strategic importance of the British West Indies and British responsibility for security in the region. The Great War itself caused major upheaval to Britain's transatlantic shipping and trade and diverted capital to financing the war effort, with obvious repercussions for trade and investment in Cuba. The island's two principal agricultural products suffered contrasting fates during the war; sugar was indispensable and in high demand as a staple commodity in Western diets, while cigars were a luxury and wholly expendable. Most Cuban cigar factories were forced to close early in the war due to the cancellation of European orders.[1]

The First World War and Beyond

Britain had developed an increasingly sweet tooth during the nineteenth century. Sugar consumption in the country rose fourfold between the 1830s and 1890s, reaching the giddy annual level of 70 lb per head.[2] Before the First World War, beet sugar from Austro-Hungary and Germany was supplying more than two-thirds of British import requirements. The outbreak of conflict precluded Britain from purchasing beet from these two wartime enemies, and to make a difficult situation worse, large agricultural regions of French sugar beet cultivation soon converted into the Western Front. As a result, Cuba benefited from increased demand and higher prices for its sugar. Constituting a foodstuff of high calorific value, Britain took emergency measures to secure the import of this essential commodity when panic hit London's market in 1914 and sugar prices doubled in two months. The Royal Sugar Commission, the first state-managed food control institution during wartime, bought and sold sugar, and regulated its production from August 1914. And the Admiralty obtained powers to requisition vessels for the conveyance of sugar imports from major outlets.[3]

During the 1914 to 1915 period Britain obtained most of its sugar, both raw and white, from Eastern suppliers in Java and Mauritius. But from 1916 the actions of German submarines and military exigencies provoked a serious merchant shipping shortage. Remoter sources of sugar in the East had to be abandoned, and priority given to those imported via the shorter and more defensible sea route across the North Atlantic. For the rest of the war, Britain was heavily dependent on Western suppliers, and particularly on Cuba, whose raw sugar production dwarfed that of its British West Indian neighbours. Soon after the United States entered the war in April 1917, Washington and London coordinated sugar purchases and allocation between the Allies in Europe and North America, anxious to secure sufficient supplies and avoid exploitative speculation by suppliers during years of crucial demand.[4] War and a commonality of national interests thus led to a rare example of coordinated Anglo–American policy toward the island.

As in 1905, armed rebellion followed the re-election of a Cuban president in 1916. Insurgents in Oriente province destroyed cane fields and threatened to halt grinding operations in sugar mills. In Santiago de Cuba, rebels compelled a branch of the Royal Bank of Canada to hand over government funds under duress. The British minister informed his US counterpart that responsibility for protection of British property lay with the United States.[5] Washington did soon again feel compelled to send troops and arms. The revolt by supporters of former President José Miguel Gómez pushed westwards as far as Las Villas, but had to admit defeat to Menocal's better-organized troops, enjoying US military support. In the course of this tumult, 13 Jamaicans were shot dead at Jobabo near Santiago. The resulting court martial and acquittal of two Rural Guard officers led to protracted complaints by His Majesty's Government, not finally resolved until 1921 when compensation was paid to ten victims' families. US marines remained in Oriente province until 1922, ostensibly for the purpose of training.

Apart from higher demand for sugar and lower demand for cigars, Cuba was largely unaffected by the war. British Minister in Havana Stephen Leech estimated that around 70 per cent of Cubans supported the Allies. The remainder, including Spaniards, were either indifferent or pro-German, these latter views expressed in the Spanish-owned newspaper *Diario de la Marina*.[6] With Cuban hearts not in the war, the British minister described insidious elements that fomented anti-American and pro-German propaganda. Havana's strategic position as a port of call for ships en route to and from Spain and Mexico also made it a centre for political intrigue related to the Mexican Revolution.[7]

An official British mission to Latin America in 1918 attempted to recover economic ground lost to the United States. During four months a mission led by Maurice de Bunsen visited 11 countries, fully utilizing the services of British railway and river navigation companies established in Latin America, travelling over cordillera at 14,000 feet and through the Panama Canal before arriving at Havana, its last port of call.[8] De Bunsen enjoyed a gala performance at the National Theatre and a banquet at the Country Club, and visited the British-owned Henry Clay & Bock Company cigar factory.[9] The mission seemed to satisfy the desire of Cuba's political elite to sit at the top table with a leading power. But the first subsequent attempt to reciprocate would end with an abortive official visit of leading Cubans to Great Britain and much recrimination.

Leech's concern over pro-German elements increased later in 1918. Additionally, he was perturbed at the absence of harmony between US officials in Havana from different government departments (State, Justice, War Trade Board, Army, Navy) and Minister William Gonzales, who he described as more 'the representative of President Menocal in Washington than the representative of President Wilson in Cuba'. On a visit to Washington, Leech reported these worrying developments to Frank Polk in the State Department and denounced Menocal's 'Cabinet of subservient and lazy Ministers'. The British minister remarked on the frankness with which US officials referred to their 'quasi protectorate' and their reticence with regard to Gonzales. Within a week of his visit, the Cuban authorities had interned 14 Germans.[10]

A recurring quandary for the Foreign Office concerned the physical protection of British interests in Cuba during periods of political unrest. In British eyes, Cuba was a US domain and Washington would resent Royal Navy intrusion into its sphere. The issue went to the heart of British attitudes towards Cuba, and highlighted a tendency to defer to larger US interests and liabilities. When disorder erupted or threatened, to the detriment of British interests, the Foreign Office automatically turned to the United States. However, problems arose when US marines did not so readily land on the island to quell unrest.

In 1919, the British fretted over a railway strike that threatened the sugar supply. Foreign Office opinion was divided over making a request for US protection, with particular opposition from senior department officials. British embassy staff in Washington raised the issue with their

US counterparts. Under terms agreed with the United States, Britain depended on Cuba for 65 per cent of the year's sugar supply. The passivity of the US embassy in Cuba, reluctant to embroil itself constantly in Cuban politics at the risk of domestic and international criticism, invoked British requests for a more proactive policy.[11] Evidently, a less overtly interventionist US policy did not always suit Britain's interests.

In the event, the British chargé d'affaires and the Foreign Office were left aghast when two Royal Navy 'men of war', the HMS *Dauntless* and HMS *Devonshire*, anchored in Havana's harbour. Unbeknown to diplomats, and to the expressed amazement of Acting Foreign Secretary Lord George Curzon, the prime minister had charged the Admiralty with protecting Cuba's sugar supply.[12] According to Vice Consul Denys Cowan, the presence of navy bluejackets had a salutary effect on both the Cubans and Gonzales, with the US minister invited aboard for dinner. The whole visit had been a 'remarkable piece of propaganda', Cowan wrote, 'carrying on a most successful process of plucking the Eagle's feathers without the Eagle knowing it, in fact rather enjoying it'. He looked forward to further naval visits and making Cubans aware that the British had 'not resigned [them]selves completely to American predominance'.[13] The importance of an uninterrupted sugar supply meant that another department had trumped Foreign Office policy. Despite fears, there were no reports of a negative US reaction to the British naval presence.[14]

In the immediate aftermath of war, there was massive speculative investment and expansion in Cuba's sugar industry in order to satisfy increased demand and benefit from higher prices. This led to financial ruin when boom was soon followed by bust in a period known as the 'Dance of the Millions'. The US Sugar Equalization Board, responsible for allied supplies from Cuba, decided to abandon control of the sugar market in December 1919. British civil servants were reluctant to pay the excessive prices soon demanded by Cuban planters and negotiated the purchase of Mauritius's whole crop for 1920, while the United States turned to the East for its supplies. Reduced British dependence on the Cuban crop, plus the release of strategically held stocks, reversed the earlier price surge and provoked a rapid price collapse. When the price of Cuban sugar plunged to 4 cents per pound at the year's end from its May peak of 22½ cents, Britain purchased 100,000 tons of the island's chief commodity.[15]

The main effect of the Great War on Anglo–Cuban relations was a wholesale reverse in the balance of trade between the two nations. Prior to the conflict, the balance favoured British exports over Cuban imports.

Table 2 Comparison of Cuban trade with the US and the UK
(as percentage of total trade)*

Year	Exports from Cuba to:		Imports into Cuba from:	
	US	UK	US	UK
1904	86%	6.5%	40.9%	13.4%
1910–11	87.8%	3.9%	52.8%	11.8%
1913–14	80.2%	10.7%	53.3%	10.9%
1919–20	75.1%	14.8%	73.8%	3.1%
1920–21	85.2%	5.9%	76.1%	3.4%
1922	80%	11.5%	66.8%	5%
1925	74.6%	15.7%	62.8%	4%
1928	72.8%	16.3%	60.8%	5.2%
1930	69.3%	15.2%	56.5%	5.4%

*Statistics compiled from UK reports on 'Trade and Commerce' and
'Economic Conditions' in Cuba in the years 1913, 1914, 1922, 1925, 1929
and 1932 (details of reports listed in bibliography).

But following the cessation of hostilities, and for the next four decades, Britain would import far more than it exported (see Table 2). This was mainly due to disruption in the world sugar trade. In 1923, the British acting consul general in Havana reported that Cuba had 'entirely taken the pre-war place of Austria and Germany as supplier of sugar to Great Britain'. From Cuba's perspective, this benefit was diminished by the sudden (but temporary) disappearance of Britain as its most lucrative cigar market. Meanwhile, the British export of woollens 'was lost' to US competitors, whereas merchants of 'the finer textiles' continued to hold their own. The volume of British shipping, even by 1923, was 'still far below the pre-war standard'.[16]

Just as worrying were attempts by European competitors to capture Britain's share of manufactured goods exports to Cuba. The Belgians, the French and the Germans were offering 'very important competition to British made goods'. Germany, also, was 'very active' in shipping, competing for both passenger and freight traffic.[17]

Reciprocal Anglo–Cuban Missions

With the Jobabo controversy still unsettled, and a further dispute over British ownership of land titles at Paso Estancia unresolved in 1920, the Cuban government pressed ahead with a reciprocal visit to Britain. But there was a serious problem with the mission's composition because it included three individuals unpalatable to the British. In their eyes, the mission's head, Secretary of State Pablo Desvernine, had displayed a most 'unaccommodating and unsatisfactory attitude', and had done little to settle both outstanding cases. General Eduardo Pujol, meanwhile, was ultimately responsible for the troops who had committed the murders at Jobabo. And Frederick Berndes, a naturalized Cuban, was German by descent. During the war, both his father and brother were German subjects and notorious 'black-listers' (forbidden from trading with British nationals).[18] On receipt of such information one official in London commented: 'A visit by a number of Germans disguised as Cubans seems to be almost a farce.' The Foreign Office communicated these concerns to Cuban Minister in London Carlos García Vélez, a political rival of Desvernine.[19]

García Vélez stood in a long tradition of Latin American politicians rewarded with a diplomatic post abroad in order to distance them from domestic politics. He telegraphed his government to postpone the mission, promising to discuss the issue personally with the president and Desvernine on his imminent return to Cuba. But the mission was already in New York, awaiting its passage to Portsmouth on board the SS *Pocahontas*, and had no option but to return ignominiously to Havana. García Vélez, meanwhile, did not arrive as planned. Cuban newspapers whipped up a storm at the 'affront to national dignity' and the British minister feared demands for his expulsion.[20] Such a reaction, he wrote, was to be expected from 'a young people who combine great sensitiveness with the arrogance of newly made wealth'.[21]

Months later, the French minister in Havana confirmed the Foreign Office suspicion that García Vélez had exaggerated British opposition to the mission in order to further his ambition to succeed Desvernine.[22] The son of independence hero Calixto García, himself a former minister to London, García Vélez would gain political notoriety from 1923 as president of the Veterans' and Patriots' Association, representing those who had fought in the nineteenth-century independence wars.[23] In this case, however, he had managed to unsettle Anglo–Cuban relations by involving them in factional domestic politics.

In 1921, the presidency of Cuba passed into the hands of the elderly Alfredo Zayas. After viewing his inauguration, the new British Chargé d'Affaires Geoffrey Haggard commented on the presence of the 'plain figure' of General Enoch Crowder: 'A spare man of 60, looking in his soiled United States uniform for all the world like a Salvation Army preacher – to whom the new Government owes its existence, and without whose support it is doubtful if it can continue.'[24] Crowder came with a colourful military background. He had fought against Apache leader Geronimo in 1886 and Sioux chief Sitting Bull in 1890, and had previously served under US Governor Magoon in Cuba.[25]

At Haggard's first meeting with the new president, Zayas immediately raised the issue of the aborted mission to London, and both his personal hurt at its failure and desire to resurrect it. But several other bilateral issues needed resolution for it to go ahead. Britain desired compensation for the families of the Jamaicans murdered at Jobabo. In the case of Paso Estancia, the various claims on land titles since 1912 were so unclear that the case had become moribund. For Cuba, there remained the issue of an extraordinary British war tariff on cigar imports, still in operation to the detriment of Cuba's second most important export. Haggard also reported pressure from British businessmen in Cuba whose trade had suffered due to embittered local feelings.[26]

To soothe British sentiment, former President Menocal was now proposed as head of the resurrected mission instead of the objectionable Desvernine, and the Jobabo victims' families received payments from lottery funds. Britain reciprocated by repealing its tobacco import tax. However, indicative of the island's delicate political relationship with Washington and their close economic ties, the Cuban government was keen that news of the forthcoming mission be presented in Havana as a British initiative. Haggard described Cuban apprehension over Americans 'trying to "queer" the mission'. Although there would be a commercial delegate in the Cuban mission, he would arrive untitled for fear of antagonizing Washington.[27] Additionally, the five Cuban delegates would travel via Paris in order to deflect US suspicions. With an impending luncheon organized at Buckingham Palace, King George V was keen to know if the delegates spoke English, if there would be any 'Americans' among them, and whether they were 'white or coloured'.[28] The assistant under secretary replied that the five English-speaking Cubans could be described as white, although 'they may present a somewhat yellow appearance'.[29]

Diplomacy and Diplomats

There were calls from several quarters within the British government to improve the country's representation and commercial strategy in Latin America, and counter both its weakened position and aggressive US intrusion. After the war Britain was unfortunately too weak financially to fund the plans of those who advocated a more effective commercial approach. In 1920, the British ambassador to the United

States urged his government to direct its efforts from Washington, where most eminent Latin American statesmen resided. A proposed Spanish-speaking embassy functionary might convince them that a British alternative existed to US commercial domination.[30]

With regard to the British diplomatic mission in Havana, the overriding concern was cost. From the establishment of the Cuban Republic in 1902 until the 1951 elevation of Britain's legation to embassy status, His Majesty's diplomatic representatives in Havana repeatedly complained about the exorbitant cost of living in the Cuban capital. Due to its skewed trading relationship with the United States and unique tariff arrangements, practically everything available to buy in the island was imported. This made costs for British representatives and their government extraordinarily high, way above those in other countries. The island's climate, its frequent cyclones, the millstone of commercial work, and the difficulty of carrying out diplomacy in a US domain, all added to the burden for Britain's men in Havana.

Cuba was the last country visited by Comptroller of Commercial and Consular Affairs Victor Wellesley, on his tour of inspection of various Latin American missions and consulates from 1919 to 1920. His report on Cuba commenced as follows:

> Of all the posts I visited in the course of my tour of inspection none stands in more urgent need of immediate and serious consideration than the Legation and Consulate General at Havana, if something like a catastrophe is to be avoided.

Such would be the cost of maintaining an adequate diplomatic post and staff in Havana that Wellesley hesitated recommending it as a serious proposition. But the legation and consular buildings, he continued, gave the impression that His Majesty's Government was 'in the last stages of financial decrepitude'. Despite the undoubted importance of Havana as a 'post of observation' over all Caribbean trade, he recommended the drastic and urgent reorganization of the legation and its staff structure. The cost of living meant that the minister, still burdened with accreditation to Haiti, was exceeding his official income by £4250 per annum! The cost of living in Havana was 30 per cent dearer than even New York or Buenos Aires.[31]

Wellesley tentatively suggested an expedient but politically unpalatable solution: accredit Britain's minister in Mexico to Havana and leave commercial and consular work in the less costly hands of a chargé d'affaires. The Foreign Office discussed the pressing matter with the

Treasury. Was Cuba worth the expense of keeping the legation on its current footing? The political importance of the post to Britain was 'comparatively small' and there existed a 'predominance of American financial and political interests'.[32] One official in London asked whether it was 'not the fact that Cuba is not wholly an independent country but under some form of American protection?'[33] The implication was that Washington's interests and therefore responsibilities were far greater, so why not ride on the back of its political representation and extract commercial benefits with the minimum of expense?

Stephen Leech, evidently a man of some considerable private means, had urged the Foreign Office to put the legation and its staff (minus the minister himself) on a firmer financial footing in 1917. None of the mission's employees in Cuba's 'exhausting tropical climate' had enjoyed even a day's leave for over three years and living costs had increased by an average of 94 per cent.[34] A compromise solution amalgamated the posts of minister and commercial secretary.[35] The new chargé d'affaires was Geoffrey Haggard, a recently promoted consul in the Consular Service, and nephew of British novelist H. Rider Haggard, famous for adventure stories set in colonial Africa. In the words of a senior official, 'A rather special and exceptional post is created to save a large sum of money.'[36] Haggard was the first of two successive consular officials to be entrusted with the downsized British legation in Havana. Initially, the expense to the British taxpayer was reduced, but the cost to Anglo–Cuban relations would prove high.

Washington grew decidedly uneasy with the financial management and general conduct of the Zayas government. President Warren G. Harding's 'special representative' in Havana, General Enoch Crowder, forced the mass resignation of the Cuban cabinet in 1922, and Washington submitted the names of new ministers for approval. Haggard remarked that the new cabinet, later nicknamed the 'honest Cabinet', was 'almost entirely American in complexion'. He was disappointed with the replacement of Secretary of State Rafael Montoro – with whom he had maintained excellent relations – and reported an 'unfriendly' reception from his successor, Dr Carlos Manuel de Céspedes. He had lengthy experience in the United States, and was the son of a nineteenth-century Cuban patriot with the same name. Haggard feared that Céspedes would prove detrimental to British interests.[37]

With the ending of wild price fluctuations during the 'Dance of the Millions' period, Cuba's volatile economy and politics achieved relative stability under Washington's close supervision. Foreign Office diplomats made the very obvious link between the condition of the island's sugar trade and its politics. Haggard described Cubans' ready acceptance of Crowder's rise to ambassadorial status in 1923. Because of the recent rise in the price of sugar, he wrote, their present frame of mind was 'seeing everything *couleur de rose*'. In London, David Kelly – the author of an invaluable treatise on British diplomacy years later – commented sagely and accurately, 'Apparently U.S. prestige fluctuates with the price of sugar.'[38] Recovery in the Cuban market did not go unnoticed by the Board of Trade. It observed that the island appeared on the cusp of renewed prosperity, and alongside Mexico, lagged behind only Argentina, Brazil and Chile as Latin American markets for British goods.[39]

The British West-Indian Problem

The success of the Cuban mission in the same year, plus the expressed desire by President Zayas to keep on good terms with the British legation, had appeared to herald a period of improved Anglo–Cuban relations. And the expense of diplomatic representation in Cuba had been resolved through compromise. But problems for Anglo–Cuban relations loomed from a different quarter, and related directly to Cuba's all-important sugar industry.

Following US intervention in 1898, there had existed a virtual ban on black immigration to Cuba. After the 1912 revolt, large sugar corporations and mills contracted thousands of Haitians, Jamaicans and 'antillanos' from other Caribbean islands as seasonal labourers for the sugar industry. The presence of British West Indians at Jobabo was naturally related to this seasonal immigration. The exigencies of war created more demand for Cuba's main product and therefore for labour, not wholly satisfied by Spanish and Haitian workers. In 1919 alone, nearly 24,000 Jamaicans came to the island.[40] But thousands of labourers were dismissed when crisis hit the sugar industry two years later, many without payment of wages. Groups of wandering destitute men naturally became a security problem.[41]

Quarantine in unsanitary conditions greeted new arrivals to Cuba. British West Indian labourers complained that unscrupulous mill-owners paid them with worthless vouchers and then colluded with armed rural guards to quell their protests. Limited repatriations to their home islands took place, but only if home governments funded their passages. On rare occasions when murder cases involving rural guards did reach court – as with the earlier Jobabo incident – guilty verdicts and prosecutions never resulted. Furthermore, Cuba's own agitated labour force in the 1920s militated against the interests of seasonal foreign workers, stirred by such factors as a nationalist anti-foreign discourse, an embryonic labour movement, and pervasive racial prejudice in an ex-slave society.[42] Describing local attitudes, Haggard's successor wrote, 'A strong racial hatred prevails against all negroes, and when times are bad the Cubans regard the Jamaicans as interlopers and the cause of all their poverty and distress.'[43] To add to the legation's woes, the oppressed West Indians were quick to proclaim both their status as British subjects and recourse to Crown protection, employing these defences when they suffered arbitrary abuses.[44]

The evidence demonstrates that the British government took the matter extremely seriously. The Colonial Office received numerous complaints and was under considerable parliamentary pressure to take action. Lengthy and vociferous private and newspaper correspondence from the Caribbean landed on the desks of royalty, politicians and officials alike. From the official British point of view, the Cuban government, despite numerous representations, had done little to alleviate injustices perpetrated against West Indian workers. The issue evoked memories of Caribbean slavery and the abolition movement of decades past. British officials in Cuba were caught in the crossfire of British government reaction, official Cuban inaction and a barrage of individual complaints at consular establishments throughout the island. The personal views of diplomats on the British subjects in question often stood out starkly when contrasted with official policy. Haggard, at least, viewed the issue in wholly negative terms: 'It is unfortunately true that these coloured people are mere drones in the hive of the British Empire. They are quarrelsome and lazy, and bring nothing to us in business, in taxes or prestige.'[45]

Yet, it was left to this same official to formulate an official strategy to resolve the issue in conjunction with the Colonial Office. Gradual and increasing pressure on the Cuban government, they thought, would result in better treatment for the migrant workers. The British government would publish a White Paper containing all the correspondence between the legation and the Cuban State Department. They would also disseminate a rumour that British West Indian governments were considering the restriction of emigration from their territories. It was a toothless and unenforceable threat. Large numbers of migrant workers were still eager to earn better wages abroad, and some authorities were reluctant to prevent them leaving. Haggard wrote of the Cuban government, 'Bring the thing home to them, and they will react as we wish.'[46] Although the arrangement satisfied the Colonial Office's wish to take overt action, it contained a 'bluff' that reflected poorly on the Foreign Office.[47]

The policy was in many respects unworkable, and above all counterproductive. Jamaica, the most important colony, had a surplus of labour, and with workers still willing to make the journey to Cuba, a ban would threaten social unrest.[48] And, as the Cuban secretary of state pointed out, migrants would still enter clandestinely. Dr Céspedes was taken aback by Britain's serious stance. An unpalatable truth was that official harsh treatment of black migrant workers in the 1920s and beyond was not an unpopular policy for a Cuban public fed with gossip and newspaper stories about desperate and murderous savages on the loose. And when the British parliament presented its two proposed White Papers, the Cubans responded in kind with a Grey Paper to their Congress. Britain's acting chargé described this riposte as 'clever and effective'.[49] In Cuba, the White Papers raised a storm, not against the mistreatment of black British subjects, but against the British Empire's high-handedness.[50] The island was already dominated by one imperious power, and did not appreciate being lectured to by another.

In the same period, powerful financial interests in the United States exerted their influence over Cuba's economy. The island's House of Representatives passed the Tarafa Bill in August 1923, providing for the consolidation of Cuba's railways and the closing of many private ports used by sugar companies. The new law pitted railway against sugar interests, both blessed with abundant US capital. British fears related to the nationalization or Americanization of United Railways, and possible action against the new and successful marketing operation of the Anglo-Mexican oil company. Donald Gainer, in charge during Haggard's absence from June to December 1923, took his chance to impress with perceptive analyses of the real power acting behind the scenes. For him, the Bill was 'the struggle of one vested American interest against another, played on the Cuban stage'. That country had now 'captured and bound Cuba hand and foot, and will not let go'. It was not so much the US government as finance that was pulling the shots. While Washington had done much good in Cuba, he argued, the country's financial interests were unscrupulously exploiting the island while its politicians acquiesced.[51]

A Low-point and Improving Anglo–Cuban Relations

When Haggard's successor arrived on the island in late 1924, he reported the real possibility of a rupture in diplomatic relations, a fate suffered by Anglo–Mexican relations some years earlier.[52] In addition to coping with the loss of three cases in transit to Cuba – one containing his irreplaceable collection of Oriental rugs – Thomas Morris encountered a 'good deal of soreness and irritation' on disembarking in Havana, and a government attitude he later described as 'distinctly hostile and almost insolent'.[53] The situation would need careful handling. Morris was a Boer War veteran with 14 years' service in the Sudanese Civil Service, and, like Haggard, had a consular service background.[54]

Keen to view conditions on the ground, he made an early tour of both Cuba's interior and Jamaica. In overly familiar language to the head of the American Department, the experienced diplomat Robert Vansittart, Morris advised a more conciliatory approach:

> The Cubans are a stubborn lot and after a certain point would just dig their heels in and delight in defiance. They hate all niggers (and so would you if you lived out here) & have little use for ethical niceties or the Rights of Man.[55]

Morris readily passed judgement on the Cuban character during his near seven years in Havana, but not always in such extreme terms.

Morris urged and soon formulated a new approach to dealing with the British West Indian problem, recognizing the counterproductive effects of his predecessor's strategy. While the United States had not objected to British policy, it feared that a prohibition on Jamaican labour would impact negatively on US-owned sugar estates. His Majesty's Government, he judged, had no easy means of applying pressure, and should not continue with its 'denunciatory policy'.[56]

After his tour of Cuba and Jamaica, Morris formulated a pragmatic approach to the problem, inspired no doubt by his military experience. He saw a need to tackle the problem at its source. The Jamaican government would finance an 'Inspector for Labour Questions' attached to the British legation. He would deal with complaints on the ground in Cuba's interior, and maintain a list of sugar estates (and rural guards) implicated in mistreatment and non-payment of labourers. The inspector would liaise with the Cuban authorities directly, lifting the burden of complaints from British representatives.[57] The formula worked. Complaints heard in Havana and London reduced sharply, and Morris was not slow to highlight his accomplishment. Anglo–Cuban relations under the new chargé d'affaires and consul general improved markedly from their lowest ever ebb.

During his near seven years in Cuba, Morris repeatedly highlighted the potential of Cuba as a market for British goods. In Morris's analysis, Cuba was the second biggest importer by value of foreign goods in

Latin America after Argentina.[58] As with previous envoys, he repeatedly emphasized the richness of the island's market and the chief obstacle to British trade, the 20 to 40 per cent preference given to US goods under reciprocity. However, he was prone to exaggeration, not only in reference to trade matters, but also in regard to the value of his own achievements. His letters portray a man who suffered delusions of grandeur, and who repeatedly sang the praises of Cuba's controversial president, General Gerardo Machado (1925–33), a man with a similar background and physical appearance to Morris: a squat bespectacled ex-military man with a puffy complexion.

Perhaps Morris's greatest success was to conclude a Parcel Post Agreement with Cuba in 1926, a project first proposed in 1904. The Treasury and the Board of Trade finally satisfied themselves that the removal of a small fine on Cuban cigar imports would be outweighed by increased revenue from luxury goods exports such as dress cloth, boots, spare parts and samples. These items had previously been shipped via France or Germany, incurring extra cost, delay and the subsequent disinterest of Cuban consumers. For Cuba meanwhile, the new direct parcel service facilitated greater exports of its prime luxury product, cigars, to their biggest traditional market.[59]

Machado's government enacted a subtle shift in emphasis away from the interests of the landlord class towards those in commerce and manufacturing. His was the first government willing to challenge – but only to a limited degree – the entrenched hegemony of the United States, and echo growing nationalist anti-American sentiment in the island. Tariff reforms in 1927 were thus more a manoeuvre to bolster legitimacy than to seriously upset the privileged US position in Cuba, to which the island's privileged economic classes were so bound and from which they benefited so much.[60] Morris presented the new opportunities for British exporters as results of his own diplomacy and the pro-British sentiments of Machado's government, appreciative of the growing market for the island's sugar in the United Kingdom. While preference for US imports remained unaltered, new tariff rates on many articles imported from Europe reduced by as much as 50 to 95 per cent. The Foreign Office greeted Morris's achievement with enthusiasm and the hope that British exporters would be suitably inspired.[61]

Writing in 1928, Morris described Machado's government as 'unquestionably the best the country has ever had'. The president, a man of 'considerable political sagacity', extracted dividends during a visit to Washington in March 1927 in the form of US moral and financial commitments to his administration. Having instigated a number of expensive projects of infrastructure under a national programme of 'honesty roads and schools', the Cuban president desired President Calvin Coolidge's support. At the same time, he extended a personal invitation to the US president for the inaugural meeting of the Pan-American Conference in Havana in 1928. Later in 1927, Machado and his supporters outmanoeuvred their political opponents by rushing a 'Prorogue' Bill through Congress that extended his administration's term in office until 1931.[62]

In advance of the Pan-American Conference, Morris highlighted Washington's showcasing of the island as an example to the rest of its Latin and especially Caribbean neighbours.[63] The visit by President Coolidge and his inaugural address, wrote British Ambassador to Washington Esme Howard, was a 'most exceptional proceeding', given the rarity of presidential visits to foreign countries. The US press had highlighted the negative view held by Latin American nations of Washington's paternal and patronizing attitude, and their increasing disinclination to accept it following recent US interventions in Central America, and Nicaragua in particular. Howard described the various newspaper depictions of Uncle Sam's countenance in advance of the conference as 'a cross between the benevolent Nordic viking, the stern nurse who slaps naughty children who make trouble in the nursery, and the cat which has devoured the canary'.[64] The Latin American republics planned to voice their opposition to US policies. In the event, however, the Havana conference highlighted their disunity, and US representatives skilfully outwitted and divided their hemispheric neighbours.[65]

A year later, Machado inaugurated a new Capitol building in the centre of Havana, modelled on its equivalent in Washington. Like a new central highway that now traversed the island, it was one of several grand projects instigated by the Cuban president. The Foreign Office liaised with the French and Italian governments over the status of their diplomatic representation for the event, not wishing to outrank each other on the day. The Spanish went out on a limb, however, and sent naval ships – including the *Almirante Cervera* – and dignitaries for a demonstrative outpouring of Hispanic brotherhood.[66]

Unfortunately, the inauguration of the expensive new Capitol building was ill timed, occurring in the midst of a severe economic hardship provoked by the Wall Street Crash. Morris described the lack of 'enthusiasm and spontaneity' among the Cuban crowds. Robert Craigie, head of the American Department, commented that 'the picture of the listless and starving populace amongst all this display is reminiscent of Paris in the days before the French Revolution'.[67] Revolution in Cuba, however, was still four years away.

When the question arose of strengthening Britain's mission in Havana, the Foreign Office cited the island's value as 'a vantage point for observing the developments of United States policy in the Caribbean' in its application for increased Treasury funding.[68] Among the statistics available, the most convincing was a league table of Latin American countries by total value of UK imports and exports, where Cuba was placed fourth behind only Argentina, Brazil and Chile.[69] Compared to conditions prevailing ten years earlier, when the British mission was downsized, Cuba's capital city had become a leading tourist centre, with Cunard already doing good business on its recently inaugurated New York–Havana winter route.[70]

The Foreign Office named Sir John Joyce Broderick as British minister to Havana in 1931, leaving Morris reportedly feeling 'very sore at his transfer back into the Consular Service'. His achievements were recognized, not least by himself, and Machado marked his departure by releasing a number of British West Indians from Cuban jails and deporting them.[71] Given his character and earlier comments about black British subjects, Morris would perhaps have been the last person to see the irony of the president's conciliatory gesture.

Broderick was the type of envoy recommended by the 1929 D'Abernon Mission to South America. Its findings had reported criticisms of diplomatic representation in the continent, 'chosen rather with a view to dignity and correctness than to active economic development'. The mission advised that the Department of Trade and the Foreign Office utilize 'men of special knowledge and special aptitudes'. Such envoys could exploit commercial opportunities and reverse the post-1914 trend of US domination.[72] Broderick, having served as assistant commercial advisor (1915–19), commercial secretary (1919–20) and commercial counsellor (1920–31) at the British embassy in Washington, had considerable experience in a dynamic business environment, and one of particular relevance to Cuba. He had also spent more than sufficient time in the United States to turn native when it came to judging the island and its inhabitants.

Broderick's appointment stood in contrast to Washington's reformed policy to appoint a series of enormously wealthy businessmen to ambassadorships in important Latin American countries such as Mexico, Peru and Cuba. In the latter case, the new US incumbent of the Havana embassy from 1929 was Harry Guggenheim, the son of an aeronautics billionaire. He set up and paid for 'expert' personnel to add to his existing diplomatic staff, who, according to Broderick, all led a rather insular existence alongside the US colony. In his opinion, 'Neither they nor the Ambassador himself can be said to have quite got the hang of the tangled political situation in Cuba.'[73] A recently arrived Broderick sought and gained London's permission to purchase a Humber Pullman limousine for the British legation. He confessed to being 'sick of going about in an old American machine' and hoped the new Humber would be 'a good ad[vertisment] for British makers'.[74] The continental initiative and the new minister appeared to herald renewed Anglo–American competition in the Cuban market.

But Cuba was in a very depressed economic position when Broderick took up his post two years after the Wall Street Crash. The bottom had dropped out of the island's sugar industry, lower prices exacerbated by the failure and counterproductive effects of international and unilateral moves, in the case of Cuba, to limit production and hence raise prices. From 1926, the deliberate restriction of sugar production in an effort to stem falling prices simply stimulated exports from other parts of the world. To add insult to injury, prices remained depressed.[75] Renowned British economist John Maynard Keynes was a successful commodities speculator in the 1920s and 1930s. In 1929, he closely analysed the 'paradox of artificial limitation in Cuba' and 'enormously increased production' in Java, its great sugar cane rival. Keynes judged that after its 'once bit is twice shy' experience, Cuba would be unlikely to attempt 'artificial control' again.[76]

In 1930, the Hawley–Smoot Tariff Act increased US duty on Cuban sugar imports. Morris's final annual report of 1930 outlined the 'severe shock' meted out to the island's sugar industry by current conditions, the country's sudden relegation to a position of secondary economic importance and its general 'gloomy' outlook.[77]

Broderick's first annual report, written in mid-1932, offered an expert analytical overview of Cuba's political and economic relations with its overbearing northern neighbour. He placed particular emphasis – three decades after their inception – on the workings and effects of the two treaties that formalized US–Cuban relations: the long-reviled Platt Amendment and its economic counterpart, the Reciprocity Treaty. He reminded his readership that the economic treaty was the gilded pill offered to leading Cubans following their marginal acceptance of the earlier political agreement. But in his view, Cuba had derived no price benefit for its sugar from reciprocity since 1910, and the position of US exports relative to other nations was no better now than it was in 1914. Nevertheless, Cuba enjoyed the enormous benefit of a guaranteed market for 65 per cent of its sugar. And, while the Cubans might complain about reciprocity, the fact was that if sugar producers such as Java were allowed to compete fairly with Cuba's main product (i.e. by not paying duties), the island's economy would be ruined.[78] In the midst of a severe economic depression, however, such a benefit appeared illusory to the vast majority of Cubans.

Broderick encapsulated Cuba's rhetorical ambivalence towards the United States in romantic fashion: 'Flirtations with other countries may satisfy her vanity, but there will be no infidelity.' He also disabused the Foreign Office of Morris's rosy picture of Cuba's rich market for British exports. They had been deluding themselves; the dice were loaded against British interests and they could but continue their efforts to minimize traders' losses while the current depression endured.[79] Such was the predicament of British interests and official representation in Cuba, left to gather the crumbs fallen from the island's rich table, where dominant US concerns enjoyed first pickings.

Britain was also severely affected by the world economic crisis. Political and financial strains in adhering to the gold standard, the country's exchange rate and currency system, brought down the Labour Government in August 1931. A new Conservative-dominated national government suspended the gold standard and allowed the pound to devalue by 25 per cent. Britain then finally acceded to pressure from its imperial interests at the Ottawa Imperial Economic Conference in 1932. After decades of internal disagreements, the new government finally committed Britain to a policy of trade tariffs, favouring empire goods, food and raw materials. The new system of imperial preference gave Britain's exports reciprocal advantages in empire markets, and soon extended benefits to its colonies as well as dominions.

As for Cuban politics, Broderick described a new movement of professors, students, professional men and women, and other non-political elements, lining up in opposition and resorting to ever more ingenious and desperate methods to unseat the dictatorial Machado. There was, for example, the ABC society, based on a hierarchical cell-system, where rank-and-file operatives carried out terrorist actions on the orders of faceless leaders. But despite the Depression, violence and political uncertainty, Broderick considered there were hardly any British or US businesses that wanted to see Machado replaced. While few were prepared to envisage the future trajectory of his political fortunes, the minister did relate the prediction of US Ambassador Guggenheim, who 'foresees financial collapse in the near future, followed by a military *coup d'État* and the seizure of the Government by the head of the army'. Despite Broderick's previous questioning of the US embassy's political nous, this affirmation would turn out to be remarkably accurate.[80]

Britain again found its interests dragged into Cuba's political imbroglio between 1931 and 1932, and again the Foreign Office faced a protection dilemma.[81] In 1930 there had been worrying signs that opposition elements in Cuba were targeting British interests in an attempt to provoke intervention, due to Washington's evident reluctance to take action. His Majesty's Government was again averse to sending a naval presence, preferring instead to rely on US protection. Here was more proof of Britain's hesitance to assume responsibility when it could defer to US preponderance instead.

At the start of an illustrious career in the Foreign Office, Harold Caccia was the first to add his comments to one of Morris's last despatches from Havana on the acute economic situation and its accompanying violence. Caccia underlined the potential repercussions of US intervention in Cuba for Herbert Hoover's administration in two spheres: domestic politics and hemispheric relations. But owing to a considerable volume of trade with Cuba, the island was of 'considerable interest and importance' to Britain. Vansittart, now assistant under secretary, proffered the opinion that 'If the worse comes to the worst the hand of the USA will be forced.'[82] On the same subject three months later, Craigie wrote that 'it is certainly the business of the U.S. Govt. to afford the necessary protection for foreigners'.[83] Again, the reliance on and assumption of US protection was evident.

British interests were targeted again in August and September 1931. A small bomb landed in the garden of the legation residence, and four days later a heavy bomb explosion caused serious damage to a large branch of the Royal Bank of Canada in Havana.[84] Broderick considered that the actions responded to Cubans' general belief that the 'point of maximum provocation' was lower in London than Washington. There was the possibility that Machado's enemies, having failed to provoke US intervention directly, were now trying to achieve this aim through the medium of the British. Broderick counselled strongly against an official British reaction.[85] The issue of protection for foreign interests was closely bound up with the Platt Amendment and Washington's right to intervene in the island. Cuba's political elite, in government and in opposition, frequently attempted to manipulate this right to their advantage.[86]

Conclusion

In his 1928 annual report, Morris had provided an excellent summary of Britain's 'triangular position' in Cuba. Such was the strength of the United States' position, he argued, that Britain – as with other foreign powers – was constantly aware that Washington was the 'final arbiter' on most issues. Furthermore, if the Cuban government had any inkling that a foreign power was attempting coercion by means of cooperation with the United States, it tended 'to adopt at once an unaccommodating attitude'. Cuba's political class might denounce US dominance, but sheltered behind Washington's protection when it suited them. Thus foreign governments had to navigate with the utmost circumspection 'the narrow channel that lies between this Scylla and Charybdis'.[87]

Broderick, meanwhile, highlighted the inadvertent benefits of close US–Cuban relations. The range of Britain's stake in the island was remarkably similar – although on a much smaller scale – to that of the United States. In 1932, these responsibilities and interests were:

- approximately 1000 white British subjects (and 60,000 British West Indians);
- United Railways of Havana;
- three Canadian bank operations;
- English and Canadian insurance companies;
- the Shell-Mex oil company;
- a submarine cable company;
- ten to twelve English landowners (in sugar, fruit cultivation and cattle-ranching).[88]

In the minister's point of view, these British enterprises desired the 'assurance of peaceful conditions', and had 'come to regard the Platt Amendment and the watchful eye of the United States Government as far better safeguards than any which an absolutely independent Cuban Government could offer, even under unhampered diplomatic pressure from London'. None of these interests, in Broderick's opinion, would view Cuba's release from US subordination in a favourable light.[89] But then having spent so long in the United States, the knighted British minister was apt to adopt a US perspective on Cuban issues.

Broderick had discussed intervention contingencies during discussions at the Foreign Office before his journey to Havana. The resulting view from these deliberations was that Washington's hand could be easily forced because of the entrenched position of US banks and commercial firms, in addition to pressure from foreign interests. Therefore, if Britain needed to make representations, it should do so through the US government in Washington or the US embassy in Havana.[90] Conspicuous by its absence was the mention of British recourse to the Cuban government in Havana or the Cuban legation in London. A revolution in Cuba in 1933 would put the Foreign Office's accepted wisdom to the test.

4
Beyond Recognition: Grau's 100-Day Government

The refusal by President Franklin D. Roosevelt's administration (1933–45) to formally recognize Ramón Grau San Martín's revolutionary government from September 1933 was the principal reason that its 100-day rule collapsed in January 1934. The episode provided an early test case for Roosevelt's 'Good Neighbor' policy in Latin America, a new US hemispheric approach that eschewed the direct intervention of previous governments. Benjamin Sumner Welles, the president's protégé and closest adviser on Latin American affairs, initially enforced the policy in Cuba. He arrived in Havana in May 1933 to mediate a political settlement between an increasingly unpopular and autocratic President Machado and his opponents, when social and political unrest threatened substantial US economic interests on the island. Machado eventually resigned in August and his successor, selected by Welles, governed for just three weeks.[1] British policymakers then agonized about recognizing Grau's radical government in contravention of US wishes, during a period of notably discordant Anglo–American relations.

Recognition versus Intervention

There was nothing new about the thorny question of political recognition of new Latin American regimes by the United States and Britain. When the first major revolution of the twentieth century broke out in Mexico, the continent's leading power – under the presidency of Woodrow Wilson – used recognition as a new tool with which to intervene in the affairs of its neighbour.[2] The episode of US non-recognition of Victoriano Huerta's dictatorship in Mexico was the most notorious of several cases involving Washington's delayed or withheld official recognition following a change of regime in a Latin American republic. Great

Britain incurred US anger when, after much deliberation, its government officially recognized Huerta's government against Wilson's wishes. Following recognition, British investors – some with substantial interests in railways and mining – received better treatment than their US rivals, although London was at pains not to press home its advantage. The aforementioned Sir Lionel Carden, British minister to Mexico during the latter part of Huerta's dictatorship, was a strong advocate of his government's continued recognition, but became the object of controversy and US demands for his recall.[3]

Intervention and outright occupation were onerous not only for the US military who had to undertake such missions, but on public opinion in the whole of Latin America, where interventionist policies were widely criticized and provoked resentment. In the midst of economic depression in the early 1930s, Washington again began to stipulate conditions under which regimes that had achieved power by force – through *coup d'état* or revolution – would receive recognition. A renowned case involved the regime of El Salvador's General Maximiliano Hernández Martínez from December 1931, following his ousting of Arturo Araujo's popularly elected government in a military coup. Washington was perturbed by this interruption to constitutional order, in contravention of a treaty signed between five Central American governments and the United States in 1923. As in the earlier Mexican case, opinion in London and Washington diverged as to both the conditions for recognition they should demand and the timing of an announcement. After considerable procrastination, US and British naval destroyers deployed to Central American waters, and the Foreign Office informed Washington that it could postpone recognition no longer.[4]

In such a way, the United States was criticized both when it directly intervened in Latin America and when it did not. Deploying a naval presence and withholding official recognition fell somewhere between these two stools.

Anglo–American Disagreements

Unresolved issues over disarmament and war debts were running sores for Anglo–American relations during the 1920s and 1930s. Mutual resentment and suspicion were – according to British historian Donald Cameron Watt – a result of generational mistrust between the foreign policymaking establishments of both nations.[5] From the British side, the hostility resulted from the US role in the First World War and unrelenting pressure by Washington in the 1920s over a wide range of issues, including war debts and disarmament. Britain wished to link the debts to reparations, while the United States did not. In 1933, President F.D. Roosevelt accepted Britain's manoeuvre to settle the ongoing dispute, but Congress then vetoed it. At the World Disarmament Conference in 1932, Washington was unable to force Britain into alignment with US interests. The British were loath to limit arms – especially for the Royal Navy – in view of their two-to-one cruiser superiority over the United States.

The United States was already annoyed by the principle of imperial preference, agreed at the Ottawa Conference in 1932. In 1933, the World Monetary and Economic Conference in London attempted to check world depression by means of currency stabilization and economic accords. But unbridgeable disagreements among the participants and US indifference made the summit a total failure. According to Professor of Economics Charles Kindleberger, Washington was 'uncertain in its international role. It felt that the British were shrewder, more sophisticated, more devious in their negotiating tactics, so that the United States came out of international conferences losers.'[6] Following the conference's break up, customs and currency restrictions became increasingly stringent throughout the world. Both Britain and the United States turned even further inwards, concentrating on resolving problems in their own domestic economies.

The irony of Anglo–American antagonism was that several of the top officials in the Foreign Office – diplomats who readily commented on faltering US diplomacy in Cuba in 1933 and 1934 – had American wives, including Robert Craigie (head of American Department), Ronald Lindsay (ambassador in Washington) and Robert Vansittart (permanent under secretary). This paradox had already led to 'snide comments about Foreign Office officials being unable to face their American wives across the breakfast table'.[7]

F.D. Roosevelt's 'Good Neighbor' Policy

Democrat F.D. Roosevelt assumed the US presidency in early 1933, his country still suffering acutely from economic depression. In the wake of the London conference, the British embassy in Washington noted the introversion of the new government and its focus on domestic problems. In the international field, the British minister there wrote that the 'administration and state department have turned their eyes away from Europe and towards South America'.[8] The new president heralded a non-interventionist approach in the hemisphere, embodied in his

'Good Neighbor' policy, with a promise to respect the political autonomy of Latin American governments. Its first major test would occur in neighbouring Cuba.

The US government viewed the deteriorating political and economic position in Cuba with increasing concern. In the last year of Hoover's presidency conditions in the countryside became ever more desperate as the price of sugar, the lifeblood of the island's economy, continued to decline. Production of the commodity dropped a full 60 per cent between 1929 and 1933, and the island's share of the US sugar market dropped from 49.4 per cent in 1930 to 25.3 per cent in 1933.[9] Labour unrest undermined social order. Student and middle-class political organizations vied for supremacy in opposition to the ever more dictatorial and repressive Machado, and employed violence in order to settle scores.

At the start of 1932, British Minister Joyce Broderick reported on the factional strife that had plagued the island for two years. New splinter groups, disgusted with politicians, were organizing themselves away from political parties. He expressed surprise on hearing 'university professors and lawyers and doctors, of education and intelligence' attempting to justify nightly bomb attacks in the capital. One such group, the notorious ABC Revolutionary Society, contained a mixture of the middle classes and young students.[10] The ABC Society appeared to embrace nationalist and right-wing ideologies, and was organized around a clandestine pyramid cellular structure that made it extremely difficult both to fathom and to infiltrate.

At the year's end, Broderick described a meeting between Harry Guggenheim and the two main opposition leaders (Mario Menocal and Miguel Mariano Gómez) at the US ambassador's Long Island estate, giving rise to the 'wildest political rumours' in Cuba. In Broderick's opinion, Washington was now more disposed to ease Machado out of power, but not before US bankers had been repaid a loan of some $3 m, given to help settle an $8 m public works debt. His prediction that President Machado would be safe until the summer of 1933 was accurate and prophetic, judging that opposition groups were agreed in their desire to oust the president but would fall out after achieving their objective.[11] Washington thus faced disorder, but desired a solution that both settled Cuba's difficulties and minimized damage to substantial US interests.

After two years in Havana, Broderick was rewarded with the most prestigious diplomatic post in Latin America – the ambassadorship to Argentina.[12] Chargé d'Affaires Hugh Border wrote in the spring of 1933 that a lull in political activity had been followed by a succession of grisly murders of young men, shot by the authorities 'while trying to escape'. Guggenheim protested to the Cuban foreign minister on behalf of the family of a missing young man, who crawled mortally wounded into a first aid station (to die some hours later). He had used language 'more forcible' than any to which the Cuban government were accustomed, informing the Cuban minister that 'a big stick' was about to be employed. Mimicking the events of previous years, the ABC Society attacked British interests with the intention of 'inducing His Majesty's Government to bring pressure to bear at Washington'.[13] Under the terms of the Platt Amendment, Cubans had grown to anticipate US interference in their affairs when conditions of unrest threatened their neighbour's interests. Overt military intervention, however, was not going to be the order of the day.

Welles's Mission

Cuba represented a serious early challenge for Roosevelt's 'Good Neighbor' policy. The president appointed family friend Sumner Welles as his new ambassador to Cuba, considered the State Department's foremost expert on the region. He had assisted the president in formulating his new hemispheric policy, and had served in several Latin American posts, aiding General Crowder's mission to Cuba in 1921, for example. As the newly appointed assistant secretary of state he was involved in preparations for the forthcoming Pan-American Conference in December.[14] At Montevideo, Latin American nations anticipated more concrete statements and promises of action from the US delegation, or, failing that, the opportunity for vehement protests against empty promises to abandon hegemonic policies and promote hemispheric harmony.

The core of Welles's mission in Cuba was to 'seek a legal solution and avoid a revolution', which threatened Roosevelt's 'Good Neighbor' policy.[15] Among the tools at the ambassador's disposal were a stick in the form of the Platt Amendment and the carrot of a new trade treaty.[16] His instructions from the US president were to resolve the political situation and place the US–Cuban economic relationship on a new footing. According to various reports, Washington was willing to negotiate a new reciprocal trade agreement with more generous tariff conditions, on condition that Cuba resolved its political unrest.[17] Hugh Border reported his diplomatic colleague's activity and numerous interviews, but also an admission from Welles that 'he was losing some of his optimism'. A local 'feeling of hope' following his appointment and arrival had soon given way to 'the old spirit of despondency'.[18] The official record shows how nine days after his arrival, Welles cabled to Roosevelt, 'The situation here is both more precarious and more difficult than I had anticipated.'[19]

A new British minister arrived two months after Welles to begin the first of two terms in Havana.[20] Herbert Grant Watson, the son of a diplomat, was familiar with diplomatic representation in situations of political unrest. From 1920 to 1928 he had served as chargé d'affaires in Portugal during the last years of its liberal Parliamentary Republic (1919–26) and the first years of General de Fragosa Carmona's dictatorship (1926–32), a period when coups and counter-coups were regular occurrences.[21] He was then minister to the Central American Republics (1928–33). Based in Guatemala City, he was witness to Washington's evolving defence of its interests in that region, and again, to frequent political upheaval.

In his first significant despatch from Havana, Grant Watson reported on Welles's progression to mediation between Machado and opposition groups, and opinion from all sides that the US ambassador was 'developing the United States policy with great caution and great skill'.[22] By the start of August, however, the situation had developed considerably, and although the British minister considered Machado to be in full control of the government, 24 bombs had rocked the capital, one directed at His Majesty's legation. Just weeks into his mission, he wrote, 'Unfortunately these occurrences are taken for granted and have come to be regarded as normal incidents in the everyday life of this immature republic.'[23] By the time the Foreign Office received this despatch, however, Machado was already out of power.

Machado Unseated

Matters came to a sudden head in late July when a bus strike developed into a general strike with other sympathizers, rapidly spreading throughout the island. At 5 p.m. on 7 August, a radio station made a false announcement that Machado had resigned, sending jubilant crowds into the capital's streets and parks, only to be fired upon from armoured cars. David Kelly, a British diplomat with first-hand experience of US policy in Latin America, wrote on 10 August, 'In view of the Platt Amendment and the overwhelmingly greater interest of the U.S. in Cuba I think we can regard U.S. intervention as almost inevitable should anarchy happen.'[24] His prediction paid no heed to Roosevelt's new non-intervention policy. With pressure from Welles to resign and the army persuading him that further resistance was useless, Machado boarded a Sikorsky at an aerodrome outside Havana and flew to Nassau on 12 August, never to return to the island. Grant Watson pointed to his mixed legacy, in the grandiloquent prose that typified the final paragraphs of his despatches:

> He was the strong man who established order in a rich country. Foreign capital rushed in and foreign bankers threw their loans at his feet. With their aid he raised many monuments which testify to his work, a rebuilt capital, architecturally, one of the fine cities of the world, the massive building of the Capitol, the famous arterial highway, numerous institutions, &c., but the accounts were heavy. In order to carry out his programme, he had to overcome the Opposition, and he did so in a ruthless manner, and thus to-day he will be remembered, not by his public works, but rather by the cruelty of his administration.[25]

The minister might have added that Machado had the misfortune to rule during the deepest of economic depressions.

Grant Watson had little contact with Welles during the US ambassador's residence in Havana. One rare meeting took place on 9 August, when the minister informed him about damage to British property in the interior and deprecated a Reuter's report that a Royal Navy cruiser had been sent to Cuba. The British could at least take some comfort in the knowledge that Spanish citizens and property, higher in number and value respectively, suffered more violent attacks than their own.[26] On writing to US Secretary of State Cordell Hull on the day that Machado departed, Welles indulged in self-congratulation. The solution, he wrote, 'has been worked out solely by the Cubans themselves and represents in my judgement the expression of the volition of very nearly the totality of the Cuban people'. He ended his message, 'I now have confidence that the situation has been saved and that no further action on the part of the United States Government will be necessary.'[27] In stark contrast, a junior official in London wrote the same day,

> The Americans have now, by inducing President Machado to relax his grip, set in motion a revolutionary force which will not easily be checked. If matters really grow serious (as seems probable enough), I fancy that Americans in Cuba will have no very happy time.[28]

A Reuters report in the *Manchester Guardian* described the wild jubilation of mobs in Havana and the looting of houses and government buildings. Some carried off beautiful silks and women's dresses and a crowd seized the piano from the presidential palace. A mob paraded the streets dancing the rumba, but torrential rain and an intense electrical storm dampened the high spirits.[29] Grant Watson vividly described the vengeance directed against Machado's secret police by his opponents on learning of his departure, scenes that would 'remain for ever a painful recollection for those who beheld them'. Next to the British legation, mobs ransacked the home of a prominent senator:

> The sackage of this fine residence was a revolting sight, for, while Negroes fought for gramophones and nursemaids for shawls, well-dressed families drive up in Packards and Cadillacs, seized Louis XV cabinets and gilded chairs and drove away with the spoil. In a few minutes not a piece of furniture was left in the house.[30]

Carlos Manuel de Céspedes took oath as Cuba's president at 9 a.m. the next day, an event which for Grant Watson 'was received with acclamation throughout the republic', adding portentously, 'It was known, too, that he was the special nominee of the United States Ambassador and could count on the support of Washington.'[31] He had earlier been Cuba's ambassador to Washington, and returned to serve in Zayas's 'honest Cabinet'. But he was better known in the island as the son and namesake of an illustrious independence movement father.[32]

Two US Navy destroyers arrived in Havana harbour on 14 August. Welles welcomed their 'moral effect', and recommended their withdrawal within 48 hours if the strike ended and local conditions calmed down.[33] His messages in the following days expressed a desire to end his mission in Havana and pass the diplomatic reins to a successor. He endeavoured to persuade the State Department to expedite his recall, and facilitate his participation in the forthcoming Montevideo Conference. In doing so his reports were far more sanguine than those of his British counterparts. A week after Machado's resignation he suggested a departure date of 1 September, justified by the fact that Cubans had a government which 'commands their confidence' with little likelihood of 'any grave political disturbances' in the near future. Furthermore, he added, no one was criticizing his relationship with the new Cuban government and the United States was now 'more popular in Cuba than it has been since the early years of the independence of the Republic'.[34]

The British embassy in Washington summarized the optimism reported in US newspaper reports and the hailing of Welles's 'brilliant piece of work'. The *New York Herald Tribune*, for example, called his mediation 'a complete success'. But the embassy also detailed reports that preceded Machado's demise, propagated 'sedulously' in Washington and Hyde Park (Roosevelt's upstate New York home), and alluding to foreign pressure on Welles to encourage US intervention and protect British and Spanish lives and property.[35] Such details received little attention while seismic political events were unfolding, but days later the British unleashed their anger. Unable to gain US cooperation in a number of recent instances, they jumped to the conclusion that Washington was acting in an underhand manner by trying to implicate foreign governments in its decisions.

When Grant Watson reported how his Spanish colleague had been a 'victim of the same calumny', London's suspicion immediately fell on Sumner Welles. David Kelly, who knew him from a previous posting, evidently harboured considerable disdain, and wrote, 'I would not trust him an inch'.[36] On receipt of the Washington embassy letter two weeks later, a junior official wrote, 'We must hold him responsible for the scheme of the U.S.G[overnment]. to throw on us and on Spain the responsibility for any intervention which they might find it necessary to make [...] I think we shall have to keep our eye on Mr Welles.' Kelly again gave vent to his feelings:

> I think Mr Welles was at the bottom of this – it would be quite typical. I knew him in Buenos Aires in 1919; and when some time later, he left the Diplomatic Service, his U.S. colleagues openly expressed relief, regarding him as an unprincipled adventurer & intriguer. He has now returned through political influence [... He] speaks English with the exaggerated blasé Anglicism cultivated by a certain type of sophisticated American, and is ultra-snobbish.[37]

Welles pinned the blame on scurrilous newspaper reports, probably based on the State Department's misreading of a Havana embassy telegram and a leak.[38] Whatever its source, the Foreign Office closely monitored the rise of Sumner Welles through the ranks of the State Department. He would be a bête noire of British diplomats for many years to come.

After the Cyclone

Welles's optimism soon dissipated. He reported the return to the country of several political opposition leaders and on 24 August 'a general process of disintegration' and anarchic conditions throughout the island.

He now considered that Céspedes had an insecure hold on power.[39] Grant Watson described confusion in government, with effective rule by two entities: the official Céspedes government and the ABC directorate. One morning at 2.30 a.m., students and ABC members roused the British minister at his residence. They demanded Machado's extradition from the Bahamas (a British territory) and that he inspected the bodies of murdered students. Wearing only his dressing gown, he managed to usher them away politely.[40]

While the country's provisional president was touring the interior of the island to inspect hurricane damage, non-commissioned army officers mutinied on the evening of 4 September and seized control of the country in alliance with radical students. In conversation with Secretary of State Cordell Hull, Welles passed on the disturbing news that a 'Sergeants' Revolt' had set up a revolutionary government composed of the island's most extreme radicals.[41] Students had made common cause with a mutiny of disaffected non-commissioned officers to depose both the Céspedes government and senior army command. The event was a new departure in Cuban politics. For the first time since its nominal independence in 1902, elements that were not under Washington's control governed the island.

The British minister deplored the amateurishness of US policy when describing the sequence of events that had led to the new rebellion. Céspedes had been imposed on the Cubans, and the rapid withdrawal of US destroyers from Cuban waters had left his provisional government without protection.[42] On Welles's advice, 150 US families moved into the recently inaugurated Hotel Nacional. In advance of his planned departure on 14 September, and with his house lease expired, the US ambassador also installed himself in the hotel, only to be followed two days later by 300 deposed officers of the Cuban army. Grant Watson offered his legation as refuge for the British colony, but in the absence of anti-British feeling, no Britons took up his offer. Destroyers of the US Navy, conspicuous by their absence in the days before 4 September, now encircled the island.[43] Thirty vessels cruised offshore, ostensibly as a contingency for the evacuation of US citizens. Roosevelt and Hull played down their presence, but their moral effect was evident.[44]

Grant Watson reflected on the altered position of his US counterpart. In referring to the traditional 'governor' status of his position, he was making an analogy with the type of proconsular role occupied by officials in British colonies and protectorates. The British minister viewed Welles's position in Havana as much weakened, with the new government set up against his wishes. He was not slow to highlight the farce in his diplomatic colleague's predicament:

> Thus we end the week in Cuba under a *de facto* Government which has not been recognised, under an army led by sergeants, with the United States Ambassador living in an hotel surrounded by soldiers and machine guns, and the island surrounded by United States men-of-war.[45]

An official in London added acerbically, 'He only made a laughing stock of himself by first recommending U.S. citizens to concentrate in the Hotel Nacional and then moving in there himself.' Such a direct challenge to the US ambassador's authority in Cuba, he wrote, was unprecedented.[46]

As on previous occasions, the Foreign Office debated sending a naval presence for the protection of British citizens and interests. Familiar questions arose again: Would Washington oppose such a move? Would US forces offer the desired protection? Grant Watson did not in fact request navy assistance because the Cubans were providing adequate protection. Taking a keen interest in the events unfolding in Cuba, the British embassy in Washington urged caution, judging it prudent to 'stand entirely aloof' in case their actions were resented or misconceived by an 'anxious and disappointed President and State Department'.[47] Past experience had shown that Washington would naturally intervene before the British government was impelled to act, owing to far weightier US interests. However, the new dimension of the 'Good Neighbor' policy dictated less inclination to intervene, forcing the British to contemplate more seriously their own action. The false stories about British pressure on the United States to act greatly concerned the Foreign Office, suspecting that Washington wanted to unburden itself of the odium it was bound to incur.

It was of course unknown how far the US government was prepared to go in upholding its new non-intervention policy. Not only Washington, but Britain also – on the coat tails of US policy – was entering uncharted territory in Cuba. Time would tell whether in the final reckoning Britain would actually flout its self-imposed policy of leaving important decisions in the island to the United States.

Presented with a new set of circumstances, the United States followed an ad hoc policy, mindful of both conditions on the ground and previous proclamations of non-intervention. The all-important Montevideo Conference – a litmus test of Pan-American unity – loomed on the horizon, while 30 US Navy vessels patrolled Cuban waters. For the British embassy in Washington the US administration found the situation 'unpleasantly embarrassing'. Welles's 'masterly diplomacy' had within three weeks turned into a 'fine quandary'. The State Department was in a 'state of nervous indecision' and 'at a loss how to proceed'. Journalists, accustomed to receiving regular updates there on Cuban affairs, now encountered 'a restless and uncommunicative atmosphere'. The reaction in London to such reports was uncharitable: 'I rejoice over the discomfiture of Mr Welles, whom we have no reason to like', wrote one official. Another judged that there was no end in sight for the complications set in motion by Welles, and that US attempts to make Britain a 'scapegoat' for its malfunctioning Latin American policy had floundered.[48]

Contacts between the State Department and its ambassador demonstrate that it was most reluctant to intervene, while Welles was not against such action. After conferring with the president, Secretary of State Cordell Hull discounted intervention of any kind unless the US embassy was in immediate physical danger. In Hull's opinion the future of the new provisional government revolved around the army. The United States would only intervene if it was compelled to because, he wrote, 'if we have to go in there again, we will never be able to come out and we will have on our hands the trouble of thirty years ago'. As for the new ruling revolutionary junta of five men (the Pentarchy), including university professor of medicine Dr Ramón Grau San Martín, Welles would not even contemplate recognition.[49] With the Montevideo Conference in mind, the State Department summoned diplomatic representatives of Latin America (minus El Salvador and Cuba) to inform them that the large navy deployment to Cuban waters did not presage an intervention. But despite Hull's expressed opposition, Welles still suggested a 'strictly limited intervention'.[50]

Hull reiterated the president's policy of non-intervention to Joseph Daniels (US ambassador to Mexico) by telephone on 9 September, telling him, 'I would rather walk from here to the South Pole than to have to intervene'. In the event the Pentarchy dissolved after a week, leaving Grau as provisional president. Fulgencio Batista, a mixed-race stenographer to the former army chief of staff, was the leading sergeant mutineer. He had already been promoted to the rank of colonel and became new army chief of staff. From Havana, Welles stressed the radical nature of the new government and its pressing need for US recognition. On 12 September, light and electricity were cut off in the Hotel Nacional, forcing Welles and other US residents to leave, while deposed army officers had little choice but to remain. After a two-hour meeting with Grau on 17 September, Welles described him as 'utterly impractical and visionary'. At the same time he reported diminishing respect for the United States, and the widely held belief that its wishes could now be 'flouted with complete impunity'.[51]

Even in Welles's eyes, the US–Cuban relationship – around which British policy pivoted – had undergone a fundamental change. The more detached British minister referred to the 'comic opera revolt' that had led to the hotel's occupation by 'pantomime colonels and captains'. Kelly in London remarked that 'Mr Welles' position – the discarded author of the revolution – is becoming ludicrous.' With bands of students roaming the streets, the deposed president Carlos Manuel de Céspedes had sought asylum for himself and his wife in the British legation. As Céspedes' life was not in danger, and acceptance would have contravened his standing instructions, the minister refused – an action supported by his superiors.[52]

Grant Watson corroborated Welles's view of a deteriorating situation, with food shortages and people openly carrying arms. A newly announced maximum eight-hour working day perturbed the legation's cook, who, threatened with a beating if he did not obey, took to his bed – leaving Grant Watson to eat restaurant food. 'Everybody talks "política," "política," ' he wrote, 'and at times it seems exactly as if we were living in a mad-house.'[53]

Grau's provisional government was indeed radical, quickly announcing a series of reforms. It immediately and unilaterally proclaimed abrogation of the despised Platt Amendment. Under the banner of 'Cuba for the Cubans', a '50 per cent' labour decree promised to regain for Cuban-born workers many of the job posts occupied by foreigners. It cancelled, for example, existing low-wage contracts for imported West Indian labour. A new maximum eight-hour working day, worker's insurance, and a minimum wage for sugar cane cutters, all attracted popular support, but alienated business circles and long-established interests.[54]

In Grant Watson's judgment, 29 September was the day that Batista became Cuba's dictator. His forces had successfully broken up a demonstration organized for the repatriation of Julio Antonio Mella's ashes from Mexico (where the Communist student leader had been assassinated in 1929), collecting and burning the red flags of the protesters. Once again, the British minister received warning that the ABC planned to attack British property in order to pressure the United States into intervention. Three days later on 2 October the soldiers and deposed officers finally ended their month-long standoff at the Hotel Nacional and fought a life or death battle for definitive control of Cuba's armed forces. After ten hours of intermittent but increasingly heavy fighting, the officers hoisted a white bed-sheet of surrender, and soldiers under Batista's command claimed victory. In its aftermath, Grant Watson related the criticism of Cubans who made Welles responsible for the chaos, ensuring Machado's downfall but having no viable replacement. He added his own verdict on the US ambassador, who, he noted, 'remains aloof, confides in no one and keeps studiously apart from his colleagues'. The French minister in Havana denounced US policy as 'scandalous'. Grant Watson asked why Washington now held off after meddling in Cuban affairs for 30 years. They had first let loose the forces of revolution and then proclaimed non-intervention, he wrote. With hatred and vengeance in the air, the island was now worse off than it had ever been.[55]

On reading this report, colleagues in London readily added their own adjudications on US policy. A junior official wrote, 'Perhaps the U.S. will learn from their difficulties with the Philippines and from the dreadful mess into which they have got themselves in Cuba that as an imperialist power they do not excel.' Another commented,

> U.S. policy – personified in Mr Sumner Welles – has been deplorably inept. The Dept. of State must bitterly regret that by meddling with President Machado they have brought the whole fabric down about their ears. The ridiculous situation in which the U.S. finds itself must be intolerably galling.

Head of the American Department Robert Craigie, with diplomatic experience in Washington, was no less scathing: 'I should like to know how Mr. Welles and Mr. Hull defend their policy – first of intervening when they ought to have stood clear then of holding aloof when their former meddling made them morally responsible for the mess.'[56] Such comments were made in light of wider Anglo–American differences and existed for internal consumption only.

In a face-to-face meeting with Batista following the Hotel Nacional siege, Welles described the new army chief of staff as the only figure of authority in Cuba. For Roosevelt – reading press reports in Washington – the imprisonment of the deposed army officers had consolidated the government's position. Hull's response, urging 'some latitude' in recognition policy, signalled an important strategic shift. But Welles strongly disagreed about consolidation of the new government, emphasizing the opposition of all financial and business elements, and an increasing split between the army and civilian elements. After a second meeting of the diplomatic corps, Welles reported Grant Watson's 'considerable alarm' at the state of disorder. Pointing out that only Mexico and Uruguay were maintaining official relations with Grau's government, the US ambassador affirmed that no other diplomats justified such recognition.[57]

To Recognize or Not to Recognize

After the Hotel Nacional battle, the question of recognition started to receive serious attention in London. On 9 October, Cuban Minister in London Dr Patterson requested that His Majesty's Government 'take the lead' in recognizing Grau's provisional government. Craigie replied that his government had lately avoided use of the word 'recognition' in Latin America; instead – where appropriate – it employed the formula that 'nothing had occurred to interfere' with political relations, a turn of phrase the Cuban minister liked. The Foreign Office would make enquiries, but consultation with the Dominions might cause delays. However, it 'would not be slow' if convinced of the government's 'stability' and 'intentions to protect and promote British interests in Cuba'. The next day, on receipt of a telegram from Grant Watson describing an obscure but improving situation, Craigie stated there could 'be no question of recognition' so long as Washington remained opposed to Grau. Difficulty arose because US officials were 'notoriously bad guides in such matters' and influenced primarily by the compliance of any Cuban administration to their influence.[58]

The quandary of whether or not to recognize ahead of Washington would play out for the next three months, and had much less to do with the Cuban government's protection of British interests than it did with fear of a negative US reaction. The Foreign Office, as on previous occasions, was most reluctant to operate outside the margins of US acquiescence in Cuba, even during a period of embittered Anglo–American relations. The perfidy of Albion, sheltering behind Washington's exposed position, was evident in an admission by Craigie the following day, admitting he had given Dr Patterson's request a sympathetic response but that Britain would avoid friction with the United States 'at all costs'. With an improvement in the situation officials might 'exert a little influence at Washington', but the time was not yet ripe.[59] Ronald Lindsay in Washington now added his contribution to the delicate matter of opposing US policy in Cuba. He judged that the State Department was holding out in the hope that Grau's government would collapse, prepared to maintain its non-intervention policy in the face of great provocation.[60]

Britain was not alone in concentrating on the recognition question. Spain recognized on 12 October, a 'premature' decision in Grant Watson's opinion and done for 'sentimental reasons' according to Welles.[61] Brazil's government was reportedly anxious to follow the US lead.[62] In the midst of an apparent 'impasse', Welles analysed the situation at length, stating arguments for and against recognition and a compromise position of withholding judgment. He continued to express a somewhat rosy view of the support Céspedes had enjoyed, resentful that the government of his own invention had been so short-lived. Meanwhile, he took a dim view of the radical elements that had – in his opinion – transformed an army mutiny into a political revolution. After meeting political opponent Carlos Mendieta at the end of October, he predicted a change in government, and suggested to Hull that he be relieved in Havana.[63] In doing so he was being wildly optimistic, but then his urge to be involved at Montevideo was all-consuming.

In anticipation of the harvest season, Grant Watson underlined the importance of the sugar crop. If mills could not grind due to labour disorder, economic calamity would ensue and prove fatal for Grau's regime. In the meantime, his administration was arranging truces between workers and employers to give the semblance of order and thus attract recognition from foreign governments.[64] Dr Patterson again urged the British government to recognize Grau's regime on both 18 October and 1 November, but he did not receive a positive response. Deputy Under Secretary of State Victor Wellesley remained wary and urged further delay.[65]

At the start of November, Grant Watson described 'general disintegration' and 'quite unbelievable' confusion in government. Eighty strikes were said to be in progress, and US prestige was at an all-time low.[66] An armed uprising by the ABC movement on 8–9 November was the fourth revolt in as many months. Defeat for the ABC persuaded Grant Watson – at least temporarily – that the army and hence Grau's government had consolidated their strength, if not popular support, and should receive British recognition. The ABC had proved weak and other opposition groups were disunited.[67] The minister's recommendation led to two months of indecision and procrastination by the Foreign Office, but not recognition.

Welles's reaction to the ABC revolt was very different, but then the ambassador's diplomacy and his country's interests were far more exposed. He proposed returning to the United States to discuss the

Cuban issue directly with the president, a meeting that took place at Warm Springs, Georgia on 19 November. Welles was conscious of his compromised position in Havana. The apparent failure of his mission to Cuba now led him to suggest his imminent substitution by Jefferson Caffery, if – as he suspected – Washington's policy was about to change.[68]

In London, American Department officials referred to the El Salvador precedent when considering recognition. Naturally, they also contemplated US sentiment and the degree of resentment that British recognition might provoke. But had the United States shown such concern in spheres vital to British interests? US policy in Cuba had been a 'lamentable failure' and 'so universally condemned' that an independent British position might attract wider approval. Therefore, there could 'scarcely be any question of *consulting* the United States Government', but the balance of argument was in favour of notifying Washington.[69] Pragmatism, not to mention realpolitik, led to the presentation of these views to the Washington embassy.

Lindsay, it transpired, had not discussed the issue with the State Department. British recognition was 'bound to cause some resentment' and he urged delay ahead of the Roosevelt–Welles meeting.[70] Anticipating possible US recognition after the Warm Springs meeting and not wanting to be left behind, the Foreign Office consulted the Dominions of the British Empire. It also contacted its Egyptian and Eastern departments, where Britain's dominant position mirrored that of the United States in Latin America. To what degree had US policy followed Britain's lead in Egypt, Iraq, Kuwait and Palestine? In receipt of their replies, Craigie judged that the British owed the Americans nothing.[71] Even so, delay and not decision reigned in London, and a volte-face by their minister in Havana did not help the situation.

With the momentum of Foreign Office opinion tending in the direction of recognition, an adjustment in Grant Watson's position checked it. First and foremost, he argued, other European diplomats in Havana were not recommending recognition. Furthermore, Grau's government had provided adequate protection for British interests over ten weeks. A subsequent letter demonstrated that the Warm Springs meeting and Washington's reiteration of non-recognition had altered his position. He feared creating an 'impression of hostile rivalry' between Britain and its ally.[72] Grant Watson was evidently loath to carry such a heavy burden.

A rumour that Britain was close to recognizing Grau's government then caused 'considerable anxiety if not alarm' in US circles. Craigie was pleased that Washington had been galvanized into fresh activity, but concerned over a possible leak from a British Dominion.[73]

A syndicated US newspaper column propagated the rumour that the Irish Free State had given a friendly hint to the State Department about imminent British recognition. A week later, the same column explained that Roosevelt's midnight announcement of Welles's replacement by Caffery was misinterpreted by pressmen as indicating his early recall from Havana, a decision actually made (without specifying a date) three months earlier.[74] It is debateable whether rumours of imminent British recognition affected the timing of the president's announcement following his 19 November meeting with Welles, contributing to a subtle shift in US strategy. Welles had certainly become a hindrance to US policy in Cuba. On 6 November, for example, Acting Secretary of State William Phillips had conceded that Welles was 'doing no good in Havana'. But the ambassador was a long-standing friend of the president. Secretary of State Cordell Hull, meanwhile, had a fractious relationship with Welles, and thus resented his closeness to Roosevelt.[75] Such internal animosities, of course, did nothing to facilitate effective decision-making.

A visit to the Foreign Office by the United Railways chairman, outlining his company's potential ruin by failure to harvest the annual sugar crop, galvanized British officials into a more proactive policy. Craigie instructed his ambassador in Washington to abandon his remoteness from the State Department and broach the subject of Cuba. Lindsay obeyed, to be told unofficially by Acting Secretary of State Phillips that the change of ambassador signified a 'readjustment' of US policy. Recognition would follow within 30 days of Caffery's arrival if the Cuban government 'showed any disposition to be reasonable'. Washington would not now be 'too exacting either as regards stability or on political grounds'.[76]

With the Montevideo Conference a few days away, as well as the sugar harvest, matters appeared to be coming to a head. Grant Watson was surprised by Welles's estimation of opposition strength during their final meeting in Havana. In the wake of failed conciliation talks between government and opposition, the departing US ambassador expected a large-scale revolution by the opposition. Permanent Under Secretary Vansittart annotated, 'This looks like a most futile & undignified proceeding. Is this all the U.S. can do?' To which Craigie replied directly, 'I agree – but we have got rid of Sumner Welles – that is the important thing.'

Now in a less passive mode, Lindsay spoke again to the State Department about recognition. Phillips was very pessimistic about the Cuban situation; Washington would seize on any pretext to recognize, but none existed. Grau was 'mentally unstable and possibly addicted to drugs'.

On reading this Vansittart commented, 'If all this is true, it doesn't seem as if we c[oul]d. well recognise either! But is it?' Clearly, with regard to US policy in Cuba, the permanent under secretary lacked faith in Washington's reasoning. When Grant Watson called on Caffery on 23 December, he again expressed his fear for the sugar crop and the possibility of United Railways' expropriation by the fiercely nationalistic government.[77]

Meanwhile, the Pan-American Conference (3–26 December) had ended, without Welles's participation. Its most significant outcome was the US delegation's acceptance of a 'Convention on the Rights and Duties of States', affirming that 'no state has the right to intervene in the internal or external affairs of another'.[78] While it could not contravene previous agreements between states, its spirit clearly ran counter to Washington's long-standing right under the Platt Amendment to intervene in Cuba. The new departure in non-intervention signified a modification of the Monroe Doctrine and a repudiation of his fifth cousin T.R. Roosevelt's 'Corollary' to the doctrine in 1904.[79]

The first ten days of 1934 saw more indecision in the Foreign Office. Grant Watson made a further volte-face on New Year's Eve and recommended recognition again as the best way of checking opposition activities and thus securing protection for British interests. Support for Grau's government was greater, he judged, than Washington appreciated. In London, US sentiment continued to dominate thinking. In order to force the issue, Grant Watson received instructions to drop a hint to Caffery about imminent British recognition.[80] Caffery's response to Grant Watson was non-committal because his own plan had yet to be formulated. The Foreign Office also spoke to the US embassy in London, requesting closer cooperation over the matter and emphasizing the 'urgent interests of British capital in Cuba'. Craigie acknowledged that were it not for the 'U.S. complication' it would be worth taking the risk, while Vansittart was more assertive, keen to know what the new ambassador had 'under his hat'. If the Foreign Office was to continue following the US line, its allies should at least bring it up to date.[81]

The dilemma was very real. Kelly's comments on 11 January went to the heart of it and portended the troubled US–Cuban relations of a quarter-century later:

> The [British and US] standpoints are perhaps irreconcilable and unfortunately we cannot really disentangle our relations with Cuba from Cuban relations with the U.S. It is doubtful whether any Cuban Government can survive long without U.S recognition unless it were

purely Communist and isolationist, and even this experiment would probably break down owing to the need of the sugar industry for foreign capital & direction, and to the pressure which the U.S. could exercise by economic blockade.[82]

On hearing that Grant Watson still had no new news, this most astute observer of US policy in Latin America compared Washington's recognition policy in Cuba to that over Huerta's dictatorship in Mexico two decades earlier. It seemed that British interests in both cases were reconciled to the same fate: Britain would be expected to slavishly follow Washington's policy, but its allies would take no responsibility for British interests. Furthermore, Britain would be left with less bargaining power vis-à-vis the resulting administration. This was a 'heads they win, tails we lose' policy. Deputy Under Secretary of State Victor Wellesley, who, unlike Vansittart, never erred towards offending Washington, derided the 'unenlightened self-interest' of US policy, but determined the cost of opposition as too high. By the time Kelly's insightful thoughts had been sent to Lindsay in Washington, Grau had resigned as president.[83]

The British government was clearly not going to recognize Grau's government without first informing Washington. And it was not on the cusp of doing this when the State Department informed Cuba's ambassador in Washington that his radical president would never be recognized, information that precipitated Grau's resignation.

'Goliath's Ankle'

Evidence shows that Grant Watson arrived at similar conclusions to Welles as to the competence of the Grau government, but he differed considerably as to the strength of opposition against it. Writing as early as November, he considered that Welles had failed to distinguish between intervention and protection, and through diplomacy ('persuasion, protests and threats') could have secured immunity for US companies.[84] Just a few days before actual recognition, he judged that the 'open opposition' of Washington and Welles had been a political mistake. Instead, they should have recognized the government and 'tried to regain control by suasion rather than adopting a policy of hostility, backed by economic pressure'. He warned, 'Nationalism and socialism in Cuba are rather artificial products, but I am convinced that they are factors with which we must reckon.'[85]

Following recognition of the government led by Colonel Carlos Mendieta, the American Department of the Foreign Office and its

Washington embassy carried out a post mortem into the episode. British diplomats in the US capital considered that the United States might – among other 'creatures' – be compared to 'A young lady, just "out", with a great sense of her own importance, thin-skinned, and not really quite sure of herself', or, 'a raw-boned young man, full of energy, full of crude half-baked sensibilities, and withal slightly selfish'. They advised against 'sticking a pin into Goliath's ankle', because of whatever its feet or boots were made, they were 'capable of administering a very formidable kick'.[86]

This ornate letter elicited the reactions of Craigie, Wellesley and Vansittart in London. For the department head, the letter did not alter his opinion that 'U.S. policy throughout the Cuban crisis was inept, hesitating and secretive – and that this made the position of a Power like Great Britain, with big interests at stake, unnecessarily difficult.' According to the deputy under secretary, 'Whether a young lady, a young gentleman, a baboon or a diplodocus America is always a very bad bedfellow.' In the opinion of the Foreign Office's chief civil servant, 'No one surely dreams of annoying the pretty – and still pretty rich – creature; but I think, contrary to the Embassy, that it is her turn to do a bit of the embracing, in the faint hope that once bitten she may not be half so shy.'[87] In the realm of wider Anglo–American relations, fall-out from Cuba was just one of several contentious issues. These included ongoing and unresolved negotiations over Britain's war debt to the United States, and stalled talks between the allies and Japan over naval limitation.

Grant Watson highlighted the failure of British embassy staff in Washington to analyse the 'inconsistent' nature of US policy in Cuba. He cited the complaints of British interests, who asked why the United States had intervened and let loose long pent-up forces if it did not intend to control them. He also repeated Cubans' likening of Sumner Welles to a 'Sorcerer's apprentice', who learned from his master the incantation for putting forces into motion, but not the remedy to rein them in.[88]

Conclusion

The main features of Britain's policy had been procrastination and deference to US wishes. While its diplomats privately criticized US policy and its main proponents, their own overriding strategy had been to wait for decisive US action. Only the prompting of a large capital interest in the island, United Railways, had induced the Foreign Office into a more assertive attitude. Experience had shown that the United States forces would intervene, and by default protect British interests. Roosevelt's new non-intervention policy, however, forced Cubans and Britons alike to adapt to new circumstances. From initial scepticism, the Foreign Office finally realized that Washington's policy really had changed.

Even Welles's own colleagues criticized him. Under Secretary William Phillips later lauded his intellect but criticized his 'unbending personality'.[89] An academic analysis of his actions in Cuba condemns his 'rigid, dogmatic, and opinionated characteristics', so that while he expended 'an inordinate amount of time on trivial matters, he often missed the larger picture'.[90] One cannot help feeling that Welles's view of Grau's government might have been rosier, had it not so easily unseated the ambassador's nominated replacement for Machado – Carlos Manuel de Céspedes. This action both tarnished Welles's reputation and thwarted his participation in Montevideo.

Welles lacked a diplomat's necessary acumen. In Grant Watson's opinion, he had 'misjudged the social forces which are at work in this island' and lacked 'sound political sense'. Britain's representative prioritized the grinding of the sugar crop and analysed the social unrest that threatened it, because British interests such as United Railways depended on the harvest. Roosevelt's ambassador held Grau's government in contempt from the beginning, and therefore never considered coercing it. The combination of non-recognition and non-intervention left the United States' far larger interests extremely exposed. The shell-marked façade of the new Hotel Nacional, a building underwritten by a British insurance company, was proof of Welles's failure.[91]

5
Sugar and the Anglo–Cuban Commercial Treaty

At the end of January 1934, Grant Watson reflected on the short-lived and tumultuous presidency of Ramón Grau San Martín: 'Students of Cuban history will remember his term because a great change came over Cuba. The rule of the sugar magnates was shaken, at any rate, for the present – perhaps forever.'[1] With Grau in exile, and Welles back in Washington, Roosevelt's administration concentrated on restructuring close US–Cuban politico-economic ties. In 1934, the abrogation of the terms of the Platt Amendment (excepting the clause on US retention of the Guantánamo naval station), and the negotiation of a new reciprocity agreement, fundamentally altered the basis of their relationship. Under the Jones–Costigan Act of May 1934, the US duty on Cuban sugar imports fell from 2 cents to 1.5 cents and in August reduced further to 0.9 cents per pound. The 1934 Reciprocity Treaty guaranteed Cuba an annual percentage of the US sugar market while giving preferences to specific US manufactures.[2] Roosevelt had intended to offer these carrots to Machado or his successor, but they were never offered to Grau's radical regime. Instead, negotiations to readjust the US–Cuban relationship soon took place with the new government of Carlos Mendieta.

After the two severe shocks of economic depression and political revolution, the island's 'productive forces' – the economic elite of industrial and commercial classes – made strenuous and ultimately successful efforts to bolster the foundations of their valuable export trade. Having secured an agreement with their all-important US market, they turned their attention to their second best customer, Great Britain, determined to place exports of sugar and cigars to this traditional importer on a much firmer footing. The United Kingdom was Cuba's best customer after the United States, importing 70 per cent of all sugar not exported to its close neighbour, and one third of all Havana cigars.[3]

Sugar and Stability

During the worst period of economic depression from 1929 to 1933, 38 sugar mills (mostly Cuban-owned) ceased production, not only creating unemployment, but affecting the entire rural communities and provincial towns in their localities. Over the next four years, however, 32 of the mills reopened. Aided by protective state regulations, Cubans recaptured a significant proportion of their sugar production in the 1934 to 1939 period. As Cuba sugar industry expert Brian Pollitt states, 'From 1934, powerful and identifiably Cuban interests in large- and small-scale sugar growing and in sugar manufacture effectively linked the sugar economy to the political state and, within limits, imposed their authority upon the state and the institutional machinery.'[4] The island's *colonos*, especially, attained and wielded significant political power, benefiting domestic sugar interests.[5] During the post-1933 period, Washington was prepared to sacrifice short-term business interests in order to maintain the longer-term objective of enduring stability in Cuba. US hegemony was less overt during the rest of the decade, years when Batista headed the armed forces behind a series of puppet presidents. Meanwhile, petty disputes between congressmen frequently paralyzed the island's legislature.[6] Government was not autonomous, but instead an extension of army power headed by its commander-in-chief, the former sergeant, Colonel Batista.[7]

In 1909, the United States had absorbed all of Cuba's sugar exports. In the 1920s, before the Wall Street Crash, it had taken between 75 and 80 per cent. But following economic depression in 1929, it bought less than half of the island's chief export.[8] Or rather, Cuban sugar had a 50 per cent share of the US market in the early and mid-1920s, dropping to a 25 per cent share by the early 1930s.[9] Despite a reduction in the US tariff on the island's sugar under the new quota system, and an improved price for the commodity in the United States, Cuba became increasingly dependent on the lower price and diminishing scope of the 'free' world market. The 'free market' did not constitute a market without customs duties, but rather defined that part of the world sugar trade to which special trading arrangements, such as those governing Cuban sugar exports to the United States, did not apply.[10]

For Cuba, production in excess of both domestic consumption and the US allocation was sold in the free market, upon which it increasingly depended in the 1930s. The principal buyer of sugar in the free market in this period was Great Britain, whose sugar policy, like that of the United States, was subject to the competing claims of large world producers and their dependencies.[11] Contentious debate surrounding worldwide sugar production and quotas continued among the producing, consuming and re-exporting countries, leading to various international conferences and binding agreements in the mid- to late 1930s.

Cuban Calls for a Treaty with Britain

Renewed calls from Cuba's productive classes to place their export trade on a more secure footing were seen as early as February 1934 in the pages of their chief organ, the monthly economic journal *Cuba Importadora e Industrial* (of the National Association of Commission Agents). Various articles implored Cuba to pay more attention to its best customers through new commercial treaties, while denouncing existing agreements with low-volume buyers of the island's produce. Several demanded straightforward reciprocity – *comprar a quien nos compra* ('buy from those who buy from us'). One pointed to the disaster for the sugar industry threatened by forthcoming agreements by Java and Peru, rival producers of Cuba's dominant primary product. Export statistics provided evidence of the British market's importance to Cuba. But worryingly, no commercial agreement had bound the island to its second biggest customer since the republic's foundation. In February 1935, an editorial described the rope thrown to Cuba in the middle of an economic storm in the form of the Jones–Costigan Act, while pointing out that its permanence was not guaranteed even during the Democratic Party's rule in office. The island's trade stood in danger of perfect isolation.[12]

For the first time in the history of the Cuban republic, calls for a treaty with Britain now received the endorsement of the United States. This reflected the recent political and economic upheaval in the island and the altered dynamics of US–Cuban relations. At a meeting of Cuban sugar manufacturers in April 1935, US Ambassador Jefferson Caffery pointed to the possible limited duration of the recently agreed Trade Agreement and Jones–Costigan Act. He also underlined Cuba's 'vital interest' in the world sugar situation, and its 'most precarious' position in the British market, absorbing 25 per cent of the island's sugar exports. It was possible that larger volumes of sugar beet production and increased supplies from its colonies could soon obviate the need for Britain to import from outside its empire. In such an eventuality, Cuba's national income 'would be slashed'.[13]

In London, the question of an Anglo–Cuban commercial treaty brought back memories of the drawn-out and ultimately frustrated negotiations in the first years of the Cuban republic. The possibility of a treaty had been raised again several times in the 1910s and 1920s, but the Board of Trade was always reluctant to recognize formally the United States' exceptional position by signing a most-favoured nation treaty that accepted US–Cuban reciprocal arrangements.[14] Acceptance of this precedent risked repetition elsewhere in a competitive and depressed world market. While the Foreign Office pointed to the anomalous case of Cuba, without a treaty with Britain, it had no political arguments to add to the economic case made by the Board of Trade, which cited the constant objections of Britain's commercial community to US preferences in the island.[15]

While British officials often highlighted the trade balance in favour of Cuban exports, a rare insight into Cuba's perspective is provided by a memorandum from its commercial attaché in Washington, setting out the island's basis for treaty negotiations in 1927. Balance of trade figures considered exports in isolation, and ignored 'invisible payments' earned by Britain in Cuba. These were principally the dividends of United Railways and premiums to insurance companies. There was also the lucrative re-export of Cuban raw sugar imports from Britain after refining and the very large exports of rice from British India to Cuba. The attaché prioritized the removal of British duties on Cuban sugar and cigar imports, and complained about both the British subsidy to its beet industry and the 'serious menace' of preferential sugar duties applied to imports from the British Empire.[16] Nevertheless, the fact was that Cuba exported to Britain much more than it imported. According to Board of Trade figures, the United Kingdom bought seven times what it sold, and even Cuban statistics showed the trade balance was four to one in its favour.[17]

When the treaty question raised its head in spring 1934, the Foreign Office again anticipated objections from the Board of Trade.[18] While the United States negotiated mutual tariff arrangements with Havana's new government, under pressure from US beet growers to reduce the island's quota, Cubans attached great importance to London's free market for their sugar exports. But two officials in London considered Britain's export position in Peru – another Latin American sugar exporter – to be much stronger, and commented ominously that there was some considerable margin to sacrifice Cuban sugar to that of the Andean nation.[19]

Peru, unlike Cuba and the many sugar-producing dependencies of Britain and the United States, did not benefit from preferential access to any market. The influential sugar interests of both Latin

American countries pressured their respective governments to negotiate treaties with London. As with the important meat-producing nations of Argentina and Uruguay, they were dependent on the British market, and thus belonged to the few select nations in Latin America where Britain still possessed effective leverage in the 1930s. The British government's abandonment of free trade, the floating of the pound and the extension of preferences to her Dominions during the Imperial Conference in Ottawa in 1932, all had serious repercussions for such Latin American nations, who hence sought reciprocal arrangements with London.[20] For Cuban producers, the news of Anglo–Peruvian negotiations served as a wake-up call, although they reassured themselves that heavy (Panama) canal duties on their rival's sugar exports minimized any competition with their own. But the fact that Peru was the first to break away from the Chadbourne Plan was further evidence – in the words of a letter published in the leading daily *Diario de la Marina* – that the moment was approaching 'when each one thinks for himself'.[21]

Cuba had joined six other sugar producers in 1931 to sign the Chadbourne Plan, an attempt to boost depressed prices by restricting production for five years. But restriction by some producers simply caused others outside the agreement to increase their production and fill the void, including those in and under the control of the United States, with devastating results. Cuba's share of the US market dropped from 49.4 per cent in 1930 to 25.3 per cent in 1933. Chadbourne signatories had produced half the world's sugar in 1929–30, but their share dropped to a mere quarter in 1932–33. To make matters worse, the price of sugar also plummeted.[22] The Cuban economy thus suffered a double hammer blow.

Britain required sugar for its much-expanded refining industry. In just a few years, Britain had become a large and profitable exporter of refined sugar that depended on a reliable supply of inexpensive non-empire raw product in order to compete with foreign refiners.[23] Cuba was the primary producer of free-market raw sugar for these refineries, and while Britain had no wish to see the price of this sugar rise substantially, it recognized that a further price drop threatened the continuation of this essential supply. With the recent political and economic problems suffered in Cuba, and the susceptibility of the free-market price to excess production and 'dumping', the risk of supply disruption was very real.

The refinery market leader in Britain was Tate & Lyle, an amalgamation of two companies with origins in Liverpool and Scotland, known respectively for their production of sugar cubes and syrup (among other items). The erstwhile competitors joined in 1921 to form a new and dominant company, with eight refineries in Liverpool, and six in both London and Greenock. Along with other refiners, Tate & Lyle maintained close and fruitful relations with the British government in the interwar period, a 'golden age' for the industry. Like New York, London's Mincing Lane was a principal centre for trading world sugar, just as it had once been for the slave trade. Its largest international broker was C. Czarnikow & Co. Ltd, for decades a dominant player in Cuban sugar imports to Britain. Like the refiners, Czarnikow maintained close links with the British government.[24]

Changed Conditions in the Island

Abrogation of the Platt Amendment and the signing of a new Reciprocity Treaty not only altered US–Cuban politico-economic relations, but also changed fundamentally the position of British interests in the island. Grant Watson reported that these interests regretted the removal of the safeguards offered by the Platt Amendment. And according to the minister, the 'more serious minded among the Cubans' realized that along with 'complete independence' came 'greater responsibility'. They apparently found the change sobering, not at all convinced that Cuba could police itself without outside interference. From London, David Kelly judged that without Washington's constitutional right to intervene in the island, Britain would be freer to send warships and decide its recognition policy should another revolution occur.[25] Nevertheless, Britain would always have at least one eye on US policy towards Cuba.

Grant Watson called at the Board of Trade in transit to his next posting and described how the Cuban government was keeping as many sugar mills open as possible. They were making no profit from sugar exports to Britain, but owners preferred to keep their mills functioning, confident that prices would ultimately rise. With the disappearance of the Platt Amendment, he explained, Cuba was now in the same position vis-à-vis the United States as other producers, and now 'absolutely dependent' on Washington's goodwill for marketing its chief export.[26]

The next day, the minister designate to Finland wrote to Craigie from the St James's Club, Piccadilly, 'I must say that I enjoyed my stay in Cuba and if, later on, I were asked to return to Latin America I would not be sorry to be there again.'[27] When the ship carrying his household goods (but not the minister himself) was shipwrecked off Norway after his re-transfer to Havana in 1937, he might have regretted this private correspondence of two years earlier.[28]

Tom Snow's posting to Havana was his first at the rank of minister, having just ended his second term in Spain (1923–24, 1934–35). He had entered the Foreign Service in 1914 and had a good knowledge of the island's politics and economics though periods spent in its American Department, evidenced by his frequent minutes on such subjects as war claims and proposals for a commercial treaty in the years from 1921 to 1922 and 1926 to 1929. Judging by the energy he showed in urging and pursuing the signing of an Anglo–Cuban treaty, Snow was keen to impress.

Members of a Peruvian delegation in London, resentful at what they viewed as the dumping of cheap Cuban sugar in the British market, suggested that the Board of Trade retaliate against the island for its discrimination in favour of US over British goods. The reaction to the proposal in London was lukewarm, considering that decisions concerning the complex sugar problem could only be reached in an International Conference.[29]

From Havana, Snow reported that the Cubans had got wind of Peru's proposed surcharge. They were nervous about it and US representatives shared their anxiety. The new minister seized on their fear as a stratagem for securing better treatment for Britain's two chief interests in Cuba: namely United Railways (with £30 m of invested capital) and various insurance companies – earning an annual premium income of £600,000 (excluding life assurance). He argued that the department's old 'somewhat doctrinaire view', opposed to a treaty because of its tacit acceptance of US preferences, might now be abandoned. As Snow explained, only Washington's largesse had saved Cuba from bankruptcy, and unlike other Latin American markets, they 'could actually rely on United States cooperation in seeking for an increase in Cuban purchases of British products'. He also reported that Washington was not seeking favourable tariffs on certain products, in order to encourage Cuba to agree commercial treaties with other countries.[30]

While the Board of Trade deprecated the 'crumbs' that Washington had 'allowed to fall from the table', Snow insisted they were 'not crumbs but bones!' The United States had made 'commensurate sacrifices, including the interests of their domestic beet and overseas cane sugar industry', with a resultant increase in Cuban prosperity. In such times, Cubans were 'lavish spenders'. Snow reasoned, 'The British public and/or British exchequer benefit from cheap Cuban sugar: the U.S. public and/or exchequer have forfeited this benefit.' Washington's actions had also diminished Japanese competition, mainly to the benefit of Britain's textile manufacturers.[31] According to the minister, therefore,

Britain could gain indirectly from Roosevelt's enlightened self-interest and largesse towards Cuba.

As Washington altered its relations with Havana following revolution, new openings appeared for the island's second customer and supplier. The unburdening of onerous US–Cuban ties had worked to the advantage of Britain, resulting in what it had sought for so long: opportunity without responsibility. Need for US acquiescence had not changed, but the margins within which British policy operated had widened considerably. Would Britain now be able to exploit this unprecedented set of circumstances? Tom Snow, at least, weeks into his first ministerial post, seized on the opening and appeared eager to pursue it.

Cuba's Chaotic Governance

A difficulty for British diplomacy was the chaotic administration of the Cuban government in this post-revolutionary period. In May 1934, Grant Watson had described a 'weak and vacillating' administration, combating attempts by extremists to overthrow it by 'systematic disturbances'.[32] In February the following year, he described a situation as confused as ever. While the army was the strongest element, Colonel Batista's position was delicate. Washington pressured him to hold elections, but these risked bringing an anti-military government into power. But when a series of strikes paralyzed Cuba, the British minister remarked on Batista's ascendancy. His display of 'skill and moderation' belied his lack of political experience and attested to his 'remarkable powers of assimilation'. More and more people, he wrote, were making the short journey to Camp Columbia to consult the colonel on vital matters.[33]

Batista operated in the background as an *éminence grise*, holding key power behind a series of weak puppet presidents. Cuba's politics and presidents were generally of a provisional character, and Washington's tutelage – mainly exercised through its ambassador in Havana – became less visible. In mid-1935, this took the form of pressure on Cuba's government to hold early elections and place itself on a constitutional basis. Roosevelt's non-interventionist 'Good Neighbor' policy could not admit the direct and overt interference of previous administrations.

Snow underlined the threatened interests of British and Canadian insurance companies in Cuba as the best motive for opening commercial negotiations. As early as 1930, legislation threatened to deprive foreign insurance companies of their near monopoly in the island by obliging them to maintain 70 per cent of their technical reserves in Cuba. The whole basis of their operations depended on the distribution of their policyholders' risks abroad rather than in one country. A complication for Snow's representation of these interests was the antagonism between Lloyd's – who wrote their insurance in London and offered reduced rates owing to avoidance of Cuban taxes – and the local and other foreign companies who felt unfairly advantaged. The two warring parties refused to cooperate with each other in combating Cuban legislation, at considerable embarrassment to the British minister.[34]

Adding to the woe were the ailing interests of United Railways. For the fifth successive year in 1934 to 1935, the company had lost money and was unable to pay interest on invested capital. Its General Manager in Havana, the seven-feet tall Lightly Simpson, lamented the series of labour laws that militated against the profitable operation of his company, and the tendency of Cubans to view railway companies as 'foreign vampires' rather than national institutions.[35] United Railways did not perceive the Cuban government as antagonistic, but instead as 'weak and incapable of resisting the demands of labour however unreasonable'.[36] Generally in Latin America, and particularly in Argentina, the British government viewed the railway companies' London directors as unbending and out of touch with local conditions, and consequently marginalized their claims against those of other interests.[37]

Snow's insistence that the Board of Trade allow him to open negotiations with the Cuban government initially met with a lukewarm response, but the minister persisted and finally wore down the department's conservativeness. The first official approach came from new Cuban President José Barnet in January 1936, when the Board of Trade was discussing arrangements for an international conference on the restriction of sugar exports, keen not to repeat the failure of the 1933 World Economic Conference. An early Board of Trade suggestion aimed at better treatment for Britain's invisible earnings in Cuba (i.e. from insurance remittances and United Railways) by threatening to limit Cuban sugar imports. But the international sugar question was finely balanced, and the British government preferred to keep its hands free rather than upset the sensibilities of other sugar-producing nations, including Peru, who were soon to convene around the negotiating table.[38]

The British minister countered this proposal by emphasizing the importance of British invisible earnings in Cuba and the island's readiness to offer concessions rather than sell its sugar elsewhere. While the United States and Cuba had settled their respective exporting interests,

Britain had only to concentrate on its capital interests in the island, with little to concede in return.[39] Snow described President Barnet as a non-party man with a broad-minded view, who wished to stabilize Cuban trade. Likely successor Miguel Mariano Gómez was unlikely to 'resist "patriotic" opposition' to such concessions.[40] Would Britain not be advised to seek better treatment before Cuba achieved its objectives at the forthcoming sugar conference?[41]

Snow repeated his line of argument in a private letter to Craigie. For him 'the light of pure reason' hardly influenced the Cuban government at all, and instead,

> What has weighed with them has been the fact that the big sugar and tobacco interests have made very strong representations to them in the sense that Cuban exports to the United Kingdom would suffer if British insurance companies were damaged.

Snow suggested connecting the insurance question with the matter of Cuban exports.[42] Attending an inter-departmental meeting in London to discuss a draft treaty, he insisted a formal agreement was the only way to safeguard insurance and railway interests, and to 'strengthen the hands of our well-wishers in Cuba against pressure from nationalists'.[43]

London authorized Snow to make tentative contacts with the Cubans to ascertain their desiderata and gauge their reaction to his proposals. Departments wished to move slowly so as to leave their hands free with regard to possible restrictions on Cuban sugar exports. While Britain sought to protect the operation of insurance companies and United Railways, Cuba desired protection for large sugar and cigar sales in the British market. British capital invested in the tobacco industry meant it was not a bargaining tool in the same way as sugar. The Board of Trade's long-standing and principled opposition to limitation of the most-favoured nation clause – on account of the United States preferential position – finally dissipated. An official recognized that to 'now swallow this rather bitter pill' went 'very much against the grain', but it would 'make it more difficult for the United States of America to object to Imperial preference'.[44] The altered international position with regard to respective US and British trade blocs thus contributed to ending long-standing opposition to a commercial treaty with Cuba.

During the course of 1936, the British insurance companies in Cuba became more pessimistic, and worked closely with Tom Snow, the Foreign Office, and the Board of Trade. They discussed tactics and strategies to ward off the 'obnoxious legislation' that threatened to both end their operations in the island and set a dangerous precedent for endangered companies in other Latin American countries.[45] On leave again in the summer of 1936, Snow insisted that it was the local agents of insurance companies in Cuba who could influence Congress. To that end he concurred with a proposal for a leading sugar-importing interest to engineer a 'calculated indiscretion', implying possible British discrimination against Cuban sugar imports. In addition, a parliamentary question and answer would highlight the unfavourable trade balance between Britain and Cuba. Two government departments shared responsibility for enacting the strategy.[46]

When Cuban Secretary of State Dr Cortina asked Caffery for his advice about treaty negotiations with Britain in June 1936, the US ambassador replied they were 'highly advisable'. Two months later, Cortina informed the ambassador that Cuba's main objective for the treaty was to obtain a 15 per cent reduction in British duties on tobacco, the island's second export commodity.[47]

Back in Havana, Snow described a deteriorating political situation. Congress was wasting time in 'undignified squabbles over patronage', while public dissatisfaction increased over the legislature's growing 'incompetence and venality'.[48] As for US–Cuban relations and the politico-economic well-being of the island, he reported that all eyes were on November's US elections, where only Roosevelt's re-election promised to maintain Cuba's all-important sugar quota. Order within the island depended on Colonel Batista, with public support for the government weak.[49]

Despite their earlier hopes of mustering congressional support, the insurance companies now agreed that a commercial agreement was their 'sole means of staving off obnoxious legislation'. By the year's end, and in the absence of such a treaty, they were counselling delay as the best method of obstruction. The British minister, meanwhile, reported the year's third presidential inauguration (*el viejo político*, Federico Laredo Bru), the fourth since his arrival on the island, and accompanied by yet another set of new ministerial appointments.[50]

Snow's Frantic Last Efforts

The first two months of 1937 were a frantic period for Snow as he prepared to exchange posts with Grant Watson and redoubled his already considerable efforts to terminate negotiations for an Anglo–Cuban Treaty of Commerce. For Britain, protection for its insurance companies was the crux of the matter. While the Board of Trade suggested to

Snow another 'hint' by the London-based sugar broker Czarnikow in order to concentrate responsible Cuban minds, the minister described the 'disturbance' caused by the previous indiscretion and recommended they hold fire. For political purposes, Batista had committed himself to favouring Cubans at the expense of foreigners, but not to the extent – in Snow's judgement – of damaging the island's most important interests.[51] Given his key role in treaty negotiations, the Board of Trade asked Snow to delay his departure to Helsingfors and tie up loose ends.[52]

A two-week delay to Snow's departure was given a perfect and coincidental justification when a shipwreck sunk the personal effects of his replacement, Herbert Grant Watson. Meanwhile, United Railways decided to negotiate with the Cuban government, attempting to combat another raft of labour legislation that threatened to exacerbate its loss-making operations in Cuba. The treaty as it stood offered it a formula of words that was meaningless in any practical application. Snow judged that new Secretary of State General Rafael Montalvo, a man of 'determined and forceful personality', gave a well-needed stimulus to the negotiations and counteracted his department's earlier opposition. Snow attended a lunch at his sugar mill 50 miles west of Havana on 2 February, guarded by 16 soldiers. There he also conversed with Montalvo's predecessor, Dr Cortina, and the ex-minister to London and ambassador-designate to Washington, Dr Martínez Fraga.[53]

Snow had a late opportunity to converse with Batista and President Laredo Bru, accompanying them for the first hour of a train journey to Santiago de Cuba. Pertinent to their surroundings – given their mode of transport – they attempted to iron out an apparently insurmountable obstacle in the way of alleviating the position of United Railways. Indicative of real power relations in Cuba, Snow was about to alight the train with his efforts finally frustrated, when Colonel Batista – with the president out of hearing – told the British minister he would send private instructions to Montalvo concerning the treaty.[54] A subsequent avalanche of inward and outward telegrams, many sent by Snow between midnight and 3 a.m., impressed Board of Trade officials, and attested to the diplomat's 'ability & enthusiasm'.[55] On the day he set sail for Miami, a final telegram described a recent conversation with the US ambassador. Snow reported that Caffery 'seemed pleased with the result', telling the outgoing British minister,

[Britain] could continue to count on his co-operation particularly (he characteristically added 'if consulted') with Colonel Batista. He considered that the latter would be the decisive factor in any difficulty and that the opposition to ratification would centre on [the] insurance article.[56]

As Snow sailed towards colder climes in Finland, his successor faced a further year and a half of difficulties in achieving congressional ratification of the signed Treaty.

Internal Disputes Frustrate Ratification

Experience might have taught Cubans to expect Washington's hostility, but those anticipating US opposition to the Anglo–Cuban Treaty were left disappointed. Stabilization of the Cuban sugar market was as much a US objective as it was Cuban, with the United States desiring political stability in the island without any intervention. The treaty's second article committed the United Kingdom to grant Cuban imports 'treatment in every respect not less favourable than that granted to similar goods the produce or manufacture of any other foreign country'.[57] In other words, sugar and tobacco would not attract higher import duties than those from elsewhere. But Britain had not agreed to any minimum import of Cuba's sugar, or more importantly, of its cigars.

The treaty provoked a heated debate in the Cuban press. Grant Watson identified local insurance companies and professional associations as the treaty's main opponents. They expected to benefit from social and labour legislation limiting foreign employees in companies such as United Railways, and new employment opportunities in insurance. Senators complained about the treaty's unconstitutionality; it had not passed through their chamber for approval and therefore trespassed on their legislative powers. They rejected its protocol by 18 votes to 11, and criticized several of its seven articles.[58] But most letters and editorials in the prestigious *Diario de la Marina* warned against rejecting the treaty and antagonizing Cuba's second best sugar market. Expressing the misapprehension that Britain had first proposed the treaty, they counselled against shutting the door in its face. In the case of Java's sugar exports to India, one argued, an opening in a market had been lost and never regained. An editorial sounded a menacing note: 'We already know that while the English are late to react, they always react effectively and powerfully.'[59]

José I. Rivero, director of the newspaper, referred to a recent speech by US Ambassador Caffery, describing Cuba's position in the British market as 'very precarious' and advising it to strengthen Anglo–Cuban bonds:

The situation is that the Americans know they cannot absorb all Cuba's exports and have had the good faith and rectitude to advise us to consolidate our position with another client, in order not to find ourselves 'in the street without a key'.[…]

Cuba's current economic position in the United States, based on a sugar quota with an artificial price, is unsecure and ephemeral, and possibly of short duration.[60]

Mediodía, a popular weekly magazine edited by writer Nicolás Guillén, adopted an opposing view. An editorial affirmed,

Cuba has to be free but will not achieve this by making new agreements with Europe. Only true independence will save our economy from the subordinate position in which it finds itself, and will enable Cubans to enjoy the wealth previously denied them. The Anglo–Cuban Treaty, meanwhile, will only subject us to greater international subjection.[61]

One of several articles on the topic of labour lamented, 'The news of the treaty agreement has made a great impact and been rejected unanimously by the Cuban people. The workers see in it their ruin, and all Cubans, the ruin of their country.'[62]

In consideration of the opposing views, Britain played on the anxieties of the island's 'productive classes', those fearing the loss of Cuba's second export market. If the influential players in Cuba's sugar and tobacco interests were given the necessary ammunition – it was hoped – they would fight Britain's battle on its behalf, recognizing a commonality of interests.

Fighting Britain's Fight

The Foreign Office repeatedly affirmed that the Cuban government bore British interests no ill will. Officials simply feared that it was susceptible to accusations from its political opponents of conceding to foreign interests. As for Washington's support, one official in London was against a united Anglo-American front, with Ambassador Caffery 'very shy of appearing to tender advice' to the Cubans, and Sumner Welles, still at the State Department, described as 'no great friend of the U.K.' Instead, an ideal opportunity to give the treaty's supporters 'practical help in overcoming the resistance of Congress' came at the International Sugar Conference, launched by the League of Nations and held in London from April to May 1937.[63] Ahead of the event, Cuba had been afraid that British colonies enjoying preferential rates, such as Mauritius and Jamaica, would marginalize Cuban sugar in London's 'free market'.[64]

Attended by delegates from 23 sugar-producing countries, former Prime Minister Ramsay MacDonald opened proceedings in London with a call for 'stability and order' that would be 'fair to both producers and consumers'.[65] With little progress towards ratification of the Anglo–Cuban Treaty, a Board of Trade official suggested they might 'get at' Batista – the key person – if they could 'really frighten' the Cuban delegates at the Sugar Conference. Initially reluctant, Chief Economic Adviser Sir Frederick Leith-Ross drafted a letter to Cuba's chief delegate, asking that Gómez Mena use his influence in order that his country show 'similar goodwill' to British wishes as the conference hosts were offering to Cuban wishes. Three days later, the Cuban delegate reported that the head of the sugar industry (leading Senator José Casanova) had been informed and had already offered reassurances to the British minister in Havana.[66]

Before the conference had ended, Grant Watson was reporting that the Cuban administration had 'reached its lowest ebb'. Batista was 'remaining aloof from political affairs', controlling the government bureaucracy 'through his partisans'. The press had published extracts from Leith-Ross's letter, and 'powerful sugar and tobacco interests' were clamouring to secure ratification. But in June, the British minister described the island's administration as 'practically at a standstill' and the Senate as 'paralysed'.[67] Such chaotic circumstances bode extremely badly for the treaty's ratification. Fear that Batista would establish a fascist dictatorship and threaten lucrative senatorial positions prompted the 'highest paid legislators in the world' to improve their behaviour, but it was short-lived. Batista's role as military overseer mutated to that of advanced social reformer and he embarked on a Three-Year Plan to transform the island.[68] In order to concentrate Cuban minds, the Foreign Office (on the minister's suggestion) arranged publication of a short news extract describing 'concern' in 'responsible circles' over Cuba's failure to ratify the outstanding treaty.[69]

The Senate did ratify the treaty on 23 August, but with 'reservations' that completely destroyed the agreement's value in Britain's eyes. Of prime importance was the repudiation of Article 4 on British insurance enterprises, stipulating that Cuba not impose 'more onerous' conditions. Another 'reservation' nullified Article 5 on the operation of United Railways, now in its centenary year in Cuba, although the commitment to 'recognise the special necessity of alleviating the position' of the company was never of any practical value.[70] Progress through Congress's Lower House of the so-called Portocarrero Bill posed a serious threat, resurrecting the proposal that foreign insurance interests deposit 70 per cent of their technical reserves in Cuban securities.[71] One insurance representative was reportedly 'seriously perturbed' by the threat, not only to the elimination of his business in Cuba, but also its knock-on effect in Central and South America (Brazil particularly). He recommended 'frightening the Cuban Congress' through threat of retaliation. A Cuban note reporting the five reservations went unanswered while the Foreign Office and Board of Trade considered their strategic options in consultation with the country's insurance and sugar interests.[72]

Their agreed strategy was a threat in the form of possible discrimination against Cuban exports.[73] Because there were no Cuban insurance interests in Britain, no pressure could be applied in this field. Insurance companies, however, urged the Board of Trade to take action 'in some field other than their own'. Tobacco was out of the question, due to customs revenue earned through cigar imports, and large British interests in the industry. They were left with sugar. But Britain could only discriminate against a Cuban import by citing discrimination against British exports to Cuba under the US–Cuban Reciprocity Treaty, wherein US goods enjoyed preferential duties.[74] Another complicating factor was the recent Sugar Agreement of May 1937, considered an 'all too rare success'. Convened on Britain's initiative and held in London, the Board of Trade feared that Cuba, holding the most seats on the newly formed International Sugar Council, might withdraw from the international agreement under threat of discrimination and 'smash' it 'out of spite'.[75]

While government departments debated official action, the Board of Trade contacted 'the [sugar] trade' in Britain – namely London-based international sugar brokers Czarnikow and refiners Tate & Lyle – to ascertain the possible negative effects of proposed discrimination. The companies acquiesced and Czarnikow facilitated a 'calculated indiscretion' to its 'Cuban friends' to the effect that Britain was 'considering' discrimination against sugar imports from the island. Both government and 'the trade' hoped this less drastic option would work, fearful of counterproductive consequences if the threat was carried out.[76] By the end of January 1938, Czarnikow reported that its friends had stimulated 'quite an agitation'.[77] But ratification was not imminent. The Board of Trade was concerned that Cuba, having received satisfaction for its sugar interests in the new international agreement, might be adopting a negligent attitude towards British interests.[78] United Railways could at least point to an achievement in early 1938, when the Cuban government paid its long outstanding debt of $3 m pesos through a bond issue to pay off public debts.[79]

Deliberations over the use of the threat extended to other spheres, including Washington. Government departments were confident that the Cuban Congress would ratify the treaty, but when push came to shove, would the British be prepared to carry out their threat? Bluff was a high-risk game to play, as they discovered to their cost in Mexico during the same year. Long unhappy with limited economic returns from foreign oil companies established in his country, Mexican President Lázaro Cárdenas announced their expropriation on 18 March 1938, leading Britain to sever diplomatic relations with his country. Nevertheless, Grant Watson judged on 27 April that only a threat of retaliation would ensure ratification of the Anglo–Cuban Treaty. He also suggested repeating the tactic of the previous year – a hint to Cuban delegates, this time at an International Sugar Council meeting. The Foreign Office acted, and Colonel Balfour of the Sugar Commission agreed to 'drop an informal and kindly hint' to the Cuban delegation.[80]

Repeating previous form, a complication arose in Washington when British policy in Cuba threatened to set an awkward precedent. Ambassador Ronald Lindsay baulked at informing the US State Department of the proposed threat. He strongly urged the Foreign Office to reconsider the proposed action, insisting that the US government would have the perfect excuse to discriminate against British imperial preference. In London, the Foreign Office did not support Lindsay's arguments. After considerable effort, it had already gained the agreement of the Board of Trade, the Treasury and Customs for the course of action. Furthermore, as one official argued, its justification for imperial preference was that Dominions were not foreign countries. The same could not be said of Cuba. A solution might be found if the threat could be carried out without citing the United States by name.[81]

First informed he had liberty to use the threat, Grant Watson then received instructions not to inform his host government of a 'special duty on Cuban sugar'.[82] Yet another inter-departmental complication had arisen. Events in Cuba, however, superseded these deliberations.

Ratification: At Last

According to the British minister, there were two opposing political groups in Cuba: the island's working classes on the one hand, and its 'productive forces' on the other. Ordinary workers identified with the extreme social reforms and nationalism practised by President Lázaro Cárdenas in Mexico. But the economic elite aligned itself with Washington's proclivity for moderate capitalism, foreign enterprise and development of natural resources.[83] At a mass meeting of workers convened at the Polar Stadium in Havana on 1 May, speakers spoke in sympathy with the Mexican president's policies. A demonstration in honour of Mexico by 15,000 people took place at the same venue on 12 June. A press report described speakers who eulogized Mexico's revolutionary politics. One orator 'denounced the imperialism of the United States and the capitalism of Great Britain'. A single prominent Cuban was in attendance, the Senator Ramón Zaydín – opposition leader in the Senate.[84]

In late June, one of the Cuban delegates to the London sugar conference, Arturo Mañas, described to US Ambassador J. Butler Wright a meeting involving himself and the secretary of agriculture. They had tried to persuade Senator Pujol and Colonel Batista to exert their influence on the Senate and break the impasse in favour of treaty ratification, rather than Cuban insurance interests. According to Mañas, Batista had no great knowledge of the subject, but would favour treaty ratification if a form of words could be found for senators to save face.[85]

Cuba's conservative 'productive forces' organized a counter manifestation in homage to the United States and Great Britain at the beginning of July. Ninety commercial, economic and financial associations attended a banquet on 3 July, attended by two guests of honour, the British minister and the US ambassador.[86] Grant Watson described both the 'continuous' pressure on the Senate by economic bodies and the press to ratify the Anglo–Cuban treaty, and of the organizers' desire to show that support for Anglo-Saxon nations – as opposed to Mexico – was in the ascendancy.[87] In mid-July he reported widespread belief in sugar and tobacco circles that Britain would retaliate because of the failure to ratify.[88]

The battle for ratification of the treaty played out in Cuba's Senate. President Laredo Bru, according to Grant Watson, had been convinced of its 'vital importance', and summoned senators to the Presidential Palace for interviews in groups of three.[89] Some 32 years after Senators Sanguily and Bustamante had fought over the ratification of an Anglo–Cuban Treaty, supporters of the new treaty such as Casanova and Casabuena lined up against its detractors (figures such as Lucilo de la Peña and Zaydín) in the new surroundings of Havana's Capitol building.[90] At midday on 27 July the British minister finally reported ratification of the treaty without reservations, by 21 votes to 4.[91]

Conclusion

After four years of persistence, Britain had achieved ratification of a commercial treaty with Cuba. Tom Snow could take considerable credit for pushing the idea in the face of initial indifference in London. But even Washington's indirect support for the treaty was not wholly decisive. Junior Foreign Office official John Beith identified the decisive stimulus to ratification: 'This satisfactory decision, which enables us to suspend any plan of retaliatory action, would not have been taken but for the representations of Cuban sugar interests.'[92]

It was these and other economic interests that had initially requested treaty negotiations with the objective of securing the British market for their sugar and cigar exports. But after obtaining a sizeable 'free market' sugar quota in a separate international agreement, Cuba procrastinated. Britain had to threaten discrimination against the island's sugar and resort to a ruse in order to indirectly coerce its Congress and secure ratification. The British government did not carry out its empty threat against sugar, and Cuba obtained the treaty it had first proposed. But it offered no protection for Cuban sugar and tobacco in the British market.

Britain collaborated not so much with Cuba's political elite, but with the island's economic elite. Britain held considerable bargaining power owing to the importance of its market to the island's sugar industry. The British government co-opted the 'productive classes' in Cuba by calling in favours from 'the [sugar] trade' in London, in order to gain protection for their insurance companies' lucrative business in Cuba. British insurance companies, however, were not the only beneficiaries of the treaty, as Grant Watson later highlighted. On account of cheap Cuban sugar imports, often bought at below production cost, UK sugar refiners were able to compete with their international competitors. Beith affirmed that this was 'the one advantage to set against all the obvious commercial disadvantages we suffer in Cuba'.[93] Britain had its cake and was eating it; a cake confected at considerable effort with cheap Cuban sugar.

6
The Second World War: Sugar without Cigars

The Anglo–Cuban Treaty of Commerce had been ratified for barely a year when Britain declared war on Germany in September 1939. While the First World War had delivered a hefty blow to Britain's commercial position in Latin America, leaving it reeling on the ropes, the Second World War left it floundering on the canvas. When the conflict ended, increased US penetration had further compromised Britain's export position in Cuba.

Following its nominal independence in 1902 the island's foreign policy was apt to follow Washington's lead, and the Second World War was no exception. Following the Japanese attack on the US naval base at Pearl Harbor in Hawaii, Cuba declared war on Japan on 9 December 1941 and against Germany and Italy two days later. The island was henceforth a belligerent on the side of the United States and its wartime allies. On the political front, Colonel Fulgencio Batista stepped out of uniform in July 1940 to triumph in presidential elections against his only opponent, Dr Grau San Martín. Batista enjoyed support from the army and the police, and from both the political right and Communists. When the former commander-in-chief became constitutional president, a new Constitution of sweeping and radical character came into force. It outlawed discrimination on the basis of race, sex and class. For workers it stipulated a minimum wage, a maximum 44-hour week, paid holidays and social insurance.[1]

Cuba and the War

Shortly before his definitive departure from Havana in early 1940, Grant Watson reported on Cuba's parochial attitude towards the Second World War. The prevailing local outlook was one of neutrality, tempered by the realization that Cuba must follow the wartime policy of its dominant US neighbour. The minister described predominant local concern for the island's economy. Rather than take sides, he wrote, Cubans condemned all belligerents alike for disrupting trade and commerce.[2]

As with the previous conflagration of 1914 to 1918, Cuba came to profit economically from the disturbance to world markets, owing once again to the wartime importance of its mainstay export and essential foodstuff, sugar. But its second product, tobacco, suffered a British restriction early in the war. While wartime Prime Minister Winston Churchill was a prodigious consumer and a walking advertisement for the world's finest cigars, his country's Treasury considered them a luxury item and not an essential staple. It prohibited imports of Cuban cigars in January 1940 to conserve valuable dollar exchange. The measure hit Cuba's second industry hard. Britain had been its largest market for rolled tobacco for decades. Cuba naturally reacted negatively to the blanket restriction, but when its government referred to the recently ratified Anglo–Cuban Treaty, it contained no guarantee of protection for tobacco exports. Despite this fact, Cuba regarded the embargo as a breach of the spirit of the agreement.[3]

Thus the war and its tumultuous events did not herald an uninterrupted boom for the Cuban economy. In the first period of the war, increased demand for Cuban products in the US market was offset by interruption to shipping and disruption in European markets. As a postwar British economic report defined it, '1941 and 1942 were years of expansion; 1940 and 1943 years of frustration. But in 1944 Cuba entered on a period of continuous and growing prosperity'.[4]

Our Wartime Man in Havana

His Majesty's Minister in Havana for most of the war, Sir George Ogilvie-Forbes (1940–44), was a Scottish veteran of the First World War (serving in Gallipoli, Egypt and Mesopotamia). While chargé d'affaires in Spain (1935–37), he had withdrawn the British embassy and British subjects from Madrid to Valencia alongside the Republican Government, when Franco's forces – bolstered by recognition from Hitler and Mussolini – descended on the Spanish capital in December 1936.[5] Burdened with the pressures of attempting to negotiate with government and local authorities, while protecting British lives and interests amidst the chaos of civil war and under criticism of Britain's 'neutral' policy, he took solace in playing his half-sized bagpipes.[6] From 1937 to 1939, he served at the British embassy in Berlin, and was again embroiled in traumatic events.

Given his humanitarian efforts in Spain on behalf of Republican refugees, Ogilvie-Forbes (a devout Catholic) was the object of unflattering press gossip in Cuba, particularly from the conservative newspaper *Diario de la Marina* and its pro-Falange editor José I. Rivero.[7] The political sympathies of many of the approximately 300,000-strong Spanish 'colony', the backbone of the island's mercantile class and constituting the leading figures in the Catholic Church, were not on Churchill's side. According to the British legation, the merchants' principal newspaper of choice published 'daily broadsides' against Britain and its allies.[8]

Correspondence by the British minister was characterized by strong denunciation of Cuba's government, and pessimism about both the future prospects for Cuba, and his country's interests in the island. In late 1940, he described 'a country where a teeming population lives in abject poverty side by side with a wealthy, ostentatious and thoughtlessly selfish minority, who pay practically no direct taxation, and who manipulate without scruple the Government to their own interests'.[9] Months later, he pointed to 'a set of professional politicians whose sole aim and object are their own financial betterment'.[10] The government was 'controlled by politicians, 90 per cent of whom are completely ignorant of the duties entrusted to them, and who have attained their positions by questionable means'.[11] Official British views of Cuba's politicians and economic elite had never been very high, but during the war and the post-war period they were particularly low. In fact, their opinions differed little from those sent from the US embassy in Havana.[12]

Ogilvie-Forbes worried about a fall in the sugar price and the general trend of events, pointing to the possibility of 'internal revolution ending in some form of Communism'. With a subsequent economic improvement, he judged the 'day of reckoning' to have been postponed, at least temporarily.[13] Although there was greater wealth owing to increased US purchases of sugar, minerals and foodstuffs, wider prosperity had not increased. 'There is no doubt that these benefits were not properly distributed, and that the Cuban people will one day have cause to regret the growing disparity of wealth amongst the various classes of the community.'[14] In this judgement, the British minister would be proved correct.

While US dominance in the Caribbean protected Cuba militarily and strategically, Britain's propaganda machine was active in the island from an early stage, prior to US entry into the conflict. Ogilvie-Forbes controlled a British Bureau of Information in Havana, despatching pro-ally literature to a mailing list of some 15,000 with the help of some

20 part-time volunteer ladies. A British Auxiliary Service unit of men provided an all-night guard for the exposed consulate general. The formation of this unit under the minister's supervision worried his head of department in London, judging that it might be viewed as 'a breach of Cuban neutrality' in a country that was 'virtually a dependency' of the United States.[15]

On the home front, Hitler's land forces threatened British shores after overrunning the Low Countries and France from May 1940, leading to the mass evacuation and repatriation of the British Expeditionary Force from the northern French port town of Dunkirk. In the same month, Winston Churchill replaced Neville Chamberlain to become prime minister of a coalition government. In preparation for a planned invasion of Britain, Hitler's Luftwaffe attempted to control the skies over the English Channel and neutralize the Royal Navy. The Royal Air Force (RAF) defeated these German ambitions in the Battle of Britain from July to October 1940. But from September 1940 to May 1941, the Luftwaffe launched a *Blitzkrieg* of night-time bombing raids against industrial and port cities such as Coventry, Liverpool, Manchester and especially London. The RAF retaliated by bombing towns and strategic military targets in Germany.

In anticipation of severe interruption to international trade, the British government introduced food rationing for bacon, butter and sugar in January 1940, followed later by sweets, tea, eggs, cheese and red meat. In late 1939, in the absence of immediate sugar and meat shortages, the British Cabinet had been reluctant to upset public opinion by rationing them. With regard to sugar, the government feared upsetting Empire producers and having to pay higher prices for free-market imports. But a rise in consumption, and worries about supplies, convinced Cabinet members to favour rationing of sugar and meat in order to conserve foreign exchange and economize on shipping. In May 1940, the Ministry of Food reduced the weekly sugar ration from 12 to 8 ounces a week. For the rest of the war and beyond, British households were dependent on a ration book of coupons to purchase essential foodstuffs.[16]

In Havana, the British minister frequently found himself in delicate positions. Many were a result of new wartime alliances, and his government's close relationship with the dominant foreign power in Cuba, the United States. During the early period of the war, he was critical of the US ambassador's 'excessively flattering' treatment of Batista's government. At the same time, he suppressed his own inclination to criticize Cuba's war contribution.[17] Reading his despatches in London,

Foreign Office colleagues occasionally sensed a lack of objectivity in his comments. When he reported 'widespread agitation' against Spanish property and mercantile business, one official commented, 'Sir Og[ilvie] Forbes is not, of course, a very safe guide in Spanish matters, & some of this may be wishful thinking.'[18] On the same subject, another colleague noted a few days later, 'The telegram does not conduce to a balanced assessment'.[19] This and other examples of disenchantment were evidence of a certain divergence of opinion between the Foreign Office and its man in Havana.

Anglo–American Cooperation

Churchill was in desperate need to strengthen Britain's military capability following French capitulation, as the country confronted Germany and Italy alone. The prime minister requested the loan of 40 to 50 destroyers from Franklin Roosevelt's government until British shipyards could supply the Royal Navy. The US president was fearful of a negative response from Congress, in mind of the Neutrality Acts and reluctance to embroil itself in war. A formula eventually resulted in the 'Destroyers for Bases' agreement in September 1940. The accord stipulated that Britain would acquire 50 second-hand ships from the US Navy, and in return, concede 99-year leases on air and naval military bases in Antigua, the Bahamas, British Guiana, Jamaica, St Lucia and Trinidad. It gave up its Bermuda and Newfoundland bases in perpetuity.[20] While Churchill viewed the deal as essential to Britain's defence during a perilous early period in the war, it signified a further diminution of his country's historic military presence in the Caribbean.

With regard to economic aid for its allies, the United States continued to be wary because of the debts still owed it from the First World War. Washington preferred a different mechanism, under which it extended a series of credits and loans to nations at war with Germany and Italy, and later Japan. The wartime programme of 'Lend-Lease' aid proffered food, military goods, oil, industrial production and services to US allies. Britain was its first beneficiary and received over half of the total wartime aid, proving essential to its war effort. But there were enduring drawbacks for Britain. The United States drove a hard bargain in deferring payment for its goods and services until after the war. Economist John Maynard Keynes, the principal British negotiator, felt impelled to agree to the unrestricted opening up of Britain's home and empire markets to US trade and commerce.[21] This was only part of the price paid for accepting Washington's self-interested benevolence.

In order to guarantee the supply of essential foodstuffs, Washington also agreed a series of commodity purchasing agreements with Latin American nations. To safeguard the supply of sugar it naturally turned to neighbouring Cuba. The United States agreed to purchase the entire harvests for 1942 to 1944, and under 'Lend-Lease' the United Kingdom henceforth received its imports of Cuban sugar direct from the United States.[22] In coordination with Washington, Britain purchased the entire Dominican Republic and Haiti sugar crops for 1942, while the United States bought their harvests for the following two years.[23] In one stroke, Britain gained security of supply, but lessened its bargaining power with Cuba. Unlike the 1930s, it could no longer apply pressure with the overt or implied threat to source its sugar elsewhere. When defending its vulnerable interests in the island, it had lost an important weapon in an already limited armoury.

The Communist Party in Cuba vocally supported Russia's entry into the war against Germany, and made friendly overtures to Ogilvie-Forbes. With the United States not yet a belligerent, and far less disposed than Churchill's government to cooperate with a communist power, the minister could hardly mimic his country's new understanding with Russia and in turn antagonize the US embassy in Havana.[24] But this was a minor distraction when compared to direct US participation in the war. When Japan declared war against the United States in December 1941, Cuban public opinion threw itself more firmly in support of its neighbour.[25] Three days after the Japanese attack on Pearl Harbor, Batista's government followed its neighbour's lead and declared war against the Axis powers.

Anglo–American intelligence cooperation in the Caribbean led to the only execution of a German spy in Latin America during the Second World War. British intelligence in Bermuda intercepted the secret-ink letters of a German resident in Havana, Heinz Lüning, holding a Honduran passport and living in a flat overlooking the capital's harbour. The allies accused him of communicating the details of ship movements via his short-wave radio to enable their sinking by German U-boats. He was nicknamed the 'canary man', on the supposition that he kept chirping birds in order to conceal his noisy radio transmissions.[26]

It was a good story that produced a mild sensation in Havana, especially as German submarines were sinking allied shipping in the early years of the war. For example, 336 allied ships suffered this fate in the Caribbean and Gulf of Mexico in 1942.[27] But an in-depth study of the case alleges that the basis of the accusations was untrue. For a start, Lüning's radio never worked, and his main motivation for residing in

Havana was to avoid German military service. But the allies desperately needed a good propaganda story while Hitler's forces threatened, and even the Abwehr (German intelligence services) welcomed the distraction from other Caribbean-based spies. A Cuban firing squad eliminated this supposed threat to allied shipping.[28]

During the Battle of the Atlantic (1939–45), coordinated sea-air operations protected transatlantic convoys of merchant shipping, providing a supply lifeline for allies such as Britain. In the early years of the war, such ships and their naval escorts were extremely vulnerable to German U-boat attack, and effective protection for them did not exist until the end of 1943. In order to ensure the supply of vital raw materials such as bauxite and oil from the South American continent, the United States bolstered Caribbean defences with a protective shield of air and naval bases. In June 1942, Batista's government agreed to Washington's request for military planes from the United States and the RAF to use its air base at San Antonio de los Baños (and later at San Julián) for anti-submarine operations.[29]

US Preponderance

The Foreign Office was clearly alive to further US encroachment upon Britain's strong second position in the Latin American market during the course of the Second World War. But the British increasingly realized the weakness of their position in the continent vis-à-vis the United States. While Britain was none too happy with this state of affairs, and considered strategies to regain lost economic ground as the post-war period approached, it ultimately had little option but to shelter behind US political preponderance.

While the British and North American 'colonies' in Cuba maintained good relations and actively supported the war effort, cooperation between British and US embassy officials in Havana was less harmonious. Ogilvie-Forbes underlined the particularly special position of the United States in Cuba, relations that served as 'a model' for its relations with other Latin American countries. He reported 'anti-British elements' at the US embassy, and alleged that it kept a 'British Activities' file.[30]

On the initiative of new Ambassador Spruille Braden, the US embassy increased its staff to over 150, including a contingent from the Federal Bureau of Investigation (FBI).[31] The high-handed activities of FBI agents operating in Havana provoked Foreign Office indignation. From the British legation's point of view, these agents enjoyed virtual impunity, acting as 'a kind of Gestapo under the cloak of the Cuban police'.[32] For example, the FBI arrested, interrogated, and interned one British citizen as a suspected criminal. The fact that he had attended the same Roman Catholic school as Ogilvie-Forbes led US authorities to believe he was the minister's friend. But this detail was an unfortunate coincidence. After an Anglo–American exchange of views, the Foreign Office was satisfied that the FBI became more circumspect in its treatment of British citizens.[33]

Due to Lend-Lease scarcities and shipping disruption, Britain lost nearly all of its visible exports to the island, such as cloth, hardware, coal, whisky and pharmaceutical products. By 1943, the minister reported that 'our trade with Cuba has lost very heavily to the Americans, not only in commodities but also in goodwill and possibility of recovery'.[34]

He questioned the objectives of the US 'Good Neighbor' policy with regard to Cuba: the US embassy in Havana regarded Cuba as a 'stepson', and was warning Britain to 'KEEP OUT from nosing into Cuban affairs'.[35] There was no possibility of Britain's acting as an 'honest broker' in Cuba, given US dominance there. Cuba's commercial class, meanwhile, would 'seek the best market regardless of political considerations'. Though Americans were increasingly unpopular, he judged that Britain must not to be played off against them while the choice was limited to Batista or the alternative of chaos. With an eye to the war's end, and with an impressive prescience of 16 years, Ogilvie-Forbes wrote,

> As the Americans with the concurrence of His Majesty's Government, insist on being the cock of the walk we must wait and see whether they can permanently control the situation in the new world of the future or whether – to change the metaphor – they are weaving a rope with which to hang themselves and then our chance may come and our collaboration may be appreciated.[36]

Momentum swung in favour of the allied forces towards the end of 1942 and the beginning of 1943. The Soviets finally defeated German invaders at the siege of Stalingrad and the United States claimed several victories in the Pacific. Axis forces suffered defeat at the hands of the British 8th Army in North Africa, and British and US forces invaded Sicily in July 1942.

A 1943 Foreign Office communication by Head of the South American Department Victor Perowne invited all British missions in Latin America to consider their local position, the threat posed by the United States and the possibility of Britain acting as an 'honest broker' between the region and Washington. His memorandum on 'The United States and Great Britain in Latin America' recognized that the United States had 'no predisposition to collaboration' but instead tended to regard Britain as a possible rival. Perowne saw a 'double necessity' of maintaining the British position in Latin America and avoiding 'all dangerous friction' with the United States. The latter was evidently the more important of these two priorities, considering that US cooperation was 'the paramount British interest'.[37] The importance of US entry into the war to assist in the defeat of Hitler and the Axis powers was evident, as was the weakness of Britain's position. It recognized that the United States had a regional 'concentration of "fire power" (in the form of financial and economic assistance and cultural and political propaganda)' with which it could not possibly compete.[38]

British officials contemplated how their economic position might develop once the dust of war had settled. From their Washington embassy, Ambassador Ronald Campbell envisaged a rise in the general standard of living and a broader demand for consumer goods, providing increased opportunities for both Britain and the United States in Latin American markets.[39] Perowne questioned this assumption, noting, 'Can we have good political relations with a country of whom we are the keenest commercial rivals on their own back doorstep, so to speak?'[40] Robin Humphreys, seconded from the Royal Institute of International Affairs to the Foreign Office during the war, highlighted that British vested interests – in the form of extractive and public utility industries – were 'in an extremely precarious position as the result of the movements of economic nationalism'. He advised that Britain would 'need the Latin American States as markets and as sources of supply in the future still more than in the past [...] but that we must avoid any such clash in trading interests and trading policy as it is likely to impair our good relations with the United States'.[41] Again, these official views highlighted the perceived prime importance of harmonious Anglo–American relations over and above commercial considerations.

In reply to a request from London to report Anglo–Cuban 'bones of contention', the Havana legation again cited a list of perennial issues in 1944. These included discriminatory labour legislation affecting 40,000 British West Indian workers, and the continuing threat against the operation of foreign insurance companies in Cuba. For United Railways, Britain's principal capital interest, the war was proving a mixed blessing. A government decree had increased wages to compensate for higher living costs, and the Cuban government had accumulated a large debt to the company. But after a decade of low sugar prices and annual losses from 1932 to 1942, United Railways was benefitting from general prosperity and heavy demand for sugar, and hence increased rail freight income. War enemy Japan now controlled sugar production in Formosa, the Philippines and Java, reducing competition from that part of the world and raising prices of the commodity and its derivatives. Another boon for the railways was the wartime shortage of petrol and tyres, impacting negatively on its freight rivals in road transport. Cuba, meanwhile, complained about the sudden and ongoing loss of the British market for its cigars, and Britain's disinclination to upgrade its Havana legation to embassy status.[42]

The position of insurance companies related to the 1937 Anglo–Cuban Treaty of Commerce, under which both British and Canadian companies enjoyed some protection. According to the companies and the Foreign Office, the Cuban government had put 'a damaging gloss' on the interpretation and application of the article providing protection, attempting to impose a tax on foreign company balances held abroad. But the British position was weak. Even the Board of Trade admitted that only occasionally could it 'hang some protest on an interpretation of a clause' in which only the British believed. And as Ogilvie-Forbes revealed from Havana, the treaty only expressly covered the operation of British, not Canadian companies. It was the latter who possessed far weightier insurance interests in Cuba, and who looked to him for protection under Article 4 of the treaty. The Foreign Office and its man in Havana concurred with the Board of Trade position that the treaty was already 'out of date', and that they would just have to 'rub along during wartime'. Following the end of conflict, they might well possess more 'bargaining power'.[43]

Before leaving Havana in May 1944, Ogilvie-Forbes fired a parting shot at his host government. While he applauded the Cuban public's sympathy for the Allied cause and its enthusiasm for Winston Churchill, he was less impressed with the island's official war effort. He considered it only paid lip service to the cause, and he was pessimistic about the future of British interests in Cuba.[44] At the same time, the Foreign Office was contemplating raising the status of some of its Latin American missions from legations to embassies, with a corresponding elevation in status for diplomats from the rank of Minister to Ambassador. Compared with other legations in Peru, Mexico, Uruguay, Colombia and Venezuela, it was judged that Cuba possessed fewer British interests, and that the record of the Cuban government was poor, both in its administration and treatment of British interests. In Havana, one newspaper interpreted the transfer of Ogilvie-Forbes to Caracas as a symptom of Anglo–Cuban difficulties, exemplified by the refusal to elevate the status of the Havana legation.[45]

Even Winston Churchill found time amidst his pressing workload to offer his judgement on the issue:

> I must say I think Cuba has as good a claim as some of the other places – '*la perla de las Antillas.*' Great offence will be given if all the others have it and this large, rich, beautiful island, the home of the cigar, is denied.[46]

But the intervention of the cigar-smoking prime minister did not alter the diplomatic status of the British mission in Havana. In Europe, US Army General Dwight D. Eisenhower commanded the successful Anglo-American armed landing at Normandy in northwest France. The land war on the European continent began on D-Day, 4 June 1944, resulting in the Allies' final defeat of Hitler and the Axis powers in 1945.

The Cuban government appeared very keen to upgrade its legation in London, and tried to force the British government's hand by uni-lateral action. But Foreign Office concern at the 'scandalous treatment' of British West Indians dominated opinion, and it refused to budge.[47] At the same time, Cuba and Canada also considered the establishment of diplomatic missions in Ottawa and Havana respectively, an initiative that bore fruit at the end of the war.

While Cuba received no joy regarding renewed cigar exports to Britain, the Admiralty did respond positively to an attractive offer from the Bacardi Company for a bulk sale of rum. After wrangling in Cuba over which distillery companies should benefit from the purchase, and the question of export tax, the Admiralty paid $366,320 (tax free) for 832,723 litres of the Cuban spirit. In July 1944, 4695 barrels left the port of Havana for the Royal Navy.[48]

Grau's Return

Batista did not seek presidential re-election in 1944. At the start of the year, Ogilvie-Forbes defined Dr Carlos Saladrigas, the general's nomi-nee, as a 'certainty' for the presidency, describing him as 'friendly [to Britain], well educated, and conversant with the insurance problem'.[49] The British legation later noted that all sides viewed the election as fair, and commended Batista for his conduct. Ambassador Spruille Braden had ensured that neither candidate received campaign funds from US business interests, and by default, the favourite Saladrigas forfeited an expected $2 m from US sources. Nevertheless, he was still expected to win, and Britain hoped its interests would benefit under more favourable conditions.[50]

But like the 1945 British general election, when Prime Minister Winston Churchill basked in the victory of war, the favourite candidate did not prevail. Just short of 11 years after his brief tenure from September 1933 to January 1934, the mild-mannered Professor of Anatomy Ramón Grau San Martín won the election by a comfortable majority. On the one hand, the Foreign Office hoped he could clean up Cuban politics and prove less corrupt than his predecessors. But on the other, he was considered a threat to foreign capital. His party had campaigned under the slogan 'Cuba for the Cubans', attracting popular support. The nationalistic character of his earlier short-lived administration, including its 'Fifty-per-Cent Law' concerning the employment of Cubans, appeared to bode poorly for British concerns like United Railways and British West Indians.[51]

The island's sugar crop for 1944 was the largest since 1930, and attracted its highest price since 1924.[52] Like his predecessor, new British Minister James Dodds and his colleagues in the British legation derided the Cuban government. The vice consul judged that the war's impact was scarcely felt on the island, apart from shortages of certain commodities and a rise in the already high cost of living. Inhabitants were entirely concerned with their own political and economic affairs. Far from suffering from the war, Cuba had in fact profited, he wrote. Between the election and Grau's inauguration, Batista's administration had been busy 'cleaning up', and when the new president took office he 'found the Treasury bare'.[53]

Owing to the nationalistic nature of Cuban labour law against the employment of foreign workers, the British 'colony' in the island – of whom about 40 per cent were Canadians – was steadily diminishing.[54] Since 1898, all Canadian diplomatic and consular interests had been handled by Britain's legation. And like the 1914–18 war, bilateral Cuban–Canadian trade had increased significantly during the Second World War. An important development for Anglo–Cuban relations in May 1945, therefore, was the separation of Canadian from British interests with the appointment of Canada's first minister to Havana.[55] British diplomats generally viewed the new situation as beneficial. Many of the invisible earnings accrued by Canadian banks and insurance interests were previously denoted as British, a factor that Cubans were reportedly prone to exaggerate in Anglo–Cuban negotiations.[56] The new Canadian minister would enjoy harmonious and close relations with his British counterpart, but the 'indefatigable' newcomer was apparently not 'animated by any strong sentiments of friendship for the United States'.[57] In this respect, Britain had also gained a new diplomatic ally. Canada occupied a similarly awkward triangular position vis-à-vis Washington; that is, mindful of troubled historical antecedents and weightier interests, but endeavouring to gain commercial advantage in the island.

The re-establishment of a direct freight service to Cuba was at least a positive sign of some normalization in trade towards the end of the war. The Pacific Steam Navigation Company renewed its direct sailings from the United Kingdom with a vessel calling at Cuba every two months.[58] Prior to this, exports to Cuba had to travel by ship via New York, incurring port expenses and considerable delay.[59]

The disruption of war, as well as interrupting the flow of normal business between Britain and Cuba, also affected regular reporting. In September 1949, the first secretary at the British legation published the first report on 'Economic and Commercial Conditions in Cuba' since 1937, a document previously published every three or four years. It described how the US exporters had supplanted most business lost by British and other European firms. In the export of cotton manufactures, a newly developed domestic industry had edged out Britain. Insurance premium earnings had doubled for UK and Canadian companies between 1939 and 1945, but they had trebled for Cuban companies and quadrupled for US companies in the same period. By 1945, Cuban companies were receiving twice the value of premiums as their second-placed Canadian competitors. To complete the picture of bilateral trade decline caused by war, Cuban cigar exports to the United Kingdom had plummeted from a value of $1.72 m in 1939 to $5436 in 1946.[60]

Conclusion

There was no doubt that, commercially, Britain had lost out heavily to the United States in Cuba during the war. In 1939, Cuba had imported $78.4 m worth of goods from the United States and $3.1 m from Britain. In 1946, these figures were $227.4 m and $4.3 m respectively.[61] In the seven years between 1937 and 1944, UK exports to the whole of Latin America fell by three-quarters.[62]

In order to fight the war and safeguard its sovereignty from the Nazi threat, Britain had liquidated many of its foreign assets, amassed sizeable debts and relied heavily on US financial aid. Sterling thus ended the war a much-weakened currency.[63] To sustain its war effort, Britain had relinquished two-thirds of its export trade, while its merchant shipping suffered a reduction of 28 per cent. In total, the country lost about a quarter of its wealth, to the value of approximately £7000 m.[64]

With almost indecent haste, the United States cancelled the Lend-Lease agreement the moment the war ended, leaving Britain with an immediate $650 m debt, just when it lacked the means to pay it off. The incoming Labour government under Clement Atlee negotiated a massive loan from the United States, to be repaid over 50 years. As a price of the agreement, Britain reluctantly agreed to US demands that it convert its sterling currency within a year.[65] The United States ended the war with its economic dominance enhanced, especially compared to defeated nations like Germany and Japan, and victorious but economically crippled countries like Britain. Furthermore, the US dollar became the world's dominant currency, a role once performed by sterling.

Unquestionably, the decisive entry of the United States into the war had ensured the military defeat of the Axis powers. In the sphere of international relations, Churchill's close wartime relationship with F.D. Roosevelt replicated itself as a transatlantic alliance between the two Anglo-Saxon nations. By the conflict's end, Britain's intimate bond with the United States was the most important element in its foreign policy. With President Harry S. Truman in attendance, the ex-prime minister first defined a 'special relationship' between the two transatlantic allies in March 1946.[66] While Britain had been sensitive to US reactions to its policy in Latin America before the war, the region was now even more a litmus test of the country's increased subservience to US interests.

7
Cold War: Democracy to Dictatorship

A new bipolar world emerged in the aftermath of the Second World War. The Soviet Union came to dominate a sphere of communist satellites in Eastern Europe, while the United States headed an alliance of capitalist countries in the West. The ensuing political and military standoff between two 'superpowers' heralded the Cold War. Washington announced the Marshall Plan in 1947, a programme of economic aid for the war-devastated European countries that aimed to hasten their recovery and reduce their susceptibility to Soviet influence.

At the end of the Second World War, Germany was divided into four occupied British, US, French and Soviet zones. The Soviet Union imposed a partial blockade on Berlin in 1948, a city divided between the four powers but located deep within the Soviet zone (later the Democratic Republic of Germany: East Germany). When the western powers unified their zones into a new country, West Germany, the Soviet Union severed overland routes into the allied-controlled areas of West Berlin, initiating the 'Berlin Blockade'. Britain and the United States opposed this effort to starve the city into submission, and their planes initiated a massive airlift of supplies to Berlin. To assist the airlift, the United States deployed B-29 bombers to airbases in Britain, planes capable of both carrying atomic bombs and reaching Moscow.[1] In taking such action, Harry Truman had committed the United States to aiding Europe's defence, and Joseph Stalin abandoned his blockade after 11 months.

Out of the Berlin crisis, western allies formed the North Atlantic Treaty Organization (NATO), a mutual defence alliance of western European countries and the United States (plus Canada). Another legacy of Berlin was an arms race between the Soviet Union and the United States involving nuclear technology, later embracing a race into space. Wartime Anglo–American military cooperation, renewed during the Berlin airlift, also continued in the field of shared intelligence. Confronting a mutual adversary, the British Secret Intelligence Service (SIS) cooperated with the CIA in espionage and counterespionage against their Soviet counterpart, the KGB. The United States considered Britain its most dependable intelligence ally.

From a position of dominance before the First World War, Britain emerged from the Second World War a junior partner relative to the United States and the Soviet Union. Labour Prime Minister Clement Attlee (1945–51) inherited from Churchill a devastated post-war economy and a huge financial debt to the United States. For the first time in its history, Britain was financially insolvent.[2] Atlee enacted a severe economic programme of post-war austerity. With low gold and hard currency reserves, there was an urgent need to cut imports and increase exports in order to reduce Britain's trade deficit. Rationing became more severe, and domestic production was reorganized to increase exports.

Post-War Anglo–Cuban Relations

If anything, the immediate impact of these global events on Cuba was positive. The island's sugar industry continued to prosper after the war while European and especially Asian sugar producers awaited full recovery. An intent of British post-war policy in Cuba after the war was to profit from its prosperity and abundance of hard currency and export to this dollar-rich market. Tempering these hopes was the oft-repeated expectation that extended economic prosperity – due to consistently large sugar exports – was bound to end and plunge Cuba into recession. More positively, British officials anticipated a reduction in US economic largesse to Cuba in the form of a revised preferential trade agreement, resulting in new export opportunities. Meanwhile, His Majesty's government continued to rankle over what it perceived as poor Cuban treatment of its interests, while Cuba pressured Britain to reverse its blanket restriction on cigar imports. Highlights for Anglo–Cuban relations in this period were a trade agreement in 1951, and the Cuban government's nationalization of United Railways in 1953.

Most official British criticism of Cuban politics in the 1930s had related to its chaotic nature, with a succession of puppet presidents and partisan congressional squabbles. During and following the war, British diplomatic reports carried strong denunciations of the venal nature of Cuban politics and politicians. In 1943, Robin Humphreys viewed a country that had not yet found 'a stable balance between chaos and dictatorship in its internal affairs, which continued to be characterised by maladministration, corruption, extravagance and violent political feuds'.[3] All four British ministers and ambassadors in Havana described these facets of Cuban political life in the period between the Second World War and another revolution in 1959. Of course, there was always an element of colonialist British haughtiness in these criticisms. And in the case of Cuba, such reproaches inherently blamed the United States for failing to nurture a mature political tradition in a country under its influence. But it is also possible that the two Cuban government administrations after 1944 really were more corrupt than their predecessors.

The return of Grau San Martín as president provoked restrained optimism in the British legation. Surely, it was hoped, this 'man of high ideals' would be an improvement over Batista. The minister's caution was justified, not least on account of the return of a virulent nationalism for which Grau was already known. According to British Minister James Dodds, his 'Cuba for the Cubans' mantra made the foreign 'capitalist' 'easy bait', and there was soon a renewed campaign against the 1937 Anglo–Cuban Commercial Agreement.[4]

A year later, Dodds continued to highlight this nationalistic targeting of foreign interests in Cuba: 'It seems clear that, if they could, the ambitious, greedy political element in Cuba, though *not* the best business element, would gladly see the end of the United States or British control in any Cuban activity.' Grau's personal popularity had, according to Dodds, suffered a severe decline, and the 'gilt was off the gingerbread'.[5] A further year on, the minister described Cuba as 'wholly disillusioned with President Grau [...] awaiting apathetically the election of his successor. Corruption is as blatant as, if not more so, [...] ever in Cuba's history'. Were it not for the 'unprecedented wave of prosperity', he continued, 'a revolution of some kind would certainly have broken out by now'.[6] Like Ogilvie-Forbes, he envisaged a direct link between an economic downturn and political upheaval.

But their estimations were only partially realized; unlike the political fracture of 1933, the economy was prospering when a revolution triumphed in 1959. The actual catalyst for this revolution was an unexpected interruption to Cuban democracy in 1952. From this juncture a new post-1933 generation of middle-class Cubans again invoked the island's nineteenth-century independence struggles and their national hero, José Martí. They demanded restoration of the 1940 Constitution, and with it, a raft of social and nationalist reforms that included land reform.

Post-War Economics

Despite greatly increased US imports of Cuban cigars during the war, a delegation from the island visited London in December 1945 to seek the reopening of the British market. In a meeting with their Cuban counterparts, Board of Trade and Treasury officials argued that the United Kingdom bought far more from the island than it sold in return, and that sugar imports far outweighed cigars in importance. In order to seek better treatment for its interests, the British legation in Havana was keen to make a 'friendly gesture' in the form of a modest cigar quota (20 per cent of its pre-war imports). To Cuba's acute annoyance, Britain was now purchasing cigars from its colony in Jamaica. As part of the sterling area, these imports caused no drain of precious dollars from British coffers.[7]

In an earlier period, Britain might have used sugar as a weapon to defend its interests. It had already resumed purchases of Cuban sugar following the end of lend-lease. But the post-war economic recovery period was a 'seller's market', and London could not use its sugar purchases as a bargaining tool until the island's rival producers recovered pre-war production levels. The Cuban cigar question provoked interdepartmental disagreement in London. The Foreign Office and Board of Trade suggested that what they termed a 'little sweetening' might improve their relations with Cuba. But the Treasury saw no reason to accede to 'blackmail', arguing that they should not be forced into a 'substantial concession' just to obtain proper treatment for British interests. In the Treasury's opinion, cigars were '(1) dollars goods; (2) luxury goods; (3) the preserve of the rich'. An exception for a luxury dollar item would provoke headline news and demands for other dollar imports. Furthermore, the government would be criticized for authorizing unnecessary dollar expenditure.[8]

From Cuba, Dodds defined the 'Havana cigar' as an issue 'distorted by national pride'. Cubans attached great importance to 'the one article of true quality and undoubted superiority which they produce'. For them, the loss of the British market for their leading brands was out of proportion to its real value 'in dollars and cents'. As evidence of Cuban strength of feeling, he enclosed a local Communist newspaper article titled, 'The Havana cigar is being ousted from the British market by the most treacherous methods'.[9] These reactions perhaps typified the disdain of an emasculated imperial power on one hand and the tetchiness of a resentful ex-Spanish colony on the other.

Britain, meanwhile, was keen to resolve the problems of British-owned United Railways. Cuba's Public Works Department had initiated a programme of highway construction that encroached on the company's land and property, seriously affecting its daily operations. And Grau's government already owed it a debt of $2.58 m. Dodds wrote to the Cuban Minister of State, highlighting the fact that Britain was 'no longer a creditor but a debtor country', and now under 'an "austerity" regime'.[10] His comments reflected the troubled state of Britain's post-war finances.

Sir William Rook from the Ministry of Food visited Cuba and met its 'sugar people'. He attempted to bluff them, hinting at the stimulation of sugar production in the colonies, and Britain's increasing independence from the Cuban market. To British government colleagues he confessed they would be in no position to dispense with Cuban sugar for at least three years. Dodds outlined an apparently iniquitous imbalance: 'Britain in her present impoverished state' was paying $80 m a year for Cuban sugar, while Grau's government owed a $3 m debt to United Railways.[11] The annual bilateral balance of trade was $59.7 m in Cuba's favour, with British invisible earnings, which the Cubans often cited in riposte (e.g. insurance premiums), earning roughly $10 m. The Cubans proposed a scheme, unpalatable to British officials, for them to purchase sugar in sterling rather than dollars. An official from the Bank of England turned the idea on its head, commenting, 'The answer, we feel, to the Cubans is not sterling for sugar but railways for sugar.'[12] In the final analysis, the British wanted to sell the railway outright and have done with its problems.

Britain continued to examine frequently the US–Cuban economic relationship. Cuba's dependency on its preference agreement with Washington was described as the 'backbone of Cuban foreign trade', an 'umbilical cord' through which trade flowed. Britain speculated about modifications to this agreement, and possible benefits such as increased Cuban dependency on the British market for sugar and tobacco exports. In this way, it was envisaged, Britain might have a weapon to protect its railway and insurance interests, under constant threat of anti-foreign legislation and treatment. With Anglo–American discussions in progress on trade and tariffs and changes to preferences and barriers, Dodds wrote,

> For the first time [Cuba] saw herself confronted with the possibility of a radical change in her foreign commercial relationships and of being obliged to face the world, as it were, out of leading strings. On the whole the prospect has filled most Cubans with something approaching dismay.[13]

He suggested reminding his host government that sugar producers like the Philippines were recovering production, and that Britain was an 'assured market' for Cuban exports. In London, one official drily remarked, 'I should have thought that the Cubans are too busy making hay while the sun shines to pay over much attention to it.'[14]

The 1947 sugar crop of 5,750,000 long tons was the largest harvested in the island's history, prolonging again wartime prosperity, and providing an income of around $640 m. Dodds wrote, 'Not only has she a very substantial favourable trade balance, but this consists exclusively of the coveted United States dollar. Cuba, therefore, presents a most desirable market at the present time'.[15]

A 'Setting of Luxury and Make-believe'

Fortunately, the spouse of the new British Minister to Cuba Adrian Holman from 1949 sent regular correspondence to a friend in Britain. So, in addition to diplomatic despatches, there exists a female insight into life on the island and the domestic problems of running a diplomatic mission in the tropics. Betty Holman was the daughter of Sir Gilbert Fox, former partner in a sugar merchant based in Liverpool and Mincing Lane (London). After the First World War, he had headed the Sugar Commission on its visit to the United States and Cuba. She mentioned her background to Cuba's Chief of Protocol on arrival, providing the Holmans with 'the most wonderful entrée to all the sugar barons'. They attended parties that flew in *paté de fois gras* and caviar from the United States, but such extravagance was at odds with their sprawling and dilapidated residence opposite the Biltmore Golf Club, a home built by Gerardo Machado's son-in-law, and formerly used as a brothel.[16]

Following sterling crises and repeated deficits on Britain's balance of payments, Clement Atlee's Labour government devalued the pound from $4.03 to $2.80 in 1949, stimulating demand for the country's exports by making them cheaper abroad, but making imports more expensive. For the Holmans, ostentatious Cuban displays of wealth contrasted with their meagre Foreign Office allowance, which had not risen since devaluation. Currency restrictions also meant that they had little access to their British savings. In order to pay their grocery bill they sold part of their duty-free whisky and gin allowance to other diplomats. When they were not at Mr du Pont's private golf course at Varadero, the Holmans played rounds alone at their neighbouring course for fear of losing against friends and having to buy their clubhouse drinks. When HM Inspectors did eventually arrive they more than doubled their allowance from £3000 to £7000. They could then at least afford to entertain friends such as Mary and Ernest Hemingway, and an old acquaintance from diplomatic service in Paris – the Duke of Windsor.[17]

In his first annual report, Adrian Holman described the 'Hollywood smile and flair for political jobbery' of new Cuban President Carlos Prío (1948–52), plus his 'considerable skill in dividing his opponents'. Political graft and corruption continued, while 'gangsterism' produced a further 20 political murders in 1949.[18] By the following year, Holman was writing of Prío's 'spectacular canter' having slowed down to a 'dull trot'. He had lost initiative and his prestige and popularity had suffered. But still, he had managed to steer a 'devious political course' through the year, holding the main body of his party together and keeping his opponents divided. Such, it seemed, was the archetypal Cuban politician of the period; poor at managing or reluctant to manage the affairs of the country, but adept at out-manoeuvring and appeasing his opponents and the US ambassador. Political assassinations and corruption continued, the shining example of immorality occurring at the court trial of former President Grau for his alleged embezzlement of $174 m, when all the prosecutor's documents were stolen from the courtroom.[19]

Labour unrest and the cowing of successive governments to union pressure aroused much comment from the British legation, especially because of its effects on the affairs of United Railways. With roads being driven through the company's property without compensation, an already considerable government debt continued to increase.[20] The company's chairman spent some eight weeks on the island in 1947, hoping to collect arrears, and, if possible, sell the railway. Hours before his departure, he managed to secure $800,000 of repayments, but not a prospective buyer.[21]

The inaction of successive governments was mainly due, according to the minister, to the stranglehold on public opinion that labour unions and the press held over the government. In such an environment, the government was loath to be seen bowing to foreign pressure instead of the virulent demands of unions. Buffeted by a combination of falling income, high wages and increased road competition, United Railways announced it would reduce expenses by dismissing staff and reducing wages. The Cuban government responded by assigning an 'interventor' to manage the company's affairs, which only resulted in increasing its debt by a further $2.8 m, and even more urgent efforts to sell the concern and end its misfortunes forever.[22]

There was a rare success for British exports in 1950. Lancashire-based Leyland Motors Limited signed a contract to supply 620 buses to Cuba, breaking a US near-monopoly on vehicle exports to the island. Millionaire businessman William Pawley established a new bus operator in Havana, Autobuses Modernos. Pawley was the former US ambassador to Brazil and Peru. He was also a well-known Republican Party supporter and associate of President Eisenhower and CIA Director Allen Dulles. Turned down by 11 US banks to finance a bus deal for his new company, and facing direct competition from established transport rival Omnibus Aliados, he approached what one US news magazine described as 'dollar-hungry Britain'.[23]

The government's official credit insurers, the Export Credits Guarantee Department (ECGD), guaranteed 85 per cent of the $10 m deal, until then Britain's largest ever single dollar-export order. But with the all-steel single-deck buses under construction, Pawley came extremely close to abandoning the whole scheme due to labour obstruction and a lack of government support in Cuba, a decision that would have left the ECGD to pay out Leyland on its sizeable loss.[24] Pawley had strategically purchased the assets of Havana's tramway company and ripped up its tramlines, eliminating competition from that mode of transport. Forced into supporting the scheme in the face of a grave lack of public transport in the capital city, Prío's government appointed an 'interventor' and nationalized Autobuses Modernos. With their bargaining position strengthened, Leyland and the ECGD renegotiated the purchase agreement in order to receive direct remittances from collected passenger fares.[25] In this way Havana's public obtained its buses and the British their money. And crucially, Leyland had gained a foothold in a traditional US market. This strengthened its chances of receiving further lucrative contracts in Cuba, something the company achieved in 1959, and controversially in 1964.

As with the two world wars, the 1950 conflict in Korea and resulting disturbance to world markets benefited Cuba through a rise in price and demand for the island's sugar, postponing again the day of economic reckoning for the country's lopsided dependence on the United States. Increased prosperity led to lavish expenditure on a scale that Holman compared to the post-First World War 'Dance of the Millions'.[26] A visiting ECGD official drolly described what he encountered in 1951:

> Havana is a city with an equable climate and a warming sun, frozen daiquiris, vulgar tourists – chiefly from the East End of New York at this time of year – breathtaking prices, a tendency to put off till tomorrow anything your friend cannot do for you to-day, and politicians who hope to clear the till at the end of their term of office and

settle in Miami. The population of the country is divided into a relatively few excessively rich people and a multitude of ultra poor labour which is considerably attracted to communistic doctrine.[27]

His depiction of the island during the Auténtico years was replete with both British condescension, and derision of the island's political class, spiced with a tinge of anti-Americanism.

The benefits of Cuba's prosperity were indeed unevenly spread, and the country did not take the opportunity to diversify its economy away from sugar dependency. The working class demanded job security, but the seasonal nature of the sugar harvest inflicted periodic unemployment. The trade-union movement had split in 1947 into Communist- and Auténtico-controlled organizations, leading to even greater labour militancy against the capitalist-friendly minority who directed the economy.[28] In defending Britain's economic interests in Cuba, its diplomats naturally sided with capitalist business interests as opposed to the radical labour unions that defended ordinary Cuban workers' rights.

Washington's reduction of the Cuban sugar quota, intended to strengthen prices, induced the island to seek larger alternative outlets for its main crop. In 1951, Cuba signed trade agreements with both Germany and the United Kingdom, and undertook negotiations for another with France. Britain agreed in advance to import Cuban cigars to a value of $0.5 m in 1952 and 1953, and to buy 1.5 m long tons of sugar from 1951 to 1953. Following an 11-year hiatus, the British market had finally opened again to Cuban cigars. In return, Cuba undertook to concede to 82 British tariff items the same customs duties as those applied to US-origin goods. Meanwhile, Prío's government was spending vast sums on an extensive public works programme, and making little effort to diversify its economy away from sugar production, as recommended by an International Bank report.[29] But a further record sugar crop of seven million tons in 1952 and the inability of consumer countries – due to their lack of hard currency – to absorb all the surplus not bought by the United States, finally put an end to Cuba's prolonged period of prosperity.[30]

Following the end of his presidential term in 1944, Fulgencio Batista went to live in Daytona Beach, Florida. At the end of 1948, Dodds reported the reappearance in Cuba of this 'sinister figure', the 'strong, determined, [and] unscrupulous' type that 'Cubans, perhaps all Latin Americans, admire and fear'.[31] On 10 March 1952, he instigated a *coup d'état* supported by the armed forces. Batista's unexpected and unconstitutional return to power came as a shock to Cubans and diplomats alike. In its immediate aftermath, Britain's ambassador – along with his neighbouring Canadian counterpart – ventured by car to the centre of Havana to get a first-hand view of the practically 'bloodless revolution'. With Cubans considering their country a 'leader of progress and democracy' in the region, Holman wrote, the *coup d'état* 'struck a rude blow at their *amour-propre*'.[32]

Considering the manner in which it had come to power, there was no urgency in Washington or London to bestow political recognition on the new regime. Given that Batista had 'flirted with the communists' in an earlier decade, Foreign Office officials worried about his 'ambivalent' or 'ambiguous' attitude to communism. But they also hoped that a 'strong government' would deal with organized labour more effectively and resolve the United Railways impasse. When it received notification of imminent US recognition, the Foreign Office instructed Holman to confer British recognition a day earlier.[33] Both Washington and London viewed Batista as generally friendly to US interests, thus avoiding the recognition complications of 1933. But Holman was astute with his general observation that 'once the Constitution has been flagrantly violated, it is frequently difficult to return to normality without a struggle and even violence'.[34] A daring assault on military barracks in eastern Cuba 16 months later proved Holman correct. The date of 26 July 1953 hence became resonant in Cuba's revolutionary history.

The general's return to power prompted the retired James Dodds to write to his old department, 'I am most interested to see in today's press that Batista has done it again in Cuba. I was always attracted by Batista and it was possible to do business with him, which one could hardly say of either of his successors.'[35] The statement by the ex-ambassador would faithfully reflect British official views. In his new incarnation as military dictator, Batista tackled obstreperous labour unions and quickly resolved points of friction in Anglo–Cuban relations. In contrast to his Auténtico Party predecessors, Batista got things done. And unlike their views on his political contemporaries, British diplomats had little reason to dislike him. A year after the coup, practically all outstanding bones of contention had been settled on an amicable basis, including the sale of United Railways and a final instalment payment to Leyland Motors.

Britain made a special one-million-ton bulk purchase of Cuban sugar in April 1953, proving highly satisfactory to both parties; Britain bought the sugar at an exceptionally cheap price and ended its post-war rationing ahead of schedule in September, while Cuba had disposed of its entire yearly crop along with an unsold surplus from the previous year. British children also had reason to rejoice in 1953 with the de-rationing of sweets. They emptied their piggy banks and gorged on confectionary. Added to the reopening of Britain's market to Cuban cigars, this new period of harmony and reciprocal deals was proving economically beneficial to both governments. There was even light at the end of the tunnel for United Railways. Britain's main capital interest in Cuba had been unprofitable for most of the previous two decades, and a target for nationalist sentiment and labour agitation. Formerly a source of prestige (and dividends for investors), the company had long since become a burden for British diplomats in Havana. After stalling for four years, the Cuban government signed a preliminary agreement for the purchase of United Railways for $13 m cash. The Foreign Office breathed a sigh of relief that this tiresome and prolonged irritant to Anglo–Cuban relations was exorcized at last.[36]

Batista, however, struggled in the domestic political sphere. Seven months after his coup, Holman described the general's difficulties in imposing his will. Having come 'in as a dictator and then behaving as a democrat', he had 'fallen between two stools'.[37] Despite these shortcomings, however, the ambassador viewed the general in a favourable light, describing him as 'a real man and born leader and a cut above ex-President Prío with his gang of predatory relations and hangers-on'. Ahead of a second general election victory (14 years after his first electoral triumph in 1940), Holman wrote, 'I know him well and like him and I am sure that he would be a happier man and a better leader as a constitutional President. If I were a Cuban, I would vote for him without the slightest hesitation'.[38] In the event, all the opposition candidates (including ex-President Ramón Grau San Martín) alleged fraud and withdrew before the November 1954 election. Batista won overwhelmingly, but was denied the meaningful democratic victory he craved.

The outgoing British ambassador noted that Batista had 'forfeited from the outset any popular support' due to his unconstitutional assumption of power in 1952. And he had 'somehow failed to win any appreciable increase in popularity' by 1954.[39] Indeed, political legitimacy proved elusive for Batista throughout the 1952 to 1958 period. Harvard Professor of Government Jorge Domínguez asserts that he was 'an inefficient dictator', criticized by some of his supporters for not being 'harsh enough'.[40]

Holman had arrived as minister and left as ambassador. Following years of deliberation, His Majesty's government finally upgraded its diplomatic mission in 1950, and abandoned its legation in the suburb of Vedado for a newly designated embassy in downtown Habana Vieja. The British embassy henceforth stood midway between the Presidential Palace and the seafront, in close proximity to the capital's harbour entrance. Although inconsequential at the time, the new embassy occupied an elevated position on the top three floors of a nine-storey building, making it an excellent vantage point for observing ships entering and leaving the harbour.[41]

In April 1954, the departing ambassador evidently felt more freedom to describe Cuba's 'setting of luxury and make-believe'. After a 34-year diplomatic career, and on the point of sailing into retirement with his wife Betty and their beloved dachshund, he wrote of his five-year term as Britain's man in Havana,

> Much of what has been reported from this post may appear to have been exaggerated or verging on the ridiculous. It may have given rise to suspicious smiles and scepticism. But Cuba is indeed a country of a particular musical comedy variety, where frivolous intrigues and plots abound and so often change into ghastly tragedies over night.[42]

In the same year, the renowned British writer Graham Greene made his first visits to the island. Much later, he recalled 'the *louche* atmosphere of Batista's city', its 'brothel life, the roulette in every hotel', and a 'nude cabaret of extreme obscenity' in the Shanghai Theater. Despite its political problems, Cuba was enjoying a tourist boom in the mid-1950s and an explosion of new hotel and casino construction. Greene's experiences in 'this extraordinary city, where every vice was permissible and every trade possible' made him recall a film sketch for an intelligence satire he had written and abandoned in the mid-1940s, set in pre-war Tallinn in Estonia. He realized that 'among the absurdities of the Cold War' in Cuba, there was 'a situation allowably comic'. He returned in 1957 to undertake research for what became his iconic spy-fiction novel, *Our Man in Havana*.[43]

United Nations and European Competition

In the late 1940s and beyond, Cuba's temporary seat on the United Nations Security Council brought dividends for Britain. In this forum, Cuba's support (or lack of opposition) bolstered Britain's standing during a period of decline for the country, its empire and its prestige. For example, the British colony of India was granted independence in 1947, and both Burma and Ceylon followed suit in the following year.

Cuba served as an elected 'non-permanent member' of the UN Security Council from January 1949 to December 1950, and again from January 1956 to December 1957. In struggling to maintain a balance of power in the Middle East that protected its interests, Britain considered other nations' support at the United Nations as crucial. For this reason it coveted Cuba's vote in crucial ballots, such as those concerning Cyprus and Suez. Due to its former centuries-long status as a Spanish colony and henceforward as a pseudo US protectorate, the British were wary of Cuban sensitivities over such colonial issues. As Holman put it, this was hardly surprising given that the island had only 'just completed some fifty summers of independence and has barely overcome her own initial birth pains'.[44]

But according to Britain's first secretary in Havana, Cuban delegates at the United Nations could usually be relied on to either support or refrain from embarrassing Britain.[45] British officials lobbied the Cubans both in Havana and New York. In the British crown colony of Cyprus, the Greek nationalist movement's demands for union with Greece transformed into a guerrilla war against British rule in 1955, while Turkish Cypriots advocated partition of the Mediterranean island. The Cuban UN Delegation moved from opposition, to abstention, and then to support for Britain's position on Cyprus. Overall, an official commented, Britain 'could hardly have expected more'.[46] Again, a year later, the Cuban government's attitude to British policy in Cyprus was described as 'appreciative' and 'even sympathetic'.[47]

But Batista's government was taken aback when Britain took a strong line over the case of a British merchant sailor, Mr J. Topham, who was shot and partially paralysed following a Cuban bar brawl in February 1956. Delays in the case coming to court and the victim receiving compensation led to questions and even a debate in the House of Commons. A letter from the UK deputy representative in New York reported a meeting with his Cuban counterpart, relating his country's frustrations after 'staunchly' supporting Britain at the United Nations.[48] Batista's government viewed London's protestations over the case as unreasonably strong, but it was not a problem that went away. The Topham case was a persistent fly in the ointment for Anglo–Cuban relations, only resolved by a compensation payment in 1964, a gesture of gratitude to Britain for breaking the US economic blockade of communist Cuba with Leyland bus exports.

For all the apparent success of British trade in dollar-rich Cuba in the 1950s, accomplishments had to be measured against the relative progress of competing Western nations for market share. The fact that much of this competition came from recently defeated or occupied nations, such as Germany and Japan, made Britain's own lack of export penetration all the more galling. In essence, the British economy was underperforming, and its exports were uncompetitive compared to European rivals and Japan.[49] As in the past, trade missions to Latin America were as much attempts to recoup lost ground as to stay ahead of the field. Their observations often made sobering reading. A Board of Trade mission to the region in 1952 highlighted Cuba's 'highly price-conscious market'.[50] An economic and commercial overview of Cuba in 1954 reported mixed fortunes for British companies. Insurance firms continued to do well, despite the frequent occurrence of major and minor cyclones. But Japanese exporters offered goods at 'very low prices' and Germans employed 'painstaking attention to Cuban market requirements and aggressive salesmanship'. The only items of British export success were chamois leathers, stout beer and linen.[51]

Competition from Western European nations increasingly impinged on Britain's export position in the 1950s to the chagrin of London, with France and Germany agreeing barter deals with the Cuban government.[52] The French won a $28 m contract to build a road tunnel, linked to a covert sugar barter deal. The Germans, also with a sugar deal, exported locomotives, and a Canadian firm, with no purchase of sugar, gained a contract for rails that British companies had hoped to win. Britain was generally disappointed at its failure to export more capital goods to Cuba.[53] In a visit to London, President of Cuba's National Bank Dr Sáenz pointed out that the British were very bad salesmen compared with the Americans and the Germans. He mentioned the helpful German habit of sending items like locomotive engines for trial and approval.[54] Britain did better in 1956 by more than doubling its exports, selling Viscount Aircraft to airline company Cubana de Aviación and British ships to the Cuban navy. But again, the threat of increased competition from Germany, Holland and Japan was a serious concern.[55]

A 1957 memorandum on British trade with Latin America emphasized that despite its past notoriety for revolutions, the continent was now one of the world's safer areas to do business. A top priority for British exports was hard currency markets such as Latin America's dollar area.[56]

Two 26th of Julys

The year 1953 was the centenary of José Martí's birth. A new rebel movement led by trained lawyer Fidel Castro revived Cuba's revolutionary tradition and mounted a bold but unsuccessful attack on the Moncada military garrison in Santiago de Cuba on 26 July 1953. Castro was a disaffected member of the Ortodoxo Party, formed from a faction of the Auténtico Party to oppose its rampant corruption under Grau. Batista's coup had thwarted Castro's plan to run as Ortodoxo congressional candidate in the 1952 elections. In the July 1953 assault, his rebels hoped to seize arms and depose Batista. Instead, the dictator's army repelled the attack, tortured to death many of the 183 rebels not killed in the initial action and captured Castro outside Santiago days later. He made his own defence speech, and received a long prison sentence on the Isle of Pines. Both he and fellow members of the *26 de julio* movement received an amnesty in 1955 and went into exile to Mexico, where they planned and trained for their next revolutionary attempt.[57]

British Chargé d'Affaires Peter Oliver would prove justified in writing in May 1956 that 'it would be rash to attempt to forecast what is likely to happen over the next two years'.[58] The arrest of 20 Cuban émigrés (including Fidel Castro) in Mexico City a month later, alleged to be plotting to assassinate Batista, ruffled few feathers in the Foreign Office. An official in London played down the event's significance, commenting, 'We have no information about any of the participants, who I suspect are just a bunch of rogues with too little to do'.[59] London had far more pressing matters to worry about than Cuba's distant political affairs.

One of these preoccupations was Egypt's Gamal Abdel Nasser. His nationalization of Egypt's Suez Canal on 26 July 1956 rocked the British government, coincidentally three years to the day after the Moncada attack. The ensuing Suez Crisis was the nadir of post-war Anglo–American relations. Approximately two-thirds of Europe's oil imports passed through the canal. Mindful of their country's disastrous pre-war appeasement of Hitler, the two main British protagonists in the crisis, Prime Minister Anthony Eden and Chancellor of the Exchequer Harold Macmillan, decided to act forcefully against the Egyptian president. But they seriously misjudged the reaction of President Eisenhower's US administration when planning military action against Egypt in collusion with France and Israel.[60] Following the initial invasion there was intense lobbying in the United Nations. Severe US economic pressure against sterling forced the previously hawkish Macmillan into a dovish stance. In the crucial final week of a re-election campaign, President Eisenhower acted quickly and decisively to rebuke the British government and force a cease-fire and humiliating military withdrawal.[61]

Eden soon resigned on grounds of ill health just 18 months after Churchill's long-postponed retirement had bequeathed him the position of prime minister. Harold Macmillan headed the Conservative government from January 1957, with Selwyn Lloyd continuing as foreign secretary. A major concern of the new administration was the rebuilding of the Anglo–American alliance, reciprocated by Washington's contrition over the harsh treatment of its transatlantic ally. A much-chastened Macmillan made a definite and successful effort to cultivate and re-establish good relations with Eisenhower.[62] A remarkable recovery was brought about with reconciliation definitively sealed at the Bermuda conference of March 1957, and a prime-ministerial visit to Washington later in the year that heralded announcements of a 'new spirit' between the two allies.[63] But Britain, and especially Conservative politicians, continued to resent US actions over Suez for many years to come.

The Sierra Maestra Campaign

Just three weeks after presenting his credentials as Her Majesty's new ambassador to Havana, Stanley Fordham reported a fresh revolutionary outbreak in Santiago de Cuba on 30 November 1956.[64] Two days later, 82 rebels from the Castro-led *26 de julio* movement landed by boat from Mexico in eastern Cuba. The group included Fidel's younger brother Raúl, and asthmatic Argentine doctor Ernesto 'Che' Guevara. Remnants of this group fled into the Sierra Maestra hills to establish a base of guerrilla operations, from where they hoped to organize a countrywide insurrection and topple the Fulgencio Batista regime. During this period, Anthony Eden was recuperating (23 November to 14 December) at the 'Golden Eye' residence of James Bond writer Ian Fleming on the neighbouring Caribbean island of Jamaica, following the prime minister's physical collapse at the height of the Suez Crisis.

During the first months following the *Granma* landing, Castro's guerrillas entrenched themselves in Sierra Maestra, attacking nearby army posts and seizing arms and ammunition. Far from the seat of insurrection in eastern Cuba, British embassy staff in Havana witnessed a daring attack in March 1957 by the *Directorio Revolucionario*, a rival group to Castro's *26 de julio* movement. At a distance of just 200 yards, Fordham and his colleagues observed the group's attempt to storm the Presidential Palace and assassinate Batista. Stray machine-gun fire narrowly missed the embassy window from where they viewed the attack, but a stray bullet did kill an American tourist on a nearby hotel balcony.[65]

In the same month, Anglo-Dutch Shell inaugurated a new $25 m oil refinery with daily capacity for 25,000 barrels. Tankers moored directly at the Regla refinery in Havana's harbour, bringing crude oil from Shell's facilities in Venezuela.[66]

Fordham had spent most of his foreign service in the Americas, mostly Latin America, and had a Peruvian wife. For one year he had been Counsellor (Head) of the American Department in the Foreign Office (1949–50), until illness forced his replacement by Donald Maclean, one of the 'Cambridge spies' uncovered as a KGB mole in 1951.[67] Fordham scrutinized the US–Cuban relationship during the two years of guerrilla activity leading up to the 1959 revolution. He noted deterioration in these relations to the point of US concern and then disapproval over the 'increasingly dictatorial nature' of Batista's rule. Britain's ambassador highlighted Washington's dilemma. It supported the dictator 'because he could be trusted to combat communism', but he was an 'embarrassment' due to 'his betrayal of the very principles on which Americans purported to set most store'.[68] Herein lay a conflict of interests, and one that would provide a rare opportunity for the British to exploit commercial advantage.

The United States had traditionally supplied Cuban defence needs under its hemispheric Military Assistance Program (MAP). Its terms prohibited utilizing supplied equipment for internal security purposes. In the latter part of 1957, it became obvious that Batista was conspicuously using US arms for internal defence, for example, in suppressing an armed rebellion at the Cienfuegos naval base in September.[69] Washington, worried at the turn of events in Cuba, began to relate the question of arms supplies to the holding of elections. Assistant Secretary of State for Inter-American Affairs Roy Rubottom wrote to the secretary of state in January 1958: 'We believe that if we work with the present regime, while holding a tight rein on the manifestations of cooperation with it, we stand the best chance of encouraging acceptable elections and an orderly transfer of the government to a successor to Batista.'[70] Internal debate over arms sales to Cuba highlighted a division between the Department of Defense – against an embargo on ideological and strategic grounds and keen to continue their support for Batista's stand against Communism – and the State Department, wanting to avoid an escalation of the conflict in Cuba that could threaten the totality of their military and economic interests.[71]

In March 1958, the State Department suspended export licences for arms, informing its embassy in Havana, 'In taking this action [the] Department considered [the] failure of [the] G[overnment] O[f] C[uba] to create conditions for fair elections and [the] deteriorating political situation.'[72] Batista reacted by following up on previous enquiries to non-US arms suppliers. Indicative of its recognition of close US–Cuban relations, the Foreign Office had instinctively questioned the motives of an enquiry to them in late 1957. Why, considering that Cuba had for so long received its arms from the United States, should it now be seeking them elsewhere? As important was the matter of whether to seek Washington's approval, especially considering the recent harmonization in Anglo–American relations following the debacle of Suez. In London, one official commented that the query might offer excellent commercial possibilities, a remark indicative of London's pragmatic approach and concentration on economic advantage.[73]

A lack of competitiveness with trade rivals, a continuing fall in its share of world trade and further sterling crises in 1951 and 1955, were all evidence of malaise in the British economy. But here was a rare export opening in Cuba, appearing because of Washington's change of policy. The British government was loath to reject this sudden gift of a new dollar-earning opportunity.[74]

Several conflicting opinions over the arms proposal permeated Foreign Office debate. One official took a cautious view, asking, 'Are we quite sure that we wish to supply arms to Cuba unbeknown to the Americans?' He added, perhaps facetiously, 'What about the "New Spirit"?' A supporter of this line of argument suggested that Washington would justly feel annoyed at a British intrusion into its sphere of influence. A more senior official took a different position, pointing out that their transatlantic allies had never hesitated to push sales in spheres of great interest to Britain.[75] The debate echoed the fact that the postwar boom decade of arms sales, a virtual monopoly for Britain and the United States, had ended. Furthermore, US arms exports were increasingly impinging on Britain's markets as its influence diminished.[76]

British diplomats in Washington, meanwhile, were keen to avoid friction with the US government. A first secretary in the US capital stressed the need – before being asked for his views – to avoid creating another of 'those tiresome irritants to Anglo–American relations'. He emphasized that any possible embarrassment to Anglo–Cuban affairs would be but a 'minor point' when compared to the potential damage to Anglo–American relations. As it transpired, there was no objection to Britain selling arms to Cuba, although US officials did recommend caution, given the uncertain political situation in the island.[77]

The exchanges highlighted British sensitivity to US reactions. Washington, meanwhile, in being so forthcoming and granting acquiescence to its British allies, demonstrated a desire to continue arms supplies to Batista. It had changed its own policy but wanted its transatlantic partner to maintain the underlying strategy of not completely abandoning the dictator in the absence of an alternative to Castro. In this instance, Britain could pursue commercial advantage due to a clash of concerns for the United States in its 'backyard'; these being domestic pressure within Congress and from Cuban exiles and disagreements between policymaking departments.[78] As Head of the American Department Henry Hankey correctly discerned, the 'arguments which make the Americans hold back simply do not apply in this country'.[79] Here was the sort of opportunity that Britain had been seeking for years, but in the midst of a Cuban insurrection, it was not without risk.

Without any firm order to supply, the Foreign Office asked its ambassador for his assessment of events on the ground. Fordham deemed it unlikely that the dictator would be overthrown, and that the value of future orders plus long-term advantage in gaining a foothold in this new market outweighed the risk involved.[80] In May, the Cuban air force requested a quote from the Hawker Siddeley group for 25 Sea Fury fighter-bomber aircraft. The Arms Working Party, the cross-department group that recommended sales and issued export licences, approved the deal in principle. The opportunity to offload outdated piston-engine fighters, to be paid for in dollars and without credit terms, had proved a most enticing prospect.[81]

Isolated from most rebel activity in Oriente province, Fordham's confidence in the dictator's hold on power fluctuated during 1958, but actually strengthened as the year progressed. He had been very noncommittal in April, writing, 'No one can guess as to what will happen in the next few days, let alone months. For what it is worth my guess is that Batista will survive. But I shall not be much surprised if I am proved wrong'.[82] In May, his department placed more weight on the criticism it may incur than on commercial considerations. Fordham, meanwhile, thought it unlikely Batista would be overthrown, but admitted that sales would be a gamble.[83] His most important diplomatic contact, US Ambassador Earl T. Smith, was a Republican political appointee with no previous diplomatic experience. Late in 1958, he personally encouraged Britain – through Fordham in Havana – to continue its arms supplies to the Cuban government.[84]

Indicative of one British government department's keenness to find a market for obsolescent war material, the Ministry of Supply contravened standard procedure and directly offered surplus Comet tanks to the Cuban Government via the Havana embassy in July 1958, without having the offer approved in the normal way. With events going badly for Batista's demoralized forces, a swift reply from the Cuban government expressed an interest in their immediate supply.[85] Well aware of the failure of Castro's call for a 'general strike' in April, the Foreign Office paid scant regard to the similar fate of Batista's 'summer operation' in July, intended to flush out the rebels from the Sierra Maestra. Considering that the rebellion had lost most of its momentum, a memorandum by Hankey ventured that Castro's chances of coming to power were now remote, and recommended the sale.[86]

In the wake of the vitriolic local reaction to Vice President Richard Nixon's ill-fated tour of Latin America in April–May 1958, the Foreign Office analysed the tensions provoked by post-war US policy in the continent.[87] It criticized Washington's failure 'to adapt policy to changing conditions' and recognize the hemispheric tendency 'against dictatorial forms of government'. Instead, it had prioritized 'relatively "stable" authoritarian forms of government' over the 'unpredictable flux' of democracies. British officials judged the US approach as 'clumsy and tactless', for having 'concentrated excessively on the cold war' and taken Latin American support for granted, despite giving it proportionally little financial aid compared to other parts of the world. US preponderance had 'aroused the same kind of antipathies' there as Britain in the Middle East.[88] It is instructive that officials in London equated local reactions in a British sphere of influence with those in a region under long-standing US tutelage.

A contract was signed in late August 1958 for the sale of 17 Sea Fury fighter-bomber aircraft. Within a month, irate telegrams of protest reached the prime minister's office from Cuban exiles in the United States. Bearing the protests in mind, the Foreign Office requested a report on the political situation in Cuba. It was reluctant to call off the arms sale and prejudice discussions with the Cuban government over several large industrial contacts.[89] These talks came to fruition in early November with the announcement of a £10 m contract for the construction of port facilities at Mariel, west of Havana. Other substantial commercial opportunities were evidently influencing Britain's policy on arms sales.[90]

In Cuba, meanwhile, from the hideout of Castro's guerrillas in the Sierra Maestra hills, *Radio Rebelde* broadcast denunciations of the British government. How could it sell heavy arms to a right-wing dictatorship after Hitler's wartime bombardment of British cities? On 19 October 1958, the rebel radio station declared,

Does not England have enough with its conflicts in Cyprus, in Egypt, in the Middle East, in British Guiana, in British Honduras, and all over the world where it may try to support its decadent colonialism, without provoking conflicts in Cuba? [...] The times of colonialism and unpunished interventions in the affairs of the small nations are over.[91]

Selling arms to the rebels' archenemy was not the best means of fostering their goodwill. The *26 de julio* movement made threats against both British economic interests and diplomats in the island. 'Law No. 4 of the Sierra Maestra' urged Cuban citizens to boycott *productos ingleses* that included Gordon's Gin, as well as any Shell Company products.[92]

Our Man in Havana

During research for his forthcoming novel, Graham Greene visited *26 de julio* representatives in Santiago de Cuba in November 1957, conveying winter clothing for the rebels in the hills.[93] In the same month he began the manuscript for *Our Man in Havana*, finishing it in June 1958.[94] The novel appeared in bookshops on 6 October 1958. Only two hours after returning from another trip to Cuba later in the same month, Greene wrote to Hugh Delargy MP, 'If only to prevent anti-British feeling on the part of the man who is likely to be the next ruler of Cuba, cannot you raise some opposition to the sale of these planes in the House of Commons?'[95] Here was concrete evidence of his support for the rebel cause. This letter to a sympathetic Labour MP was instrumental in initiating parliamentary opposition to the Conservative government's arms sales. Just 11 days after Greene's letter, Hankey wrote, 'There is very little reason to suppose that Fidel Castro will come to power in the foreseeable future.'[96] Underlying the Foreign Office point of view was its confidence that when push came to shove, Washington would go to some lengths to avoid the suspected radical Castro from reaching power, and Britain's risky arms sales policy could shelter with confidence behind the US position.[97]

Delargy tabled a parliamentary question on 19 November, asking if the government had knowledge that 'civil war is raging in Cuba?' Foreign Secretary Selwyn Lloyd's less than combative reply angered the Cuban ambassador to London, who felt that Britain owed a debt to General Batista for his help over Suez (unique among Latin American countries). Hankey accepted this claim, admitting that Cuba's record at the United Nations had been generally very favourable to Britain, particularly over Suez.[98] On 24 November 1956, Cuba was one of ten countries to abstain on a UN resolution calling for the 'evacuation forthwith' of Anglo-French forces from Egypt, with 63 votes for the resolution and 5 against. Hankey began to acknowledge the seriousness of the insurrection in Cuba, and the inherent risk to Britain's arms policy. The Head of the American Department described how Castro's 'group of twelve men' had expanded 'to an army of over 10,000' within two years. In a mournful tone, Ambassador Fordham wrote a personal handwritten letter to Hankey, remarking on the multitude of rumours and the scarcity of reliable news in Havana. It was extraordinarily hard to evaluate the local situation, and many Cubans and US citizens were blaming Washington for the turn of events.[99]

By the middle of December the arms sales question was even more contentious. The opposition Labour party had learnt that a boat was preparing to sail for Havana with '100 tons of rockets'. After a lengthy and rowdy debate, in which the government was accused of doing a 'dirty deal... behind the backs of the British people and of Parliament', the embattled minister for foreign affairs pledged that 'no further weapons of any sort' would be sent without first informing the House of Commons.[100]

The minister's assurance created a degree of unease in the Foreign Office because an outstanding order for five aircraft awaited shipment. Embarrassment vis-à-vis Batista's government – a reliable voting ally in the United Nations to which it would now have to withhold contracted arms – was to prove short-lived.[101] But a parliamentary row with the opposition over a foreign affairs matter, just two years after the Suez Crisis, was an unwelcome development for Macmillan's government. Even more perturbing was the potential embarrassment of having to deal formally with the rebels after selling heavy arms to their foe Batista.[102]

Conclusion

Only on 12 December did the Foreign Office recognize that Cuba was in a state of civil war.[103] It not only instructed its embassy in Washington to inform the Americans of its arms embargo, but also issued the following instruction: 'Inform them we are seriously disturbed by the trend of events in Cuba, that we still suspect the best course might have been to enable the Government to crush the rebels finally before they virtually got out of control.'[104] It was almost laying the blame for the situation at Washington's door. Herein perhaps is the underlying belief that had permeated Foreign Office policy throughout Castro's guerrilla campaign; surely the United States – given its strategic and economic interests in the island – would not permit Castro to take power, starkly revealing British perceptions about US responsibility and capacity to dictate Cuban affairs.[105] This position was inconsistent and hypocritical. After Nixon's April 1958 tour of Latin America, British officials had criticized Washington for heavy-handedness in the region, and yet now they complained about the US refusal to overtly support a repressive regime.

Fulgencio Batista took advantage of subdued end-of-year revelries to board a plane for the Dominican Republic in the early hours of 1 January 1959, never to return to Cuba. The Foreign Office immediately faced difficult questions about its decision to approve arms sales to the dictator so late in the day.

8
Revolution:
Anglo–American Cooperation

Embarrassment was the dominant sentiment in the Foreign Office when Castro's hirsute revolutionaries swept into power on 1 January 1959. Just two days later, *The Times* published a letter from Graham Greene that began, 'The welcome success of Dr Fidel Castro in overthrowing the dictatorship of Batista reminds us again of the extraordinary ignorance of Cuban affairs shown by the British Government'. His scornful correspondence continued: 'Any visitor to Cuba could have given Her Majesty's Government more information about conditions in the island than was apparently supplied by our official representatives'.[1] The slowness of shipping meant that a cargo of 15 Comet tanks had arrived in the port of Havana on 17 December 1958, two days after the minister's arms embargo pledge to the House of Commons.[2]

At least Macmillan's government could claim that its arms sales to Cuba were restricted when the revolution triumphed. But this had only happened at the Labour opposition's behest, and because Greene had first requested an MP acquaintance to intervene. A *Guardian* editorial affirmed that rather than relying on its embassy in Havana for news on the ground, the Foreign Office would have been better advised 'to sit at home reading the newspapers'.[3]

Criticism led to an internal Foreign Office enquiry. The department found that its decisions 'were not above criticism', and there had been a 'lack of reliable information' from Washington. Fordham's analysis pointed to his 'commercial considerations' when recommending the sales, unfortunately timed at the lowest point of Castro's fortunes in April 1958. He described the 'divided views' emanating from the US embassy in Havana, a reflection of inter-departmental squabbling in Washington, and his difficulties in liaising with US Ambassador Earl T. Smith, describing him as a 'self-willed and not too intelligent amateur'.[4]

Anglo–Cuban Rapprochement

Fordham conveyed British official recognition of the new provisional government within an hour of Washington doing so on 7 January.[5] Fortunately, trials of Batista's alleged accomplices and other events in the heady weeks of early 1959 deflected attention away from the ill-timed British arms sales. Castro sought a conciliatory gesture from the Foreign Office to make amends for the export of tanks and planes to Batista, and although they considered it, none was forthcoming.[6] The revolutionary leader highlighted the two countries' mutual interest in trade during a speech at the Shell refinery in early February 1959. Britain was a sugar importer, he affirmed, and Cuba should buy from those countries to which it sold. Castro lifted the unofficial boycott of British products and services.[7] Fordham was similarly pragmatic, suggesting that whatever their doubts they had to live with the new government, and there would be 'considerable commercial advantages – & possibly some political ones in meeting it half-way'.[8]

The day after Castro's victory caravan of bearded guerrillas arrived in Havana atop captured jeeps and tanks, the *Diario de la Marina* published a summary of Anglo–Cuban trade during the life of the republic. The statistics were evidence of an historical trade imbalance, overwhelmingly in Cuba's favour. Only before the First World War had British exports to Cuba outweighed imports from the island (see Table 3). The revolutionary leader's speech and his Treasury's trade statistics pointed to the rich British market for Cuban exports. It was appropriate that Castro spoke at the Shell refinery, the dominant British capital investment in Cuba, inaugurated four years after the 1953 sale of United Railways.

Apart from Shell, British interests within Cuba were small. Glaxo Laboratories ran a small packaging plant in the island. Cable & Wireless maintained three telegraph offices, in Santiago, Havana and Cienfuegos. Some 15 authorized British insurance companies still operated, enjoying limited protection under Article 4 of the 1937 Anglo–Cuban Commercial Treaty. And Her Majesty's Government had consular responsibility for an estimated 40,000 British West Indians, in addition to approximately 700 UK nationals resident on the island.

Anglo–American Differences

British officials naturally made analogies between their recent reverse at the hands of Nasser at Suez and Washington's setback in the US

Table 3   Anglo–Cuban trade, 1902–57[9]

Five-year periods	Cuban imports from UK	Cuban exports to UK
1902–06	$60,183,000	$29,996,000
1907–11	$65,298,000	$30,690,000
1912–16	$78,362,000	$131,524,000
1917–21	$68,120,000	$376,122,000
1922–26	$58,667,000	$197,178,000
1927–31	$49,982,000	$154,219,000
1932–36	$18,556,000	$77,128,000
1937–41	$20,831,000	$84,336,000
1942–46	$20,666,000	$162,373,000
1947–51	$49,664,000	$498,359,000
1952–56	$67,740,000	$380,364,000
Total 1902–57*	$572,388,000	$1,975,694,000

*Individual figures for 1957 were $21,319,000 (imports) and $43,581,000 (exports).

hemisphere. The 1956 Suez Crisis and the 1959 Cuban Revolution marked pivotal Cold War events for the respective transatlantic allies, and important tests of Anglo–American cooperation. Castro ratcheted up his anti-American rhetoric and actions through the course of 1959. Like their US counterparts, British diplomats were appalled by the ferocity of Castro's speeches and his denouncements of US interference in Cuba, describing his 'ranting demagogy and gesticulations' and 'a frenzy almost amounting to paranoia'.[10] This demonization of Castro was similar to that of Nasser a few years earlier. Both allies were perturbed at the temerity of these Third World nationalist leaders, challenging British and US ascendancy and endangering their long-standing economic interests.

By 1960, Cuba had transformed from an issue of minor importance to a serious bone of contention. The allies' distinct approaches to dealing with the revolution threatened harmony in the transatlantic relationship. Friction centred principally on two related issues: trade and shipping. Washington's strategy to combat the radical revolutionary government was to isolate it through a trade blockade. But the British government, particularly its economic departments, was most averse to instigating such measures, due to reliance on trade and shipping for economic prosperity. Furthermore, it was wary of export competition, particularly from European rivals. Britain was loath to set a dangerous precedent in Cuba, arguing that economic measures were not suitable for political ends. It also doubted they could bring down Castro's revolutionary government, soon benefitting from close economic and political links with the Soviet Union.

Fundamental and long-standing differences existed between Britain and the United States over restrictions on shipping. These were partly a legacy of the 1812 war between the erstwhile imperial master and colony. A *casus belli* of this conflict was a dispute over the Royal Navy's right to search neutral vessels and blockade ports. The United States was trading with belligerents, namely the French adversaries of Britain.[11] Drawn out legalistic disputes over such maritime issues continued well beyond the cessation of war and the declaration of the Monroe Doctrine in 1823, when the United States asserted itself more stridently in the Americas. A more recent antecedent was 1954 and Foreign Secretary Anthony Eden's forthright defence of British merchant vessels' right to continue trading when Eisenhower's administration attempted to isolate the Jacobo Arbenz government in Guatemala.[12]

Castro landed in Washington aboard a Britannia airplane on 15 April 1959 for his first visit to the United States following the revolution. President Eisenhower famously went to play golf at Augusta in Georgia, and the bearded revolutionary leader met with the vice president instead. Richard Nixon noted Castro's leadership qualities, and judged he was 'either incredibly naive about Communism or under Communist discipline'.[13] Surprisingly, Cuban officials avoided discussing the question of US economic aid to their island during the visit. In the following month, Castro's government promulgated an Agrarian Reform Act, expropriating farm estates over 1000 acres and banning land ownership by foreigners, with many thousands of peasants receiving titles to land.

Planes Exchange

When Batista fled, five of the 17 Sea Fury aircraft remained to be delivered. Britain decided its arms policy in consultation with Washington in March, and acceded to the US request to suspend all arms supplies to the Caribbean.[14] Incipient rivalry between Castro and Rafael Trujillo's government in the Dominican Republic had created tension in the area and led to a series of armed raids against both territories. Both regimes made enquiries to foreign arms suppliers during 1959.

Despite the new restrictions, competitors including the United States continued to sell limited amounts of arms. The British found justification therefore in supplying Cuba with the five outstanding aircraft in mid-May. But subsequent dialogue with Washington uncovered the

perturbing fact that the United States had supplied Cuba with five helicopters in mid-June owing to a 'serious administrative error'.[15] This was
potentially embarrassing for the Foreign Office because it had been pla-
cating its arms manufacturers with arguments about a general arms
embargo.

Bus exports were less problematic, at least in this early period of the
revolution. Just three months before the sudden implosion of Batista's
dictatorship, Leyland Motors Ltd followed up on its 1950 success and
obtained a letter of intent to supply 300 more buses to Cuba. But delays
in agreeing payment terms and revolutionary upheaval stymied the
deal. In July 1959, further negotiations between the new revolutionary government's Ministry of Transport and Leyland resulted in a signed
contract for 200 buses valued at £1.5 m ($4.2 m), backed by five-year
credit terms.[16]

In August, the Admiralty strongly supported British boat manufacturers, enticed by Cuba's requirement for 15 'customs/coastguard patrol
boats'. Pressured to maintain the embargo, the Foreign Office was anxious that Washington compel other competing European firms not
to supply. As with another enquiry about helicopters, government
departments weighed up the offensive and defensive capabilities of
such exports, concluding that the boats could be used as 'troop carri-
ers' and refusing them an export licence. In doing so, however, they
were denying work 'over a long period' to one boat manufacturer in
a region of 'gross unemployment'. The Foreign Office, most eager to
appease Washington, recognized that sentiment in other departments
and among manufacturers was 'running very high' over US determi-
nation to keep them 'out of the arms and aircraft market in Latin
America'.[17]

A much bigger arms quandary for Britain arose from Cuba's request
to exchange all the recently delivered Sea Fury aircraft for new Hawker
Hunter jets. The arms manufacturer Hawker Siddeley agreed the deal
in July, but it required British government approval. Cuba would
pay $189,000 for each Hawker Hunter jet and receive $80,000 for
each piston-engine Sea Fury returned. Such a substantial deal was of
course very attractive commercially, but there were a whole host of
considerations, not the least of which was the fragile Caribbean arms
embargo.[18]

Unlike European competitors, Britain was constrained by its relationship with the United States that acted against its natural inclination to
accede to the Cuban request.[19] Foreign Office officials highlighted pressure from industry and other government departments, and possible

repercussions should foreign competitors win the business.[20] Fidel Castro, meanwhile, declared that he would consider Britain's decision a 'touchstone' of its attitude to his new government.[21]

During the course of 1959, Foreign Office officials questioned the wisdom of Washington's policy towards Cuba and its estimations of radicalization in the Castro-led administration. US diplomats were far quicker than their British counterparts to discern communism within the island. One official in London, for example, described Washington's tendency to define all left-wing neutralism or anti-Americanism as 'communist'.[22] While there was undoubted difficulty in assessing communist influence in the island, US fears of a communist throttlehold were deemed 'much exaggerated'. As late as October 1959, when leading Cabinet members were debating a decision on the planes exchange, Castro's revolution was still being described in London as 'a nationalist and agrarian movement with neutralist tendencies in some sectors'.[23]

While the Board of Trade was keen not to ignore increased export opportunities in what had suddenly become its third largest market in Latin America (behind Argentina and Venezuela), the Foreign Office argued that 'British special interests sometimes had to be subordinated to our broader world interests of which the Anglo–American partnership was the most important.'[24] The announcement on 8 September of a general election and subsequent political campaigning, suspended ministers' decision-making until voting on 8 October. Harold Macmillan and his Conservative administration subsequently won a 100-seat majority and a further term in office.

In October, several factors exacerbated an already complex situation. The State Department first heard about Cuba's request for an aircraft exchange from a news agency report on 12 October.[25] Without consulting the British government, it called a press conference on 16 October. The following day, *The Times* reported,

> The United States is understood to have expressed strong opposition to the possible sale of British jet fighters to Cuba. A State Department spokesman said to-day that it was no secret that the United States did not like and was not happy about moving arms into the Caribbean area, and it had made this clear to Britain 'in forthright language'.[26]

According to British officials, Washington had commented on the possible Hunter deal in the clumsiest possible way, giving the impression of exerting overt pressure on Britain. The indiscretion galvanized their debate on the aircraft exchange. It might now be wiser, some argued, to ignore the United States and its short-sighted policy.[27] The best justification for allowing the exchange had now been found and even Harold Macmillan became involved. On the very day of the report, his private secretary wrote to the Foreign Office, 'The Prime Minister said this morning that if there was any question of our giving way to the State Department in the matter of arms for Cuba, he must be consulted before any decision is taken'.[28] Supporters of the deal were emboldened, arguing for a strong defence of the proposed deal. The best tactic would be to announce the decision to Washington, rather than trying to obtain its approval, expecting a negative response.[29]

A memorandum set forth arguments for the foreign secretary in advance of a Cabinet meeting on 29 October. It advised that it would be embarrassing to snub the left-wing Castro, struggling to carry through (even if misguidedly) an idealistic programme, after supplying aircraft to the right-wing dictator Batista. The Cubans were determined to be less dependent on US equipment, and, if rebuffed, would almost certainly turn elsewhere. This could lead to a 'whole series of chain reactions within [the] Egyptian model'. Furthermore, US fears of a communist stranglehold in Cuba appeared much exaggerated.[30] The analogy with Nasser was striking. Britain had learned harshly the lessons of its treatment of the Arab leader.

Foreign Secretary Selwyn Lloyd informed his Cabinet colleagues that he would carefully present Britain's decision to proceed with the deal to his US counterpart. After all, the United States had already supplied Cuba with helicopters and transport aircraft. He explained to US Secretary of State Christian Herter the reasons that made him want to accede to the Cuban request. Castro's threat to go behind the Iron Curtain for arms was his most potent argument. If some people thought that unlikely, he asserted, this had been Britain's 'opinion about Nasser in 1955, and look where that got us'. He highlighted the State Department error: 'We are now put in the position that if we refuse to allow the exchange we shall be considered as having given in to United States pressure.' Lloyd timorously informed Herter, 'I feel that I must authorise the exchange as soon as the present effervescence and violent feelings have died down.'[31]

Macmillan, a notorious interferer in the work of his ministers, wrote to Lloyd congratulating him on the wording and substance of his message and hoping for no further delay. Evidently still in a bellicose mood more than two weeks after Washington's indiscretion, and three years after Suez, he wrote, 'I should judge it wise as soon as Herter has made some acknowledgement. He must see how weak they are about their own behaviour.'[32]

Lloyd's mention of 'effervescence' related to a string of political incidents in Cuba that coincided with Washington's imprudent statement. These included the resignation of Army Commander Huber Matos on 19 October, alleging communist penetration of the Cuban government as his motive. Two days later, recently exiled Cuban Air Force Chief Pedro Díaz Lanz dropped counter-revolutionary leaflets over Havana from a plane. In late October, a plane carrying army commander Camilo Cienfuegos went missing. There followed a Cabinet reorganization that ousted moderate members in favour of suspected radicals such as Raúl Castro, Fidel's younger brother.[33]

US policy hardened in reaction to these events and a resumption of inflammatory speeches by Fidel Castro. Assistant Secretary of State for Inter-American Affairs Roy Rubottom decided that Castro's anti-American outlook was a 'fixed proposition'.[34] By early November, even moderate US Ambassador Philip Bonsal (Earl T. Smith's successor) felt there were tremendous and perhaps insurmountable obstacles to establishing good relations with revolutionary Cuba.[35] It was in this context that Britain attempted to gain the State Department's consent for the aircraft exchange deal, leading to continued British prevarication and delay in making a definitive decision.

In further high-level contacts, Herter highlighted a deteriorating political situation in Cuba, the risk of supplying arms to Castro, and the need to maintain the arms embargo. US–Cuban relations appeared beyond the point of no return. Importantly, Lloyd now acknowledged a worsening outlook in Cuba, and substance in US reports. He wrote in his diary on 23 November, 'It looks as though we dare not do it – if he were to fall just after, as Batista did last year, we should look very silly.'[36]

A belligerent Macmillan, evidently unaware of the latest developments and correspondence, wrote to his foreign secretary on 25 November,

> I hope you will have a word with me before deciding about the Cuban Aircraft. I am told by Billy Rootes[37] that our exports to Cuba are all the time increasing. The Americans of course are very jealous of this. There is no embargo policy, for the Americans have already sold them aircraft, as they always do when they are under pressure from their own industry.[38]

Despite the prime minister's letter, Lloyd informed his Cabinet colleagues of continuing US opposition to the aircraft exchange. Balancing
a negative US reaction on the one hand and the size of the export order
on the other, he recommended rejection of the deal. The prime minister noted Britain's flourishing trade with Cuba, and wondered how
payment would be secured. The Chancellor of the Exchequer ventured
that the cost to Anglo–American relations would outweigh the economic benefits of expanded trade with Cuba. The Cabinet agreed to
turn down the aircraft exchange.[39] Later the same day, Lloyd described
his 'long wobble' in Cabinet. His colleagues had quietly accepted his
finely balanced decision to decline the Hunter deal.[40] As with previous
cases of decision-making, when push came to shove over Cuba, Britain
prioritized the Anglo–American relationship.

Cuban sentiment reacted strongly to Britain's decision to turn down
the deal with the excuse of 'tension in the Caribbean region'. Its daily
newspaper *Revolución* claimed it bore the stamp 'Made in the U.S.A.'
It asked why the previous year's 'bombing of open cities' by Batista had
not been considered 'tension' when selling him arms. Another article
proposed that 'Cuba can very well do without Perfidious Albion', and
that the 'insignificant colony of the United States – England – obeys and
obeys faithfully. It is a case of a decadent nation.'[41] Castro had promised
to treat Britain's decision as a 'touchstone' of its attitude towards the
revolution. The British decision, and Cuban reaction, marked an inauspicious beginning for Anglo–Cuban relations in the post-revolutionary
period.

From Close to Distanced Relations

The year 1898 had signalled the beginning of direct US involvement in
Cuba. But 1959 witnessed a quick unravelling of their close relations and
a visceral reaction to Castro in the United States, much like the loosen-
ing of British–Egyptian ties and Eden's loathing of Nasser earlier in the
decade.[42] After a series of what Washington perceived as anti-American
actions, including expropriation of US-owned properties without compensation, an official in London made an analogy with Suez: 'As we
ourselves have found elsewhere, it is hard to be objective in one's own
back-yard.'[43] *The Economist* made a similar point when it compared the
'uncontrolled exaggeration' of US newspapers and politicians towards
Castro to those of Britain towards Nasser, recognizing that US business
interests – dominant in the island for half a century – had no reason to
welcome the revolution's antipathy.[44]

Washington's policy evolved with the further perceived radicalization of Castro's regime. It also responded to internal pressure. In early 1960, US business firms with interests in Cuba became more insistent that Eisenhower's administration adopt a firmer attitude. Its chief weapon, short of economic sanctions or military intervention, was the sugar quota.[45] Soviet Deputy Prime Minister Mikoyan inaugurated a Soviet exhibition in Havana in February 1960, and announced that his country would buy 1 m tons of sugar from Cuba for the next five years.

As it became increasingly evident that Cuba was set on a path of political accommodation with the Soviet Union, Eisenhower's government embarked on a policy of communist containment in its hemisphere. British officials sympathized with Washington's foreign policy dilemma, but US policy towards Cuba was exceptional, newly formulated to deal with a fresh problem close to home.[46]

Questions surrounding the supply of 'strategic' material to the island became increasingly problematic for Britain as this traditional market expelled more US economic interests and others withdrew. When explaining the sale of sea-rescue helicopters in early 1960, the Foreign Office – under pressure from industry and wary of losing the business to other European suppliers – went to the extreme of detailing their flight range as proof they had no militarily capability against the neighbouring Dominican Republic.[47] Fearing parliamentary and press criticism for further weakness in the face of US pressure, and still entertaining thoughts of 'exercising a moderating influence' on the Cuban government, the British stood firm and sold the helicopters.[48]

Britain's largest economic interest in the island was the Shell oil refinery, operating since March 1957, and now valued at $27 m. Cuban controls on foreign exchange imposed in 1959 meant that foreign oil companies could not make remittances to their oil suppliers. This local affiliate of the Shell Group, a multinational company with both Dutch and British shareholders, had accumulated a debt of $17 m dollars in non-transferable Cuban currency for crude oil supplied from Venezuela since May 1959.[49] A more serious challenge followed in June 1960 when the Cuban government asked the island's three foreign oil companies – Shell, plus US-owned Esso Standard Oil and Texaco – to refine half their oil from Soviet sources. The Cuban request provided Eisenhower's government with its first opportunity to implement a new 'get tough' policy towards Cuba. After travelling to confer in Washington, the State Department informed the three companies that a negative response to Castro would be in line with official US policy.[50]

There was fear in London that Shell's decision to adhere to State Department policy would cause Cuba to erroneously discern British government interference in the decision, prejudicing other British interests in the island.[51] Shell had informed the Foreign Office of its decision to comply with Washington's wishes in a last-minute fait accompli. The Foreign Office appreciated Shell's position; acceptance of crude oil from other sources would seriously dent its profits. But British diplomats also identified in the concerted action of the big three oil companies a bullying monopoly, because Cuba only possessed two small refineries of its own. Britain's efforts to maintain amicable Anglo–Cuban relations without hampering US efforts to undermine Castro were becoming harder to reconcile.[52] Britain was at risk of 'being dragged along by the coat tails of U.S. policy'.[53] Washington policymakers were informing rather than consulting their British counterparts, who could soon stand accused of both failing to adopt an independent line and prejudicing their commercial interests.[54] In the event, the US-owned Esso and Texaco refineries suffered expropriation, while Shell was only 'intervened', meaning the assumption of its management but not its ownership.[55]

In an interview for the *Financial Times*, Che Guevara (president of the National Bank) affirmed that his government would not have 'intervened' the Shell company had its boss 'gone to London for instructions instead of Washington'. He mentioned opportunities in Cuba for British trade and his hopes of obtaining export credit.[56] Meanwhile, Conservative backbench MPs – compelled in part by their constituents – evoked memories of oil disputes in other Third World countries under radical nationalist leadership. They pressured their government to defend more vigorously British investments overseas, citing such unhappy antecedents as Cárdenas in Mexico (1938), Mossadeq in Iran (1951) and Nasser in Egypt (1956).[57] In London, the US embassy asked Britain to discourage its tanker owners from carrying Soviet oil to Cuba. The Foreign Office responded that even during the Persian oil crisis in the early 1950s, when Iran nationalized the Anglo Persian Oil Company (later British Petroleum), it had not employed or sought powers to restrict UK-flag tankers.[58]

Anglo–American Dialogue

Revolution in Cuba and the radicalization of Castro's regime made Washington increasingly fearful of communist contagion in its hemisphere. But while the United States worried about the possible emergence of another Castro and wider Soviet incursion into the region,

London was more preoccupied with the ongoing process of decoloniza-tion in various British colonies and possessions in the Caribbean. After ten years of negotiations, the British established the West Indies Federa-tion in 1958, an ultimately short-lived attempt to establish political and economic union among several island colonies. It dissolved in 1962, the year that Jamaica and Trinidad and Tobago obtained their inde-pendence. The British government judged Castroist subversion in the Caribbean as unlikely, with the possible exception of British Guiana.[59] But even here, it took severe pressure from the new J.F. Kennedy admin-istration to convince the British government that such a danger existed. An interdepartmental briefing paper, for example, considered that while some countries might undergo a phase of extreme radical nationalism, the region was unlikely to go communist.[60] Furthermore, British officials considered that much of Latin America's anti-American sentiment and lukewarm support for Cold War issues in the United Nations contained 'an element of bluff ', an attempt to extract 'a higher price' from the Western camp.[61]

In British Guiana, Macmillan's government initially deemed US esti-mations of Indian People's Progressive Party leader Cheddi Jagan as a communist to be exaggerated, and opposition to independence under his rule to be hypocritical. Jagan was victorious in 1961 elections, and Britain was keen to facilitate independence in the colony. But alarm bells rang in Washington, where officials saw a correlation between recent radicalism in Cuba and political events in British Guiana. The new prime minister had made equivocal statements about communism, and had visited Cuba under Castro's rule in 1960, discussing trade and a possible $5 m loan from the revolutionary government for hydroelectric projects.[62]

Unlike Washington, the British government did not view its colony as a potential Soviet satellite. Colonial Secretary Reginald Maudling told the President's Special Assistant Arthur Schlesinger, 'If you Americans care so much about British Guiana, why don't you take it over? Nothing would please us more'. From London, it appeared that Washington crit-icized British colonialism on the one hand, but selectively undermined the independence process on the other. Macmillan wrote in his diary, 'They are ready to attack us as Colonialists when it suits them. They are the first to squeal when "decolonisation" takes place uncomfort-ably near to them.' President Kennedy and his officials were convinced that a second Cuba threatened to establish itself in the South American continent, and managed to browbeat their British counterparts into servile submission. The imperatives of Cold War realpolitik dictated that

US wishes for the colony eventually prevailed. Britain had no overriding strategic interest in British Guiana, and prioritized the Anglo–American relationship instead. The CIA, initially without British permission to interfere, fomented labour and racial unrest in the colony to subvert Jagan's rule, ensuring his downfall and decades-long banishment to the political wilderness.[63]

With regard to Cuba, British diplomats were sensitive to accusations of susceptibility to US pressure at the expense of commercial interests, and were wary of becoming embroiled in a US–Cuban wrangle.[64] While 1959 differences over arms exports to Castro's government had been conducted between British Foreign Secretary Selwyn Lloyd and US Secretary of State Christian Herter, a new dialogue proceeded at the highest level. A flurry of letters between Macmillan and Eisenhower highlighted mutual concern over Cuba's political trajectory, but also the potential for Anglo–American discord over economic warfare. The president highlighted US patience in the face of Castro's hostility, and outlined US–Cuban relations from January 1959: (1) a 'testing phase' of about six months; (2) a second phase of roughly a year where the 'hard line' was not practised, but when it was made clear that the 'deteriorated situation was of Castro's making'; (3) an 'active phase' from July 1960 in which Washington 'would establish conditions which will bring home to the Cuban people the cost of Castro's policies and of his Soviet orientation'. A reduction in Cuba's long-standing sugar quota was an early manifestation of this new policy.[65]

Cabinet Secretary Norman Brook was struck by an Egypt–Cuba parallel and Eisenhower's 'very frank approach'. While the president might be wary of Soviet intrusion in his sphere, he wrote, Britain had felt much the same about Nasser. Brook advised that if the British were going to diverge from US policy they should make this clear from the start, affirming, 'We know only too well as a result of 1956, that the worst thing of all is for ourselves and the Americans to become divided on an issue like this'.[66] British officials reacted with scepticism to Eisenhower's portrayal of US commitment to non-intervention in its hemisphere and his affirmation of 'respect [for] the rights of weaker nations'. One observer remarked caustically that it had 'a curious ring for anyone who has heard Latin Americans talking about U.S. colonialism in relation to Guatemala, Panama, Haiti, Cuba and her economic policy throughout Latin America'.[67]

The Foreign Office identified in Eisenhower's first letter a request for British support in three areas: (1) the United Nations; (2) restriction of free-world tankers transporting Soviet oil to Cuba; (3) a tightened arms embargo. Britain's first reaction was to refuse support over shipping.[68] Macmillan replied that his government could not embark on measures suitable only 'in times of emergency' (e.g. war), not to mention the practical difficulties in instigating such action.[69] There existed a world surplus of available tankers and Her Majesty's Government had no control over their owners. Overall, the prime minister doubted the effectiveness of the US strategy, relying as it did on economic denial and thinly disguised support for counterrevolutionaries. He instead advocated letting 'the yeast rise of its own accord', with less obtrusive support from Washington. In yet another analogy with Britain's Arab world, he wrote, 'After all, we have been through it ourselves and know the difficulties and dangers'.[70]

From July 1960, Cuba and the United States carried out a mutual series of tit-for-tat economic reprisals. The US Congress gave President Eisenhower the authority to cut the Cuban sugar quota, and Castro reacted by nationalizing many established US companies on the island. The Soviet Union then announced that it would take all the Cuban sugar not purchased by the United States. Shell did not figure among the long list of expropriations. Instead, Cuban authorities continued to run the affairs of the 'intervened' company, although the practical effect was the same. Shell lost control of its own refinery, while the accumulated Cuban debt to the company (plus compensation for its large investment) remained unpaid.

While the British advocated patience and subtle encouragement of internal opposition, the State Department was subject to intense domestic pressure for quick results. It was 'far more difficult for them than for us to reach objective conclusions', one Foreign Office brief asserted.[71] At a meeting in New York, Permanent Under Secretary Sir Frederick Hoyer Millar again counselled caution to his US allies, summarizing British advice as 'be careful and don't be in a hurry'.[72] Rumours were already circulating of a planned armed intervention in Cuba with the support, but not necessarily the active participation, of the United States.[73]

The Foreign Office agreed with the ultimate goal of ending Castro's revolutionary government, but differed markedly over the means for doing so. Henry Hankey enunciated this point of view: 'In general we agree with the U.S. thesis that Castro's régime should be brought to an end if possible. But we fear that excessive pressure from without, particularly from the U.S., may have a counterproductive effect in Cuba'.[74] Britain's strategy to deal with the Soviet Bloc eschewed isolation and advocated engagement. British policymakers did not view Cuba as a threat to Western security and disagreed with Washington's retributive policy, particularly with regard to trade restrictions.[75]

Scepticism over the efficacy of US strategy was evident. In anticipation of discussions with the State Department, diplomats considered that their US counterparts had indulged in 'a certain amount of wishful thinking about Cuba'. The British had a whole list of arguments against such 'undue optimism', judging that Washington's approach responded to 'intense pressure' from public opinion and business interests. Such demands meant that Washington desired to be seen as proactive in negating an increasingly communistic threat.[76] While Britain's geographic distance and the Suez experience bred caution, US proximity and domestic pressure provoked impatience and necessitated overt action.[77]

Trade

Anglo–American differences over trade with Cuba continued to create tension. The British were not prepared to pander slavishly to US policy, especially when it acted against their own interests. The country faced its own domestic pressures, not least of which was the clamour of industry and manufacturing to take advantage of new export opportunities. Britain's share of world trade had declined throughout the 1950s. While exports from 'defeated' nations such as Germany had risen 150 per cent, and from Italy by 180 per cent, Britain saw an increase of just 28 per cent. In a period when Germany enjoyed an economic miracle and the United States a trading surplus, Britain stood out as the sick man of Europe. Successive British governments keenly felt their loss of status as a first-class trading power, as well as the mountain of debt owed to the United States following their post-war settlement.[78] Furthermore, factors such as the country's 'stop-go' economy and an adverse balance-of-payments situation concentrated the minds of Macmillan's government. The prime minister announced a fresh export drive in mid-1960.[79] The British government once again attempted to stimulate growth in its sluggish economy, wary and resentful at losing exports to Western competitors.

Within Whitehall's bureaucracy, contentious decisions over exports to Cuba accentuated philosophical differences between predominantly political and economic departments. The Caribbean island had become such a highly charged political issue for the United States that practically any British export had the potential to create hostility between London and Washington. Subsequently, serious differences of opinion arose between departments such as the Foreign Office and the Board of Trade. Even senior officials in the Foreign Office, primarily a political rather than an economic department, recognized the problem. The British rankled not just over Suez, but also the post-war eclipse of their global trading position. A British journalist recently returned from Cuba highlighted these sentiments:

> At the moment, despite British blunders at the end of 1958, Cuban feelings towards this country are remarkably warm. On the British side there is the obvious reluctance to profit by United States misfortunes – though a similar reluctance did not deter the Americans from filling quite a few British 'vacuums' in Latin America during World War Two.[80]

British Ambassador to Washington Harold Caccia revealed similar thoughts in connection with yet another thorny case of British export to Cuba. One of his country's most experienced and high-ranking diplomats, soon to be permanent under secretary at the Foreign Office, he evidently harboured resentment over Britain's compromised trade position in the continent and pointed to its main cause:

> I realize that if we do not supply, Cuba may well get what she wants from elsewhere and that this may accelerate Communist penetration. I am also aware that in two world wars, while we were fighting for freedom, United States firms scooped our trade in Latin America.[81]

In the same month, the British agreed to the terms of a US 'aide-memoire' listing arms and aircraft components for embargo. But, almost inevitably, there arose a series of marginal cases that pitted one government department against another, and London against Washington, in defending or opposing individual exports to the island.[82]

After nearly four years in Cuba, Stanley Fordham left for a new diplomatic post in Bogota. His ambassadorship had begun during the capitalist bonanza era of Batista's dictatorship, weeks before the Castro-led insurrection. He then became embroiled in the British arms-to-Batista controversy. Fordham was leaving – in his own words – under 'a new dictatorship', seemingly 'headed straight for communism'. Given free rein to express his true feelings, he wrote in his valedictory letter, 'To have watched at close quarters the debauchment of a country one is fond of has been an interesting experience, but it has not been a pleasant one.'[83]

In company with the incoming ambassador to Havana, Fordham passed through Washington to share reflections on Cuba with both

British embassy and State Department officials. Harold Caccia described to London the US State Department's 'rather optimistic estimates' that economic shortages would 'arouse discontent' amongst Cuba's population against the Castro regime.[84]

Herbert ('Bill') Marchant was a former assistant master at Harrow School (1928–39) and had worked at the Government Code and Cypher School (later GCHQ) at Bletchley Park during the Second World War. He acted as Deputy Head in Hut 3, responsible for translating and process-ing German Army and Air Force intelligence.[85] Before Havana, he had worked at other Foreign Office postings in Bucharest (1948–49), Zagreb (1952–54), North Rhine/Westphalia (1954–55), Düsseldorf (1955–57) and San Francisco (1957–60).

The new British ambassador soon identified Cuba's need to keep European countries and Canada 'warm and sweet' and meet a poten-tial shortfall of goods from Soviet Bloc sources.[86] Marchant thought this reflected both a genuine desire for quality goods no longer supplied by the United States, and a way of gauging British support for US pol-icy. He also considered that Castro's government might want to 'drive a wedge' between policies formulated in London and Washington.[87] Cuba's request for more Leyland buses in 1963 would be a case in point.

As the United States hardened its policy, the Foreign Office questioned the wisdom of instigating an economic embargo. The announcement of more robust controls on exports to Cuba came with a minimum of warn-ing to the Foreign Office. US Vice President Richard Nixon announced it was time 'to put Cuba into international quarantine', undermining in British eyes the official US line that the embargo was a commercial rather than political reprisal.[88] In December, a Foreign Office memorandum stated,

> The Americans did not consult us before they imposed their trade embargo. We regard it as an unfortunate policy which the Americans probably adopted for political reasons during the election campaign. We consider that its effect is to drive Cuba more rapidly and com-pletely into economic dependence on the Sino-Soviet bloc. It is questionable whether it contributes more effectively to the difficul-ties of the Castro regime than to its consolidation. The Americans are therefore asking us, in effect, to help them to impose a policy which we do not support.[89]

Hankey recognized in October 1960 that British trade with Cuba was 'in a very difficult position'. On the one hand Cuba was potentially a good market, but on the other the United States stood to be easily offended. Other Western nations, including Japan, were not as scrupulous as the British in avoiding offence to Washington, and Castro's regime was consolidating itself by the month.[90] He advocated a middle course of '(a) maintaining a foot in a potentially good market, and (b) doing nothing which might cause major offence to the Americans by seeming to take advantage of their eclipse in Cuba'.[91]

Such a compromise position was practical while the volume of potential exports was low. But as Washington tightened its embargo, more trade opportunities arose. While the Soviet Bloc countries met most of the shortfall, they could not supply all quality goods required. Furthermore, the Cubans desired both reinsurance against the loss of that market, and maintenance of alternative contacts in the West, along with accompanying political dividends. Considering Washington's hypersensitivity to East–West trade with Cuba, Hankey's 'middle course' became increasingly difficult to steer.[92]

Rupture in US–Cuban Relations

In anticipation of an inevitable rupture in US–Cuban diplomatic relations, the State Department sounded out its British allies with a view to their representing US interests on the island. Considering the closeness of Anglo–American relations and their obvious language affinity, Britain seemed the obvious choice.[93] The Foreign Office's American Department debated both the opportunities and dangers for British relations with Havana, and was on balance in favour of acceding to the US request.[94] But in receipt of reactions from the Havana embassy, Foreign Secretary Lord Home stated his aversion, principally because the value of the embassy as an intelligence 'listening post' would be compromised if it was closely identified with the United States.[95]

In the event, the Swiss agreed to Washington's request and expanded their small mission in Havana in order to take on the burden of extra work. The British, meanwhile, agreed to provide the State Department with political and economic intelligence from Havana via their Washington embassy.[96] On receipt of instructions from London, the British embassy in Havana confirmed it would send Washington 'two copies of all general correspondence, with the exception of anything directly affecting United Kingdom commercial interests'.[97]

The break in relations, despite the expectation and discussions surrounding it, came suddenly and with little notice to the British. Two weeks before the presidential inauguration of John F. Kennedy, the outgoing Eisenhower administration severed diplomatic relations when instructed by Castro's government to reduce its diplomatic staff in Havana from 300 to a total of 11. In London, the decision was judged 'more a matter of emotional impulse than of rational consideration'. Hankey concluded, 'The Cubans have succeeded in manoeuvring the Americans into doing what they always told us they didn't want to do – taking the initiative in actually making the last break.' From Havana, Marchant added his adjudication: 'I would give this particular round, without any doubt at all, to Castro'.[98]

Kennedy's inauguration commenced one of the more successful presidential–prime ministerial relationships. Despite a wide age gap, the sexagenarian British premier and the Anglophone US president (23 years his junior) hit it off and enjoyed a personal chemistry. Both leaders suffered in common from chronic pains, the legacy of wounds and injuries from the First and Second World Wars respectively. And Macmillan, like Churchill before him, had an American mother. The ambassadorial appointment of a Kennedy family friend to the British embassy in Washington also assisted the burgeoning relationship. David Ormsby Gore was a perfect conduit for the flow of information and advice that passed between London and the US capital during a crucial period in the Cold War.[99]

Invasion Rumours

The rapid transformation of Cuba from a US market into a Soviet satellite was remarkable. Bill Marchant wrote in early 1961,

> Cuba has wiped out the classic pattern of her foreign trade and, for better or for worse, placed her economic existence at the mercy of the Sino/Soviet Bloc [...] Cuba is going into 1961 with an economy which is seventy-five per cent State socialism, most of it mortgaged up to the hilt to communist countries, all of them situated more than five thousand miles away.[100]

While complications continued to arise for the British government in deciding its trade policy towards Cuba, the Bay of Pigs debacle confirmed for British policymakers that US policy was misguided, counterproductive and designed for internal consumption. Before the turn of the year, the Cuban authorities had already received intelligence reports about an imminent US-backed invasion. In January 1961, the military authorities mounted an anti-aircraft machine-gun nest on the roof of the British embassy building, to the dismay of diplomats inside. The placement of armed defences directly above their heads suddenly made them a potential target for enemy attack.[101]

When rumours of an imminent invasion reached a climax in early April 1961, just days before the actual Bay of Pigs invasion, Marchant was unequivocal in his assessment:

> Prospect of badly organised landings planned on the assumption that internal opposition is strong enough to give decisive support continues to cause considerable concern to me and to all my European colleagues. [I]f the American assessment is based exclusively on counter-revolutionary sources it is almost certainly wrong.[102]

On reading this telegram in London, one official commented, 'Nothing w[oul]d restore revolutionary zeal to its 1959 pitch more effectively than a landing by exiles, for which the U.S. w[oul]d certainly be blamed.'[103]

Kennedy's ill-judged endorsement of CIA advice resulted in one of the Cold War's most infamous episodes. Some 1400 mercenaries and Cuban exiles, financed and trained in Central America by the CIA, launched an amphibious invasion at the Bay of Pigs on the island's southern coast. Their plan was to establish a beachhead and foment a mass internal uprising against the revolution. But the Cuban authorities had arrested thousands of suspected counterrevolutionaries before the ill-conceived military operation. And a pre-emptive attack by B-26 bombers only destroyed half of Cuba's air force. Ironically, it was a Sea Fury fighter-bomber plane – sold to Batista by the British in 1958 – that sank the main supply ships of the proxy invasion force at the Bay of Pigs. This was the turning point of the CIA-sponsored fiasco and came the very day after Castro first declared the 'socialist' nature of his revolution.[104]

In the United Nations, a Mexican draft resolution against the use of foreign territories for military operations against Cuba placed Britain's representative in New York in a difficult position. President Kennedy made a personal appeal to Ambassador Caccia for the British to vote against rather than abstain.[105] In Cabinet, Lord Privy Seal Edward Heath (Foreign Office) defined the resolution as awkward, while the prime minister advised that they must support the United States when it was in trouble.[106] In Parliament, the government faced a barrage of criticism for being seen to accede to US pressure. In one combative intervention, Labour MP Emrys Hughes asked Heath whether he agreed with the public's desire 'to see Her Majesty's Government licking the boots of the

Americans a little less and speaking up for the people of this country a little more'.[107]

In Hankey's opinion, allies of the United States had been placed in an 'impossible position' at the United Nations and in the face of domestic public opinion by their reluctant support for Washington's 'open infraction of international law'. He described Britain's 'high degree of cooperation' in Cuba over the arms embargo, economic policy and the Bay of Pigs. His mention of agreement to the contingency of making Caribbean territories available to invasion-force aircraft hinted at British foreknowledge of the operation.[108] Indeed, Kennedy had informed Macmillan beforehand about a simpler plan to put 200–300 partisans ashore and establish a resistance base in the mountains, similar to the Castro-led *Granma* landing in 1956.[109]

In the eyes of the Foreign Office, the Bay of Pigs fiasco emphasized more than ever the narrow set of options open to the United States for the downfall of Castro's regime. Furthermore, the debacle undoubtedly strengthened his hold over Cuba. Following Kennedy's error of judgement over the Bay of Pigs invasion, the British ambassador to Washington was asked to remind the US administration that excellent reports had been supplied by the British since the US–Cuban diplomatic break, and would continue 'in the hope that perhaps better use will be made of them in Washington in the future'.[110] Harold Caccia judged that such counsel was not prudent at this particular juncture. With a parallel British case in mind, he replied 'they are still sore and our observations would be no more welcome than theirs were after Suez'.[111]

Four-and-a-half years after the Suez campaign and their high-handed treatment at the hands of Washington, British diplomats might be forgiven for feelings of *Schadenfreude* towards their transatlantic ally. Both the British government, followed by the United States government, had suffered the ignominy of failed military interventions in their spheres of influence. And the respective nemeses of the transatlantic partners, namely Nasser and Castro, came through the botched invasions with increased prestige and a surfeit of nationalist sentiment on which to draw.[112]

Caccia analysed Washington's 'post mortem' on the debacle, and described a 'baffled and angry' mood in the country after a series of 'hard knocks'. Kennedy had reacted well to the crisis by taking full responsibility, with the likelihood he would redouble his efforts to bring the 'wayward American government machine' under control. But considering the US strategy to tackle the communist threat, the ambassador feared 'American impatience and impetuosity and a failure to comprehend the real nature of the struggle'.[113]

1961 had been declared the 'Year of Education', with a mass mobilization of literacy teacher brigades to all parts of the island. Marchant identified its 'avowed objective' as teaching every Cuban to read and write, when in reality it was 'a monster exercise in mass indoctrination'.[114] On reading the ambassador's long exposé, a senior official in London commented, 'I do not think we had realised how rapidly Cuba was turning into a fully-fledged Communist state.'[115]

The Cuban Revolution's increasingly radical nature posed analytical challenges for the diplomats of both allies, with the Caribbean island now implicated in superpower Cold War rivalries. Rumours began to circulate in the island about the arrival of sophisticated Soviet weaponry. A July 1961 despatch from the British embassy cited a source who had seen the arrival in port of tubes 10 m long and 2 m in diameter, eight with Russian characters in blue, the remainder in red.[116]

Credit Where It's Due

Britain's 'stop-go' economy, pressure on sterling and interventions by the Bank of England in the face of balance of payments deficits were factors that encouraged the Conservative government to promote an export drive from mid-1960. In order to stimulate and hasten the effectiveness of this initiative, the Economic Relations Department (a section of the Foreign Office) acted in conjunction with the Board of Trade and improved the government's credit policy.[117] From 1960 to 1961, President of the Board of Trade Reginald Maudling extended the scope and length of the financial guarantees offered by the ECGD to British companies with export opportunities.[118]

Within the British government, different departmental responsibilities dictated attitudes to trade and shipping restrictions. From the 1950s, the Foreign Office and the Ministry of Defence tended to align themselves with Washington's point of view, highlighting Cold War security priorities and vital relationships with the United States. But economic departments such as the Treasury and the Board of Trade, with the support of business and public and parliamentary opinion, had a more liberal stance on trade with the communist bloc.[119] They targeted reducing the balance of payments deficit and the weak British economy.

Questions surrounding trade to Cuba continued to exercise minds in various British government departments. It was difficult for economic departments to assess the levels of Soviet economic support and Cuba's foreign exchange, and hence its likelihood of repaying credit. The ECGD, acting on the advice of bankers and businessmen, was proud of its independence and track record of correct commercial judgements

on export credit extended over varying repayment periods. It therefore resented Foreign Office attempts to introduce political criteria into
credit decisions on exports to Cuba. After an exchange of prickly letters in April 1961, Maudling wrote to Edward Heath in the Foreign
Office, 'I would not wish to risk damaging the export credit insurance
machinery by using it for a purpose for which it was not designed or
intended.'[120]

Companies with firm and lucrative export offers from Cuba pressured
departments such as the Ministry of Aviation and the Board of Trade
to represent their interests more assertively in opposition to the Foreign Office, always sensitive to US reactions. The US aide-memoire from
1960 listed prohibited military equipment for Cuba, but many items
fell into a grey area between civilian and potential military use. Tyres
for tractors were a clear-cut non-controversial case, but not tyres and
tubes for aircraft, or likewise, radio transmission and radar surveillance
equipment.

Conclusion

The Kennedy administration, still in its first year, licked its wounds after
the Bay of Pigs embarrassment and planned new ways of bringing down
a regime enjoying increasing levels of Soviet economic support. With
this objective in mind, the president endorsed a 'Program of Covert
Action' (dubbed Operation Mongoose) in November 1961. It proposed
the sabotage of Cuban economic assets, from industrial and military
installations to shipping and transport facilities.[121]

Fidel Castro confirmed Washington's worst fears on 1 December when
he founded a new United Party of the Socialist Revolution and declared,
'I am a Marxist-Leninist, and I shall always be one'. Marchant assumed
that the Cuban Revolution now required 'greater and greater demands'
on the Cuban people and that 'a new faith, a new cause' was needed 'to
make new sacrifices palatable'.[122]

The Foreign Office prepared a brief for the prime minister ahead
of a meeting with Kennedy in Bermuda. It defined Cuba as 'a bit-
terly emotional issue in American politics', and advised Macmillan to
be wary of any US request for British cooperation. The Castro regime
was 'firmly established with the support of the Communist hard core,
a well-armed Militia, and a ruthlessly efficient Secret Police; nothing
short of outright United States military intervention would dislodge
it'. The brief advised the West to leave Cuba alone and concentrate
on more progressive approaches to Latin America, citing Kennedy's

recently-announced 'Alliance for Progress', a programme of economic and social development partly financed by the United States.[123]

In his end-of-year report for 1961, Marchant reflected on the April debacle at the Bay of Pigs. He judged that the reverse for the United States had 'made the Suez campaign look like a successful picnic'.[124] The respective 1956 and 1961 crises had certainly diminished the prestige of the two allies that instigated them. But the much graver Cuban Missile Crisis in the following year would risk the annihilation of millions of people around the globe.

9
Shipping, the Missile Crisis and Buses

British and US estimations of the threat posed by a communist Soviet-backed regime in Cuba varied widely, mainly due to the geographical proximity of the Caribbean island to the United States. Washington perceived that communism was expansionist and constantly sought ways to sow and exploit instability in the US 'backyard'. US policymakers therefore desired stability in Latin America and active containment of any communist outbreak.[1] During the early 1950s, Senator Joseph McCarthy fomented paranoia about communist bogeymen in the country's midst and encouraged witch-hunts against supposed 'reds under the bed'. The United States cried wolf many times over communist subversion within its own borders and in Latin America. For example, fearing that Guatemala's purchase of East-bloc arms (and other signals) presaged a communist takeover, the CIA instigated a successful military coup against the mildly reformist Jacobo Arbenz government in 1954.[2]

Castro's Marxist-Leninist Revolution confirmed the United States' worst fears about the spread of communism and Soviet ambitions, and threats to its capitalist way of life. Early manifestations of Castro's radical anti-American outlook and his political accommodation with the Soviet Union made the revolution the most important and enduring hemispheric reverse since the declaration of US independence. The Cold War had suddenly and disconcertingly arrived in Latin America.

Coexisting (or Not) with Communism

Communism and Marxism were European creations, and all countries in the continent had an active socialist Left, split into a smorgasbord of political groupings. Socialist movements in the United States, on

the other hand, had always been marginalized.[3] Britain had coexisted
with European communism for decades, and lived within strike range
of offensive Soviet nuclear missiles. When US atomic weapon bases
became operational in Britain in the early 1950s, Churchill noted that
his country had made itself 'the bull's eye of a Soviet attack'.[4] When
Castro accepted Premier Nikita Khrushchev's audacious offer to locate
nuclear missiles in the Caribbean island in 1962, the Cuban leader – like
the British government a decade earlier – converted his country into an
aircraft carrier for foreign weaponry, risking an overwhelming military
response from his US neighbour.

Less than a month before the Cuban Missile Crisis, Conservative
Foreign Office Minister Joseph Godber formulated a memorandum
in response to 'very disturbed' US opinion about Cuba. With mid-
term congressional elections approaching in November 1962, Kennedy's
opponents were making political capital out of an apparent Soviet military build-up in Cuba, and the refusal of NATO allies like Britain
to curtail their shipping to the island. Godber's sympathy for the
US predicament only went so far. He considered that the Monroe
Doctrine had historically made Europeans consider the Americas a 'particular sphere of interest of the United States', and Cuba 'a problem
largely related to the American continent'. While Britain, like the United
States, was 'deeply and irrevocably opposed' to the 'abhorrent' doctrine
of Communism, it had been 'imposed by the Cubans themselves' and
not by Soviet Russia. With large doses of British understatement and
Schadenfreude, he added, 'We have, of course, been used to living for a
long time now with Communism on our doorstep. We understand and
sympathise with the regrettable fact that the United States now has a
similar experience.'[5]

The memorandum judged that Washington's strategy was flawed
because there was 'no likelihood' that economic sanctions or a blockade would bring down Castro's regime. They would simply facilitate
more dependence on the Soviet Union, and redirect blame for Cuba's
shortcomings on the West. Matter-of-factly, the minister stated, 'No one
would insult the United States by thinking that Cuba represents a military threat against her.' Air-reconnaissance photographs soon proved
this statement wildly misinformed.[6]

CoCom

The Coordinating Committee for Multilateral Export Controls
(CoCom) – an informal arrangement between NATO countries (minus

Iceland) and Japan – operated a Western strategic embargo against the Soviet Bloc from 1950.[7] But the United States and Britain often disagreed over the choice and scale of embargoed goods, a reflection of fundamentally different practical and philosophical points of view. Britain's economy was far more dependent on exports than the largely self-sufficient United States. In this regard, Macmillan's government repeated the mantra, 'Britain must trade in order to survive'.[8] With many economic difficulties in the early 1960s, it was desperate for new export markets, especially in the dollar area. Economic departments were extremely reluctant to extend the list of prohibited CoCom items beyond those of a strictly military or advanced technological nature.[9]

When discussing trade policy towards Cuba, the Foreign Office often cited Washington's 'extreme sensitivity', Britain's isolation in NATO, and the wider interest of amicable Anglo–American relations. Its officials criticized the Board of Trade's 'rigid attitude', its 'doctrinaire' arguments, and its solidarity with Treasury and ECGD officials.[10] But whatever the Foreign Office arguments, the Board of Trade refused to accept them, defending a point of principle. It would not concede economic ground to satisfy a diplomatically expedient concession to the United States and its irrational fears over Cuba. In a 'thin edge of the wedge' argument, the Board of Trade feared that any concession to the United States would invite further unreasonable demands.[11] It also opposed treating Cuba as part of the Soviet Bloc, entailing its formal inclusion on the CoCom list and reporting export credit granted to the island. It considered such efforts as US attempts to use CoCom as an instrument to wage economic warfare – a purpose, it argued, for which it was not set up. Looming large in its thinking was the potential criticism of Parliament and industry if it did concede this principle.[12]

The Ministry of Defence also sided with the Board of Trade, arguing that Kennedy's administration 'would like nothing better than to be able to tell Congress that their allies are co-operating in denying strategic goods to Cuba. Such a declaration would go down very well with the American public', but was indefensible in Britain.[13]

From a low level, the CoCom debate rose to heads of department and then to ministers. Foreign Secretary Lord Home was correct when suggesting Foreign Office and Board of Trade views only differed in their respective estimations of 'vulnerability to American pressure'. He underlined US 'distress', a possible 'major row' with Washington, and the 'heavy cost in goodwill'. In an attempt to contextualize US fears, he explained to President of the Board of Trade Fred Erroll that 'The existence of a Communist regime in the Caribbean must be a matter of deep concern to us, but to the Americans it is a calamity.'[14] But the Board of Trade's resistance continued. Erroll suggested that the Foreign Office had not explained Britain's 'consistent policy' on Cuban trade clearly enough to the United States.[15]

Macmillan stated that he 'strongly disagreed with the whole idea of COCOM' at a meeting of senior British and US officials in London. He stressed that 40 per cent of Britain's gross national product consisted of overseas trade, and the comparable US figure was a mere six per cent. US Secretary of State Dean Rusk acknowledged the British 'lived by trade', but also that they 'must defend themselves against those who would like to cut their throats'. Lord Home reassured his US counterpart that Britain was 'very unlikely' to extend credits to Cuba. The prime minister, in person at least, expressed no objection to 'merely reporting' credit.[16] The issue divided Cabinet opinion. Erroll recommended resistance and defence of a principle. Chancellor of the Exchequer Selwyn Lloyd advised telling Washington it was not 'sensible', but favoured falling into line with consensus in NATO. One member questioned agreeing to such 'nonsense', but another emphasized strong US feelings on the issue. Lord Home was conciliatory but not wholly convinced, and Macmillan took a similar line. The Cabinet approved NATO's recommendation to report export credits extended to Cuba.[17] Even so, the British government had not agreed to stop granting these credits.

Shipping

NATO shipping to Cuba was another ongoing bone of contention, still not resolved to Washington's satisfaction. Eisenhower had commenced an economic denial programme in 1960 when he reduced the US quota for Cuban sugar. Kennedy inherited the presidency and the problem of Cuba in January 1961, and set about establishing an economic 'embargo' of the island, prohibiting the export of a range of goods to this traditional and well-established US market.

Eisenhower's attempts to persuade NATO allies to restrict merchant shipping to Cuba came to nothing in 1960. But in 1962, President Kennedy renewed attempts to cut off the lifeline of Soviet and other goods by pressuring US allies to halt the flow of maritime trade to the island. His administration initially attempted to do this in the forum of NATO, but when this failed, it targeted non-complying countries individually. One of the worst and most recalcitrant offenders in US eyes was Britain. Alongside Norway, another nation heavily dependent on trade, these allies' registered shipping carried half of all the goods entering Cuba.[18]

In view of an increased Soviet military build-up in the island, a highly perturbed Washington increased pressure on NATO governments to cease the transport of Bloc country supplies to Cuba. British shipping came in for particular criticism during the summer and early autumn of 1962. But Macmillan's government and British shipping companies were most averse to setting a precedent that would interrupt maritime trade, the lifeblood of their island economy. They would not contemplate a policy designed (in their view) to assuage US public and congressional opinion, rather than deal effectively with the Cuban problem. Furthermore, the British government insisted it had no legal powers to control the operation of its shipping during peacetime, and was not about to legislate for them. Such powers would be controversial and unpopular, especially for British owners who already resented US discrimination and subsidies against their shipping.[19]

The issue became red hot in the United States. Chancellor of the Exchequer Reginald Maudling stoked the flames further during a 'meet the press' session in the United States. His hosts jumped on his remark that 'Cuba is essentially an American problem', when explaining British responsibilities in other parts of the world. Asked if his country would help the United States over Cuba, he explained that Britain shared US feelings, but didn't always accept its measures.[20] At the same time, a senior British diplomat wrote from New York, 'There is considerable heat here both in Press and Administration circles over continuing Western trade with Cuba.' The campaign accused Western allies of continuing 'for their own selfish profit to trade with Cuba', while the United States was 'left alone to face the Cuban problem'.[21] The British embassy in Washington reported that Congress and particularly the House of Representatives had been 'on the rampage' over the question of NATO merchant shipping.[22] Republican Senator Barry Goldwater was a particularly vociferous critic of British policy, declaring, 'If this blockade means blockading our two-timing allies like the British, let's blockade them.'[23]

At the start of October 1962, weeks before the Cuban Missile Crisis, Kennedy told Home that 'he simply couldn't understand' why Britain 'could not help America by joining in an embargo on trade'. On the same day, Macmillan told his foreign secretary, 'I hope we shall not agree to COCOM or anything approaching it. There is no reason for us to help the Americans on Cuba'.[24]

The head of steam in the United States resulted in a drastic proposal to close US ports to any ships carrying goods to Soviet-Bloc countries and Cuba, thus threatening Britain's entire trade with the United States.

British officials fretted over this threat to freedom of navigation, practically a founding principle of their trade policy, and contravening the longstanding 1815 Convention of Commerce with the United States.[25] They were reluctant to mention the convention to Washington, fearing ridicule and a negative reaction from the US public.[26]

The British government publicly rejected the US proposal for a wholesale shipping boycott of Cuba. British ships carrying goods to Cuba fell under several categories. They could be British owned and registered, British registered and foreign owned, or British registered but under charter to communist countries. Some long-term charters even allowed British ships to be manned by Russian crews. Legislating for such a variety of shipping would be complicated in the extreme, and was without precedent in peacetime. Furthermore, there was a surplus of Soviet Bloc or neutral shipping available to fill any hole left by NATO-controlled ships.[27] The British considered the proposal and its potential effects on the Cuban economy as futile, an empty gesture that would harm Britain's economy and prove unpopular with its public.

In Cuba, the British rejection of Washington's proposal provoked headlines and a satirical cartoon. It showed a British lion refusing to remove a thorn (identified as Cuba) from the bleeding foot of Uncle Sam, designated as the slave Androcles (see Fig. 1).[28] Making an analogy with the legend of a Roman slave, the Cuban newspaper asserted that Britain owed no debt of goodwill to the United States. There had been no past favour and there was nothing to reciprocate, however great was Washington's pain. Perhaps the cartoonist was making a parallel with recent events at Suez, and the American Revolution against British colonial rule in the late eighteenth century.

But the build-up of Soviet arms in Cuba continued unabated. Cuban authorities arrested two British journalists in early September, sent to report on the presence of Russians. Cuban exile group Alpha 66 attacked a British freighter off the coast of Cuba and threatened to carry out more acts of sabotage against foreign merchant shipping that traded with the island.[29]

Over the next year, several attacks were launched from the British crown colony of the Bahamas. After local police arrested nine Cuban exiles preparing a raid in April 1963, Castro made good on his threat to take action if British or French islands in the Caribbean were used in this way again. In August, his armed forces landed and arrested 19 Cubans on Anguilla Cay, an atoll in the Cay Sal Bank. The Foreign Office made a strong protest after it had established the facts of the case, but Castro later made a private verbal apology and an

EL LEON Y ANDROCLES   Por Nuez

Figure 1 'El León y Androcles', René de la Nuez, *Revolución* (Havana), 6 Oct. 1962.

assurance of restraint that calmed British anger over this incursion into their sovereign territory.[30]

By 1963, it suited Washington to keep a lid on the actions of Cuban exiles based in Florida and Puerto Rico that used various islets in the Bahamas as staging posts for hit-and-run raids against Cuba and foreign shipping. On the one hand, overt suppression of the raids and the raiders could prove unpopular among the US public, particularly the exile community. But the actions also provided Castro with ammunition to castigate both the US and British governments. The transatlantic allies therefore cooperated in exchanging intelligence and physically preventing the raids, as well as keeping publicity about them to a minimum.[31]

Cuban Missile Crisis

Renewed US attempts to gain NATO support for a shipping embargo paralleled the build-up of Soviet arms and military personnel in the island during 1962. Conservative estimations of the size and scope of the Soviet military arsenal in Cuba proved wide of the mark when a US Air Force U-2 spy plane identified intermediate range nuclear missiles in the island, sparking the most dangerous crisis of the Cold War.

Throughout the year, the British embassy in Havana made a significant contribution to gathering low-level intelligence for the United States, adding to its information from other sources.[32] This found its way to Washington via the Joint Intelligence Bureau (JIB) in London. In March, the JIB outlined to Marchant the importance of photographic evidence and requested more precise information on specific military vehicles, affirming that that he was their 'only source in Cuba'.[33] Michael Brown, working in the British embassy in Havana since late 1960, visited the Pentagon en route to London in September, along with Iain Sutherland, a Washington-based British diplomat with recent experience in Havana.[34] British consul Stanley Stephenson (based in Santiago de Cuba) also visited the State Department to meet officials from the United States Information Agency (USIA) and the Department of Intelligence and Research.[35] The problem for accredited British diplomats in obtaining intelligence was that it often required taking risks. They wondered if their US allies did not already have 'detailed photographic cover of every inch of this little island' to pass onto the JIB. If not, they would 'crane [their] necks over hedges and round corners' to obtain it.[36]

The British embassy enjoyed an elevated view of the port's harbour entrance and the approaches to a new arterial tunnel linking the city with the main coastal highway. Without leaving the embassy, therefore, staff could report important road and shipping traffic before, during and following the Soviet military build-up and the epochal Cuban Missile Crisis in October 1962.

In the summer of 1962, 45,000 Soviet troops accompanied their country's nuclear deployment of tactical medium- and long-range ballistic missiles to Cuba. Soviet equipment and personnel arrived in Cuba's main ports and travelled on its limited road network.[37] Marchant witnessed a 'noticeable increase' in Soviet shipping in mid-August 1962 and reported that 'Persistent rumours, sometimes from reasonably good sources, of the recent arrival of Russians and new equipment are not without some foundation.' A colleague had seen 'bulky deck cargo' on a Soviet ship. Two others saw at a camp near Havana around 200 men, '99% certainly Russians', with radio trucks and aerial systems. The ambassador passed an escorted military convoy in the west of the island, including two trucks with trailers and equipment under tarpaulins. In London, a memorandum described press reports of a military build-up as 'partly true but much exaggerated' when compared to Marchant's telegrams.[38]

These estimations proved to be erroneous in the light of new incontrovertible evidence. A US Air Force U-2 spy plane took high-altitude photographs showing the installation of nuclear-armed missiles in Cuba. President Kennedy offered this photographic evidence to the world on 22 October. Some in Britain questioned initial US intelligence reports about Soviet missiles in Cuba. These included Shadow Leader Hugh Gaitskell and Denis Healey of the Labour party.[39] But their scepticism was unfounded. Kennedy and his advisors had no such doubts and announced a naval 'quarantine' of the island, demanding that the Soviet Union remove its missiles. People around the world contemplated the very tangible prospect of a nuclear conflagration to end all wars.

Anglo–American contacts during the crucial days of Cuban Missile Crisis have been well documented.[40] Macmillan played a supporting but not crucial role. In nightly phone conversations with Kennedy he acted as a 'sounding board' for the president's evolving strategy in dealing with Premier Nikita Khrushchev's audacious deployment of nuclear missiles to Cuba.[41] In an initiative to pacify Soviet concerns over US nuclear weapons in Turkey, the prime minister offered to immobilize Thor missiles stationed in Britain. The US Department of Defense ruled out this bargain. For Marchant, writing from the 'unnatural calm [...] in the edge of a cyclone', the roles of Cuba and Castro were 'incidental' to the high-stakes game of brinkmanship between the two superpowers'.[42] The status of Berlin, meanwhile, a wall dividing its Soviet- and Western-controlled sectors since 1961, was considered vital in the decision-making of Kennedy and Khrushchev.

In the midst of the crisis, British shipowners worried that their cooperation over a US naval blockade of the island – a measure of questionable legality according to the Foreign Office – was setting a dangerous precedent.[43] The British government objected to Washington's analgesic term 'quarantine' to describe a blockade. Shadow Foreign Secretary Harold Wilson insisted on television that the problem should have been taken to the United Nations before the unilateral imposition of a blockade.[44] The prime minister and the foreign secretary had to field probing questions about it in the House of Commons. In private, Lord Home told his UN representative to 'leave it to the Americans to defend the legality of their blockade'.[45]

The Lord Chancellor Lord Dilhorne, the government's legal consultant, advised the Cabinet to put its reservation of legal rights over the blockade in writing to Washington. Lord Hailsham, meanwhile, advised that they were 'in danger of making asses' of themselves by citing international laws formulated for 'the sailing ship and the cannon' during an 'age of the nuclear warhead and the rocket'.[46] Dilhorne responded, 'I am concerned lest our tacit acquiescence in interference with British ships on the High Seas on this occasion should come to be regarded as a precedent justifying similar action in the future.'[47]

On the one hand the government needed to show its shipowners and the general public that it was defending vital national interests, but on the other, it wanted to avoid offending its main Cold War ally during a world crisis.[48] Lord Home wrote to Macmillan, 'I am very anxious that we should not publicly take sides against the United States by saying that Her Majesty's Government doubt whether the blockade is legally justified.'[49] Britain took a legalistic stance when its national interests were under threat. But another vital national interest was its relationship with the United States, the most important element in its foreign policy. With Soviet missiles overtly threatening major US cities, Britain had to delicately balance its range of interests during the crisis.

From Havana, Marchant urged the United States to increase its Voice of America (VOA) broadcasts to 'news hungry' Cubans in the absence of more balanced reporting. The island's subservient satellite status should be brought home to them, he advised. Washington took note and expanded its VOA transmissions to Cuba.[50] Embassy staff remained vigilant, and often only had to look out of the window to spot heavy vehicles and ships passing the embassy building, often travelling to or from the port of Mariel, west of Havana.[51]

In the high-stakes game of international brinkmanship Khrushchev blinked first, and agreed to withdraw Soviet nuclear warheads from Cuba in exchange for US missiles being withdrawn from Turkey. Kennedy also made a commitment that US forces would not invade Cuba. Amidst the fallout of the superpower confrontation, diplomats hoped that in pursuing either the hard or the soft line over Cuba, Washington would consult their allies, and would not henceforth anticipate greater allied cooperation in the economic field.[52]

Staff in the British embassy were well placed to report the withdrawal of the military equipment and provide details not visible from US air surveillance. They traversed the island in an effort to provide Washington with the information it required, and enable Kennedy's government to assuage domestic opponents who distrusted Khrushchev's word. A new British consul drove from Santiago de Cuba in the east to Havana in the west on 4–5 November and back again (via another route) on 8–9 November. Frustratingly though, tarpaulins often covered military equipment and identification was based on outline only.[53]

Ground reconnaissance by the British embassy in Havana was Anglo–American cooperation practised on a micro scale. In 1960, the United States had agreed to sell Britain the Skybolt air-to-ground missile system. In return, Britain allowed the US military to construct a nuclear submarine base at Holy Loch in Scotland. But only weeks after the Cuban Missile Crisis, President Kennedy abandoned the controversial Skybolt programme, the only weapon that gave Britain nuclear power status. Against State Department advice at a summit of the two allies at Nassau in December 1962, Kennedy acceded to Macmillan's request for Polaris, a submarine-launched nuclear missile system. The new deal boosted Britain's defence credentials, but also made the country completely dependent on the US nuclear technology for its strategic defence capability.[54]

New Negotiations with Leyland

In March 1963, the French ambassador in Havana told Marchant how he had been 'practically seduced' by Cuba's Ministry of Foreign Affairs. Cuba was suddenly treating Western governments favourably in the commercial field, with quick arrangements to pay long outstanding debts.[55] According to the British embassy's annual report, Castro's visit to the Soviet Union from 26 April to 4 June was the island's most significant event of 1963. Following the unilateral Soviet decision to withdraw its missiles, the report identified Moscow's desire both to reduce its economic commitment and soothe Castro's feelings. The Cuban leader's reaction, meanwhile, displayed his desire to moderate Russian influence, mindful of his country's embarrassingly dependent and precarious position. This manifested itself in a definite move by the revolutionary leader to cultivate Western embassies in Havana and increase trade outside the Soviet Bloc.[56]

Marchant urged a rethink of his country's cautious commercial policy in May. Companies were reporting increased trade opportunities and competition. It was a 'changing picture', he insisted, which in view of the national need to export could not be ignored. Britain's trade policy of the last two years to 'let trade find its own level' was now outdated. In an obvious reference to Charles de Gaulle's recent decision to veto Britain's entry into the European Economic Community (EEC) in January 1963, he wrote, 'We may be losing a far more important slice of cake than the slice under consideration when this policy was evolved – and we are losing it to Germany and worse still, to French competition.' He asked, 'How are our exporters going to feel if they now see more fruitful opportunities slipping away to Common Market countries?'[57] The French president's rebuff had thwarted the Conservative government's economic recovery plan, exacerbating even further its need to export.[58] But despite Marchant's pleas, diplomatic colleagues in London continued to prioritize political objections over the stimulation of trade with Cuba.

When the ECGD received tentative credit enquiries for exports to Cuba in the early summer of 1963, its first reaction was to speculate about the official credit offered by European rivals.[59] A Board of Trade paper recommended caution by British exporters, and offered 'little justification for H.M.G. to encourage exporters to offer credit terms'. The picture of Cuba's economy was too opaque to inspire more optimism.[60]

Leyland's negotiations in Cuba from July 1963 transformed the attitude of the Board of Trade and its subsidiary the ECGD. Cuba's public transport system was suffering from regular breakdowns and shortages, and was forced to rely on unsuitable Soviet Bloc vehicles. Bus numbers in Havana halved to 800 between 1961 and 1963, and reliable replacements were a government priority.[61] Leyland buses from the original 1950 contract were still running on Havana's streets, but the so-called *enfermeras* (nurses) had received a battering from aggressive tram-turned-bus drivers, and many vehicles had been cannibalized for spare parts.[62]

Leyland's sales manager for the Americas returned from Havana at the end of July with a letter of intent to purchase 450 buses.[63] The company then applied pressure on the British government's economic departments, anticipating political objections. Deputy Chairman and Managing Director Donald Stokes emphasized his company's existing relations with Cuba, and the continuing standardization of the island's transport system with Leyland vehicles. Offering appropriate government-backed credit would lead to a 'major prestige contract', with an equally lucrative after-sales income in spare parts.[64]

The ECGD now considered the risk 'not unreasonable', but also anticipated political repercussions.[65] The Board of Trade also changed its tune, and told the Havana embassy to encourage British companies to pursue new opportunities, but 'as unobtrusively as possible so as to avoid recrimination from the U.S.A.'[66]

In August, the Export Guarantee Committee heard debate and submissions from five different departments. The Treasury reported that the ECGD was receiving regular repayments from the 1959 Leyland deal, but there were other outstanding debts and the Cubans were 'desperately short of foreign currency'. Added to the political objections in Washington and NATO, the Treasury judged that cover should not be granted.[67] The ECGD underlined that it was for ministers to make credit cover decisions. For the Board of Trade, the contract would have a 'direct bearing on the unemployment situation' and was 'a particularly attractive piece of business'. The Foreign Office argued that given its worst harvest for twenty years and a 'disastrous' economic climate generally, credits to Cuba 'must be completely ruled out of court'.[68]

A submission to ministers summarized the contrasting arguments that left the Board of Trade and the ECGD – those departments favouring credit – in a minority of two. Leyland, according to the Board of Trade, deserved 'the fullest possible support' on account of its previous Cuban contracts and possible 'further replacement business'. Despite a lack of reliable information on Cuba's trade and payments position, it noted a 'slight improvement' in its foreign exchange earnings. But this would be the first credit-backed contract by a NATO country since 1961. To reach a final decision, departments would have to submit their views to their respective ministers.[69]

Battle continued at ministerial level between departments. The Foreign Office told Chancellor of the Exchequer Reginald Maudling that important political considerations reinforced the economic case against approval, and disagreed with the Board of Trade's claim that US reactions could not be predicted. They were predictable, and they were 'bound to be disagreeable'.[70] At the same time, the President of the Board of Trade asked Maudling to support Leyland. Emphasizing a more sanguine view of Cuba's creditworthiness, Fred Erroll wrote, 'I have the impression that if it were not for fears of upsetting the Americans, a more generous view might have been taken.' And comparing Cuba favourably with other Latin American countries already receiving ECGD cover, he continued, 'I would find it hard in these circumstances to defend to Leyland an adverse decision, which would be a poor reward for their past endeavours in this market.'[71]

In receipt of these contrasting views, the Chancellor's decision on 30 August 'to treat Cuba exactly like any other member of the Soviet Bloc in trade matters' was pivotal. While admitting that Washington was 'especially sensitive about Cuba', Maudling argued that Britain had a 'considerable interest in maintaining normal trade with all members of the Soviet Bloc'. This policy should not be modified, even if it was 'unpopular in Washington'.[72] In opposition, the Foreign Office suggested offering Cuba the buses for cash. The government should also consult the French and Germans and see if they were prepared to offer five-year credit terms. If they were, they could then defend the credit-backed sales by arguing that NATO competitors were doing likewise.[73]

To diplomatic colleagues, at least, the foreign secretary was pragmatic:

> It is agreed that we would like to sell the buses to Cuba. What is not agreed are the credit terms if any. It seems to me that the Treasury must decide this in the knowledge of what competitors would be likely to offer.[74]

For the sake of its relationship with Washington, the Foreign Office did not want to appear more amenable to trade with Cuba than other competing nations.[75]

Given the respective economic and political responsibilities of the Treasury and the Foreign Office, it is notable that the former department should be seen by the latter to be emphasizing 'political' arguments. Lord Home replicated this paradox, replying to the Treasury that he 'attached great weight to the economic side of this case'.[76]

A meeting to discuss the deal was scheduled for 19 September involving Lord Home, Maudling and Board of Trade Minister Alan Green. A Foreign Office memorandum set out its latest thinking. Given continued doubts over Cuba's creditworthiness it considered political objections as overriding. Government-backed credit to Cuba, a positive encouragement to trade, would be taken 'very amiss' by the Americans'. A potential row with Leyland should not deter them, and the matter could be defended in Parliament by offering the buses for cash.[77]

At the meeting, Maudling and Alan Green recommended the extension of credit for the bus sales, leaving the Foreign Office to continue its strenuous opposition. American Department Head Dick Slater cited the fears of Ambassador to Washington Sir David Ormsby Gore:

> The Administration, and President Kennedy in particular, would go through the roof. Public and Congressional opinion will in fact leave them little option. 'British economic aid for Castro' will headline a bitter press campaign in which comparisons will be drawn between American staunchness over Indonesia and British treachery over Cuba. The Administration will be under the severest pressure to take it out of [*sic*] us in any way they can.[78]

The British government was wary of US criticism and a possible lack of support following the foundation of Malaysia in 1963, when Britain was uncompromising in its defence of the new federation, threatened with confrontation by President Sukarno in neighbouring Indonesia.[79]

Permanent Under Secretary Harold Caccia, formerly ambassador to Washington during the triumph of Castro's revolution and the Bay of Pigs debacle, was well qualified to calibrate the force of Washington's likely reaction. He weighed Britain's inter-departmental impasse against US domestic politics:

> From the p[oin]t of view of logic & trade I sympathise with the B[oar]d of T[rade] arguments. The case against is that logic alone does not rule the acts of foreign Govts & that the U.S. Govt, Congress & public opinion, are if you like mad about Cuba. We sh[oul]d therefore bear in mind that their reaction may be 'mad' & that being so, is the business worth the risk, i.e. the political risk?[80]

Evidently, Foreign Office fear over Washington's reaction was by far and away its principal objection to the deal, considering US sentiment so extremely sensitive as to be practically irrational. Crucially, Caccia's deliberation pointed to the essentially political dimension, as opposed to the economic or strategic aspects of the buses issue and East–West trade in general. Cabinet Secretary Sir Burke Trend encapsulated the dilemma for the prime minister ahead of the meeting that would decide in favour or against the deal: 'This is a clash between economic policy on the one hand and a particularly sensitive area of foreign policy on the other hand.'[81]

In the key Cabinet meeting on 24 September, Lord Home drew attention to Britain's dependence on US support and assistance in Indonesia. Washington could 'turn nasty' and retaliate against Britain and its colonies. Russia was increasingly annoyed with Cuba and might reduce its economic support, and it was far preferable to offer the buses for cash. Maudling, meanwhile, was not present during discussion of the bus exports. Fred Erroll stressed foreign competition and the probable loss of the contract without a credit offer. He argued this was commercial and not government credit, and as repayments exceeded loans, it did not constitute either aid or a subsidy. The prime minister's executive prerogative decided the matter. He instructed his foreign secretary to outline the deal carefully to Dean Rusk. The Board of Trade should enable him to present it as a normal-phased cash payment deal, avoiding the loaded term 'credit'. He should also highlight that Britain had thus far cooperated successfully with the United States over trade with Cuba.[82]

It was one of the last decisions taken by Macmillan's government in advance of the prime minister's resignation and replacement by Lord Home (soon to be Sir Alec Douglas-Home) just a few weeks later.

Reactions to Britain's Decision

The reality of official government backing for the deal led Leyland to fear a negative US reaction against its sales in the United States.[83] In the event, the immediate US response was somewhat softened by the fortuitous timing of announcements by both Canada and the United States of wheat sales to the Soviet Union. When Foreign Secretary Lord Home met with President Kennedy in Washington on 4 October the Leyland deal was barely mentioned.[84] Afterwards, the US government expressed fears that its public would link the Leyland and wheat deals, and accuse Kennedy of giving the British a 'green light'. The president himself phoned Ormsby Gore, asking the British to leak news of the bus contract ahead of his own announcement of wheat sales to the Soviets.[85] It also suited British interests to protect Kennedy from domestic difficulties, but the fabricated press leak did not induce media outlets to report the news as desired.[86]

Kennedy was assassinated in Dallas a month later. Anglo–American interactions over the Leyland deal were subsequently conducted between two new administrations, both with unelected leaders, headed by Democratic Party President Lyndon B. Johnson in Washington, and the Conservative Party Prime Minister Sir Alec Douglas-Home in London.

The Foreign Office fretted over the row that would ensue when Washington officials realized, as they had not done already, that the bus contract had ECGD credit cover.[87] A difficulty for Leyland, meanwhile, was that it was contractually obliged to find shipping to transport the buses to Havana. The companies it contacted did not wish to contravene strict US restrictions and affect future business with the United States.[88] Stokes, a consummate publicist, even went to the lengths of requesting an aircraft carrier from the Admiralty.[89] He eventually managed to charter shipping from East Germany.

Leyland and the Cuban state trading organization 'Transimport' signed the bus contract in Havana on 6 January 1964. It stipulated delivery within 12 months of 400 single-deck Olympic buses (including spare parts and interest) at a cost of £3.7 m ($11 m) with five-year credit terms, and included a future option on a further 1000 vehicles. In Washington, the State Department was disapproving and the press generally hostile. A public statement reported ongoing dialogue with the British government and US disapproval throughout. Behind closed doors, however, US officials were reportedly 'distressed' that the five-year terms offered by the British contrasted with their own estimations for the survival of the Castro regime.[90]

Critical press comment included the *Washington Daily News* accusation that the British were 'grabbing a fast buck', accompanied by advice that Johnson's government adopt a 'new and sterner policy' towards recalcitrant allies.[91] Donald Stokes, with his recognized 'gift for the provocative phrase', surpassed himself and caught the mood of the British public, exclaiming, 'these buses are not strategic material – you would look damn silly going to war in a bus'. His acerbic intervention took the wind out of Washington's assertion that buses were strategic assets for Castro's regime, although it did ignore a famous battle in the First World War.[92] Opponents of the deal could have cited the more recent and pertinent history of the Bay of Pigs, when Leyland buses transported Cuban militias from Havana to the island's south coast in order to repel a US-trained invasion force.[93]

Other comments linked the bus contract with the US–Soviet wheat deal.[94] Republican Congressman Paul Fino (New York) was critical of the US government: 'How can we in good conscience justify our criticism when we are selling £90 million worth of wheat to Russia?' When Washington defended its wheat trade with the Soviet Union by pointing to production in excess of domestic consumption, Leyland Chairman Sir William Black retorted, 'If America has a surplus of wheat, we have a surplus of buses.'[95] Indeed, the immediate reaction of Johnson's administration was somewhat muted by the unfortunate coincidence of the wheat sales. When the president was brought up to speed on the bus contract immediately after its public announcement, he was unable to discern a substantive difference between the two export deals. National Security Adviser McGeorge Bundy informed him that the British public certainly equated US wheat sales to the Soviet Union with the Leyland sales to Cuba.[96]

Meanwhile, Cuban émigrés picketed the British Consulate in Miami, one of their placards reading 'Pirates of the Caribbean, Friends of Castro'.[97] The *New York Times* analysed fundamental differences between the allies' trade policies, and conceded that Britain was a 'nation which depends on foreign trade'.[98] In London, *The Economist* defined the trade policy as a primarily political issue for the United States and a commercial one for the British.[99] In Cuba, the deal received front-page coverage and reported a gesture of defiance against US policy.[100] Embassy staff in Havana described mixed local reaction, with Cubans from various walks of life perturbed by Her Majesty's Government's credit-based estimation that Castro's government would endure for at least another five years.[101]

In the forum of NATO the United States continued attempts to rally Western allies to the cause of Cuba's economic isolation. Johnson, like Kennedy before him, had inherited the Cuban problem and the official policy to deal with it. The recent experiences of the Bay of Pigs and the Cuban Missile Crisis ruled out direct and dangerous military intervention. The economic denial programme was seen as a practical measure that stopped short of war, and the continuation of 'an acceptable response to both domestic pressures to "do something" about Cuba and foreign pressures not to do too much'.[102] It also increased the cost to the Soviets of maintaining an outpost in the Americas and served as a disincentive to any hemispheric neighbours considering a similar political path to Cuba.[103] The Foreign Office noted Britain's isolation in NATO and the likelihood that if the French came to break the embargo, they would doubtless shelter behind the recent British breach.[104] This fear was borne out when a French truck deal was announced a few days later, a decision that struck the US State Department as a 'predictable result of the British action'.[105]

Following the visit of a Cuban Trade Mission in November and introduction to 30 British firms, ECGD credit decisions were pending on contracts for a list of items: locomotives, earth-moving and building construction equipment, a rayon plant, harbour equipment, dairy equipment, a sugar bag production mill, a chemical plant and ships.[106] On the one hand the Board of Trade warned that the withholding of medium-term credit for deals would effectively curtail exports to Cuba and be strongly criticized by British industry.[107] The Foreign Office, on the other hand, naturally highlighted the political ramifications of British trade with Cuba, admitting that the case for more credit cover had been 'effectively deployed and will be strongly pressed' by the government's economic departments.[108]

The British embassy in Washington warned colleagues in London that the timing of announcements for future contracts would need careful consideration, because of a tendency to link Britain's attitude to the embargo with US assistance in other parts of the world, for example, in Indonesia and Malaysia.[109] A few days ahead of a visit by Douglas-Home, it set out the strength of feeling at the top of the administration and advised against 'flippancy'. The Counsellor and Head of Chancery warned, 'Any cracks about people not going to war in buses nowadays would go down very poorly with Mr. Johnson.'[110] Ormsby Gore wrote, 'You should be in no doubt about the strength of feelings on this subject in the administration, whatever the merits of our case, with particular regard to the E.C.G.D. aspect.'[111]

It was the credit-guarantee dimension of the bus sales that most exercised the US administration, viewing government-backed insurance as equivalent to financial aid. From Washington's standpoint, cash sales drained Cuba's scant reserves of hard currency, allowing the Soviets to devote more resources to their civilian sector without compromising military spending. Government credits were therefore regarded as tantamount to strategic assistance.[112] When reading a report that an option had been signed to buy another 1000 Leyland buses, Washington urgently queried whether ECGD cover had already been agreed.[113]

Johnson's main objectives in his White House meeting with Douglas-Home were to impress on him the strength of US feeling and pressure him to refuse credit cover for these 1000 extra buses.[114] The prime minister made no such commitment, and further antagonized his host by telling journalists afterwards that economic measures could not bring down leaders like Castro. And ignoring earlier advice about flippancy, he referred to the buses issue during a White House dinner toast. The two leaders never spoke to each other again.[115]

The strength of Washington's reaction to the signed Leyland bus deal also reflected the fact that 1964 was a presidential election year. A brief by the prime minister's private secretary ahead of the meeting had warned him he was in for a 'rough time' in Washington over Cuba, defined as 'primarily a domestic political problem, less so a diplomatic one'. The Republicans were doing everything to embarrass the president. Furthermore, he recommended strong resistance to any US attempt to 'horse-trade' British support over Cuba for US support in Indonesia.[116] Senator Barry Goldwater, the Republican candidate for the presidency, attempted to ratchet up the pressure on Johnson by saying he would use US warships to halt the shipment of British buses and French goods to Cuba.[117] Days after the visit the United States cut military aid to Britain, France and Yugoslavia because of their trade with Cuba, although this amounted to a pittance for the British.

The ECGD and the Foreign Office continued to disagree on the Cuban economy's strength and its dependence on the Soviet Bloc, the former department mentioning the build-up and 'very great pressure' of firms waiting for credit cover.[118] In a Cabinet meeting on 3 March, new

President of the Board of Trade Edward Heath stressed the urgency of a credit decision with four firms needing a positive answer if they were not going to lose orders and another 17 negotiating with the Cubans. Foreign Secretary 'Rab' Butler continued to stress the political risks of US opposition.[119]

But again, the economic departments won the day in the face of determined opposition. In a familiar pattern, the disagreement had been taken to Cabinet, discussions had continued thereafter, and the final decision had gone against Foreign Office wishes. The £4 m annual credit repayment ceiling recommended by the ECGD's Advisory Council conveniently accommodated all the Cuban deals currently on the table, although most of the exports did not proceed because of companies' fears over reprisals against their interests in the United States.[120]

Butler's Visit and Domestic Pressures

If there was any misconception as to the US strength of feeling on the matter of British credit-backed exports to Cuba, it was Foreign Secretary 'Rab' Butler who felt the full force of President Johnson's anger in Washington on 29 April. Butler had expected to discuss the bus issue in a meeting with Secretary of State Dean Rusk, but it turned out to be the central theme of an interview with the president.[121] There is little discernible divergence of view in the different published versions of the interview. According to Butler's own memoir, he had sensed trouble and had not insisted on seeing Johnson. When they did meet, the president 'launched immediately' into the issue, produced a wad of dollars from his pocket, and beseeched the foreign secretary to send the Leyland bill to his Texas ranch.[122] According to a diplomatic résumé, the talk 'consisted largely of a monologue' from Johnson on the bus deal's 'deplorable effect upon Anglo–American relations'. The trade was 'a mere drop in the bucket', and Britain should choose between him and Castro.[123]

In Britain, there was little possibility of the Conservative government yielding to US pressure, with general elections announced on 9 April. British public opinion supported continued defiance in the face of US pressure, and, with Douglas-Home's poor prospects of re-election, a policy reversal was highly unlikely.[124] The Labour Party, in opposition since 1951 and with its best chance in 13 years of returning to government, publicly supported this populist stance.[125] Opposition Leader Harold Wilson had visited Lyndon Johnson in Washington at the start of March, and Secretary of State Dean Rusk had no illusions that he

planned to change Britain's trade policy towards Cuba. The US administration warned him against making public statements about trade with
Cuba, only weeks after Douglas-Home's pronouncements to journalists,
and Wilson did indeed promise that he would not follow the prime
minister's lead of making 'domestic mileage' out of the buses issue.[126]

Wilson did not evade the president's direct enquiries about trade
in nonstrategic commodities to Cuba, and offered no prospect of a
future Labour government modifying the policy. With an eye to self-
interest, Wilson mentioned the likelihood that the Conservatives would
propagate anti-American sentiment during the forthcoming election
campaign, pointing out that there were 'still memories of Suez' within
the Conservative government.[127] While Suez was not mentioned by
name in the government's deliberations over exports to Cuba, the
spectre of the crisis and kowtowing to Washington persisted.

The French government, like the British, were pulled in the direction of credit refusal because of fears over relations with the United
States, but in the other direction by the intense pressure of industrial
and financial interests. Once the Leyland deal was announced this pressure increased, and French officials sheltered behind the action of their
NATO partners across the channel.[128] A French firm stepped in when a
British company passed over the opportunity for a £3.5m export contract for locomotives, fearing reprisals against its group's operations in
the United States. And when the British did sell locomotives to Cuba,
the Foreign Office took some comfort in the fact that the French were
exporting even more.[129]

Conclusion

Castro's government justified the ECGD's confidence in offering it
five-year credits by eventually settling all outstanding payments. Cuba
received all the Leyland buses, although a chartered East German vessel carrying 42 vehicles famously collided with a Japanese ship in the
Thames just minutes after leaving Dagenham on 26 October 1964,
beaching the vessel and ruining its cargo.[130] Given the controversy over
the sales, some have affirmed or speculated that the 'accident' was a
CIA operation. It was certainly unusual for two boats with experienced
pilots to collide in the Thames, and a big coincidence that it should
happen to a vessel carrying such a controversial cargo.[131] The sinking
occurred just ten days after Harold Wilson's narrow general election victory, and days before Johnson's electoral triumph. If the collision was
deliberate, it was perhaps a shot across the bows of the new Labour

government. But the new prime minister remained true to his word and did not reverse support for credit-backed bus exports to Cuba. Leyland did well from the sinking because the shipment was insured at 110 per cent of its value. The company received full compensation and simply manufactured and shipped the buses again without incident.[132]

The Thames collision evoked memories of the *Maine* disaster in 1898. A thorough scientific investigation 100 years after the tragic explosion in Havana's harbour, using computer modelling and simulations, failed to provide conclusive proof that it was provoked by either a coal bunker fire or an external mine. In fact, it concluded that 'The case remains open'.[133] Regarding the Thames incident, perhaps only the normalization of US–Cuban relations and the declassification of records will reveal if the CIA was involved. The common feature of both incidents is the ongoing doubt and speculation over their causes, a result of the heightened political tensions at play when they occurred.

The Leyland bus sales certainly dealt a heavy blow to Washington's attempts to gain NATO unanimity for an economic blockade of Cuba. The deal released a logjam of pending exports to Castro's Soviet-backed government and a clamour for new trade among Western competitors. Washington's transatlantic partner had unwittingly instigated a breach of its blockade, or, to use a metaphor, it had driven a fleet of buses through it. Johnson's administration readily recognized the significance of the deal, viewing the action of 'America's closest ally' as a 'major set-back' to its 'economic denial program' and lamenting the resulting 'band-wagon psychology' in the minds of other Western European governments.[134]

It was principally the domestic dimension on both sides of the Atlantic that decided policy over the bus sales. Fidel Castro, speaking in Havana's Revolution Square on May Day 1964, explained the British government's dilemma. In receipt of a cable describing the US administration's distress during 'Rab' Butler's visit, Castro told his audience that Britain had been spoken to like a US 'satellite', without mentioning his own country's status vis-à-vis the Soviet Union. The British government – according to the Cuban leader – had the choice of upsetting the US government by selling buses to Cuba or abandoning a long-held principle and alienating its own public. Castro explained that with forthcoming elections and the economy in mind, the British government preferred to conciliate its own people.[135]

Washington's position reflected fear of communist contagion on its continent and its role in holding together a hemispheric consensus against Cuba. The US public, especially in the wake of the Cuban Missile

Crisis, expected its government to act resolutely against threats from an enemy that would wish the United States harm. Moreover, Johnson's administration was domestically vulnerable to the charge that its allies were abandoning it to fight the battle against communism alone.[136]

But the British Conservative government preferred to appease domestic as opposed to US opinion. While Johnson had to select his attitude towards trade with Cuba with a forthcoming election in mind, so did his British allies.[137] They viewed Washington's position as counterproductive and emotional, responding to domestic political pressures rather than being a rational and effective strategy to unseat a Soviet-backed regime. The case set limits to British cooperation in the field of trade restrictions. Castro, meanwhile, as well as improving Cuba's run-down transport system, benefitted from the not insignificant propaganda value of splitting the policies of the transatlantic allies.

Conclusion

Anglo–Cuban relations had come full circle with the Leyland buses deal. The 1963–64 controversy was reminiscent of Britain's frustrated efforts to conclude a commercial treaty with Cuba in the early 1900s. In both cases, Lancashire-based mercantile interests pressured the British government to prioritize exports to Cuba at the expense of Anglo–American harmony. Given both the increased importance of the United States to British foreign policy, and the larger power disparity between the two allies, it is odd that the British government was less disposed to appease US concerns in the 1960s than at the start of the century.

The US Dimension to Anglo–Cuban Relations

During the trajectory of the 1898 to 1964 period, the gap in power between Britain and the United States grew increasingly wide. Contributing factors included the detrimental effects of two world wars, Britain's shrinking empire and the United States' rapid rise to displace Britain as the globe's pre-eminent economic and military power.

In the post-1898 period, Conservative and Liberal foreign secretaries prioritized harmony with Washington, or the avoidance of disharmony, despite the vociferous protestations of domestic mercantile interests. Even in 1933, the lowest ebb of Anglo–American relations during the whole period studied, the Foreign Office was most reluctant to antagonize F.D. Roosevelt's administration. The British repeatedly tested the mood in the State Department and found it unfavourable to recognition of Grau's radical government. Again, Britain was averse to taking the lead and adopting a policy in Cuba independent of its North American ally.

When we reach the insurrectional and revolutionary periods of 1958 and 1959, British eagerness to gain US acquiescence before selling arms in its traditional market is perfectly understandable, especially given the Anglo–American fallout over Suez just two years earlier. Although Macmillan appeared bellicose, the Foreign Office was reluctant to incur the wrath of Eisenhower's government by exchanging military hardware with Castro. However, the 1963 to 1964 Leyland case represented an apparent aberration. Britain anticipated an adverse reaction in Washington and did not attempt to gain acquiescence. Its policy went against US wishes, antagonizing its transatlantic ally despite the mutual Cold War security concerns of the period. Especially with regard to Britain's relative weakness and need for US support in various parts of the world, the case highlighted a departure from previous policy.

Did residual British resentment over past US actions influence the decision-making of Macmillan's Cabinet? The Foreign Office commissioned its Planning Staff to write a paper entitled 'An Anglo–American Balance Sheet' in 1964. It highlighted the transatlantic alliance as 'the most important single factor' in British foreign policy. Its conclusion was that 'bargaining' was not the way to operate the Anglo–American relationship. Britain was 'much the weaker partner' and while US support for its policies was 'virtually indispensable', British support for US policies was merely 'useful and sometimes valuable'. The paper also remarked that Britain would be 'ill-advised' to try and 'exert leverage on the Americans' and operate the relationship via a 'series of bargains'.[1] Or in other words, it would be futile trying to horse-trade a few old British nags for a stable full of US thoroughbreds. Lord Harlech in Washington disliked the idea of 'balancing concessions against each other'. As the British ambassador affirmed, this was because 'we need them more than they need us'. A 'truer picture' of their relationship would result from 'identifying where one *must* have the support of the other'.[2]

Guatemala in 1954 was a case in point. Foreign Secretary Anthony Eden had been loath to support the United States in the United Nations after the CIA-orchestrated overthrow of its government. Yet against Eden's better judgment, and in line with Prime Minister Churchill's wishes, the British reluctantly supported Washington in the United Nations.[3] Eisenhower had complained: 'The British expect us to give them a free ride and side with them in Cyprus and yet they won't even support us on Guatemala.' He vowed to 'give them a lesson' and show them that 'they have no right to stick their nose into matters which concern this hemisphere entirely'.[4] Britain and France subsequently abstained in an important UN Security Council vote on Guatemala.

In such a way, the Leyland buses aberration can be understood if British policy in Cuba, with regard to issues deemed important by the United States, is viewed in the form of a tacit bargain between London and Washington. However, it was not in the form of exchanged quid pro quos between the allies that British policy operated in Cuba. Instead, Anglo–American cooperation in Cuba represented a tradable value. Although Washington took a lead in formulating policy towards the island, given its geographical proximity and importance to the United States, British support – or restraint from opposing US policy or desires – was the price to pay for reciprocal US support (or lack of opposition) in spheres of the world deemed vital by Britain. From 1954 to 1963 there were a series of issues that strained this tacit Anglo–American under-standing, at least from Britain's point of view. Taking the examples of the Middle East and Latin America, vital spheres respectively of British and US influence, successive Conservative governments felt that their repeated support for Washington, and a lack of cooperation in return, had left them short-changed.

Prime Minister Anthony Eden's ill-judged invasion at Suez, not to mention the sudden end to his hitherto distinguished political career, can in this light be viewed as a failure to appreciate the true dynamics of the transatlantic alliance and the operation of the allies' tacit under-standing. Representing the weaker partner in the relationship, Eden had only presumed Eisenhower's acquiescence before launching a military invasion in Egypt, and felt betrayed when US opposition and not sup-port was forthcoming. The Suez Crisis left a lasting legacy of British resentment, especially among senior figures in the ruling Conservative party. These included Chancellor of the Exchequer Harold Macmillan, who became prime minister upon Eden's resignation in January 1957.

Following the Cuban Revolution, there was a lengthy list of cases where Britain supported, often reluctantly, US wishes in the island. These included, inter alia: the decision not to exchange military planes in November 1959; acceptance of a US aide-memoire on military equip-ment export restrictions in August 1960; diplomatic and intelligence reporting from its Havana embassy from January 1961; British territo-ries made available to invasion aircraft during the Bay of Pigs operation, and supportive voting in the United Nations following the April 1961 invasion; support during the Cuban Missile Crisis in October 1962.

The CIA invasion plan at the Bay of Pigs was modelled on its 1954 operation in Guatemala, but failed to replicate its success. As with its reluctant support six years earlier, the British government courted the wrath of Parliament and public opinion by engaging in devious

diplomacy at the United Nations in April 1961. All these efforts contributed to positive entries on Britain's 'balance sheet' of goodwill with
Washington. In return, the Eisenhower and Kennedy administrations
reciprocated by supporting (or not seriously opposing) British colonial
policy in such parts of the world as Cyprus, Southern Rhodesia and
Malaysia. In some cases US policy aims were aligned with those of
Britain anyway.[5]

However, on the issue of East–West trade, there was never real accord.
This partly responded to Britain's position as an insular nation, dependent on trade for its economic prosperity. As seen, the economic
departments of the British government machine resented and strenuously resisted US attempts to use CoCom restrictions as an instrument to
wage economic warfare against Cold War adversaries. Macmillan especially viewed US machinations with distrust. In the light of these views,
the Leyland sales could be seen as reciprocation for US lack of support, for example over Suez, and perceived betrayal over trade issues.
The fact that Macmillan's government as well as Conservative fortunes
generally were on a downward spiral lends to the Leyland decision the
air of a parting shot at perceived US transgressions. Forthcoming elections also concentrated minds. Any overt weakness towards Washington
risked domestic unpopularity and the greater likelihood of electoral
defeat. Credit-backing for the Leyland deal followed by defeat at the
ballot box, meanwhile, left the incoming government to deal with US
resentment.

Much in the same way as Eisenhower's reaction during the Suez Crisis,
the Leyland deal determined Britain's maximum tolerance. While the
British government respected mutual Cold War security concerns and
restricted sales of military hardware to Soviet satellites, it drew the line
at blocking sales of passenger vehicles to Cuba.

Cuba and the British Lion

The exceptional nature of US policy towards Cuba, particularly with
regard to trade and shipping, meant that British policymakers were
particularly wary of setting dangerous precedents. This took the form
of a reluctance to entertain draconian US measures, even in times of
emergency. One shining example of this occurred during the 1962 missile crisis, when British shipowners and government departments were
very wary of complying with Kennedy's naval quarantine restrictions
around the island. They worried that by taking such action they were
committing themselves to more than just a short-term national security

expedient. Thus, the British government was resistant, despite its apparent servility to US policy in Cuba, to accede to some of Washington's more outlandish plans. Donald Stokes's timely riposte about looking 'damn silly going to war in a bus' was exemplary, responding to the US notion that public transport vehicles constituted strategic goods. His assertion struck a raw nerve in Washington, but elicited a chord of sympathy from the British press.

Cuba's attitude to Britain in the light of these observations is also enlightening. After the Leyland deal was signed at the beginning of 1964, Castro immediately offered to negotiate compensation for the 1960 'intervention' of the Shell oil refinery. He found Shell's lukewarm response to the offer difficult to fathom, and was reportedly left 'puzzled and annoyed'.[6] He evidently discerned little difference between Shell's decisions and those of the British government, but the oil company actually acted of its own accord and found the offer 'embarrassing'. It had substantial interests in the United States and cooperated with US oil companies around the world.[7] Months later, to resolve a long-standing Anglo–Cuban disagreement predating the revolution, Castro's government finally offered compensation to a British sailor crippled in a bar shooting.[8] Such Cuban reactions indicate a misunderstanding of British motivation and the separation between business and government interests/decisions. They also demonstrate that Cuba, or at least its revolutionary government, saw fit to operate the Anglo–Cuban relationship through a direct exchange of quid pro quos.

In an earlier period, Britain sought to benefit its commercial interests by a congenial relationship with a 'collaborating elite' in Cuba, namely political and economic figures during the first years of the republic. The problem for Lionel Carden in the 1902 to 1906 period was that the elite prioritized collaboration with US financial, commercial and political interests.[9] In spite of efforts by errant senators like Manuel Sanguily, US–Cuban collaboration excluded the pretensions of Britain's first minister in Havana to formalize Anglo–Cuban commercial relations through a treaty.

In the late 1930s, British Ministers to Havana Tom Snow and Herbert Grant Watson targeted Cuba's 'productive classes' during a period when politicians held power fleetingly, with government administration paralysed by disputes. These economic collaborators were receptive to the British approach because they saw a duality of interests in securing their second best sugar market. Importantly but not decisively, Washington gave a green light to such cooperation with a commercial rival. In this way, collaborators did much of Britain's bidding for

Table 4   Anglo–Cuban trade, 1959–64*

	Cuban exports to Britain	British exports to Cuba
1959	$28.3 m	$43.1 m
1960	$21.8 m	$20.7 m
1961	$14.6 m	$12.9 m
1962	$19.6 m	$7.3 m
1963	$34.7 m	$6.2 m
1964	$25.5 m	$26.9 m
Total	$144.5 m	$117.1 m

*Source: Alistair Hennessy and George Lambie (eds), *The Fractured Blockade: West European–Cuban Relations during the Revolution* (London: Macmillan, 1993), p. 342. Statistics taken from Board of Trade figures.

it with the island's legislature, to the mutual satisfaction of both Cuban and British interests. And so a 'collaborating elite' in Cuba was able to secure an Anglo–Cuban treaty of commerce, three decades after Carden's frustrated efforts.

Fidel Castro was very keen in 1964 to pursue a closer relationship with Britain after its government had defied Washington's pressure and given credit backing to bus exports for his regime. The Foreign Office, however, was extremely wary of antagonizing the United States even further. Rather than a 'collaborating elite', Cuban leaders were revolutionary and communistic, and actively involved in continental subversion. They were the target of overt and underhand US efforts to undermine them, involving an economic blockade and sabotage respectively. The level of British exports to Cuba had grown in the first year of the revolution to outweigh Cuban exports to Britain for the first time since the First World War. British trade to Cuba entered the doldrums again from 1961, recovering in 1964 (see Table 4).

Perhaps the greatest manifestation of Castro's friendliness to Britain came during his visit to a British embassy reception in June 1964 to celebrate the Queen's birthday. There were elaborate security arrangements beforehand. Cuban security officials spoke to waiters and interviewed the embassy cook. After Castro's arrival (30 minutes early) the Cuban security chief insisted on filling his glass from newly opened bottles. The revolutionary commander indulged in British hospitality, starting the evening with whisky, followed by champagne and red wine. He led the toast to Her Majesty's health. In a more relaxed mood later he alternated between Cointreau and tea. Following a late dinner the revolutionary leader held forth on a sofa. He sat between the Soviet and British ambassadors, with reportedly more energy than either of them, departing the reception at 1.40 a.m.[10]

On the same day that Ambassador Adam Watson wrote to describe these proceedings to London, the head of the American department was adding his comments to a memorandum on 'Trade with Cuba'. He wrote about the paper:

> It confirms the view that we have always taken – namely, that the benefits to the United Kingdom of an improvement in relations with Cuba are infinitesimal in relation to the harm that Anglo–American relations are liable to suffer in the process.[11]

And in a reply to Watson two weeks later, following the ambassador's suggestion that Britain might meet Castro's friendly approaches halfway, Dick Slater advised against any 'gratuitous friendly gestures towards the Castro régime'. It was likely, he wrote, 'that any improvement in Anglo–Cuban relations would be at the expense of our relations with the United States – a price we are unwilling to pay'. First and foremost, Britain needed US support in other parts of the world.[12] Evidently, the Leyland deal had already debited Britain's chit of goodwill with the United States, and this arbiter of foreign policy was most wary of incurring any further debt.

British Free-riding

Of course, geographical remoteness and US preponderance gave British governments the luxury of deferring to Washington's policies and security provision in the region. In this regard, there was a certain element of Britain free-riding on the back of US actions, even more accentuated in the Caribbean than in the more distant parts of the Americas. Concrete examples of this occurred in the 1930s when officials in London deliberated over sending Royal Navy vessels for the protection of British interests in the island. On no occasion did the Admiralty receive instructions to mobilize ships to the island. British officials were most reluctant to become both directly involved and set a precedent for future entanglement in politically turbulent Cuba. It was preferable to leave responsibility for external shows of force to the United States, even if the timing of its interventions did not always concur with Foreign Office wishes.

Much like US policy in parts of the world dominated by the British, for example in the Middle East, London desired opportunity without responsibility. This attitude followed the previously mentioned precept of a tacit Anglo–American understanding. It also explains British complaints about being left to scramble for 'crumbs from the table' in Cuba. They could hardly expect to have first refusal on opportunities when the United States had invested so much, both materially and symbolically, in the development and stability of the island. While British officials might have criticized US policy and actions in Cuba, their country benefited from the island's impressive economic development following the 1898 intervention.

With the important exception of the trade blockade, and particularly the Leyland bus deal, British government policy in Cuba operated within the margins of US acquiescence throughout the period under study. Suggestions from various ministers and ambassadors in Havana to prioritize British interests against the wishes of the United States nearly always met with opposition from Foreign Office colleagues in both London and Washington, who underlined the overriding importance of Anglo–American harmony. On occasion, the British embassy in Washington proffered views on Cuban before being asked. Acting on information from counterparts in the State Department or on a rumour from London, these opinions nearly always trumped the hand of junior and marginalized colleagues in Havana or errant minds in London.[13]

Fear of US irritation or retribution often restricted Britain's freedom of action. In fact, Anglo–Cuban relations were not strictly bilateral from Britain's point of view, but were rather an adjunct of Anglo–American relations, the so-called 'special relationship'. When 'perfidious Albion' and the United States acted in concert against Cuba, they could appear as bullies. Fidel Castro saw reason to criticize such a 'pact of convenience' during Tony Blair's later government (1997–2007), denouncing an 'absolutely immoral' pact between the transatlantic allies that marginalizes Cuba's freedom of action in international affairs.[14]

At other times, Washington would have done well to listen to its ally's advice. British diplomats warned against rash attempts to unseat Castro's regime, but the Kennedy administration still went ahead with the ill-fated Bay of Pigs invasion in 1961. The British government's scepticism about the US trade blockade was also justified, viewing it as a retributive policy that was never likely to achieve its stated objective of defeating the Cuban Revolution. As they predicted, it would offer enduring propaganda value and a perfect distraction from the communist government's maladministration of the Cuban economy.

Caribbean Vacuum

Such overriding deference to US dominance in Cuba also extended less tangible benefits to Britain. Something remarkably absent during the period studied was a strong linkage between British policies in Cuba and the rest of the Caribbean islands, particularly colonies such as Jamaica (an ex-colony from 1962). Even following the 1959 revolution, and despite the movement for independence in its Caribbean possessions, there was remarkably little need for British preoccupation over revolutionary contagion.

The preservation of stability in the region, the first priority for both British and United States governments, was largely maintained in the British Commonwealth islands. But there were differences in Anglo and American approaches to the maintenance of such stability. Washington evidently took a more interventionist short-term view that was more tolerant of social injustice when it guaranteed stability.[15] However, the type of repressive right-wing regime tolerated and often supported by the United States in the Caribbean Basin in the 1950s and 1960s never developed in the British Caribbean. The British preserved their economic and strategic interests, albeit diminished ones, through a relatively peaceful and tension-free process of decolonization.[16] Britain was more pragmatic and tolerant of political pluralism in the region, and, unlike the United States, did not project communist-style subversion onto every local demand for radical change. Only in British Guiana did Britain modify its approach, and this was due to US demands.

Geographical insularity, their export of identical tropical produce, linguistic and cultural differences between the Hispanic, Francophone, Dutch and Anglophone Caribbean, as well as the lapse in time between their independence, all contributed to a remarkable lack of regional involvement between the different territories. Even the scope for trade competition in export markets between their tropical products was negated by their differing colonial heritage. Bananas from Anglophone Caribbean territories such as St Lucia and Dominica, for example, enjoyed preferential access to Britain and the Commonwealth. US multinational companies largely controlled and marketed produce from Latin America, including the Dominican Republic.[17] Cuba, meanwhile, soon found alternative export markets in the Soviet Bloc following the revolution and the US trade blockade.

Doomed Relations?

Viewed in another light, Britain's relations with Cuba were doomed to frustration. Its attempts to balance and satisfy competing commercial and political interests, both domestic and international, made the government appear indecisive and servile, and led to occasional embarrassment. When Britain was able to exploit economic opportunities, benefits were often short-lived and detrimental to other less tangible interests.

For example, after a short hiatus of four years without any large British capital investment in Cuba, the Shell oil refinery opened in 1957. Amid continuing economic prosperity, the timing seemed auspicious. Unfortunately, the $25m investment commenced operations during a period of armed insurrection. In the midst of this civil conflict, the British government could not resist an enticing cash order for planes and tanks to Batista in 1958, after the United States imposed its own arms embargo. While this opening in a traditional US market was rare, it was also risky, and the sudden demise of the general's dictatorship left diplomats looking ill informed. As Hankey later remarked, we 'burnt our fingers' selling arms to Batista.[18] Or as Foreign Secretary Selwyn Lloyd conceded, they had 'persevered' despite the risks and were 'mistaken' in their judgment.[19] Having supplied arms to Batista, it appeared inconsistent to refuse a simple exchange of military planes with Castro's revolutionary government. But Macmillan's government did indeed decline this lucrative offer, susceptible to Washington's pressure and negative reactions.

In the first years following the 1959 Revolution, practically all US economic interests abandoned the island or suffered expropriation. New export opportunities beckoned, despite Soviet Bloc intrusion. Unfortunately, inter-departmental differences and sensitivity to US reactions led the British government to deny export licences to many companies with offers, or dissuaded the companies themselves from pursuing new business. How galling that a US-imposed trade blockade and the closeness of Anglo–American relations should hinder Britain's prospects, just when the Cuban market seemed ripe for exploitation. Fate seemed destined to frustrate British opportunities in Cuba. To highlight this, only three years after its inauguration, Fidel Castro's new government 'intervened' the Anglo-Dutch Shell refinery when it acted in concert with US companies and refused to process Soviet oil. It had enjoyed precious little time to repay its original investment.

In 1963, the Cuban government presented Leyland with an opportunity to exploit its hard-won foothold in the island's transport market. After considerable deliberation, Macmillan's Cabinet came down on the side of extending official credit for this lucrative contract. Unfortunately, Washington reacted very negatively to this major breach of its economic blockade against Communist Cuba.

Heads Havana Wins: Tails Washington Loses

It would appear that Britain was destined to play handmaiden to US policy in Cuba within an international system that favours its most powerful protagonists. British servility to Washington's wishes contributed to Cuba's exposure to the policies of its powerful neighbour. From 1898 to 1958, US foreign policy was dominant and undiluted, unchallenged by the hegemony of any other nation.

But from 1959, Cuba was in control of its own destiny. As a small country, economically, politically and emotionally important to the United States, an arch-strategist like Fidel Castro was able to identify and exploit ambiguities in the close Anglo–American relationship and the allies' opposing interests and policies towards his revolution. He sought to engineer different reactions and split British and US policies. In this sense, some delicately balanced British decisions involving Cuba presented win-win situations for Castro. The Macmillan government's decisions over the arms exchange in 1959 and Leyland buses in 1963 are two cases in point. Castro's ambivalent treatment of the three foreign oil companies in 1960 is also illustrative.

A British Cabinet decision to exchange military planes with Castro's government would have demonstrated action independent of Washington. But instead, in a case that Castro immediately defined as a 'touchstone' of Britain's attitude to his revolution, Macmillan's government cowered to US pressure and offered weak excuses about Caribbean tensions. An affirmative Cabinet judgement to exchange the planes, meanwhile, would have driven a wedge between the policies of the transatlantic allies. Both outcomes had propaganda value for Castro.

As well as securing buses for Havana's dilapidated transport system, the Cabinet's credit backing for the Leyland deal demonstrated that Washington's main ally did not agree with an economic blockade of Cuba. This was also good propaganda. Despite US pressure, the British government openly disagreed with its principal Cold War ally. To most outside the United States the US blockade appeared vindictive, while

Britain's defence of a principle seemed reasonable. On the other hand, a Cabinet rejection of credit backing and a scuppered deal would have demonstrated weakness in the face of US pressure. The British public would have criticized its government's servility to the United States. And Washington would have appeared domineering, first formulating a retributive policy against its small island neighbour, and then pressuring its transatlantic ally to deny itself a desperately needed export deal. Cuba's original decision to open contract negotiations with Leyland won both ways.

In the case of foreign oil companies, Castro's government appeared to invite different reactions when he asked them to refine Soviet crude. It then treated the Anglo-Dutch Shell Company differently to the two US oil companies, despite their joint refusal. As seen, Shell acted independently of the British government, and thought in terms of its global position and other multinational oil companies. But the decision to 'intervene' the company was different to the expropriations suffered by Esso and Texaco. And when his government and Leyland signed the buses contract, the Cuban government offered to open compensation negotiations with Shell, something not offered to the US companies. He seemed determined to provoke different public responses from the two transatlantic allies. It is hardly a surprise that Cuba, a comparatively small and less powerful country, exploited such rare opportunities.

Two Events on the Thames

The dominance of the US–Cuban nexus, whether operating through formal diplomatic ties or not, severely circumscribed Anglo–Cuban relations from 1898. Britain prioritized the Anglo–American relationship, perceived as vital to its economic and international outlook. In such a way, Britain was destined to play handmaiden to US policy in Cuba.

The historical narrative presented here ends with the sinking of an East German cargo vessel on the River Thames in October 1964. Winston Churchill died three months later, and his nation honoured him with a state funeral. Even at an advanced age, he had reminisced to Macmillan about the Cuban rebel bullets that whistled over the tent he shared with his Spanish army hosts in 1895.[20] When a launch sailed Churchill's coffin down the Thames in January 1965, Port of London cranes lowered in salute to the twentieth-century statesman. The port had started the century as the biggest and busiest in the world, importing goods from all points of Britain's extensive empire and beyond. But by the 1960s, it was already in steep decline.

In terms of trade, their primary bilateral interest, Cuba had much more reason to be content than Britain. During the period from 1898 to 1964, the Caribbean island exported far more to Britain than it imported in return.[21] But Britain achieved its main objective in Cuba. With the exception of its refusal to join Washington's trade blockade, and the Leyland deal especially, it avoided upsetting the United States.

Notes

Introduction

1. 'The Cuban Insurrection: A Sombre Outlook: Fifth and Concluding Letter: By Our Own Correspondent, Tampa Bay [USA], December 14th 1895', *Daily Graphic*, 13 Jan. 1896, p. 4. Sources refer to both the English and the British occupation of Havana. While the first Act of Union had joined Scotland with England to form Great Britain in 1707, the second Act of Union in 1801 established the United Kingdom of Great Britain and Ireland. This book employs the more succinct terms Britain, British and Anglo (–Cuban and –American) to refer to interests represented by the government in London. The terms UK and the United Kingdom (of Great Britain and Northern Ireland) are used here only where they appear in official documents.
2. Martí (Guantánamo, Cuba) to Secretary of the Foreign Office (London), 27 April 1895, the National Archives of the United Kingdom (henceforth TNA): Public Record Office, London (henceforth PRO) Foreign Office papers (henceforth FO) 72/2102.
3. Stephen McGinty, *Churchill's Cigar* (London: Macmillan, 2007), pp. 133–41.
4. Martin Gilbert, *Churchill: A Life* (London: Pimlico, 2000), pp. 864–6.
5. 'Churchill and the birth of the special relationship', www.bbc.co.uk/news, 9 March 2012.
6. Graham Greene, *Our Man in Havana* (London: Heinemann, 1958).
7. *Our Man in Havana*, directed by Carol Reed, screenplay by Graham Greene (Columbia Pictures, 1959).
8. Haggard to Seymour, 5 Oct. 1921, TNA FO371/5564 A8102.
9. 'Mr Chamberlain on Cuba: The Tax on Havana Cigars', *The Times*, 4 Nov. 1921, p. 9.
10. Haggard to Curzon enclosing 'Report to His Government by General Mario Menocal, Cuban Ambassador to London, November, 1921', no. 116, 30 Dec. 1922, TNA FO371/7212 A544.
11. Haggard to Curzon, no. 85, 3 Oct. 1921, TNA FO371/5564 fols 203–5.
12. Gainer to Curzon, no. 117, 20 Sep. 1923, TNA FO371/8449 A6137.
13. Broderick to Simon, no. 77, 'Cuba Annual Report, 1931', 11 May 1932, TNA FO371/15837 A3291 par. 3.
14. Oliver to Man, 18 Sep. 1956, TNA FO371/120120 AK1052/1.
15. Zara Steiner refers to its 'educational homogeneity' in *The Foreign Office and Foreign Policy, 1898–1914* (London: Cambridge University Press, 1969), p. 19. For example, of the 16 different men who headed the British diplomatic mission in Havana from 1902 to 1964, five were Old Etonians. Of the 12 ministers/ambassadors that had studied at university, 11 were Oxbridge graduates. See Table 1.
16. George Curzon (Viceroy of India) to Lord George Hamilton (Secretary of State for India), 11 April 1900, cited in Earl of Ronaldshay, *The Life of Lord*

Curzon: Being the Authorized Biography of George Nathaniel, Marquess Curzon of Kedleston: Vol. I (London: Ernest Benn, 1928), pp. 252–3.

17. Edward Du Cann, *Two Lives: The Political and Business Careers of Edward Du Cann* (Upton upon Severn: Images, 1995), p. 214.
18. Perhaps the most notable holder of this post was Donald Maclean (Nov. 1950–May 1951), who as one of the 'Cambridge spies' fled to the Soviet Union with Guy Burgess shortly after they were uncovered as KGB moles in 1951.
19. Broderick to Simon, no. 152, 20 Dec. 1932, TNA FO371/16573 A257.
20. Broderick to Crowe, 24 Aug. 1931, TNA FO371/15089 A5043.
21. Snow (Madrid) to Craigie, private, 15 March 1935; Craigie to Snow, private, 28 March 1935: TNA FO371/18679 A3095.
22. Grant Watson to Simon, 9 Jan. 1935, TNA FO371/18675 A835.
23. Fordham to Lloyd, 3 July 1959, TNA FO371/138897 AK10113/3. Reading his letter in London, Hildyard wrote on 6 August, 'A very good defence. We should cheer Mr Fordham up and restore his morale (if this is really needed) in due course.'
24. Ramiro Guerra, *Manual de Historia de Cuba: desde su descubrimiento hasta 1868* (La Habana: Editorial de Ciencias Sociales, 1973), pp. 82–5.
25. Albion was the Greek and Roman name for Britain, probably on account of its white cliffs (Latin: *albus* = white). The term '*la perfide Albion*' is attributed to the Marquis de Ximenès (1726–1817). J.A. Simpson and E.S.C. Weiner (eds), *The Oxford English Dictionary: Volume I, A–Bazouki* (Oxford: Clarendon Press, 1989), p. 297.
26. Root to Samuel L. Parish, 1 Dec. 1899, cited in Philip Caryl Jessup, *Elihu Root: Volume I, 1845–1909* (New York: Dodd, Mead & Co., 1938), p. 300.
27. Frank Schumacher, 'The American Way of Empire: National Tradition and Transatlantic Adaptation in America's Search for Imperial Identity, 1898–1910', *Bulletin of the German Historical Institute*, 31 (2002), pp. 35–50 (41–2).
28. Cited in Michael W. Doyle, *Empires* (Ithaca, NY and London: Cornell University Press, 1986), p. 217.
29. Ezard to Henderson, no. 70, 27 May 1931; minutes by Kelly and Vansittart, 15 and 18 June 1931, TNA FO371/15089 A3693.
30. Diary entry, 17 June 1960: Peter Catterall (ed.), *The Macmillan Diaries Vol. II: Prime Minister and After: 1957–1966* (London: Macmillan, 2011), p. 309.
31. Robert Freeman Smith, 'Latin America, the United States and the European Powers, 1830–1930', in *The Cambridge History of Latin America: Volume IV c. 1870 to 1930*, ed. Leslie Bethell (Cambridge: Cambridge University Press, 1986), pp. 83–119 (96).

1   Perfidious Albion? Britain and Cuba before 1898

1. Richard Gott, *Cuba: A New History* (New Haven, CT and London: Yale University Press, 2004), pp. 32–3.
2. J.R. Ward, 'The British West Indies in the Age of Abolition, 1748–1815', in *The Oxford History of the British Empire, Volume II: The Eighteenth Century*, ed. P.J. Marshall and Alaine Low (Oxford and New York: Oxford University Press, 1998), pp. 415–39 (415).

3. Gustavo Placer Cervera, *Inglaterra y La Habana: 1762* (La Habana: Editorial de Ciencias Sociales, 2007), pp. 141–71.
4. David Syrett (ed.), *The Siege and Capture of Havana 1762* (London: Navy Records Society, 1970), pp, xiii, xxiv–xxv.
5. Cumberland to Albermarle, 2 Oct. 1762, cited in Nelson Vance Russell, 'The Reaction in England and America to the Capture of Havana, 1762', *The Hispanic American Historical Review*, 9.3 (Aug. 1929), pp. 303–16.
6. Hugh Thomas, *Cuba, or the Pursuit of Freedom* (London: Eyre & Spottiswoode, 1971), p. 55.
7. Louis A. Pérez Jr, *Cuba: Between Reform and Revolution* (New York: Oxford University Press, 1988), pp. 57–8.
8. Dick Cluster and Rafael Hernández, *The History of Havana* (New York: Palgrave Macmillan, 2006), pp. 28, 34.
9. Adrian J. Pearce, *British Trade with Spanish America, 1763–1808* (Liverpool: Liverpool University Press, 2007), pp. 67–8, 80, 83.
10. Eduardo Galeano, *Open Veins of Latin America: Five Centuries of the Pillage of a Continent* (London: Serpent's Tail, 2009), p. 79 (first published in Spanish in 1973).
11. David R. Murray, *Odious Commerce: Britain, Spain, and the Abolition of the Cuban Slave Trade* (Cambridge: Cambridge University Press, 1980), pp. 72, 100.
12. Murray, *Odious Commerce*, pp. 134, 139–40. In his book, Turnbull described slavery and his plans to eradicate it. See David Turnbull, *Travels in the West: Cuba; with Notices of Porto Rico, and the Slave Trade* (London: Longman, 1840).
13. Robert L. Paquette, *Sugar Is Made with Blood: The Conspiracy of La Escalera and the Conflict between Empires over Slavery in Cuba* (Middletown, CN: Wesleyan University Press, 1988), pp. 139–40, 143–4.
14. Murray, *Odious Commerce*, p. 145.
15. Rodolfo Sarracino, *Inglaterra: sus dos caras en la lucha cubana por la abolición* (La Habana: Editorial Letras Cubanas, 1989), p. 134.
16. Murray, *Odious Commerce*, pp. 154–6.
17. Cirilo Villaverde, *Cecilia Valdés or El Angel Hill*, trans. Helen Lane (Oxford and New York: Oxford University Press, 2005), p. 177.
18. B.J.C. McKercher and S. Enjamio, ' "Brighter Futures, Better Times": Britain, the Empire, and Anglo-American Economic Competition in Cuba, 1898–1920', *Diplomacy & Statecraft*, 18.4 (2007), pp. 663–87 (665).
19. Colin Lewis, 'The Financing of Railway Development in Latin America, 1850–1914', *Ibero-Amerikanisches Archiv*, 9 (1983), pp. 255–78 (257).
20. Oscar Zanetti and Alejandro García, *Sugar & Railroads: A Cuban History, 1837–1959* (Chapel Hill, NC and London: University of North Carolina Press, 1998), p. 25.
21. For development of the island's railways from 1853 to 1865, £1.5 m (1990 equivalent: approx. £50 m) was raised. Periods of depression and revival in the sugar industry later led to rationalization of the interdependent railway system. In 1889 several port and railway companies amalgamated to form the United Railways of the Havana and Regla Warehouses Company, with 457 kilometres of track. Richard Roberts, *Schroders: Merchants and Bankers* (Basingstoke: Macmillan Press, 1992), pp. 51, 54, 59–61, 101.

22. Leslie Bethell, 'Britain and Latin America in Historical Perspective', in *Britain and Latin America: A Changing Relationship*, ed. Victor Bulmer-Thomas (Cambridge: Cambridge University Press, 1989), pp. 1–24 (20).
23. P.J. Cain and A.G. Hopkins, *British Imperialism, 1688–2000* (Harlow: Longman, 2002), p. 671.
24. D.C.M. Platt, 'Economic Imperialism and the Businessman: Britain and Latin America before 1914', in *Studies in the Theory of Imperialism*, ed. Roger Owen and Bob Sutcliffe (Harlow: Longman, 1972), pp. 295–311 (299).
25. Tony Smith, *The Pattern of Imperialism: The United States, Great Britain and the Late-Industrializing World since 1815* (Cambridge: Cambridge University Press, 1981), p. 100.
26. Irving Stone, 'British Direct and Portfolio Investment in Latin America before 1914', *The Journal of Economic History*, 37.3 (Sept. 1977), pp. 690–722 (692).
27. Sheryllynne Haggerty, Anthony Webster and Nicholas J. White (eds), *The Empire in One City? Liverpool's Inconvenient Imperial Past* (Manchester: Manchester University Press, 2008).
28. The declaration followed a botched attempt by Prime Minister George Canning to enlist US support for a move against feared French ambitions in the continent. See R.A. Humphreys, *Tradition and Revolt in Latin America: And Other Essays* (London: Weidenfeld & Nicolson, 1969), pp. 146–8.
29. Palmerston to Clarendon, 30 Sept. 1857, cited in Humphreys, *Tradition and Revolt*, p. 182.
30. Canning (Wortley Hall) to Rufus King, 7 Aug. 1825, cited in C.K. Webster (ed.), *Britain and the Independence of Latin America, 1812–1830: Select Documents from the Foreign Office Archives, Volume II* (New York: Oregon Books, 1970), p. 521.
31. Louis A. Pérez Jr, *The War of 1898: The United States and Cuba in History and Historiography* (Chapel Hill, NC and London: University of North Carolina Press, 1998), p. 5.
32. Cited in Walter LaFeber, *The Cambridge History of American Foreign Relations: The American Search for Opportunity, 1865–1913, Vol. 2* (Cambridge: Cambridge University Press, 1993), p. 64.
33. Christopher J. Bartlett, 'British Reaction to the Cuban Insurrection of 1868–1878', *Hispanic American Historical Review*, 37.3 (Aug. 1957), pp. 296–312; Charles C. Jacobs, 'The Diplomatic History of the Cuban Ten Years' War, 1868–1878' (doctoral thesis, Birmingham University, 1973), pp. 431–2.
34. 'London, Tuesday, September 14, 1869', *The Times*, p. 6.
35. Richard H. Bradford, *The Virginius Affair* (Boulder: Colorado Associated University Press, 1980).
36. There were 53 executions, including 19 British and 15 US subjects, from a total of 52 crew and 103 passengers. Jacobs, 'The Diplomatic History', p. 317 n. 29, 327. Another British historian labels British policy in the war as 'cautious, neutral and legalistic'. See Joseph Smith, *Illusions of Conflict: Anglo-American Diplomacy toward Latin America, 1865–1896* (Pittsburgh: University of Pittsburgh Press; London: Feffer & Simons, 1979), p. 59.
37. Smith, *Illusions of Conflict*, pp. 122–3.
38. Foster (Madrid) to Gresham, 28 Sept. and 26 Oct. 1884, cited in David M. Pletcher, *The Awkward Years: American Foreign Relations under Garfield and Arthur* (Columbia: University of Missouri Press, 1962), pp. 296–7.

39. LaFeber, *The American Search for Opportunity*, p. 129.
40. Louis A. Peírez, Jr, *Cuba between Empires, 1878–1902* (Pittsburgh: University of Pittsburgh Press, 1983), pp. 31–5.
41. Dexter Perkins, *A History of the Monroe Doctrine* (London: Longmans, 1960), pp. 171–85.
42. Rory Miller, *Britain and Latin America in the Nineteenth and Twentieth Centuries* (London: Longman, 1993), p. 60.
43. D.C.M. Platt, *Finance, Trade, and Politics in British Foreign Policy 1815–1914* (Oxford, London: Clarendon Press, 1968), p. 347.
44. 'Queen's Speech Debates: Lord Rosebery Attacks the Policy of Salisbury's Government', *New York Times*, 12 Feb. 1896, p. 1; *Hansard Vol. 37, Parliamentary Debates – House of Commons*, 11 Feb. 1896, p. 52.
45. Cited in Lars Schoultz, *National Security and United States Policy toward Latin America* (Princeton; Guildford: Princeton University Press, 1987), p. 199.
46. Alfred Thayer Mahan, *The Interest of America in Sea Power: Present and Future* (London: Sampson Low, Marston & Co., 1897), p. 26.
47. Sebastian Balfour, 'Spain and the Great Powers in the Aftermath of the Disaster of 1898', in *Spain and the Great Powers in the Twentieth Century*, ed. Sebastian Balfour and Paul Preston (London and New York: Routledge, 1999), pp. 13–31.
48. David F. Trask, *The War with Spain in 1898* (New York; London: Macmillan, 1981), p. 15.
49. Charles S. Campbell Jr, *From Revolution to Rapprochement: The United States and Great Britain, 1783–1900* (New York: Wiley, 1974), p. 191.
50. The Queen Regent of Spain to Queen Victoria, May 1896; the Marquis of Salisbury to Queen Victoria, 25 May 1896: George Earl Buckle (ed.), *The Letters of Queen Victoria: Volume III, 1896–1901* (London: John Murray, 1932), pp. 44–5.
51. White to Olney, 17 June 1896, cited in R.G. Neale, *Britain and American Imperialism, 1898–1900* (Brisbane: University of Queensland Press, 1965), p. 118.
52. Sylvia L. Hilton and Steve J.S. Ickringill (eds), 'Introduction', in *European Perceptions of the Spanish–American War of 1898* (Berne: Peter Lang, 1999), p. 22.
53. Winston S. Churchill, *My Early Life: A Roving Commission* (London: Thornton Butterworth, 1930), pp. 88–90; Ted Morgan, *Churchill 1874–1915* (London: Cape, 1983), p. 74.
54. Churchill, *My Early Life*, p. 91. Churchill's remark reminds us both of Sir John Seeley's 1883 observation that the British had obtained a far-flung empire in 'a fit of absence of mind', and that it did not always suit imperialists to acquire territory.
55. 'The Insurrection in Cuba: Letters from the Front – II: From Our Own Correspondent, Sancti Spiritus, November 23rd', *Daily Graphic*, 17 Dec. 1895, p. 5.
56. Churchill, *My Early Life*, pp. 94–6. He commented that the Latins were wiser and closer to nature in their way of living than the Anglo-Saxons. At the Admiralty during the First World War, Churchill added nearly two hours to his working day by taking an hour-long siesta after lunch.

57. David Stafford, *Churchill and Secret Service* (London: John Murray, 1997), pp. 10–11.
58. 'The Insurrection in Cuba: Letters from the Front – III: From Our Own Correspondent, Arroyo, November 27th', *Daily Graphic*, 24 Dec. 1895, p. 4.
59. Balfour, 'Spain and the Great Powers', p. 14.
60. Wolff was appointed to Madrid in 1892, spending nearly nine years in Spain.
61. See Neale, *Britain and American Imperialism*, pp. 8–12.
62. Balfour to Wolff, 2 March 1896, cited in Neale, *Britain and American Imperialism*, p. 6. First Lord of the Treasury Arthur James Balfour deputized for Salisbury at the Foreign Office on the frequent occasions when the prime minister was ill. Salisbury directed foreign policy during a period when no foreign secretary was appointed.
63. 'Editor's note', Frederick W. Ramsden, 'Diary of the British Consul at Santiago during Hostilities', *McClure's Magazine*, 11, May–Oct. 1898 (New York and London, 1898), pp. 580–90 (580 n.). Ramsden was therefore a witness to the whole insurrectional period from the Ten Years' War until his death in 1898. His son Henry was British consul at Manila during the Spanish–American War. After Spain's defeat the Philippine archipelago transferred to US control.
64. Ramsden (Santiago de Cuba) to Salisbury, 14 July 1897, TNA FO72/2056.
65. Wolff to Salisbury, 17 Oct. 1897, TNA FO414/152.
66. Wolff to Salisbury, 17 Oct. 1897.
67. Pérez, *Cuba between Empires*, p. 150.
68. Mahan, *The Interest of America in Sea Power*, pp. 288–313.
69. *Daily Chronicle*, 17 Feb. 1898, cited in Charles S. Campbell Jr, *Anglo-American Understanding, 1898–1903* (Baltimore, MD: Johns Hopkins Press, 1957), p. 28.
70. Barclay to Salisbury, 17 March 1898, TNA FO72/2062.
71. Published 31 March and 2 April 1898. All cited in John L. Offner, *An Unwanted War: The Diplomacy of the United States and Spain over Cuba, 1895–1898* (Chapel Hill: University of North Carolina Press, 1992), pp. 156–7.
72. Offner, *An Unwanted War*, p. 176.
73. Campbell, *Anglo-American Understanding*, pp. 30–6.
74. Neale, *Britain and American Imperialism*, pp. 828–9.
75. Piero Gleijeses, '1898: The Opposition to the Spanish–American War', *Journal of Latin American Studies*, 35.4 (Nov. 2003), pp. 681–719 (694).
76. Thomas G. Paterson, J. Garry Clifford, Kenneth J. Hagan, *American Foreign Relations Vol. 2. A History: Since 1895* (Boston, MA: Houghton Mifflin, 2000), p. 17.
77. Cited in Gleijeses, '1898', pp. 694–5. Figures compiled by the Intelligence Division, British War Office (n. 34).
78. Joseph Smith, *The Spanish–American War: Conflict in the Caribbean and the Pacific, 1895–1902* (London: Longman, 1995), pp. 146–50.
79. Gleijeses, '1898', p. 714.
80. Bertha Ann Reuter, *Anglo–American Relations during the Spanish–American War* (New York, 1924), pp. 95–6, 99–100; Richmond Pearson Hobson, *The Sinking of the 'Merrimac': A Personal Narrative of the Adventure in the Harbor of Santiago de Cuba, June 3, 1898*…(London and New York: T.F. Unwin, 1899), pp. 156–9, 226–7, 251, 255–9. On the shifting political allegiances of the planters, see Pérez, *Cuba between Empires*, pp. 34, 118–19, 122, 137.

81. Entries of 3/5/6 July 1898: Frederick W. Ramsden, 'Diary of the British Consul at Santiago during Hostilities', *McClure's Magazine*, 12, Nov. 1898–April 1899 (New York and London, 1899), pp. 62–70.
82. 'Report on the Santiago Campaign, by Captain A.H. Lee, R.A.', *Reports by the Military Attachés with the Spanish and United States Forces in Cuba and Porto Rico* (London: War Office, 1899), p. 76: TNA FO881/7454X.
83. V.W. Baddeley, 'Lee, Arthur Hamilton, Viscount Lee of Fareham (1868–1947)', rev. Marc Brodie, *Oxford Dictionary of National Biography* (Oxford: Oxford University Press, 2004). Lee became military attaché to the British embassy in Washington in 1899. He bequeathed his Chequers mansion and Buckinghamshire estate to Britain in 1917 for use as the prime minister's weekend residence.
84. J.B.A., 'The Landing of Troops and the First Fighting in Santiago' (Siboney, 26 June 1898), *Manchester Guardian*, 25 July 1898, p. 7; idem, 'American Administration in the War: A Word for the Cuban Insurgents' (Tampa, 13 Aug. 1898), *Manchester Guardian*, 25 Aug. 1898, p. 5.
85. Gilbert, *Churchill: A Life*, pp. 107–21.
86. Thomas Pakenham, *The Boer War* (London: Weidenfeld & Nicolson, 1997), pp. 472–3, 493–5.
87. Zanetti and García, *Sugar & Railroads*, p. 235; Roberts, *Schroders*, pp. 135–6.
88. Joseph Smith, *The Spanish–American War*, pp. 160–1.
89. *London Standard* and *London Chronicle*, 7 Dec. 1898, cited in David F. Healy, *The United States in Cuba, 1898–1902: Generals, Politicians, and the Search for Policy* (Madison: University of Wisconsin Press, 1963), p. 51.
90. 'The President's Message', *Daily News*, 6 Dec. 1898, p. 4.
91. See Campbell, *Anglo-American Understanding*, pp. 12–21. On the specific case of China, see Charles S. Campbell Jr, *Special Business Interests and the Open Door Policy* (New Haven, CT: Yale University Press, 1951). In late 1899, US Secretary of State John Hay sent notes to Britain, Germany and Russia and similar messages to France, Japan and Italy. His formal 'open door' statement advocated free trade in China to those powers with established spheres of influence. Michael Graham Fry, Erik Goldstein and Richard Langhorne (eds), *Guide to International Relations and Diplomacy* (London and New York: Continuum, 2002), pp. 401–3.
92. 'Imperialist Policy in the United States', *The Times*, 10 Dec. 1898, p. 11.
93. Balfour, 'Spain and the Great Powers', p. 13.

2   Uncle Sam versus the British Lion

1. Jules R. Benjamin, *The United States and the Origins of the Cuban Revolution: An Empire of Liberty in an Age of National Liberation* (Princeton, NJ: Princeton University Press, 1990), pp. 5, 67.
2. Jerome to Salisbury, political no. 1, 3 Jan. 1899, TNA FO5/2401.
3. Jerome to Salisbury, political no. 5, 20 Feb. 1899, TNA FO5/2401.
4. 'Our New Consul-General in Havana', *Pall Mall Gazette*, 17 Dec. 1898, p. 8.
5. Jerome to Salisbury, political no. 11, 20 Dec. 1899, TNA FO5/2401.
6. Carden to Newman, personal, 27 March 1900, TNA FO5/2437.
7. Carden to Cockerall, personal, 27 Feb. 1900, TNA FO5/2437.

8. Carden to Salisbury, political no. 3, 24 March 1900, TNA FO5/2436.
9. 'Memorandum' enclosure, Carden to Salisbury, no. 8 Commercial, 9 Oct. 1900, TNA FO5/2437.
10. 'Memorandum' enclosure, Carden to Salisbury, commercial no. 8, 9 Oct. 1900, TNA FO5/2437.
11. Louis A. Pérez Jr, *Cuba under the Platt Amendment, 1902–1934* (Pittsburgh: University of Pittsburgh Press, 1986), p. 46.
12. Root to Hay, 11 Jan. 1901, cited in Healy, *The United States in Cuba*, p. 154. Pérez writes (*Cuba under the Platt Amendment*, p. 49), 'Wood predicted [in February 1901], with Cuba bound to the United States by formal ties, Washington could end the military government and reduce the North American military presence to several regiments. "What is wanted," he wrote, echoing Root's analogy with Egypt, "is the moral force to hold these people up to their work until the decent element assumes its normal position in the government of the island." '
13. Pérez, *Cuba between Empires*, pp. 326–7.
14. Carden to Lansdowne, commercial no. 2, 16 Jan. 1901; minutes by Sanderson (7 Feb. 1901) and Lansdowne (n.d.); Bergne to Carden, 7 Feb. 1901: TNA FO108/9.
15. Carden to Lansdowne, commercial no. 4, 23 March 1901, TNA FO5/2466.
16. Carden to Lansdowne, political no. 4, 24 April 1901, TNA FO5/2465.
17. Pauncefote to Lansdowne, commercial no. 35, 1 April 1901, TNA FO108/9.
18. Hermann Schürhoff to W.F. Haydon, 20 April 1901, Birmingham Libraries and Archives, Birmingham Chamber of Commerce and Industry, MS 2299 (2000/127) Box 8, Council Minute Book Vol. 1901–3, f 4.
19. Correlli Barnett, *The Collapse of British Power* (London: Eyre Methuen, 1972), p. 255.
20. In October 1902, Lord Selborne told the British Cabinet that the German navy was 'carefully being built up from the point of view of war with us'. Cited in Steiner, *The Foreign Office and Foreign Policy*, p. 54.
21. Campbell, *Anglo-American Understanding*, p. 238; Steiner, *The Foreign Office and Foreign Policy*, p. 47.
22. Carden (12 Burlington St W., London) to Villiers, personal, 10 Aug. 1901, enclosing Memorandum 'Commercial Relations with Cuba'; minutes by Cranborne and Lansdowne (n.d.); Cranborne to Carden (draft: commercial separate), 17 Aug. 1901: TNA FO108/9. Foreign Secretary Lord Lansdowne's red pen added the words 'unofficially and' to Cranborne's instructions to Carden.
23. Carden (Torquay) to Villiers, personal, 29 Aug. 1901, TNA FO108/9.
24. 'Memorandum' (anon.), 21 Oct. 1901, TNA FO108/2. 'Most-favoured nation' clause: the clause in an international trade treaty under which the signatories promise to extend to each other any favourable trading terms offered in agreements with third parties. See Graham Bannock, R.E. Baxter and Evan Davis, *The Penguin Dictionary of Economics*, 5th edn (London: Penguin, 1992), p. 295.
25. Carden to Lansdowne, commercial no. 16, 18 Dec. 1901, TNA FO108/9.
26. Board of Customs Report (forwarded to Foreign Office by Treasury) by T.J.P, 16 January 1902, TNA FO108/9.
27. Carden to Villiers, personal, confidential, 15 Jan. 1902, TNA FO108/9.

28. Minutes by Bergne, 4 Feb. 1902, Cranborne, 10 Feb. 1902, Lansdowne, n.d., TNA FO108/9.
29. Carden to Lansdowne, commercial no. 5, 13 Feb. 1902; Carden to Bergne, personal, 13 Feb. 1902: TNA FO108/9.
30. Leland Hamilton Jenks, *Our Cuban Colony: A Study in Sugar* (New York: Vanguard Press, 1928), pp. 135–6; Healy, *The United States in Cuba*, pp. 203–4.
31. Liverpool Record Office, Liverpool Chamber of Commerce (henceforward LRO), 380 COM 2/9/6, General Purposes Committee, Minute Book Feb. 1902–July 1903: meeting 25 Feb. 1902 on 'British Trade with Cuba', with annexed resolution by Mr J.E. Hawkes.
32. 'British Trade with Cuba: Important Conference', *Journal of Commerce* (Liverpool), 26 Feb. 1902, p. 5.
33. A summary of the Liverpool meeting's conclusions appeared in the press: 'British Trade with Cuba', *The Times*, 27 Feb. 1902, p. 12.
34. Reply to Liverpool Chamber of Commerce on behalf of Lansdowne, 26 Feb. 1902, TNA FO108/9 f 106.
35. Memorandum 'British Trade in Cuba and the United States' Reciprocity Treaty', Feb. 1903, TNA FO108/4. The following chambers were represented: Liverpool, London, Manchester, Birmingham, Wolverhampton, Bury, Bradford, Glasgow and Belfast.
36. Carden also suggested a Royal Navy presence at the inauguration. Carden to Villiers, personal, 2 April 1902, TNA FO5/2496.
37. FO telegram to Carden, 9 May 1902, TNA FO108/9 f 226.
38. FO telegrams to Carden, 10/13/17 May 1902, TNA FO5/2496.
39. Carden to Lansdowne, commercial no. 24, 14 Aug. 1902, TNA FO108/9.
40. Carden to Lansdowne, commercial no. 27a, 29 Sept. 1902, TNA FO108/9.
41. FO to Carden, commercial no. 11, 8 Oct. 1902, TNA FO108/9.
42. Carden to Lansdowne, commercial no. 30, 17 Oct. 1902, TNA FO108/9.
43. Lansdowne to Herbert, no. 192, 17 Oct. 1902, TNA FO5/2484 ff 222–3.
44. FO to Carden, T. no. 5, 20 Oct. 1902, TNA FO108/1.
45. Carden to Lansdowne, T. no. 10, 22 Oct. 1902, TNA FO108/1 f 164.
46. Lansdowne to Herbert, no. 201, 30 Oct. 1902, enclosing 'Copy of Memorandum reported to U.S. Government as having been left by British Minister at the [Presidential] Palace, Havana, October 9th, 1902'; Lansdowne to Herbert, no. 218, 19 Nov. 1902, TNA FO5/2484.
47. Kneer correctly describes the Foreign Office's position towards US–Cuban reciprocity as 'ambivalent'. He argues, 'Torn between the desire to placate the United States and the need to assuage commercial interests at home, their orders to Carden had been rather contradictory.' W.G. Kneer, *Great Britain and the Caribbean, 1901–1913* (East Lansing, MI: Michigan State University Press, 1975), p. 77.
48. 'The Trade of Cuba', *Economist*, 1 Nov. 1902, pp. 1680–1; 'Optimistic as to Cuba: British Minister Tells of Remarkable Progress in Island – People Energetic and Industrious', *New York Times*, 20 Dec. 1902, p. 1.
49. Raymond L. Buell et al., *Problems of the New Cuba: Report of the Commission on Cuban Affairs* (New York: Foreign Policy Association, 1935), p. 43.
50. Herbert to FO, commercial no. 15, 17 Dec. 1902; minutes by Law and Campbell (with addition by Lansdowne) (n.d.); FO to Herbert, commercial no. 13, 17 Dec. 1902: TNA FO108/9.

51. Hay (Washington) to Herbert, 20 Dec. 1902, TNA FO108/9 f 407. In reference to the US reply a 1917 Board of Trade memorandum described it as 'something very like a snub'. 'Commercial Treaties of the United Kingdom: Report to the President of the Board of Trade on the Treaty Arrangements of the United Kingdom' by Stanley, Sept. 1917, TNA BT274/24, p. 112.

52. One Liverpool representative suggested that the Foreign Office deal direct with Cuba through Carden, rather than through Washington. See LRO, Committee of the West India Section, minutes of meeting 5 Jan. 1902, 380 COM 3/10 ff 49–50.

53. George Monger, *The End of Isolation: British Foreign Policy 1900–1907* (London: Nelson, 1963), pp. 104–6.

54. 'America's Colonial Trade Policy: Shutting Out Other Nations: Action by the Liverpool Chamber of Commerce', *Liverpool Courier*, 17 Jan. 1903.

55. 'Memorandum: British Trade in Cuba and the United States' Reciprocity Treaty', 28 Feb. 1903, TNA FO108/10. The Chambers represented were: Liverpool, London, Manchester, Glasgow, Nottingham and Wolverhampton. Three MPs were also present.

56. Carden to Villiers, personal, 4 Sept. 1904, TNA FO108/11.

57. 'British Trade with Cuba', *Economist*, 17 Dec. 1904, p. 2051.

58. FO to Carden, T. commercial no. 2, 24 Jan. 1905; Carden to C.E. Ortiz, 31 Jan. 1905: TNA FO108/12. In April 1904 a member of the Liverpool Chamber of Commerce cited a letter received from Havana reporting the ambition of US rice mills in Louisiana, Texas, Georgia and South Carolina to capture the entire consumption of Cuba and Puerto Rico within four to five years. See LRO, Committee of the West India Section, minutes of meetings 29 April 1904, 380 COM 3/10 ff 97–8.

59. Kneer (*Great Britain and the Caribbean*, p. 84) describes this as a 'distinct defeat for American policy'.

60. Carden to Lansdowne, commercial no. 32, 12 July 1905, TNA FO108/12.

61. Carden (Torquay) to Lansdowne (commercial: separate), 23 Oct. 1905, TNA FO108/12. Puzzlingly, Carden referred to the 'absolute indifference' of those in England 'most directly interested' in trade with Cuba. The minister had met at least two representatives from the Liverpool Chamber of Commerce in Havana, and he could hardly have been unaware of their correspondence and deputations to London.

62. Minutes of 'Deputation arranged by Liverpool Chamber of Commerce to Meet Marquess of Lansdowne, Foreign Office, Downing St, 9 November 1905', TNA FO108/12. Delegates represented Hartlepool, Clyde, Mersey and Thames-based interests.

63. Lansdowne to Durand, 13 Nov. 1905, TNA FO800/144 ff 445–6.

64. 'Diplomatic Appointments', *The Times*, 9 Dec. 1905, p. 11.

65. 'Minister Squiers Out; Morgan goes to Cuba: [...] Cubans did not like Squiers', *New York Times*, 30 Nov. 1905, p. 8.

66. Carden to Grey, T. commercial no. 1, 20 Jan. 1906; Carden to Grey, T. commercial no. 2, 15 Feb. 1906; Carden to Grey, T. commercial no. 3, 28 Feb. 1906; Carden to Grey, T. commercial no. 5, 24 April 1906: TNA FO368/13.

67. Carden to Grey, T. commercial no. 6, 15 May 1906. He wrote: 'No useful purpose served by my remaining further.'

68. Griffith to Grey, T. commercial no. 7, 24 May 1906; minute by Law, n.d.: TNA FO368/13.
69. *Diario de Sesiones del Congreso de la República de Cuba, Novena Legislatura,* Habana: Senado, XVIII Sesión – Mayo 30 de 1906 (1906, vol. 9), pp. 5–21.
70. For more detail on the Cuban Senate debate, see Jorge Renato Ibarra Guitart, *El Tratado Anglo–Cubano de 1905: Estados Unidos Contra Europa* (La Habana: Editorial de Ciencias Sociales, 2006), pp. 245–59.
71. Minute by Grey, n.d., TNA FO368/13 f 447. Law added (n.d.) f 448: 'Our action on this occasion will be watched with interest and instruction wherever the Spanish language is spoken on the American Continent. We shall be setting an important precedent one way or the other.'
72. Alfred L. Jones (Liverpool) to Grey, 20 June 1906; minute by Law, n.d.: TNA FO368/13.
73. Memorandum 'The Cuban Treaty' by de Salis, 23 June 1906, TNA FO368/13 21335.
74. Memorandum 'Ratification of Commercial Treaty with Cuba: Notes taken at interview between Sir Edward Grey, with whom were Sir Eldon Gorst and Mr. Algernon Law, and a Deputation introduced by Mr. Austin Taylor, M.P.', 21 June 1906, TNA FO368/13.
75. Lance E. Davis and Robert A. Huttenback (eds), *Mammon and the Pursuit of Empire: The Political Economy of British Imperialism, 1860–1912* (Cambridge: Cambridge University Press, 1986), pp. 225–6.
76. Sir John Tilley and Stephen Gaselee, *The Foreign Office* (London: G.P. Putnam's Sons, 1933), pp. 248–9.
77. Roosevelt to George Otto Trevelyan, private, 9 Sept. 1906. Cited in *The Letters of Theodore Roosevelt: Volume 5, The Big Stick, 1905–1907*, ed. by Elting E. Morison (Cambridge, MA: Harvard University Press, 1951), p. 401.
78. Luis E. Aguilar, *Cuba 1933: Prologue to Revolution* (Ithaca, NY and London: Cornell University Press, 1972), pp. 27–9.
79. 'Chamber of Commerce: Trade with Cuba', *Manchester Guardian*, 11 Oct. 1906, p. 3.
80. Grant-Duff to Grey, no. 5, 'Cuba Annual Report, 1907', 15 Feb. 1908, TNA FO881/9253, pp. 36–7.
81. Numerous written and pictorial examples of US attitudes are found in Louis A. Pérez Jr, *Cuba in the American Imagination: Metaphor and the Imperial Ethos* (Chapel Hill, NC: University of North Carolina Press, 2008).
82. Sydney Brooks, 'Cuba and the Cuban Question', *North American Review* 653 (July, 1912), pp. 52–62; Leech to Grey, no. 6a, 'Cuba Annual Report, 1909', 26 Jan. 1910, TNA FO881/9645, pp. 2, 5.
83. McKercher and Enjamio, 'Brighter Futures, Better Times', p. 663.
84. FO 'Cuba Annual Report, 1909', pp. 9–10.
85. John M. Kirk and Peter McKenna, *Canada–Cuba Relations: The Other Good Neighbor Policy* (Gainesville: University Press of Florida, 1997), p. 14.
86. Leech to Grey, no. 8, 'Cuba Annual Report, 1910', 11 March 1911, TNA FO881/9847, p. 2.
87. Leech to Grey, no. 17, 'Cuba Annual Report, 1911', 13 March 1912, TNA FO881/10029, p. 2; Cowan to Grey, no. 4, 'Annual Report, 1913', 26 March 1914, TNA FO881/10433, par. 1.

88. 'The American Minister [Jackson] to the Secretary of State', Havana, 16 Aug. 1911, *Papers Relating to the Foreign Relations of the United States ... 1911* (henceforth FRUS and year) (Washington, DC: US Govt Printing Office, 1918), p. 131.

89. 'Personal letter from the Cuban Secretary of State to the American Minister', Havana, 9 Feb. 1912, *FRUS: 1912* (Washington, DC: US Govt Printing Office, 1919), pp. 278–81.

90. Leech to Louis Mallet, 8 June 1913, TNA FO371/1632 28333; Leech to Spicer, 21 Aug. 1913, TNA FO371/1632 38606.

91. Leech to Spicer, private, 21 Aug. 1913, TNA FO371/1632 38606; Haggard to Curzon, no. 113, 17 Aug. 1922, TNA FO371/7213 A5656.

92. Leech to Grey, no. 17, 'Cuba Annual Report, 1911', 13 March 1912, TNA FO881/10029, p. 6.

93. Jenks, *Our Cuban Colony*, p. 119.

94. FO 'Cuba Annual Report, 1913', par. 13.

95. FO 'Cuba Annual Report, 1910', p. 5; FO 'Cuba Annual Report, 1911', pp. 5–6; 'The Secretary of State to the American Minister', Washington, 8 Feb. 1913, *FRUS: 1913* (Washington, DC: US Govt Printing Office, 1920), p. 393; 'The Secretary of State to the British Minister', Washington, 25 Feb. 1913, *FRUS: 1913*, p. 400; FO 'Cuba Annual Report, 1913', par. 7. On President Gómez and the Villanueva/Arsenal land controversy, see Charles E. Chapman, *A History of the Cuban Republic: A Study in Hispanic American Politics* (New York: The Macmillan Co., 1927), pp. 290–2.

96. 'Cuban Railways', *Economist*, 2 Nov. 1901, p. 1614.

97. On 1 January 1906, United secured complete ownership of the Cárdenas and Jucaro Railway Company. It absorbed the Matanzas Railway on 1 July 1906. In March 1907, United acquired a controlling interest in the Havana Central, a US corporation: 'The United Railways of the Havana and Regla Warehouses, Limited', *Economist*, 3 Feb. 1906, p. 174; 'Company Meetings, &c.: United Railways of the Havana and Regla Warehouses, Limited', *Economist*, 25 Nov. 1911, p. 1112.

98. Roberts, *Schroders*, p. 136.

99. Considered in the past a US enterprise, recent research affirms that the Cuban Railroad was a Canadian corporation, with ownership divided between US, British and Canadian investors. See McKercher and Enjamio, 'Brighter Futures, Better Times', p. 671. Detail on the development of British-controlled railways in Cuba is found in Zanetti and Garciía, *Sugar & Railroads*, ch. 12, 'British Monopoly in the West', pp. 235–55.

100. Michael Cobiellas, 'British Economic Presence in Havana, 1900–1930', *International Journal of Cuban Studies*, 2.1 (June 2009), pp. 46–53 (49–51).

101. 'Report on the Trade and Commerce of the Island of Cuba for the Year ended June 30, 1913', by Vice-Consul Denys Cowan, no. 176, *British Documents on Foreign Affairs: Reports and Papers from the Foreign Office Confidential Print Vol. 2: Central America and Mexico, 1914–1922* (henceforth *Confidential Print* with volume number, region/title and year range), p. 176.

102. Oscar Pino Santos cites 1913–14 foreign investment by Great Britain and the United States in Cuba as \$216 m and \$215 m respectively: *El asalto a*

Cuba por la oligarquía financiera yanquí (La Habana: Casa de las Ameíricas, 1973), p. 37; Leech had earlier quoted what he admitted to be uncertain figures of £44 m for US and £30 m for British investments: FO 'Cuba Annual Report, 1911', p. 8; Bill Albert uses a variety of sources, including Fred Rippy and Irving Stone, to produce the admittedly 'not very reliable' figures of accumulated 1913 investment in Cuba at £48 m for the UK and £45 m for the US: *South America and the World Economy from Independence to 1930* (London: Macmillan, 1983), p. 34; Irving Stone arrived at the figure of £45.9 m for British investment in Cuba in 1913, consisting of £21.7 m in direct investment and £24.2 m in portfolio investment (£10 m in government loans, and £14.2 m in corporate securities): 'British Direct and Portfolio Investment', p. 706.

103. David Healy, *Drive to Hegemony: The United States in the Caribbean 1898–1917* (Madison, WI: University of Wisconsin Press, 1988), p. 260.
104. Jenks, *Our Cuban Colony*, p. 339 n. 3.
105. McKercher and Enjamio, 'Brighter Futures, Better Times', pp. 681–2.
106. Samuel F. Wells Jr, 'British Strategic Withdrawal from the Western Hemisphere, 1904–1906', *Canadian Historical Journal*, 49 (1968), pp. 335–56; D.C. Watt, 'American Strategic Interests and Anxieties in the West Indies', *Journal of the Royal United Service Institution*, 108 (1963), pp. 224–32. Troops withdrew from garrisons at Barbados, Trinidad and St Lucia. Naval bases at Jamaica and St Lucia closed, and Bermuda became the main station for the West Indian squadron.
107. Peter Calvert, 'Great Britain and the New World, 1905–1914', in *British Foreign Policy under Sir Edward Grey*, ed. F.H. Hinsley (Cambridge: Cambridge University Press, 1977), pp. 382–94 (394).

3   The First World War to Boom and Bust

1. Cowan to Grey, no. 20, 11 Sept. 1914, TNA FO371/1961 52868.
2. Avner Offer, *The First World War: An Agrarian Interpretation* (Oxford: Clarendon Press, 1989), p. 168.
3. Bill Albert, *South America and the First World War* (Cambridge: Cambridge University Press, 1988), p. 106; 'Second Report of the Royal Commission on the Sugar Supply, 1921', *Parliamentary Papers* cmd. 1300 (London: HMSO, 1921), p. 4.
4. 'Second Report of the Royal Commission on the Sugar Supply, 1921', pp. 4–5; William H. Beveridge, *British Food Control* (London: Oxford University Press, 1928), pp. 123–4, 134.
5. Gonzales to Secretary of State, 25 Feb. 1917, *FRUS: 1917* (Washington, DC: US Govt Printing Office, 1926), p. 366.
6. Leech to Grey, no. 10, 3 July 1916, TNA FO371/2661 143244.
7. Leech to Balfour, no. 10, 10 March 1918, TNA FO371/3193 58603.
8. *British Diplomatic and Commercial Mission to South America, 1918: Report by Follett Holt* (London: HMSO, May 1919).
9. Haggard to Curzon, no. 82, 26 Sept. 1921, enclosing 'Notes on Principal Features of Cuban Reception of the Maurice de Bunsen Mission', TNA FO371/5563 A7620.

10. Leech to Balfour, no. 71, 9 Sept. 1918, TNA FO371/3195 168894; Leech to Balfour, no. 81, 22 Oct. 1918, TNA FO371/3195 191619.
11. Cowan to Balfour, 13 Dec. 1918, TNA FO371/3705 223; FO to Barclay (Counsellor, Washington), T. no. 61, 7 Jan. 1919, TNA FO371/3705 1431.
12. Commodore Sinclair (Intelligence Dept.) to Tilley, 11 April 1919; Palmer (Admiralty) to Seymour, 24 April 1919; minute by Curzon, n.d.: TNA FO371/3705 9141.
13. Cowan to Leech, 24 March 1919, TNA FO371/3705 59126; Cowan to Curzon, 25 March 1919, TNA FO371/3705 58589.
14. Arnold-Foster (Assistant Naval Attaché in Cuba) 'Memorandum on the Political Situation in Cuba and its effect on British Interests', ('late') 1918; minute by Tilley, 17 Feb. 1919: TNA FO371/3705 23500.
15. 'Second Report of the Royal Commission on the Sugar Supply, 1921', p. 5; Victor Bulmer-Thomas, *The Economic History of Latin America since Independence* (Cambridge: Cambridge University Press, 2003), p. 159; Beveridge, *British Food Control*, p. 298.
16. 'Department of Overseas Trade: Report on the Economic Conditions in Cuba', September 1923, by St Clair Gainer (acting consul general, Havana) (London: HMSO, 1923), pp. 6, 12–13, 16, 23.
17. 'Department of Overseas Trade: Report on the Economic Conditions in Cuba', November 1925, by Kelham (Acting British Consul General, Havana) (London: HMSO, 1925), p. 6.
18. On the operation and criteria for inclusion on the wartime 'Black List', see Tilley and Gaselee, *The Foreign Office*, pp. 187–9.
19. Erskine to Curzon, no. 18, 'Cuba Annual Report, 1920', 11 Feb. 1921, TNA FO371/5565 A2178; minute by de Salis, 23 June 1920, TNA FO371/4464 A3902.
20. Erskine to FO, no. 78, 6 July 1920, TNA FO371/4464 A4619.
21. Erskine to Curzon, no. 55, 17 July 1920, TNA FO371/4462 A5348; reading a letter from Cuba's legation in London an official commented that the Cubans were 'deeply wounded at HMG's tilt at their national & judicial institutions'. Minute by Bateman, 14 Aug. 1920, TNA FO371/4464 A5610.
22. Erskine to Curzon, no. 74, 27 Oct. 1920, TNA FO371/4464 A7893.
23. Russell H. Fitzgibbon, *Cuba and the United States, 1900–1935* (New York: Russell & Russell, 1964), p. 183. The Association represented the veterans of the nineteenth-century independence wars.
24. Haggard to Curzon, 7 June 1921, doc. no. 247, *Confidential Print Vol. 2: Central America and Mexico, 1914–1922*.
25. Gott, *Cuba: A New History*, p. 117.
26. Haggard to Curzon, no. 39, 2 May 1921, TNA FO371/5563 A3661.
27. Haggard to Sperling, 20 May 1921, TNA FO371/5563 A4209.
28. Stamfordham (King's Private Secretary, Balmoral Castle) to Tyrrell, 25 Sept. 1921, TNA FO371/5563 A7011; Stamfordham (Buckingham Palace) to Tyrrell, 13 Oct. 1921, TNA FO371/5563 A7511.
29. Tyrrell to Stamfordham, 27 Oct. 1921, TNA FO371/5563 A7620.
30. Lindsay to Curzon, 30 Jan. 1920, doc. no. 36, *Confidential Print Vol. 1: South America, 1914–1922*.
31. 'Report on the Legation and Consulate General at Havana, Cuba' by Victor Wellesley, 3 April 1920, TNA FO371/4463 A3392.

32. Minute by Montgomery, 12 April 1920, TNA FO371/4463 A3392.
33. 'Report' by Wellesley; minute by Akers Douglas, n.d., TNA FO371/4463 A3392.
34. Leech to Balfour, no. 63, 22 Oct. 1917, TNA FO371/2923.
35. Montgomery to Secretary to the Treasury, 10 July 1920, TNA T162/75.
36. Sperling to Secretary to the Treasury, 12 Feb. 1921, TNA T162/75. Tom Snow (later British Minister to Cuba, 1935–37) wrote a year later, 'He is however apparently now discharging the functions of Minister, Consul & Commercial Secretary in his own person. It would appear a somewhat heavy task, & undesirable as a permanent arrangement.' Minute by Snow, 15 June 1922, TNA FO371/7214 A3373.
37. Haggard to Balfour, no. 86, 19 June 1922, TNA FO371/7214 A4331; Haggard to Balfour, no. 91, 8 July 1922, TNA FO371/7214 A5653.
38. Haggard to Curzon, no. 25, 14 Feb. 1923; minute by Kelly, 13 March 1923: TNA FO371/8449 A1459. The underlining would appear to be Kelly's.
39. Lord Aspley's Committee, paper no. 113, 'Latin America as a Market for British Goods', n.d. (1923), TNA BT90/19.
40. Thomas, *Pursuit of Freedom*, p. 540.
41. Haggard to Curzon, no. 61, 'Cuba Annual Report, 1921', 8 May 1922, TNA FO371/7214 A3373, par. 59.
42. Barry Carr describes 'racial dimensions of the nationalist and anti-imperialist discourse that developed in the 1920s and early 1930s' in 'Identity, Class, and Nation: Black Immigrant Workers, Cuban Communism, and the Sugar Insurgency, 1925–1934', *Hispanic-American Historical Review* 78.1 (1998), pp. 83–116.
43. Morris to Chamberlain, no. 55, 'Cuba Annual Report, 1925', 15 May 1926, TNA FO371/11138 A3179, par. 3.
44. Graciela Chailloux Laffita and Robert Whitney, 'British Subjects y Pichones en Cuba', in *De dónde son los cubanos*, ed. Graciela Chailloux Laffita (La Habana: Editorial de Ciencias Sociales, 2007), pp. 55–91 (58).
45. Haggard to Curzon, no. 57, 'Cuba Annual Report, 1922', 1 May 1923, TNA FO371/8451 A2920, par. 29.
46. Haggard (Llangower, N. Wales) to Warner, 17 Aug. 1923, TNA FO371/8450 A3565.
47. See: editorial, 'Treatment Meted Out to Jamaicans in Cuba', *Herald* (Jamaica), 26 July 1924.
48. Minute by Warner, 29 July 1924, TNA FO371/9535 A4508.
49. 'Correspondence between His Majesty's Government and the Cuban Government Respecting the ill-Treatment of British West Indian Labourers in Cuba', cmd. 2158 (HMSO, 1924); 'Further Correspondence...', cmd. 2245 (HMSO, 1924); Gainer to FO, T. no. 21, 10 July 1924, TNA FO371/9535 A4221.
50. Morris to Chamberlain, no. 165, 23 Dec. 1924, TNA FO371/10618 A206. In comparison, their fellow Haitian immigrant workers did not benefit from diplomatic support in Cuba. See M.C. McLeod, 'Undesirable Aliens: Race, Ethnicity, and Nationalism in the Comparison of Haitian and British West Indian Immigrant Workers in Cuba, 1912–1939', *Journal of Social History*, 31.3 (1998), pp. 599–623.
51. Gainer to Curzon, no. 109, 16 Aug. 1923, TNA FO371/8451 A5383; Gainer to Curzon, no. 130, 5 Oct. 1923, TNA FO371/8451 A6622; Gainer to Curzon,

no. 117, 20 Sept. 1923, TNA FO371/8449 A6137. For more on the Tarafa Bill, see Chapman, *A History of the Cuban Republic*, pp. 458–64.

52. Anglo–Mexican diplomatic relations were broken off in 1918, and only re-established under Plutarco Calles' presidency in 1925.
53. Morris to Warner, 25 Nov. 1924, TNA FO371/10618 ff 2–3; FO 'Cuba Annual Report, 1925', par. 5.
54. Morris had been consul in the Canary Islands for five years and chargé d'affaires in Caracas for one year. 'Obituary', *The Times*, 5 Sept. 1953, p. 8.
55. Morris to Vansittart, 23 Nov. 1924, TNA FO371/10618 A363.
56. Morris to Chamberlain, 23 Dec. 1924, TNA FO371/10618 A206.
57. Morris to Chamberlain, 23 Dec. 1924, TNA FO371/10618 A206.
58. Morris to Chamberlain, no. 24, 16 March 1926, TNA FO371/11138 ff 68–71.
59. Morris to Chamberlain, no. 3, 'Cuba Annual Report, 1926', 1 Jan. 1927, TNA FO371/11991 A744, pars 14–19; Morris to Chamberlain, no. 48, 'Cuba Annual Report, 1927', 27 March 1928, TNA FO371/12760 A2696, pars 16–17; 'Agreement between [HMG] and the Cuban government regarding parcel post with Cuba…, December 1, 1927', cmd. 3212 (London: HMSO, 1928). In 1926 the value of parcel goods sent to Cuba from the United States was a substantial $23 m.
60. Jules R. Benjamin, *The United States & Cuba: Hegemony and Dependent Development, 1880–1934* (Pittsburgh: University of Pittsburgh Press; London: Feffer and Simons, 1977), pp. 38–41, 206 n. 43.
61. Morris to Chamberlain, no. 9, 15 Feb. 1927; minute by Snow, 9 March 1927: TNA FO371/11991 A1423; FO 'Cuba Annual Report, 1927', par. 6.
62. FO 'Cuba Annual Report, 1927', pars 3 and 8.
63. Morris to Chamberlain, doc. no. 41, 29 July 1927; Morris to Chamberlain, doc. no. 55, 12 Jan. 1928: *Confidential Print Vol. 17: Latin America and the Philippines, 1919–1939*.
64. Howard to Chamberlain, doc. no. 54, 20 Jan. 1928, *Confidential Print Vol. 17: Latin America and the Philippines, 1919–1937*.
65. 'Annual Report on the United States, 1928', doc. no. 2, Aug. 1929, *Confidential Print Vol. 20: Annual Reports, 1928–1932*, p. 47.
66. Morris to Chamberlain, no. 65, 8 June 1929, TNA FO371/13482 A4344.
67. Morris to Chamberlain, no. 56, 27 May 1929, TNA FO371/13482 A4060; minute by Craigie, 26 June 1929, TNA FO371/13482 f 216.
68. FO to Secretary to the Treasury, 16 Dec. 1930, TNA FO371/14223 A8158.
69. Total UK imports and exports, 1929: Argentina – £112.1 m; Brazil – £20.9 m; Chile – £20.2 m; Cuba – £10 m; Uruguay – £9.4 m; Peru – £8.6 m. In terms of UK exports only, Cuba would have been positioned last of these six nations with a value of £2.1 m (imports from Cuba constituting £7.9 m of the total value). FO to Secretary to the Treasury, 16 Dec. 1930, TNA FO371/14223 A8158.
70. 'Memorandum: Proposed Creation of a Legation at Havana' by Thompson, 9 Dec. 1930, TNA FO371/14223 A8158.
71. Morris to Henderson, 6 April 1931, ff 34–5; minute (name illegible), 29 April 1931, f 33: TNA FO371/15089.
72. The mission visited Argentina, Brazil and Uruguay: 'D'Abernon Mission Report', 18 Jan. 1930, TNA BT60/26/2.
73. 'Heads of Foreign Missions in Cuba', 1 Feb. 1932, TNA FO371/15837 f 60.
74. Broderick to Crowe, 24 Aug. 1931, TNA FO371/15089 A5043.

75. Pérez, *Between Reform and Revolution*, pp. 251–2.
76. Donald Moggridge (ed.), *The Collected Writings of John Maynard Keynes*, *Vol. 12: Economic Articles and Correspondence; Investment and Editorial* (London: Macmillan for the Royal Economic Society, 1983), pp. 551–3; John Paul Rathbone, *The Sugar King of Havana: The Rise and Fall of Julio Lobo, Cuba's Last Tycoon* (New York: The Penguin Press, 2010), p. 78.
77. Morris to Henderson, no. 45, 'Cuba Annual Report, 1930', 1 April 1931, TNA FO371/15090 A2570, par. 34.
78. Broderick to Simon, no. 77, 'Cuba Annual Report, 1931', 11 May 1932, TNA FO371/15837 A3291, pars 5–6, 8.
79. FO 'Cuba Annual Report, 1931', pars 5, 8–9.
80. Broderick to Simon, no. 177, 15 Dec. 1931, TNA FO371/15836 A33; Broderick to Simon, no. 84, 8 June 1932, TNA FO371/15836 A3927.
81. Such was the security situation at the start of 1931 that Morris recommended that HRH Prince of Wales and Prince George should not disembark during a planned visit to Cuba en route to Argentina.
82. Morris to Henderson, no. 12, 28 Feb. 1931; minute by Caccia, 24 Feb. 1931; minute by Vansittart, 25 Feb. 1931: TNA FO371/15089 A1149. Caccia later became ambassador to Washington and permanent under secretary.
83. Minute by Craigie, 21 May 1931, TNA FO371/15090 A2570.
84. According to Machado's memoirs the diplomatic representatives of the United States, Germany and Great Britain all received death threats: Gerardo Machado y Morales, *Ocho años de lucha* (Miami: Ediciones Históricas Cubanas, 1982), p. 48.
85. Broderick to Marquess of Reading, no. 116, 2 Sept. 1931, TNA FO371/15089 A5551; FO 'Cuba Annual Report, 1931', par. 24.
86. Louis A. Pérez Jr., *Intervention, Revolution, and Politics in Cuba, 1913–1921* (Pittsburgh: University of Pittsburgh Press, 1978), pp. 146–8.
87. Morris to Chamberlain, no. 20, 'Cuba Annual Report, 1928', 31 Jan. 1929, TNA FO371/13482 A1295, par. 2.
88. Broderick to Simon, no. 24, 'Cuba Annual Report, 1932', 15 Feb. 1933, TNA FO371/16577 A1755, par. 26. A successor to the Anglo-Mexican oil company, first established in the island in 1922, Shell-Mex did not refine oil in Cuba until 1957.
89. FO 'Cuba Annual Report, 1931', par. 4.
90. Minute by Thompson, 19 May 1931, TNA FO371/15090 A2570.

4   Beyond Recognition: Grau's 100-Day Government

1. Philip Dur and Christopher Gilcrease, 'US Diplomacy and the Downfall of a Cuban Dictator: Machado in 1933', *Journal of Latin American Studies*, 34.2 (2002), pp. 255–82; Robert Dallek, *Franklin D. Roosevelt and American Foreign Policy, 1932–1945* (New York and Oxford: Oxford University Press, 1979), pp. 60–3.
2. Dana G. Munro, *Intervention and Dollar Diplomacy in the Caribbean, 1900–1921* (Princeton, NJ: Princeton University Press, 1964), p. 426.
3. Peter V.N. Henderson, 'Woodrow Wilson, Victoriano Huerta, and the Recognition Issue in Mexico', *The Americas*, 41.2 (1984), pp. 151–76; Peter Calvert,

The Mexican Revolution, 1910–1914: The Diplomacy of Anglo–American Conflict (Cambridge: Cambridge University Press, 1968), pp. 131–284.

4. 'Annual Report on United States, 1932', doc. no. 10, *Confidential Print Vol. 20: Annual Reports, 1928–1932*, p. 374; 'Memorandum by the Assistant Secretary of State [White], May 19, 1932', *FRUS, 1932: The American Republics Volume V* (Washington, DC: US Govt. Printing Office, 1948), p. 599.

5. See Donald Cameron Watt, *Succeeding John Bull: America in Britain's Place, 1900–1975: A Study of the Anglo–American Relationship and World Politics in the Context of British and American Foreign-policy-making in the Twentieth Century* (Cambridge: Cambridge University Press, 1984), p. 63.

6. Charles P. Kindleberger, *The World in Depression, 1929–1939* (Berkeley, CA and London: University of California Press, 1986), p. 297.

7. Bridgeman's Journal entry from 1929 cited in Watt, *Succeeding John Bull*, p. 59; D.C. Watt, *Personalities and Policies: Studies in the Formulation of British Foreign Policy in the Twentieth Century* (London: Longmans, 1965), pp. 39, 42.

8. Osborne to FO, T. no. 481, 27 Aug. 1933, TNA FO371/16612 A6330.

9. Robert Whitney, *State and Revolution in Cuba: Mass Mobilization and Political Change, 1920–1940* (Chapel Hill, NC; London: University of North Carolina Press, 2001), pp. 58–9.

10. Broderick to Simon, doc. no. 74, 13 Jan. 1932, *Confidential Print Vol. 8: Mexico, Central and South America, August 1931–July 1932*.

11. Broderick to Simon, doc. no. 65, 20 Dec. 1932, *Confidential Print Vol. 9: Mexico, Central and South America, August 1932–May 1933*.

12. 'Sir J.J. Broderick: From Consul to Ambassador', *The Times*, 3 June 1933, p. 14. Tragically, he died in England before assuming his new position.

13. Border to Simon, doc. no. 155, 4 April 1933, *Confidential Print Vol. 9: Mexico, Central and South America, August 1932–May 1933*.

14. Frank Warren Graff, *Strategy of Involvement: A Diplomatic Biography of Sumner Welles* (New York; London: Garland, 1988), pp. 2, 8, 25, 60. Both Roosevelt and Welles had studied at Groton and Harvard University.

15. Luis E. Aguilar, 'Cuba, c. 1860–c. 1930', in *Cuba: A Short History*, ed. Leslie Bethell (Cambridge: Cambridge University Press, 1993), pp. 21–56 (53).

16. Benjamin, *Hegemony and Dependent Development*, pp. 89–90.

17. Dur and Gilcrease, 'US Diplomacy and the Downfall of a Cuban Dictator', pp. 257–8.

18. Border to Simon, doc. no. 32, 7 June 1933, *Confidential Print Vol. 10: Mexico, Central and South America, May 1933–March 1934*.

19. Welles to Roosevelt, 18 May 1933, Edgar B. Nixon (ed.), *Franklin D. Roosevelt and Foreign Affairs: Volume I* (Cambridge, MA: Harvard University Press, 1969), p. 140.

20. Welles arrived on 8 May. Grant Watson arrived on 5 July. Watson is unique in being the only British diplomat to have served twice as head of mission in Cuba (1933–35 and 1937–40), bridged by a two-year interval in Helsingfors, Finland (1935–37).

21. Anthony Adamthwaite, 'Introduction', *Confidential Print Vol. 24: Portugal 1919–39*, pp. xv–xvii.

22. Grant Watson to Simon, no. 63, 15 July 1933, TNA FO371/16573 A5529.

23. Grant Watson to Simon, no. 70, 1 Aug. 1933, TNA FO371/16573 A5979.

24. Minute by Kelly, 10 Aug. 1933, TNA FO371/16573 A5853. Following diplomatic service in Buenos Aires (1919–21), Kelly – like Grant Watson – served in His Majesty's legation in Lisbon (1921–25). He was then posted to Mexico (1925–27).
25. Grant Watson to Simon, no. 77, 21 Aug. 1933, TNA FO371/16573 A6441.
26. Welles to Hull, 9 Aug. 1933, *FRUS, 1933: The American Republics Volume V* (Washington, DC: US Govt Printing Office, 1952), p. 345; 'British Warship on way to Havana?', 9 Aug. 1933, *Daily Mirror*, p. 19.
27. Welles to Hull, 12 Aug. 1933, *FRUS, 1933 Vol. V*, pp. 358–9.
28. Minute by Haigh, 12 Aug. 1933, TNA FO371/16573 A5923.
29. 'Presidential Palace Looted in Cuba: Celebrating General Machado's Downfall', *Manchester Guardian*, 14 Aug. 1933, p. 13.
30. Grant Watson to Simon, no. 77, 21 Aug. 1933, TNA FO371/16573 A6441.
31. Ibid.
32. Grant Watson to Simon, no. 88, enclosing 'Leading Personalities in Cuba' report, 19 June 1934, FO371/17518 A5439.
33. Welles to Hull, 14 Aug. 1933, *FRUS, 1933 Vol. V*, p. 363.
34. Welles to Hull, 19 Aug. 1933, *FRUS, 1933 Vol. V*, pp. 367–9. Roosevelt instructed him to remain in Havana until 15 September. Phillips (under secretary) to Welles, 21 Aug. 1933, *FRUS, 1933 Vol. V*, p. 369.
35. Osborne to Simon, no. 1122, 16 Aug. 1933, TNA FO371/16573 A6317.
36. Grant Watson to FO, T. no. 23, 14 Aug. 1933; minute by Kelly, 15 Aug. 1933: TNA FO371/16573 A5967.
37. Minute by Haigh, 30 Aug. 1933; minute by Kelly, 31 Aug. 1933: TNA FO371/16573 A6317.
38. Welles to State Department, T. 160, 14 August 1933, National Archives at College Park, Maryland, US (henceforth NARA) Record Group 84, Entry 13, Volume 285.
39. Welles to Hull, 22 Aug. 1933, p. 369; Welles to Hull, 24 Aug. 1933, pp. 371–3: *FRUS, 1933 Vol. V*.
40. Grant Watson to Simon, no. 81, 29 Aug. 1933, TNA FO371/16574 A6572; 'Machado in Exile: Extradition Demanded', *Manchester Guardian*, 23 Aug. 1933, p. 12.
41. 'Memorandum of Telephone Conversation', 5 Sept. 1933 (8.10am), *FRUS, 1933 Vol. V*, p. 380.
42. Grant Watson to Simon, no. 96, 9 Sept. 1933, TNA FO371/16574 A6901.
43. Ibid.
44. Bryce Wood, *The Making of the Good Neighbor Policy* (New York: Norton, 1961), pp. 76–80.
45. Grant Watson to Simon, 9 Sept. 1933, TNA FO371/16574 A6901.
46. Minute by Roberts, 22 Sept. 1933, TNA FO371/16574 A6901.
47. Osborne to FO, T. no. 491, 8 Sept. 1933, TNA FO371/16574 A6624.
48. Osborne to Simon, no. 1264, 14 Sept. 1933; minutes by Haigh and Roberts, 26 Sept. 1933: TNA FO371/16574 A6990.
49. 'Memorandum of Telephone Conversation', 5 Sept. 1933, pp. 386–7; 'Memorandum of Telephone Conversation', 6 Sept. 1933, pp. 389–90: *FRUS, 1933 Vol. V*.
50. Welles to Hull, 7 Sept. 1933, *FRUS, 1933 Vol. V*, pp. 396–8.

51. 'Memorandum of Telephone Conversation', 9 Sept. 1933, pp. 412–13; Daniels to Hull, 9 Sept. 1933, pp. 414–15; Welles to Hull, 10 Sept. 1933, pp. 416–18; Welles to Hull, 12 Sept. 1933, pp. 426–8; Welles to Hull, 17 Sept. 1933, pp. 443–5; Welles to Hull, 25 Sept. 1933, pp. 457–8: *FRUS, 1933 Vol. V.*
52. Grant Watson to Simon, no. 100, 16 Sept. 1933; minute by Kelly, 2 Oct. 1933: TNA FO371/16574 A7082.
53. Grant Watson to Simon, no. 110, 26 Sept. 1933, TNA FO371/16575 A7253.
54. Pérez, *Between Reform and Revolution*, pp. 268–9.
55. Grant Watson to Simon, no. 119, 4 Oct. 1933, TNA FO371/16575 A7580; Antoni Kapcia, 'The Siege of the Hotel Nacional, Cuba, 1933: A Reassessment', *Journal of Latin American Studies*, 34.2 (2002), pp. 283–310.
56. Minutes by Haigh, 14 Oct., Roberts and Craigie, both 20 Oct., TNA FO371/16575 A7580.
57. Welles to Hull, 4 Oct. 1933, pp. 469–72; Hull to Welles, 5 Oct. 1933, p. 472; Welles to Hull, 5 Oct. 1933, pp. 473–4; Welles to Hull, 6 Oct. 1933, p. 476: *FRUS, 1933 Vol. V.*
58. 'Record of Conversation', 9 Oct. 1933, TNA FO371/16575 A7409; Grant Watson to FO, T. no. 101, 9 Oct. 1933; minute by Craigie, 10 Oct. 1933: TNA FO371/16575 A7353.
59. Minute by Craigie, 11 Oct. 1933, TNA FO371/16575 A7353.
60. Lindsay to FO, T. no. 553, 13 Oct. 1933, TNA FO371/16575 A7462.
61. Grant Watson to FO, T. no. 103, 13 Oct. 1933, TNA FO371/16575 A7464; Welles to Hull, 11 Oct. 1933, *FRUS, 1933 Vol. V*, p. 483.
62. Gibson (Rio) to Hull, 13 Oct. 1933, *FRUS, 1933 Vol. V*, pp. 483–4.
63. Welles to Hull, 16 Oct. 1933, pp. 487–91; Welles to Hull, 30 Oct. 1933, p. 504: *FRUS, 1933 Vol. V.*
64. Grant Watson to Simon, no. 130, 21 Oct. 1933, TNA FO371/16575 A7892. Mimicking an earlier occurrence, ex-President Menocal also sought refuge at His Majesty's legation and received the same negative response.
65. Minute by Wellesley, 2 Nov. 1933, TNA FO371/16575 A7891.
66. Grant Watson to Simon, no. 136, 2 Nov. 1933, TNA FO371/16576 A8162.
67. Grant Watson to FO, T. no. 132, 14 Nov. 1933, TNA FO371/16576 A8214.
68. Welles to Hull, 13 Nov. 1933, *FRUS, 1933 Vol. V*, pp. 520–1.
69. Minute by Roberts (also summarizing Craigie's and Kelly's views), 16 Nov. 1933, TNA FO371/16576 A8214.
70. Lindsay to FO, T. no. 624, 19 Nov. 1933, TNA FO371/16576 A8345.
71. Minutes by Craigie, 21 and 23 Nov. 1933; minutes by Warner and Rendel, 22 Nov. 1933: TNA FO371/16576 A8345.
72. Grant Watson to FO, T. no. 137, 22 Nov. 1933; minute by Roberts, 24 Nov. 1933: TNA FO371/16576 A8458; Grant Watson to Simon, no. 146, 23 Nov. 1933, TNA FO371/16576 A8845.
73. Lindsay to FO, T. no. 633, 27 Nov. 1933; minute by Craigie, 29 Nov. 1933: TNA FO371/16576 A8607.
74. The column in question was 'The Daily Washington Merry-Go-Round' by Drew Pearson and Robert S. Allen, published in multiple press outlets on 22 and 29 Nov. 1933. Roosevelt made the announcement at Warm Springs, Georgia, late on 23 November 1933. See statement text in *FRUS, 1933 Vol. V*, pp. 525–6.

75. Phillips diary entry, 6 Nov. 1933, cited in Graff, *Strategy of Involvement*, p. 95; William Phillips, *Ventures in Diplomacy* (London: John Murray, 1955), pp. 90–1.
76. 'Record of Conversation', 28 Nov. 1933; minute by Craigie, 29 Nov. 1933: TNA FO371/16576 A8745; Lindsay to FO, T. no. 647, 7 Dec. 1933, TNA FO371/16576 A8895.
77. Lindsay to FO, T. no. 670, 24 Dec. 1933; minute by Vansittart (n.d.): TNA FO371/16576 A9284; Grant Watson to FO, T. no. 151, 26 Dec. 1933, TNA FO371/16576 A9299.
78. Text of convention, signed on 26 Dec. 1933: *FRUS, 1933: The American Republics Volume IV* (Washington, DC: US Govt. Printing Office, 1950), pp. 214–18.
79. Peter H. Smith, *Talons of the Eagle: Dynamics of U.S.–Latin American Relations* (New York: Oxford University Press, 2000), p. 69.
80. Grant Watson to FO, T. no. 153, 31 Dec. 1933; minute by Craigie, 2 Jan. 1933; FO to Havana, T. no. 3, 4 Jan. 1934: TNA FO371/17515 A29.
81. Grant Watson to FO, T. no. 4, 6 Jan. 1934; minute by Craigie, 9 Jan. 1933: TNA FO371/17515 A206; minute by Vansittart, 7 Jan. 1933, TNA FO371/17515 A733; Atherton (US embassy, London) to Hull, T. 7, 6 Jan. 1934, NARA RG84 Box 1363, vol. 19.
82. Minute by Kelly, 11 Jan. 1934, TNA FO371/17515 A318. Underlining in original.
83. Minute by Kelly, 12 Jan. 1934; minute by Wellesley, 13 Jan. 1934: TNA FO371/17515 A348.
84. Grant Watson to Simon, no. 136, 2 Nov. 1933, TNA FO371/16576 A8162.
85. Grant Watson to Simon, no. 5, 13 Jan. 1934, TNA FO371/17515 A833.
86. Washington Chancery to American Dept., 5 Feb. 1934, TNA FO371/17516 A1473.
87. Minutes by Craigie (28 Feb. 1934), Wellesley (1 March), Vansittart (2 March): TNA FO371/17516 A1473.
88. Grant Watson to American Dept., 5 April 1934, TNA FO371/17516 A3417.
89. Phillips, *Ventures in Diplomacy*, p. 90.
90. See Irwin F. Gellman, *Secret Affairs: Franklin Roosevelt, Cordell Hull, and Sumner Welles* (Baltimore and London: Johns Hopkins University Press, 1995), pp. 82–4. State Department colleagues Francis White and William Castle were also harsh critics.
91. Grant Watson to Simon, 'Report on the Heads of Foreign Missions in Cuba', 20 Dec. 1933, TNA FO371/17519 A295; Grant Watson to Simon, no. 5, 13 Jan. 1934, TNA FO371/17515 A833. For more criticism of Welles's diplomacy, see Irwin F. Gellman, *Roosevelt and Batista: Good Neighbor Diplomacy in Cuba, 1933–1945* (Albuquerque: University of New Mexico Press, 1973), pp. 67–8, 81–3.

5   Sugar and the Anglo–Cuban Commercial Treaty

1. Grant Watson to Simon, no. 13, 29 Jan. 1934, TNA FO371/17515 A1127.
2. Pérez, *Cuba: Between Reform and Revolution*, pp. 279–80. Negatively, the treaty stifled Cuban economic diversification and efforts to reduce dependence on

sugar. Furthermore, the US Congress allocated Cuba its sugar quota each year, affecting the industry's ability to plan and leading to general economic uncertainty. The Jones–Costigan Act allocated sugar quotas to Cuba, and to continental and offshore US producers, with a small quota given to other countries.

3. 'Department of Overseas Trade: Economic Conditions in Cuba', no. 518, April 1932, by Broderick (London: HMSO, 1932), p. 11. The following 1935 economic report stated that the UK took 'nearly one-third' of all Cuban sugar and 'not far short of one-quarter' of its cigars, 'Department of Overseas Trade: Economic Conditions in Cuba', April 1935, by Rees (London: HMSO, 1935), p. 11.

4. Brian Pollitt, 'The Cuban Sugar Economy in the 1930s', in *The World Sugar Economy in War and Depression 1914–40*, ed. Bill Albert and Adrian Graves (London and New York: Routledge, 1988), pp. 97–108.

5. Pollitt, 'The Cuban Sugar Economy in the 1930s', p. 107. *Colono* sugar growers could be poor tenant *minifundistas* or landowners. Their agricultural class was defined by its contractual obligation to supply local mills.

6. Jorge I. Domínguez, *Cuba: Order and Revolution* (Cambridge, MA and London: Belknap Press of Harvard University Press, 1978), pp. 63, 82.

7. Antoni Kapcia, 'Fulgencio Batista, 1933–44: From Revolutionary to Populist', in *Authoritarianism in Latin America Since Independence*, ed. Will Fowler (Westport, CT and London: Greenwood Press, 1996), pp. 73–92 (87).

8. B.C. Swerling, *International Control of Sugar, 1918–41* (Commodity Policy Studies, 7; Stanford, CA: Food Research Institute, 1949), p. 39.

9. Benjamin, *Hegemony and Dependent Development*, p. 180.

10. I am grateful to G.B. Hagelberg for this definition of the 'free market'.

11. 'Report of the United Kingdom Sugar Industry Inquiry Committee', cmd. 4871 (London: HMSO, April 1935), pp. 12–13, 46–50.

12. 'Los Tratados de Comercio Vigentes: Necesidad de concertar nuevos convenios y denunciar algunos que están en vigor. Conveniencia de crear una Comisión permanente de Tratados', Feb. 1934, pp. 17–18; 'El Principio de la Reciprocidad Comercial como Política Exterior de Cuba', Nov. 1934, pp. 9–10; 'Las Posibilidades Comerciales de Cuba con la Gran Bretaña: Necesidad de un Régimen de Concesiones Recíprocas', Nov. 1934, p. 11; 'Editoriales: Tratados Maltratados', Feb. 1935, p. 3: all from *Cuba Importadora e Industrial* (the monthly journal changed its name to *Cuba Económica y Financiera* from 1938).

13. Enclosure no. 8, Caffery address to the National Association of Sugar Manufacturers, Havana, 19 Feb. 1935: Caffery to Secretary of State, no. 2709, 20 Feb. 1935, NARA Record Group 84, Entry 13, vol. 329.

14. 'Commercial Treaties of the United Kingdom: Report to the President of the Board of Trade on the Treaty Arrangements of the United Kingdom', by Stanley, Sept. 1917, TNA BT274/24 (report on Cuba, pp. 111–13). The report affirmed (p. 113) that 'nothing useful' could be achieved by Britain until termination of US–Cuban reciprocity, and that 'So far we have only been "weaving ropes of sand."' '

15. Craigie to Wellesley, 24 Feb. 1928; Craigie to Secretary Board of Trade, 1 March 1928: TNA FO371/12759 A755; Fountain (BT) to Under Secretary

(FO), 28 April 1928; minute by Wellesley, 7 May 1928: TNA FO371/12759 A2869.

16. Luis Marino Pérez (Legación de Cuba, Londres) to Vansittart, 22 June 1927, TNA FO371/12759 A3754.
17. Grant Watson to Simon, no. 49, 28 March 1934, TNA FO371/17519 A2930. The discrepancy is explained by inclusion of British re-exports in Cuban statistics.
18. While on leave in Havana, the Cuban minister to London told Grant Watson that his government would propose a commercial agreement with the UK after completing its negotiations with Washington: Grant Watson to FO, T. no. 59, 3 May 1934; minute by Broad, 4 May 1934: TNA FO371/17519 A3495.
19. Grant Watson to FO, T. no. 45, 23 Feb. 1934, TNA FO371/17519 A1576; Grant Watson to Simon, no. 49, 28 March 1934; minutes by Mason and Kelly, 18 April 1934: TNA FO371/17519 A2930.
20. Bill Albert, 'Sugar and Anglo–Peruvian Trade Negotiations in the 1930s', *Journal of Latin American Studies*, 14.1 (1982), pp. 121–42; Rory Miller, *Britain and Latin America in the Nineteenth and Twentieth Centuries* (London: Longman, 1993), pp. 207–9.
21. Grant Watson to Simon, no. 146E, 13 Dec. 1934, TNA CO852 23/9; Grant Watson to Simon, no. 10, 24 Jan. 1935, containing translation from *Diario de la Marina*, TNA FO371/18675 A1336. Cuba's denouncement of commercial agreements with Japan, Portugal and Italy indicated its new attitude: Grant Watson to FO, T. no. 1, 8 Jan. 1935, TNA FO371/18679 A518.
22. Thomas, *Pursuit of Freedom*, p. 562; Pérez, *Between Reform and Revolution*, pp. 252–3.
23. 'Report of the United Kingdom Sugar Industry Inquiry Committee' (1935), pp. 6–7, 54. The Empire sources of raw sugar in 1935 were Queensland (Australia), Natal (South Africa), the West Indies, Mauritius and Fiji.
24. Philippe Chalmin, *The Making of a Sugar Giant: Tate and Lyle, 1859–1989* (New York: Harwood Academic Publishers, 1990), pp. 1, 19, 54, 131–2, 179, 190; Bill Albert and Adrian Graves (eds), *The World Sugar Economy in War and Depression, 1914–40* (London: Routledge, 1988), p. 16. The company took its name from Julius Cesar Czarnikow, an 18-year-old of Polish-Jewish origins who arrived in London in 1854. The J. Henry Schroder bank financed his company's early and subsequent trading in European beet sugar. Czarnikow Ltd was later linked to a smaller New York brokerage company, Czarnikow-Rionda, both maintaining an ongoing and close association with Cuba's sugar industry and controlling elite. See Muriel McAvoy, *Sugar Baron: Manuel Rionda and the Fortunes of Pre-Castro Cuba* (Gainesville: University Press of Florida, 2003).
25. Grant Watson to Simon, doc. no. 159, 6 June 1934, *Confidential Print Vol. 11: Mexico, Central and South America, March 1934–June 1934*; minute by Kelly, 31 May 1934, TNA FO371/17520 A4318.
26. Record of meeting between Grant Watson and Board of Trade, London, 31 May 1935, TNA FO371/18675 A5650.
27. Grant Watson to Craigie, private, 1 June 1935, TNA FO371/18679 A5278.
28. 'British Minister's Goods Lost at Sea', *The Times*, 23 Jan. 1937, p. 14. He had reportedly lost his silver, furniture, pictures and archives.

29. Willis (BT) to Craigie, 22 May 1935, attaching memorandum 'Sugar' by Board of Trade (C.R.T. Dept.), May 1935; minute by Ashton-Gwatkin, 23 May 1935: TNA FO371/18675 A4781.
30. Snow to Troutbeck, 22 June 1935, TNA FO371/18675 A6507.
31. Stirling (BT) to Holman, 4 Sept. 1935, TNA FO371/18675 A7788; Snow to Troutbeck, 11 Oct. 1935, TNA FO371/18675 A9161; Snow to Hoare, no. 86, 5 Aug. 1935, TNA FO371/18676 A7312.
32. Grant Watson to Simon, no. 67, 9 May 1934, TNA FO371/17516 A4099.
33. Grant Watson to Simon, no. 21, 28 Feb. 1935, TNA FO371/18676 A2564; Grant Watson to Simon, no. 31, 29 March 1935, TNA FO371/18676 A3517. Jorge Domínguez affirms that the period from 1933 to 1937 was one of 'virtually unremitting social and political warfare'. Governments, he wrote, 'succeeded each other [. . .] in such rapid succession that no leader had time to consolidate his rule'. Domínguez, *Order and Revolution*, p. 76.
34. Snow to Eden, 'Cuba Annual Report, 1935', no. 51, 28 Feb. 1936, TNA FO371/19780 A2640 pars 16 and 21.
35. 'Memorandum' enclosure within Simpson (United Railways, Havana) to Snow, 3 Aug. 1935, TNA FO371/18676 A7741. Lightly Simpson CBE (*c.*1870–1942), a Cambridge engineering graduate from Dalbreck (Gullane, Scotland), with over 40 years' railway experience in Argentina and Cuba. 'Siluetas Financieras: Mr. Lightly Simpson', *Cuba Importadora e Industrial*, Nov. 1937, p. 25.
36. Memorandum by Stirling (BT), 8 Nov. 1935, TNA FO371/18676 A9488.
37. Miller, *Britain and Latin America*, pp. 212–13.
38. 'Agreed minutes of a conference held at the Treasury . . . 30th January, 1936, on the proposed international conference on the restriction of exports of sugar', TNA BT 11/587 f 11.
39. Snow to Troutbeck, 7 Jan. 1936, TNA FO371/19779 A680.
40. Snow to FO, no. 8, 13 Jan. 1936, TNA FO371/19780 A420.
41. Snow to FO, no. 9, 14 Jan. 1936, TNA FO371/19780 A424.
42. Snow to Craigie, private, 7 Feb. 1936, TNA FO371/19780 A1621.
43. 'Note of Meeting held at Board of Trade, 23rd April, 1936', TNA BT 11/587 f 31. Snow met with United Railways and insurance company representatives on the same day.
44. Minute by Willis (BT), 4 May 1936, TNA BT 11/587 minute sheets (unnumbered).
45. On British insurance companies' employment of underhand methods to resist threatening legislation, see Charles Jones, 'Insurance Companies', in *Business Imperialism 1840–1930: An Inquiry Based on British Experience in Latin America*, ed. D.C.M. Platt (Oxford: Clarendon Press, 1977), pp. 53–74.
46. Snow (Exeter) to Troutbeck, 19 June 1936; minute by Allen (FO), 22 June 1936, TNA FO371/19780 A5209.
47. Caffery to Welles (assistant secretary of state), no. 501, 26 June 1936, Sumner Welles Papers, Franklin D. Roosevelt Presidential Library, Hyde Park, NY (henceforth SWP), box 144, folder 4; Caffery to Welles, no. 583, 29 Aug. 1936, SWP box 144, folder 5.
48. Snow to FO, no. 6, 21 Sept. 1936, TNA FO371/19779 A8072.
49. Snow to Eden, no. 145, 6 Oct. 1936, TNA FO371/19779 A8385.

50. Snow to Eden, 'Cuba Annual Report, 1936', no. 15, 3 Feb. 1937, TNA FO371/20628 A1356 pars 1, 14, 23.
51. Snow to FO, no. 4, 20 Jan. 1937, TNA FO371/20626 A508.
52. Minute by Allen, 3 Feb. 1937, TNA FO371/20626 A870.
53. Snow to Eden, no. 24-E, 19 Feb. 1937, TNA FO371/20627 A1867.
54. Snow to FO, no. 42, 15 Feb. 1937, TNA FO371/20626 A1249; Snow to FO, no. 43, 15 Feb. 1937, TNA FO371/20626 A1248.
55. Minutes by Stirling, 11 and 20 Feb. 1937, TNA BT 11/632 minute sheets (unnumbered).
56. Snow to FO, no. 53, 20 Feb. 1937, TNA FO371 BT 11/632 f 75.
57. 'Commercial Agreement between [...] the United Kingdom and Cuba [...] Havana, February 19, 1937', *Parliamentary Papers* cmd. 5383 (London: HMSO, 1937). British dominions and possessions did not constitute 'foreign countries' under the treaty.
58. Grant Watson to Eden, no. 32-E, 16 March 1937, TNA FO371/20627 A2239.
59. 'Impresiones', *Diario de la Marina*, 9 March 1937, p. 1 (author's translation). This misconception is repeated in a Cuban analysis of the treaty's gestation: Rodolfo Sarracino, *El Grupo Rockefeller actúa: entreguismo e injerencia anglo–yanqui en la década del treinta* (La Habana: Editorial de Ciencias Sociales, 1987), p. 21.
60. Extract of Caffery speech, *The Havana Post*, 6 March 1937, enclosure Grant Watson to Eden, no. 32-E, 16 March 1937, TNA FO371/20627 A2239; 'Impresiones' por J.I.R., *Diario de la Marina*, 10 March 1937, p. 1 (author's translation).
61. 'Editoriales: El Tratado Anglo–Cubano', *Mediodía*, 15 March 1937, p. 3 (author's translation).
62. 'La Vida Obrera: Las Leyes Sociales y el Tratado con Inglaterra', *Mediodía*, 25 March 1937, p. 16 (author's translation).
63. Minute by Troutbeck, 2 April 1937; minute by Allen, 1 April 1937: TNA FO371/20627 A2442.
64. Grant Watson to Eden, no. 3, 'Cuba Annual Report, 1937', 5 Jan. 1938, TNA FO371/21451 A1372 par. 120.
65. 'Inaugural Speech by the President [of the International Sugar Council], the Right Hon. J. Ramsey MacDonald', 5 April 1937: League of Nations, *International Sugar Conference Held in London from 5 April to 6 May 1937. I: Text of the Agreement; II: Proceedings and Documents of the Conference* (Geneva, 1937), p. 26. The five Cuban delegates were all members of the Cuban Institute for the Stabilisation of Sugar: José Manuel Gómez Mena, Aurelio Portuondo, Arturo Mañas, Rafael María Angulo and Edelberto Farrés. The Conference's resulting agreement delimited the 'free' world market, with exporting members accepting specific export quotas. See Swerling, *International Control of Sugar*, p. 56. The Agreement signed by 21 countries set up an International Sugar Council with nine executive members, to meet in London once a year. Cuba was rewarded with a free-market quota of 940,000 metric tons, only surpassed by Java with 1,050,000 tons. Peru's quota was 330,000 tons. 'World Sugar Agreement', *The Times*, 26 May 1937, p. 11.
66. Minute by Stirling, 9 April 1937, minute sheets (unnumbered); Leith-Ross to Gomez Mena, 16 April 1937, f 38A; Leith-Ross to Stirling, 19 April 1937, f 36: TNA BT11/773. José Manuel Casanova (1884–1949) had long experience

in the sugar industry. Over many years he was head or a leading member of various influential organizations related to agricultural production, including presidency of the Unión Social Económica de Cuba, which he founded in 1934. In 1936 he was elected Senator for Oriente province (Liberal Party). Fermín Peraza Sarausa, *Diccionario biográfico cubano: Tomo I* (La Habana: n.d.), pp. 67–8.

67. Grant Watson to Eden, no. 71, 2 May 1937, A3547; Grant Watson to Eden, no. 86, 1 June 1937, A4239: TNA FO371/20625.

68. Grant Watson to Eden, no. 91, 8 June 1937, A4477; Grant Watson to Eden, no. 98, 30 June 1937, A4946: TNA FO371/20625. For more detail on Batista's Three-Year Plan, see Whitney, *State and Revolution*, pp. 157–61.

69. The British minister wrote, 'Failure to ratify is due rather to inanition of the Government than to opposition.' Grant Watson to FO, T. no. 129, 6 July 1937; minute by Allen, 12 July 1937; enclosure 'The Anglo–Cuban Treaty', *Sunday Times*, 18 July 1937: TNA FO371/20627 A4769.

70. On this point, one specialist journal asserted, 'No doubt many of our readers will be wondering how far and in what manner share and debenture holders of the United Railways of Havana stand to reap any benefit from the clause in the Anglo–Cuban Trade Agreement.' 'The Anglo–Cuban Trade Agreement', *South American Journal*, 28 Aug. 1937, pp. 194–5.

71. FO 'Cuba Annual Report, 1937', pars 58–65.

72. Minute by Stirling, 30 Oct. 1937, TNA BT11/820 f 85; Memorandum 'Record of Conversation' by Holman, 28 Oct. 1937, TNA FO371/20627 A7764.

73. Using powers under Section 12 of the Import Duties Act (1932) to discriminate against countries that discriminated against British trade.

74. The arguments are best summarized in a minute by Willis, 11 Jan. 1938, TNA BT11/820 minute no. 18.

75. Minute by Willis, 12 Nov. 1938, TNA BT11/820 f 86.

76. Minutes nos 10 and 15 by Jenkins, 15 Nov. 1937 and 3 Dec. 1937; memorandum 'Question of threatening discrimination against Cuban sugar' by Willis, 23 Nov. 1937, f 87a; minutes by Willis and Carhill, 23 and 25 Nov. 1937, f 87; Ellyan (director, Tate & Lyle) to Willis (BT), 26 Nov. 1937, f 88; Rook (Czarnikow) to Willis, 7 Dec. 1937, f 92: TNA BT11/820.

77. Rook's letter contained an article 'Jugando con fuego' (n.d., f 100A) from a 'leading Havana paper', that warned of the serious consequences for Cuba's export trade if British insurance interests were damaged. Rook (Czarnikow) to Willis, 28 Jan. 1938, f 102; Willis reported a telephone conversation with Rook: 'His friends there had been able to induce a few powerful personalities interested in the new Cuban insurance companies to sever their connection with those companies in order to support what Mr. Rook described as the sugar side of the question as against the local insurance interests.' Minute by Willis, 29 Jan. 1938, TNA BT11/820 f 105.

78. Jenkins to under secretary (FO), 16 Feb. 1938, TNA FO371/21448 A1306.

79. Grant Watson to Halifax, no. 2, 'Cuba Annual Report, 1938', 4 Jan. 1939, TNA FO371/22748 A996 par. 61.

80. Grant Watson to FO, T. no. 25, 27 April 1938; minute by Beith, 2 May 1938: TNA FO371/21449 A3342.

81. FO to Lindsay, T. no. 314, 5 May 1938, A3447; Lindsay to FO, T. no. 230, 8 May 1938; minutes by Beith and Stirling, 10 May 1938, A3604: TNA FO371/21449.

82. There would not be 'any mention of the technical basis' (i.e. Cuban preferential duties on US imports) on which the action would be based. FO to Lindsay (repeated to Havana), T. no. 385, 17 June 1938, A4806; Grant Watson to FO, T. no. 39, 1 July 1938, A5144; FO to Grant Watson, T. no. 16, 6 July 1938, A5144: TNA FO371/21449.
83. FO 'Cuba Annual Report, 1938', par. 1.
84. Grant Watson to Halifax, no. 47, 10 May 1938, A4411; Grant Watson to Halifax, no. 54, 13 June 1938, A5241: TNA FO371/21450.
85. Butler Wright to Welles, 24 June 1938, SWP box 50, folder 4 (office correspondence, 1920– 1943).
86. US Ambassador Robert Butler Wright and Herbert Grant Watson were renewing an acquaintance, after both serving as diplomats in Brussels in 1912.
87. Grant Watson to Halifax, no. 62, 6 July 1938, TNA FO371/21449 A5757.
88. In London, John Beith wrote, 'Our retaliatory action is now held up indefinitely. It is satisfactory that the mere hint of a threat of such action has had a certain effect: but if the situation deteriorates and we are not prepared to implement our threats we shall look fools.' Grant Watson to FO, T. no. 21, 15 July 1938; minute by Beith, 26 July 1938: TNA FO371/21449 A5748.
89. Grant Watson to Halifax, no. 74, 25 July 1938, TNA FO371/21449 A6623. This despatch contained comments made outside Congress by an unnamed Senator to a local newspaper: 'Relations with England are becoming strained and the British Minister is warning us of the dance which our sugar and our tobacco will dance. This has alarmed the President, who summoned the Senators to the Palace.' Grant Watson denied exerting such direct pressure on the Cuban government.
90. For proceedings from the heated Senate discussions, see 'Apuntes del Senado', *Avance*, 28 July 1938, pp. 1, 4.
91. Grant Watson to FO, T. no. 46, 27 July 1938, TNA FO371/21449 A5897. Senator Casanova left a note to this effect at His Majesty's Legation that evening. Grant Watson to Halifax, no. 78, 30 July 1938, TNA FO371/21449 A6482.
92. Minute by Beith, 29 July 1938, TNA FO371/21449 A5897.
93. FO 'Cuba Annual Report, 1938', par. 40; minute by Beith, 31 May 1939, TNA FO371/22748 A996.

6   The Second World War: Sugar without Cigars

1. R.A. Humphreys, *Latin America and the Second World War: Volume One 1939– 1942* (London: Athlone/ ILAS, 1981), p. 91.
2. Grant Watson to Halifax, no. 1, 1 Jan. 1940, enclosing 'Political Report on Cuba, 1939', pp. 5–6, TNA FO371/24187 A542.
3. Ogilvie-Forbes to Eden, no. 62, 'Cuba Annual Report, 1940', 9 June 1941, TNA FO371/25933 A4808, par. 5(i). On 9 Oct. 1945, Dr Belt (Cuba's Ambassador in Washington) told the British minister that President Grau was contemplating denouncing the Anglo–Cuban Agreement because the UK was not buying Cuban cigars and was profiting greatly from invisible earnings (e.g. insurance premiums). Dodds to Bevin, no. 18, 'Cuba Annual Report, 1945', 28 Jan. 1946, TNA FO371/51535 AN492, par. 17.

4. 'Economic and Commercial Conditions in Cuba' by Brimelow (first secretary, commercial), Sept. 1949 (London: HMSO, 1950), p. 1.
5. 'A Move From Madrid: British Embassy Leaving: Withdrawal to Valencia', *The Times*, 29 Dec. 1936, p. 12; 'Obituary: Sir George Ogilvie-Forbes: A Varied Diplomatic Career', *The Times*, 12 July 1954, p. 10.
6. Sir Geoffrey Thompson, *Front-line Diplomat* (London: Hutchinson, 1959), p. 120.
7. Ogilvie-Forbes to George Messersmith (US Ambassador, Havana), 27 May 1941, TNA FO371/ 25932 A4385.
8. Ogilvie-Forbes to FO, T. no. 203, 8 Aug. 1940; Ogilvie-Forbes to Halifax, no. 98, 4 Oct. 1940, enclosing 'Memorandum on Spanish Activities in Cuba' by Stagg (n.d.), TNA FO371/24188 A3711.
9. Ogilvie-Forbes to Halifax, no. 125, 21 Nov. 1940, TNA FO371/24187 A4589/460/14.
10. FO 'Cuba Annual Report, 1940', pars 11–12.
11. FO 'Cuba Annual Report, 1940', par. 2.
12. For examples of official US opinions, see Lars Schoultz, *That Infernal Little Cuban Republic: The United States and the Cuban Revolution* (Chapel Hill, NC: University of North Carolina Press, 2009), pp. 34–6.
13. Ogilvie-Forbes to Eden, no. 54, 24 May 1941, TNA FO371/25926 A4384.
14. Ogilvie-Forbes to Eden, no. 168, 8 Sept. 1943, 'Political Report on Cuba, 1941', TNA FO461/2 (part 7 July to Sept. 1943), par. 2.
15. FO 'Cuba Annual Report, 1940', pars 11–12; minute by Perowne, 30 April 1940, TNA FO371/24187 A3066.
16. Lizzie Collingham, *The Taste of War: World War Two and the Battle for Food* (London: Allen Lane, 2011), p. 506; Ina Zweiniger-Bargielowska, *Austerity in Britain: Rationing, Controls, and Consumption, 1939–1955* (Oxford: Oxford University Press, 2000), p. 17.
17. Ogilvie-Forbes to Eden, no. 79, 2 July 1941, TNA FO371/25925 A5653.
18. Ogilvie-Forbes to FO, T. no. 307, 19 Dec. 1941; minute by Makins, 26 Dec. 1941, TNA FO371/25925 A10480.
19. Minute by Serans, 24 Dec. 1941, TNA FO371/25925 A10553.
20. Humphreys, *Latin America and the Second World War: Volume One*, pp. 76–7.
21. I.C.B. Dear and M.R.D. Foot (eds), *The Oxford Companion to the Second World War* (Oxford and New York: Oxford University Press, 1995), pp. 677–81.
22. Memorandum, 'Summary of Anglo–Cuban Relations' by Hohler, 29 April 1943, TNA FO371/33825(B) A4008.
23. L.A. Wheeler, 'War and Postwar Agricultural Problems of Latin America', in *Economic Problems of Latin America*, ed. Seymour E. Harris (New York and London: McGraw-Hill, 1944), pp. 69–91 (81).
24. Ogilvie-Forbes to Eden, T. no. 27, 27 Sept. 1941, TNA FO371/25925 A8659.
25. Minute by Hohler, 10 Dec. 1941, TNA FO371/25925 A9421.
26. R.A. Humphreys, *Latin America and the Second World War: Volume Two 1942–1945* (London: Athlone/ ILAS, 1982), pp. 5–6; 'Cuban Police Seize Key German Spy', *New York Times*, 6 Sept. 1942, p. 19; Ruby Hart Phillips, *Cuba: Island of Paradox* (New York: McDowell/Obolensky, 1959), p. 217.
27. Schoultz, *National Security*, p. 201. Thirty-five allied ships were sunk in the region in 1943 and only three in 1944.

28. Thomas D. Schoonover, *Hitler's Man in Havana: Heinz Lüning and Nazi Espionage in Latin America* (Lexington: University Press of Kentucky, 2008), pp. 89–92, 120–22, 139–40.
29. 'Agreement between the United States and Cuba for Military Cooperation, Signed at Habana, June 19, 1942', *FRUS, 1942: The American Republics Volume VI* (Washington, DC: US Govt Printing Office, 1963), pp. 267–73.
30. Ogilvie-Forbes to Eden, no. 31, 18 Feb. 1943, TNA FO371/33903 A2343.
31. Spruille Braden, *Diplomats and Demagogues: The Memoirs of Spruille Braden* (New Rochelle, NY: Arlington House, 1971), p. 255.
32. Ogilvie-Forbes to Eden, no. 87, 12 May 1943, 'Political Report on Cuba, 1942', TNA FO461/2 (part 6 April to June 1943), par. 4. A later report cited 200 employees in the US mission compared to a mere 30 in the British legation. The FBI had as many as 50 officers, but the British equivalent consisted of just one. See 'memorandum' by Hobson (n.d.), enclosure within Dodds to Eden, no. 173, 25 Nov. 1944, TNA FO371/38095 AN4675.
33. Blake-Tyler (Washington) to Ogilvie-Forbes, 16 Feb. 1943; Ogilvie-Forbes to Blake-Tyler, 24 Feb. 1943: TNA FO371/33825(B) A2662; Ogilvie-Forbes to Eden, no. 1, 1 Jan. 1944, 'Political Report on Cuba, 1943', TNA FO461/3 (part 9 Jan. to March 1944), par. 11.
34. Ogilvie-Forbes to Eden, no. 33, 19 Feb. 1943, TNA FO371/33903 A2344.
35. Demonstrating awareness of historical Anglo–American rivalry in the island, he added, 'Sir Lionel Carden would turn in his grave.'
36. Ogilvie-Forbes to Eden, no. 33, 19 Feb. 1943, TNA FO371/33903 A2344.
37. Memorandum, 'The United States and Great Britain in Latin America' by Perowne, 26 Feb. 1943; minute by Perowne, 26 Feb. 1943: TNA FO371/33903 A2230.
38. Minute by Gallop, 26 March 1943, TNA FO371/33903 A2213.
39. Campbell (Washington) to Perowne, no. 24c, 29 May 1943, TNA FO371/33903 A5359.
40. Minute by Perowne, 15 June 1943, TNA FO371/33903 A5359. Perowne's underlining. Perowne's name is associated with his department's April 1943 ' "Bones of Contention" in Latin America' communication to all its missions in the region, presaging commercial opportunities at the end of the war. It was sent again in 1946 with the objective of eliminating as far as possible 'all outstanding causes of friction' and in order to facilitate 'healthy commerce' with the region. See various documents in TNA: PRO BT11/3279; especially South American Dept. to Chancery (all Chanceries in Latin America), 31 July 1946, f 1; 23 October 1946, f 5a.
41. Dr R.A. Humphreys to Gallop, draft letter, 1 March 1943, TNA FO371/33903 A2213.
42. Memorandum 'Summary of Anglo–Cuban Relations' by Hohler, 29 April 1943, TNA FO371/33825(B) A4008; Ogilvie-Forbes to Eden, no. 86E, 11 May 1943, enclosing 'Amendment to Memorandum "Bones of Contention" in Latin America', TNA FO371/33825(B) A4690.
43. Ogilvie-Forbes to Eden, no. 9E, 11 Jan. 1944, TNA FO371/38076 AN289; Tout (BT) to Butler (FO), 2 March 1944, TNA FO371/38076 A974; untitled FO memorandum, 10 Aug. 1944, TNA FO371/38076 AN3206.
44. Ogilvie-Forbes to FO, 11 Feb. 1944, TNA FO371/38084 AN608.
45. Ogilvie-Forbes to FO, 4 Feb. 1944, TNA FO371/38084 AN5674; Hobson to FO, 10 June 1944, FO371/38084 AN2248. The Havana newspaper quoted

was *Información*. The decision evidently caused resentment in Cuban circles, especially as Britain did elevate some of its other missions in Latin America to embassy status.

46. Prime Minister to Foreign Secretary, 5 Feb. 1944: Winston S. Churchill, *The Second World War: Closing the Ring* (Boston, MA: Houghton Mufflin, 1951), pp. 693–4.

47. Minutes by Hohler (23 June 1943) and Butler (26 June 1943), TNA FO371/33825(B) A5802.

48. Hobson (Havana) to FO, T. no. 180, 28 July 1944, TNA FO371/38087 AN2939.

49. Ogilvie-Forbes to Eden, no. 9E, 11 Jan. 1944, TNA FO371/38076 AN289.

50. Dodds to Eden, no. 2, 'Cuba Annual Report, 1944' (report written by Consul General Hobson), 1 Jan. 1945, TNA FO371/44411 AN391, pars 4–5.

51. Memorandum, 'Economic Conditions in Cuba' by British consulate general (Havana), 30 June 1944, TNA FO371/38079 AN2809.

52. Thomas, *Pursuit of Freedom*, p. 735.

53. FO 'Cuba Annual Report, 1944', pars 1 and 9.

54. Dodds to Eden, no. 173, 25 Nov. 1944, enclosing 'Memorandum' by Hobson, n.d., TNA FO371/38095 AN4675.

55. Kirk and McKenna, *Canada–Cuba Relations*, pp. 17–23.

56. FO 'Cuba Annual Report, 1945', par. 34.

57. Dodds to Bevin, no. 8, 'Cuba Annual Report, 1946', 24 Jan. 1947, TNA FO371/60879 AN825, par. 22.

58. Cleugh (consulate general, Havana) to Dept. of Overseas Trade, 'Enclosure: Economic Conditions in Cuba', 21 June 1945, TNA FO371/44415 AN2175.

59. Hobson (Consulate General, Havana) to Secretary of State (BT), no. 76, 17 Nov. 1944, TNA FO371/38076 AN4605.

60. 'Economic and Commercial Conditions in Cuba', Sept. 1949, pp. 20–1; p. 30; Appendices XI and XXV.

61. Dodds to Bevin, no. 12, 'Cuba Annual Report, 1947', 31 Jan. 1948, TNA FO371/67970 AN568, par. 42.

62. Humphreys, *Latin America and the Second World War: Volume Two*, p. 223.

63. Andrew Gamble, *Britain in Decline: Economic Policy, Political Strategy and the British State* (London and Basingstoke: St Martin's Press, 1994), p. 101.

64. Alan Sked and Chris Cook, *Post-War Britain: A Political History* (London: Penguin, 1993), p. 26.

65. Peter Howlett, 'The wartime economy, 1939–1945', pp. 1–31 (19–20); Sir Alexander Cairncross, 'Economic policy and performance, 1945–1964', pp. 32–66 (39–40): both in *The Economic History of Britain Since 1700, Volume 3: 1939–1992*, ed. Roderick Floud and Donald McCloskey (Cambridge: Cambridge University Press, 1994).

66. 'Churchill and the birth of the special relationship', www.bbc.co.uk/news, 9 March 2012.

7 Cold War: Democracy to Dictatorship

1. Ritchie Ovendale, *Anglo–American Relations in the Twentieth Century* (Basingstoke: Macmillan, 1998), pp. 76–7.

2. F.S. Northedge, *Descent from Power: British Foreign Policy, 1945–1973* (London: Allen and Unwin, 1974), pp. 23, 38.
3. R.A. Humphreys (Royal Institute of International Affairs, Balliol College, Oxford) to Evans (FO), 23 Nov. 1943, enclosing 'Cuba Intelligence Report', TNA FO371/30466 A11658, p. 6. This chapter includes extracts of an article first published as Chris Hull, 'British Diplomacy in Havana from the Second World War to the Revolution', *International Journal of Cuban Studies*, 2.1 (2009), pp. 54–63 (http://cubanstudies.plutojournals.org/Portals/8/Issues).
4. Dodds to Bevin, no. 18, 28 Jan. 1946, TNA FO371/51535 AN492.
5. FO 'Cuba Annual Report, 1946', pars 1–2.
6. Dodds to Bevin, no. 12, 'Cuba Annual Report, 1947', 31 Jan. 1948, TNA FO371/67970 AN568, par. 2.
7. Havana Chancery to South American Dept., 14 Oct. 1946, enclosing 'A Statement of Current Problems in Cuba', TNA FO371/51543 AN3226; 'Agreed Note of Meeting at the Board of Trade at 3pm on Tuesday, 11th December, 1945', TNA FO277/249 f 9.
8. Patterson (BT) to Cahan (Treasury), 10 Sept. 1946, AN2780; minute by Minford (FO), 21 Sept. 1946 AN2780; Rowe-Dutton (Treasury) to Wilson Young (FO), 2 Dec. 1946, AN3675: TNA PRO FO371/51534.
9. Dodds to Atlee, no. 202, 16 Dec. 1946, enclosing summary of article from '*Hoy*' (8 Dec. 1946), TNA FO371/60881 AN37.
10. Dodds to Dr Alberto Inocente Álvarez (Ministry of State, Cuba), 9 July 1946, TNA FO277/251.
11. Dodds to Wilson Young, 7 Feb. 1947, AN784; 'Meeting to discuss the position in Cuba as regards our sugar interests and the United Railways of Havana' by Wiggin (FO), 18 April 1947, AN1456: TNA FO371/60881.
12. Dodds to Bevin, no. E.123, 31 July 1947, AN2881; Crick (Bank of England) to Eggers (Treasury), AN3975: TNA FO371/60882.
13. FO 'Cuba Annual Report, 1946', par. 9.
14. Dodds to Bevin, no. 8, 24 Jan. 1947; minute by Rundall, 6 March, 1947: TNA FO 371/60879 AN825.
15. FO 'Cuba Annual Report, 1947', pars 33–4.
16. Betty Holman, *Memoirs of a Diplomat's Wife* (York: Wilton 65, 1998), pp. 142–5.
17. Betty Holman, *Memoirs*, pp. 147–50, 183.
18. Holman to Bevin, no. 11, 'Cuba Annual Report, 1949', 18 Jan. 1950, TNA FO371/81459 AK1011/1, pars 2–3.
19. Holman to Bevin, no. 13, 'Cuba Annual Report, 1950', 19 Jan. 1951, TNA FO371/90770 AK1011/1, pars 2–3.
20. FO 'Cuba Annual Report, 1946', par. 12.
21. FO 'Cuba Annual Report, 1947', par. 12.
22. FO 'Cuba Annual Report, 1949', par. 7.
23. 'Wizard at Work', *Time*, 20 March 1950, p. 36. Pawley owned Miami's bus system and had set up Cuba's first commercial airline. In December 1958, Eisenhower sent him to Havana as his unofficial emissary in a late and unsuccessful effort to persuade Fulgencio Batista to resign. Pawley later helped plan the CIA-sponsored Bay of Pigs invasion. See Thomas G. Paterson, *Contesting Castro: The United States and the Triumph of the Cuban Revolution* (New York and Oxford: Oxford University Press, 1994),

pp. 206–11. These passages on the Leyland deal were first published in Christopher Hull, ' "Going to War in Buses": The Anglo–American Clash over Leyland Sales to Cuba, 1963–64', *Diplomatic History*, 34.5 (2010), pp. 793–822. More extracts from the same article (in Chapter 9 of this book) cover the controversial 1964 Leyland bus sales.

24. Holman to Bevin, 27 Oct. 1950, TNA FO371/81476 AK1372/10; Somerville-Smith (ECGD) to Holman, 8 Dec. 1950, TNA FO371/81476 AK1372/12.
25. Somerville-Smith to Stevenson (Treasury), 6 Jan. 1951, AK1372/2; memorandum, 'Cuba: Leyland buses' by Somerville-Smith, 8 Feb. 1951, AK1372/4; Holman to Morrison, no. 43, 13 April 1951, AK1372/6: TNA FO371/90793.
26. Holman to Eden, no. 2, 'Cuba Annual Report, 1951', 8 Jan. 1952, TNA FO371/97515 AK1011/1, par. 26.
27. Memorandum, 'Cuba: Leyland buses' by Somerville-Smith, 8 Feb. 1951, TNA FO371/90793 AK1372/4.
28. Samuel Farber, *Revolution and Reaction in Cuba, 1933–1960: A Political Sociology from Machado to Castro* (Middletown, CT: Wesleyan University Press, 1976), pp. 130–5.
29. FO 'Cuba Annual Report, 1951', pars 18–19, 22, 26–8, 45. *The Economist* ('Trade Agreement with Cuba', 18 Aug. 1951, p. 417) reported how Britain could now 'compete on what is virtually equal footing with the United States for $85 million worth of Cuban trade'. Although other countries would enjoy the same concession, Britain stood to 'reap the largest harvest'.
30. Holman to Eden, no. 1, 'Cuba Annual Report, 1952', 1 Jan. 1953, TNA FO371/103375 AK1011/1, par. 14.
31. Dodds to Bevin 'Cuba: future prospects of the new president, Dr. Prío Socarrás, and his new administration', no. 192, 30 Dec. 1948, TNA FO371/73995 AN/0021.
32. Holman to Eden, no. 35, 13 March 1952, TNA FO533/6 AK1015/12.
33. Minute by Jackson, 11 March 1952, FO371/97516 AK1015/3; minute by Jackson, 2 April 1952, AK1015/12; memorandum, 'Recognition of new Régime in Cuba' by Barclay, 21 March 1952, AK1015/13.
34. Holman to Eden, no. 36, 20 March 1952, TNA FO371/97516 AK1015/18.
35. Dodds (Beckley, Sussex) to Cecil (FO), 11 March 1952, TNA FO371/97516 AK1015/12.
36. Holman to Eden, no. 5, 'Cuba Annual Report, 1953', 12 Jan. 1954, TNA FO371/108989 AK1011/1, pars 7, 15, 18. Britain renewed its commitment for further cigar purchases to a value of $0.75 m for 1954, rising to $1 m in 1955 and 1956. Cuba was also glad to see the conclusion of a new International Sugar Agreement in August 1953, allotting the island an annual crop of five million tons and maintaining the commodity's world price at a satisfactory level. After the de-rationing of sweets for a short period from April 1949, demand outstripped supply, and sweet rationing was reintroduced four months later. Zweiniger-Bargielowska, *Austerity in Britain*, p. 35.
37. Holman to Eden, no. 148, 22 Oct. 1952, TNA FO533/6 AK1015/45.
38. Holman to Eden, no. 36, 1 April 1954, TNA FO371/108991 AK1016/1.
39. Holman to Eden, no. 36, 1 April 1954, TNA FO371/108991 AK1016/1.

40. Jorge I. Domínguez, 'The Batista Regime in Cuba', in *Sultanistic Regimes*, ed. H.E. Chehabi and Juan J. Linz (Baltimore and London: John Hopkins University Press, 1998), pp. 113–31 (127).
41. From 1958, the embassy directly overlooked the western entrance and exit to a new road tunnel, built to link Havana's main seafront avenue with the coastal highway on the opposite eastern side of the harbour.
42. Holman to Eden, no. 36, 1 April 1954, TNA FO371/108991 AK1016/1. The comedic side of British diplomacy in Cuba is highlighted in more detail in Christopher Hull, 'Prophecy and Comedy in Havana: Graham Greene's Spy Novel and Cold War Reality', in Dermot Gilvary and Darren J.N. Middleton (eds), *Dangerous Edges of Graham Greene: Paradoxical Journeys with Saints and Sinners* (New York and London: Continuum, 2011), pp. 149–65.
43. Graham Greene, *Ways of Escape* (London: Bodley Head, 1980), pp. 238–41.
44. Holman to Eden, no. 36, 1 April 1954, TNA FO371/108991 AK1016/1.
45. Oliver to Man, 18 Sept. 1956, TNA FO371/120120 AK1052/1.
46. Gallienne to Lloyd, no. 28, 'Cuba Annual Report, 1955', 2 March 1956, TNA FO371/120115 AK1011/1, par. 5; minute by McGivern, 9 April 1955.
47. Fordham to Lloyd, no. 10, 'Cuba Annual Report, 1956' (report written by First Secretary Oliver), 30 Jan. 1957, TNA FO371/126465 AK1011/1, par. 7.
48. Crosthwaite to Hood, 16 Aug. 1957, TNA FO371/126470 AK1052/1.
49. Gamble, *Britain in Decline*, pp. 118–20.
50. 'Report to the President of the Board of Trade by the United Kingdom Trade Mission to Venezuela, Colombia, the Dominican Republic, Cuba and Mexico: November–December, 1952' (London: HMSO, 1953), pp. 10, 39.
51. 'Economic and Commercial Conditions in Cuba', by Stephens, June 1954 (London: HMSO, 1954), pp. 14, 22–4, 27.
52. Gallienne to Lloyd, no. 28, 'Cuba Annual Report, 1954', 14 Feb. 1955, TNA FO371/114228 AK1011/1, par. 7.
53. FO 'Cuba Annual Report, 1955', par. 11.
54. Minute by Hoyce, 2 Aug. 1955, TNA FO371/114232 AK1151/7.
55. FO 'Cuba Annual Report, 1956', par. 11.
56. Memorandum, 'Trade with Latin America' by Foot (F.O.R.D.), Oct. 1957, TNA FO371/126104 A1153/21.
57. Gott, *Cuba: A New History*, pp. 147–52.
58. Oliver to Lloyd, no. 64, 29 May 1956, TNA FO533/10 AK1015/21.
59. Minute by D. Thomas, 31 July 1956, TNA FO371/120116 AK1015/25.
60. Anthony Gorst and Lewis Johnman, *The Suez Crisis* (London: Routledge, 1997), p. 167.
61. Eisenhower was also upset that events in Egypt distracted from the Soviet intervention in Hungary from 24 October 1956.
62. D. Cameron Watt, 'Demythologising the Eisenhower Era', in *The 'Special Relationship': Anglo–American Relations since 1945*, ed. Roger Louis and Hedley Bull (Oxford: Clarendon Press, 1986), pp. 65–85 (74).
63. 'West must unite to face Russian challenge', *Manchester Guardian*, 11 Nov. 1957, p. 4.
64. Previous ambassador Wilfred Gallienne (1954–) became seriously ill with pneumonia in late May 1956. He was flown home to Guernsey but died a few weeks later.

65. Fordham to FO, T. no. 29, 13 March 1957, TNA FO371/126467 AK1015/11; Fordham to Lloyd, no. 28, 20 March 1957, TNA FO371/126467 AK1015/13.
66. Guillermo Jiménez, *Las empresas de Cuba 1958* (La Habana: Editorial de Ciencias Sociales, 2004), p. 491.
67. Robert Cecil, *A Divided Life: A Biography of Donald Maclean* (London: Bodley Head, 1988), p. 116.
68. Fordham to Lloyd, no. 7, 'Cuba Annual Report, 1957', 13 Jan. 1958, TNA FO371/132162 AK1011/1, par. 12.
69. On MAP and US attempts to pressure Batista, see Mark Phythian and Jonathan Jardine, 'Hunters in the Backyard? The UK, the US and the Question of Arms Sales to Castro's Cuba, 1959', *Contemporary British History*, 13.1 (1999), pp. 32–61 (33–5); Schoultz, *That Infernal Little Cuban Republic*, pp. 71–5.
70. Rubottom to Herter, 17 Jan. 1958, *FRUS 1958–60: Volume VI Cuba* (Washington, DC: US Govt Printing Office, 1991), p. 9.
71. For the background and outcome to US internal debate on the arms embargo, see Morris H. Morley, *Imperial State and Revolution: The United States and Cuba, 1952–1986* (Cambridge: Cambridge University Press, 1987), pp. 58–61.
72. Herter to Embassy in Cuba, 14 March 1958, *FRUS 1958–60: Volume VI Cuba*, p. 60.
73. Oliver to FO, 11 Oct. 1957; minute by Pease, 14 Oct. 1957: TNA FO371/126479/AK1192/1.
74. Extracts of the following analysis into the British arms to Batista controversy (and the later refusal to sell arms to Castro's government) were originally published in Chris Hull, 'Our Arms in Havana: British Military Sales to Batista and Castro, 1958–59', *Diplomacy and Statecraft*, 18.3 (2007), pp. 593–616.
75. Minutes by Doyle and Andrews (11 Nov. 1957), Hildyard (12 Nov. 1957), TNA FO371/126479 AK1192/3.
76. Anthony Sampson, *The Arms Bazaar* (London: Hodder & Stoughton, 1977), pp. 107–8.
77. Jackling (Washington) to Hankey, 3 Dec. 1957, AK1192/10; Hood (Washington) to Rumbold, 14 Dec. 1957, AK1192/13: TNA FO371/126479.
78. Hull, 'Our Arms in Havana', p. 598.
79. Minute by Hankey, 18 Dec. 1957, TNA FO371/126479 AK1192/12.
80. FO to Havana, 23 May 1958, AK1191/9; Fordham to FO, Havana, 23 May 1958, AK1191/10; Fordham to FO, Havana, 25 May 1958, AK1191/11: TNA FO371/132174.
81. Hull, 'Our Arms in Havana', p. 599.
82. Fordham to Hankey, 2 April 1958, TNA FO371/132164 AK1015/20.
83. FO to Havana, 23 May 1958, AK1191/9; Fordham to FO, 23 May 1958, AK1191/10: TNA FO371/132174.
84. Fordham to Lloyd, 18 Nov. 1958, TNA FO371/132165 AK1015/62.
85. Oliver to FO, 25 July 1958, TNA FO 371/132175 AK1192/4.
86. Memorandum, 'Recommendation that we should not object to the sale of Comet tanks' by Hankey, 6 Aug. 1958, TNA FO371/132175 AK1192/6.
87. Schoultz (*That Infernal Little Cuban Republic* , pp. 68–70) details Latin America's ugly reception of the tour.

88. American Dept. memorandum, 'Relations between the United States and the countries of Latin America', 15 July 1958; minute by Hankey, 17 July 1958: TNA FO371/131844 A1042/1.
89. Various protest telegrams contained in folder AK1123/9; FO memorandum by Hildyard, 25 Sep. 1958, AK1123/10: TNA FO371/132179.
90. 'Anglo–Cuban Venture: Big Shipyard near Havana', *The Times*, 1 Nov. 1958, p. 12; *The Times* had announced a valuable order from Cubana de Aviación to buy eight civilian aircraft for $13 m on 12 Aug. 1958 ('Britannia Airliners for Cuba', p. 6).
91. Enclosure 'BBC Monitoring' transcriptions from Radio Rebelde broadcasts (19 and 20 Oct. 1958), TNA FO371/132165 AK1015/47.
92. Benest (Washington) to Hildyard, enclosure 'Coopera al boycot revolucionario: no compres productos ingleses', 23 Dec. 1958, TNA FO371/132176 AK1192/64. Other products listed were: all brands of 'English' whisky; English cars; Glaxo pharmaceuticals; English cloth; Irish linen (manufactured in Northern Ireland and therefore a UK export); English insurance company policies. This and the following chapter contain extracts from an article first published as Christopher Hull, 'Parallel Spheres: Anglo–American Cooperation over Cuba, 1959–61', *Cold War History*, 12.1 (2012), pp. 51–68.
93. Greene, *Ways of Escape*, pp. 244–9.
94. Norman Sherry, *The Life of Graham Greene: Volume Three, 1955–1991* (London: Jonathan Cape, 2004), pp. 94, 102–3.
95. Greene to Delargy, 24 Oct. 1958: Richard Greene (ed.), *Graham Greene: A Life in Letters* (London: Little Brown, 2007), pp. 232–3.
96. Memorandum by Hankey 'Anglo–Cuban Relations', 4 Nov. 1958, TNA FO371/132168 AK1051/14.
97. See Oliver to Hankey, 24 Sept. 1958, TNA FO371/132168 AK1051/1. On the chances of Castro coming to power, the chargé d'affaires in Havana wrote, 'in view of [his] declared opposition to U.S. economic and commercial interests in Cuba, Washington would probably go to very considerable lengths to prevent this happening'.
98. *Hansard Vol. 595, Parliamentary Debates – House of Commons*, 19 Nov. 1958, pp. 1133–4; minutes by Brain and Hankey, 21 Nov. 1958, TNA FO371/132175 AK1192/40.
99. Memorandum, 'Arms for Cuba' by Hankey, 18 Nov. 1958. TNA FO371/132175 AK1192/36; Fordham to Hankey, 2 Dec. 1958, TNA FO371/132165 AK1015/72.
100. *Hansard Vol. 597, Parliamentary Debates – House of Commons*, 15 Dec. 1958, pp. 763–5, 770–5.
101. Fordham to Hankey, Havana, 21 Dec. 1958, TNA FO371/132176 AK1192/63. The British ambassador reported a meeting with Dr Güell. The Cuban foreign minister resented Britain's ungratefulness following his government's support in the United Nations (often in the face of strong criticism at home and abroad) over Suez, Cyprus and other UN matters, and deals such as the Mariel shipyard contract.
102. Hull, 'Our Arms in Havana', p. 601.
103. FO memorandum by Hankey, 12 Dec. 1958, TNA FO371/132176 AK1192/57.

104. Brain to Hood, 22 Dec. 1958, TNA FO371/132176 AK1192/58.
105. Hull, 'Our Arms in Havana', pp. 601–2.

8 Revolution: Anglo–American Cooperation

1. 'Cuba's Civil War: To the Editor of The Times', *The Times*, 3 Jan. 1959, p. 7.
2. Coincidentally, the first Bristol 'Britannia' was delivered to Cuba on the same day, part of a contract with Cubana Airlines for eight civilian aircraft announced in Aug. 1958. The Anglo–Cuban Trade Agreement was renewed for a further three-year period on 24 Dec. 1958.
3. 'Our Men in Havana', *Guardian*, 8 Jan. 1959, p. 8. *The Economist* asserted ('Cuba: Hindsight Wisdom', 10 Jan. 1959, p. 108) that the affair 'made Whitehall look pretty silly, and it will scarcely help to get Britain's relations with the victorious regime in Havana off to a good start'.
4. For example, a vital CIA report (15 Aug. 1958) was only received by the FO in mid-October: FO memorandum by Hankey, 15 Jan. 1959, TNA FO371/139459 AK1192/25. A Parliamentary Select Committee concluded there had been a 'serious failure to obtain timely and accurate information' – *Second Report from the Select Committee on Estimates*, 'Sale of Military Equipment Abroad', Session 1958–59, 11 March 1959 (London: HMSO, 5 Aug. 1959). Hankey to Fordham, 12 June 1959, TNA FO371/138897 A10113/1; Fordham to Hankey, 3 July 1959, TNA FO371/138897 A10113/3. Unfortunately, Fordham was absent on leave from Cuba between 14 July and 7 Nov. 1958, leaving the less-experienced First Secretary Peter Oliver in charge of the embassy.
5. Fordham to FO, 7 Jan. 1959, TNA FO371/139429 AK1051/9.
6. Fordham to FO, T. no. 31, 13 Jan. 1959, TNA FO371/139430 AK1051/16.
7. Havana Chancery to American Dept. (FO), 11 Feb. 1959, enclosure 'Extracts from Dr. Fidel Castro's speech at the Shell refinery on Friday, February 6, 1959', TNA FO371/139431 AK1051/37. There were unsubstantiated claims that President of Shell in Cuba Julio Iglesias, who soon left the island, was implicated in the British arms sales to Batista.
8. Fordham to Hankey, 11 Feb. 1959, TNA FO371/139432 AK1051/38.
9. 'Fuertes oscilaciones en el comercio con Gran Bretaña', *Diario de la Marina*, 9 Jan. 1959, p. 6-B.
10. Oliver to Hildyard, 15 July 1959, TNA FO371/139421 AK10345/10. For similar US reactions to Castro's vituperative speeches, see Louis A. Pérez Jr., 'Fear and Loathing of Fidel Castro: Sources of US Policy Toward Cuba', *Journal of Latin American Studies*, 34.2 (2002), pp. 227–54.
11. Howard Temperley, *Britain and America since Independence* (Basingstoke: Palgrave, 2002), pp. 25–32. Britain and France were embroiled in a war that threatened each other's sovereignty.
12. Stephen Schlesinger and Stephen Kinzer, *Bitter Fruit: The Story of the American Coup in Guatemala* (Cambridge, MA and London: Harvard University Press, 2005), pp. 162–3.
13. 'Editorial Note', *FRUS 1958–60: Volume VI Cuba*, p. 476.
14. FO to Havana, London, 26 March 1959, TNA FO371/139470 AK1223/4.

15. Benest (Washington) to Hildyard, 29 July 1959, TNA FO371/139471 AK1223/25.
16. Smith (ECGD) to McCann (Havana), 18 Aug. 1959, TNA FO371/139455 AK1152/14.
17. Walworth (Admiralty) to Hildyard (FO), 4 Aug. 1959, TNA FO371/139466 AK1214/5; minute by Tristram (FO), 18 Sept. 1959, TNA FO371/139463 AK1214/15; C. Cledwyn Hughes MP (Holyhead) to Ormsby-Gore (FO), 16 Sept. 1959, TNA FO371/139463 AK1214/14; Hildyard (FO) to Miss G. Brown (Washington), 25 Sept. 1959, TNA FO371/139463 AK1214/16.
18. Hull, 'Our Arms in Havana', p. 603.
19. Phythian and Jardine, 'Hunters in the Backyard?', p. 41.
20. Brain to Hood (Washington), 20 Aug. 1959, TNA FO371/139472 AK1223/37.
21. This assertion is repeated in several documents, including FO memorandum, 'The Cuban Request for Hunters' by Hildyard, 22 Oct. 1959, TNA FO371/139473/AK1223/76.
22. Minute by Hildyard, 2 April 1959, TNA FO371/139400 AK1015/77.
23. Draft memorandum by Hildyard 'The Cuban Case', n.d. (*c*.27–9 Oct. 1959), TNA FO371/139473 AK1223/75.
24. Maudling (President of the Board of Trade) to Lloyd, 23 Oct. 1959, TNA FO371/139473 AK1223/74; memorandum by Lord Lansdowne (Joint Parliamentary Under Secretary of State, FO), 'The Sale of Hawker Aircraft to Cuba', 28 Aug. 1959, TNA FO371/139472 AK1223/46.
25. Christian A. Herter to Embassy in the UK, 14 Oct. 1959, *FRUS 1958–60: Volume VI Cuba*, p. 624.
26. 'U.S. objecting to British Arms Sales to Cuba', *The Times*, 17 Oct. 1959, p. 6.
27. Minute by Hildyard, London, 19 Oct. 1959, TNA FO371/139473 AK1223/73. Permanent Under Secretary Derick Hoyer Millar commented (19 Oct.) that the US handling of the issue had been 'lamentable', but thought the embargo should be maintained for the present.
28. Phelps (10 Downing St.) to Ackland (Lloyd's Assistant Private Secretary), 17 Oct. 1959, TNA PREM11 2622/29.
29. FO memorandum by Hildyard, 22 Oct. 1959, TNA FO371/139473 AK1223/76.
30. 'Draft memorandum by the Secretary of State for Foreign Affairs' (n.d., but evidently written between 27 and 29 Oct. 1959), TNA FO371/139473/AK1223/75.
31. Cabinet Secretary's Notebooks, 29 Oct. 1959, TNA CAB195/18 C.C.55 (59); Lloyd (London) to Herter, 29 Oct. 1959, TNA FO371/139473 AK1223/76.
32. Prime Minister's Personal Minute to Lloyd, 31 Oct. 1959, TNA FO371 139474/AK1223/94. On Macmillan's style of leadership, see Peter Hennessy, *The Prime Minister: The Office and Its Holders since 1945* (London: Allen Lane, 2000), pp. 254–6.
33. Hull, 'Our Arms in Havana', p. 606.
34. 'Memorandum of a Conversation, Department of State, Washington', 1 Oct. 1959, *FRUS 1958–60: Volume VI Cuba*, p. 617.
35. Bonsal to Department of State, 6 Nov. 1959, *FRUS 1958–60: Volume VI Cuba*, p. 659. Schoultz (*That Infernal Little Cuban Republic*, pp. 103–5)

provides more evidence of increasing US aversion to Castro and the Cuban Revolution in this crucial Oct.–Nov. 1959 period.

36. Christian A. Herter to Foreign Secretary Selwyn Lloyd, 17 Nov. 1959, *FRUS 1958–60: Volume VI Cuba*, pp. 670–1; Personal 'confidential' diary entry for 23 Nov. 1959, The Papers of Selwyn Lloyd, Churchill Archives Centre, Cambridge University (henceforward SELO), 4/33.

37. Sir William ('Billy') Rootes began as a car distributor, owning a string of national dealerships. He later moved into vehicle manufacturing and was Chairman of the new Dollar Exports Board from 1951.

38. Macmillan to Lloyd, 25 Nov. 1959, TNA PREM 11/2622/8.

39. Cabinet Secretary's Notebooks, 26 Nov. 1959, TNA CAB195/18 C.C.60 (59). The 1959 upturn in British exports to Cuba was short-lived, halving in 1960 and declining further in 1961.

40. Personal 'confidential' diary entry for 26 Nov. 1959, SELO 4/33.

41. Fordham to Hankey, 11 Dec. 1959, enclosing 'Extract from "Revolución" dated December 3, 1959', 'England against Cuban interests', 'Extract from "Revolución" dated December 4, 1959', 'Perfidious Albion and the jet planes' by Jacobino, TNA FO371/139475 AK1223/131.

42. Nigel J. Ashton, *Kennedy, Macmillan and the Cold War: The Irony of Interdependence* (Basingstoke: Houndmills; New York: Palgrave, 2002), pp. 64–5.

43. Minute by Parsons, 11 Dec. 1959, TNA FO371/139421 AK10345/23.

44. 'Living with Castro', *Economist*, 2 July 1960, pp. 16–17.

45. Havana Chancery to American Dept., 14 Jan. 1960, TNA FO371/148213 AK10345/6.

46. Hull, 'Parallel Spheres', p. 55.

47. Lloyd to Herter, T. no. 646, 15 Feb. 1960, TNA FO371/148277 AK1223/15; FO memorandum, 'Helicopters for Cuba' by Hankey, 15 Feb. 1960, TNA FO371/148277 AK1223/22; Herter to Lloyd, 21 Feb. 1960, *FRUS 1958–60: Volume VI Cuba*, pp. 805–7.

48. FO to Washington, T. no. 1093, 12 March 1960, TNA FO371/148278 AK1223/26. Secretary of State Selwyn Lloyd expressed his desire not to 'give way to the Americans'. Minute by Acland, 15 Feb. 1960, TNA FO371/148277 AK1223/15.

49. 'Climax in Cuba', *Economist*, 2 July 1960, p. 60; 'Cuba takes over British and U.S. oil plants', *The Times*, 2 July 1960, p. 8. Compañía Petrolera Shell de Cuba was wholly owned by Canadian Shell Ltd, in turn owned by the Royal Dutch/Shell Group (with 40 per cent British and 60 per cent Dutch shareholders).

50. 'Memorandum from the Assistant Secretary of State for Inter-American Affairs (Rubottom) to the Secretary of State', 2 June 1960, *FRUS 1958–60: Volume VI Cuba*, pp. 934–5; Morley, *Imperial State and Revolution*, p. 104; George D.E. Philip, *Oil and Politics in Latin America: Nationalist Movements and State Companies* (Cambridge: Cambridge University Press, 1982), pp. 103–4.

51. FO American Dept. memorandum, 'Cuba', 10 June 1960, TNA PREM11/3688.

52. FO to Washington, T. no. 2456, 13 June 1960, TNA FO371/148293 AK1531/15; minute by Edmonds, 8 June 1960, TNA FO371/148293 AK1531/11.

53. Minute by Brain, 7 June 1960, TNA FO371/148297 AK1531/63.

54. American Dept. brief for prime minister 'Cuba', 10 June 1960, TNA FO371/148181 AK1015/38.
55. FO American Dept. brief, 'The Situation in Cuba: (including the oil supply problem)', Sept. 1960, TNA FO371/148183 AK1015/71. Fordham thought the Cubans might be hoping to split the British and US governments over the oil issue. Fordham to FO, 6 July 1960, TNA FO371/148298 AK1531/85.
56. Fordham to FO, T. no. 277, 6 July 1960, TNA FO371/148298 AK1531/85.
57. Paul Williams MP to Selwyn Lloyd, 7 July 1960, TNA FO371/148303 AK1531/146; Francis W. Julian (Penzance, Cornwall) to Greville Howard MP, n.d. (*c.*20 July 1960), TNA FO371/148303 AK1531/149.
58. Fearnly (FO) to G. Brown (Washington), 8 July 1960, TNA FO371/148298 AK1531/77.
59. Report by Cabinet Joint Intelligence Committee, 'Cuban Developments and their Impact on the Caribbean', J.I.C. (61) 17 (Final), 2 June 1961, TNA CAB158/43.
60. Brief for Interdepartmental Committee, 'United Kingdom Policy in Latin America', 20 May 1960, TNA FO371/152126, SC (60) 7 (2nd revise).
61. 'Foreign Office Steering Committee Paper: British Interests in Latin America', 19 May 1960, TNA FO371/152126.
62. Stephen G. Rabe, *U.S. Intervention in British Guiana: A Cold War Story* (Chapel Hill: University of North Carolina Press, 2005), pp. 68–70.
63. Schlesinger to Bruce (US ambassador, London), 27 Feb. 1962, *FRUS 1961–63: Vol. XII American Republics* (Washington DC: US Govt Printing Office, 1996), p. 549; Macmillan diary entry, 27 Sept. 1962: Catterall (ed.), *The Macmillan Diaries Vol. II*, p. 500; Ashton, *Kennedy, Macmillan and the Cold War*, pp. 67–71; Stephen G. Rabe, *The Most Dangerous Area in the World: John F. Kennedy Confronts Communist Revolution in Latin America* (Chapel Hill and London: University of North Carolina Press, 1999), pp. 83–95; Rabe, *U.S. Intervention in British Guiana*, pp. 75–123.
64. FO to Washington, T. no. 2456, 13 June 1960, TNA FO371/148293 AK1531/15/G.
65. Eisenhower to Macmillan, 11 July 1960, *FRUS 1958–60: Volume VI Cuba*, pp. 1000–5.
66. Brook to Macmillan, 13 July 1960, TNA PREM11/3688. The prime minister annotated his agreement.
67. Minute by Hankey, 15 July 1960, TNA FO371/148217 AK10345/114. Norman Brain added (15 July), 'I think it is true that the Americans do not apprehend the depth of the hostility to them in Latin America'.
68. Minute by Hankey 'Letter of July 11 from President Eisenhower to the Prime Minister', 15 July 1960, TNA FO371/148217 AK10345/114.
69. Macmillan to Eisenhower, 22 July 1960, *FRUS 1958–60: Volume VI Cuba*, p. 1005 (n.6); Macmillan to Eisenhower, 25 July 1960, *FRUS 1958–60: Volume VI Cuba*, p. 1033. A discussion at the US National Security Council also noted that it was 'almost impossible to keep the Soviets from obtaining tankers'. 'Memorandum of Discussion . . . ', 15 July 1960, *FRUS 1958–60: Volume VI Cuba*, p. 1015.
70. Macmillan to Eisenhower, 25 July 1960, *FRUS 1958–60: Volume VI Cuba*, pp. 1032–4. In his previous letter on 22 July 1960 (p. 1005 n. 6), Macmillan had told Eisenhower, 'Castro is really the very Devil. He is your Nasser'.

71. FO American Dept. brief, 'The Situation in Cuba (including the oil supply problem)', Sept. 1960, TNA FO371/148183 AK1015/71.
72. 'Record of a meeting in Mr. [Livingstone] Merchant's suite at the Waldorf Hotel at 3 p.m. on Tuesday, September 20, 1960', TNA FO371/148183 AK1015/74.
73. In August, the Foreign Office sent a circular to all its Latin American posts outlining three invasion scenarios, and asking their estimations of local reactions if intervention did occur. FO to all Latin American Posts (except Havana), 5 Aug. 1960, TNA FO371/148219 AK10345/142. In June, the Foreign Office had passed on the following to Caccia, for repetition to the State Department: 'in our view, whatever plans the Americans have in mind, the greatest danger which must be avoided at all costs is an unsuccessful operation which would leave Castro in power, but more embittered than ever'. FO to Washington, 13 June 1960, TNA FO371/148293 AK1531/15/G.
74. Hankey to Petrie (UK Delegation, OTAN/NATO, Paris), 18 July 1960, TNA FO371/148218 AK10345/126.
75. Harold Bush-Howard sets out these arguments in 'Coming to Terms with Castro: Britain and the Cuban Revolution, 1958–1965', doctoral thesis, London School of Economics and Political Science (1997), pp. 167–217. They are repeated in Steve Wilkinson, 'Just How Special Is "Special": Britain, Cuba, and US Relations 1958–2008: An Overview', *Diplomacy & Statecraft*, 20.2 (2009), pp. 291–308.
76. FO American Dept. brief 'The Situation in Cuba (including the oil supply problem)', Sept. 1960, TNA FO371/148183 AK1015/71.
77. Hull, 'Parallel Spheres', p. 59.
78. Peter Lewis, *The Fifties* (London: Heinemann, 1978), pp. 32–3.
79. 'Ministers to tour Britain in new export drive: Mr. Macmillan asks firms for aggressive sales policy', *The Times*, 19 July 1960, p. 6.
80. 'After Seventeen Months: Cuban Question Mark' by J. Halcro Ferguson, *Observer*, 22 May 1960, p. 7.
81. Caccia to FO, T. no. 1633, 16 Aug. 1960, TNA FO371/148260 AK1151/20.
82. Hull, 'Parallel Spheres', p. 60.
83. Fordham to Lloyd, 21 Aug. 1959, TNA FO371/139402 AK1015/139.
84. Sir H. Caccia (Washington) to FO, T. no. 1405, 18 July 1960, TNA FO371/148217 AK10345/110.
85. William Millward, 'Life in and out of Hut 3', in *Codebreakers: The Inside Story of Bletchley Park*, ed. F.H. Hinsley and Alan Stripp (Oxford and New York: Oxford University Press, 1994), pp. 17–29 (26).
86. Marchant to Home, 'Annual Review, 1960', 17 Jan. 1961, TNA FO371/156137 AK1011/1, par. 8.
87. Marchant to FO, T. no. 511, 3 Oct. 1960, TNA FO371/148262 AK1152/41.
88. Minute by Hankey, 20 Oct. 1960, TNA FO371/148254 AK11345/11.
89. FO memorandum by Scott, 'U.S. request for the denial of trans-shipment facilities for U.S. goods bound for Cuba', 20 Dec. 1960, TNA FO371/156211 AK113145/1.
90. Minute by Hankey, 14 Oct. 1960, TNA FO371/148262 AK1152/43.
91. Memorandum, 'UK Trade with Cuba' by Hankey, 20 Oct. 1960, TNA FO371/148262 AK1152/46.
92. Hull, 'Parallel Spheres', p. 61.

93. Hood to FO, T. no. 523, 3 Oct. 1960, TNA FO371/148219 AK10345/158. US documents affirm that the British pre-empted and staved off the US request. The British embassy in Washington suggested an approach to the Canadians instead, an idea the State Department did not pursue. See 'Memorandum from John C. Pool of the Office of Caribbean and Mexican Affairs to the Assistant Secretary of State for Inter-American Affairs (Mann)', 26 Oct. 1960, *FRUS 1958–60: Volume VI Cuba*, pp. 1100–2.
94. Minute by Hankey, 6 Oct. 1960, TNA FO371/148219 AK10345/158/A.
95. Marchant to FO, T. no. 532, 8 Oct. 1960, TNA FO371/148219 AK10345/160/G; FO to Washington, T. no. 5175, 20 Oct. 1960, TNA FO371/148219 AK10345/158.
96. Greenhill (Washington) to Hankey, 13 Jan. 1961, TNA FO371/156176 AK103145/28. Canada, Italy and West Germany agreed to perform similar functions, but on a smaller scale.
97. Sutherland to Hankey, 2 Feb. 1961, TNA FO371/156177 AK103145/46.
98. Minutes by Scott (5 Jan. 1961) and Hankey (6 Jan. 1961), TNA FO371/156175 AK103145/4; Marchant to FO, T. no. 24, 5 Jan. 1961, TNA FO371/156138 AK1015/3.
99. D.R. Thorpe, *Supermac: The Life of Harold Macmillan* (London: Chatto & Windus, 2010), pp. 492–4.
100. FO 'Annual Review, 1960', pars 5–6.
101. Sutherland to Edmonds (FO), 19 Jan. 1961, TNA FO371/156138 AK1015/11; 'Gun Taken from Embassy Roof: Castro Demobilising', *Guardian*, 23 Jan. 1961, p. 6.
102. Marchant to FO, T. no. 267, 6 April 1961, TNA FO371/156140 AK1015/41.
103. Minute by Edmonds, 7 April 1961, TNA FO371/156140 AK1015/41.
104. For a detailed account of Sea Fury engagements, see Howard Jones, *The Bay of Pigs* (Oxford and New York: Oxford University Press, 2010), pp. 106–7; Peter Wyden, *Bay of Pigs: The Untold Story* (London: Cape, 1979), pp. 250–5. The *Río Escondido* was sunk and the *Houston* beached after being hit by fire from a Sea Fury piloted by US-trained Cuban pilot Captain Enrique Carreras Rojas; Thomas, *Pursuit of Freedom*, pp. 1358–9.
105. FO to UK Mission to UN (New York), T. no. 1620, 19 April 1961, TNA FO371/156179 AK103145/97; UK Mission to UN (New York) to FO, T. no. 746, 21 April 1961, TNA FO371/156181 AK103145/125.
106. Cabinet Secretary's notebooks, 20 April 1961, TNA CAB195/19 C.C.22 (61).
107. *Hansard Vol. 639, Parliamentary Debates – House of Commons*, 26 April 1961, pp. 406–13. Michael Foot MP (Labour) asked, 'Are we to take it from the right hon. Gentlemen's replies and from the votes cast...that the British Government condone and even support the action which the American Government took about Cuba?'
108. Memorandum, 'Cuba' by Hankey, 9 May 1961, TNA FO371/156184 AK103145/181. On British foreknowledge of the Bay of Pigs invasion, see Ashton, *Kennedy, Macmillan and the Cold War*, pp. 66–7. For British agreement to the United States using Caribbean territories for future combat operations, see L.V. Scott, *Macmillan, Kennedy and the Cuban Missile Crisis: Political, Military and Intelligence Aspects* (Basingstoke: Macmillan; New York: St Martin's Press, 1999), p. 27; 'Britain gave US use of Bahamas air base in Cuba missile crisis' by Richard Norton-Taylor, *Guardian*, 23 Dec. 1992, p. 2.

109. Macmillan diary entry, 5 May 1961: Catterall (ed.), *The Macmillan Diaries Vol. II*, p. 381.
110. Hoyer Millar to Caccia, 18 May 1961, TNA FO371/156184 AK10345/181.
111. Caccia to Hoyer Millar, 24 May 1961, TNA FO371/156184 AK10345/189.
112. Hull, 'Parallel Spheres', p. 64.
113. Caccia to Home, no. 83, 1 May 1961, TNA FO371/156145 AK1015/150.
114. Marchant to Home, 31 July 1961, TNA FO371/156151 AK1015/252.
115. Minute by Brain, 18 Aug. 1961, TNA FO371/156151 AK1015/252.
116. Sutherland to Edmonds, 6 July 1961, TNA FO371/156219 AK1195/5/G.
117. FO memorandum, 'Economic Relations Department' by Mason, 10 Dec. 1964, TNA FO371/178112 UEE1049/219.
118. 'Credit for Communists', *Economist* (UK), 22 Feb. 1964, p. 719.
119. Alan P. Dobson, 'The Kennedy Administration and Economic Warfare against Communism', *International Affairs*, 64.4 (1988), pp. 599–616 (601).
120. Maudling to Heath, 19 April 1961, TNA FO371/156214 AK1152/20. The date coincided with the Bay of Pigs invasion, and Maudling signed off, 'Of course, all this sounds a bit academic today.'
121. Schoultz, *That Infernal Little Cuban Republic*, pp. 175–8.
122. Marchant to Home, no. 63.S, 7 Dec. 1961, TNA FO371/156153 AK1015/282.
123. FO brief 'Bermuda Meeting: December 1961, Cuba', series B no. 11(d), n.d., TNA FO371/156185 AK103145/222.
124. Marchant to Home, 'Annual Review for Cuba 1961', 11 Jan. 1962, TNA FO371/162308 AK9843/5, par. 5.

9 Shipping, the Missile Crisis and Buses

1. Schoultz, *National Security*, pp. 20, 24, 38, 106.
2. Hal Brands, *Latin America's Cold War* (Cambridge, MA: Harvard University Press, 2010), p. 16.
3. Alistair Hennessy, 'Cuba, Western Europe and the US: An Historical Overview', in *The Fractured Blockade: West European–Cuban Relations during the Revolution*, ed. Alistair Hennessy and George Lambie (London: Macmillan, 1993), pp. 11–63 (13–15).
4. *Hansard Vol. 484, Parliamentary Debates – House of Commons*, 15 Feb. 1951, p. 630.
5. FO memorandum, 'Cuba' by Godber, 27 Sept. 1962, TNA FO371/162347 AK1051/1.
6. FO memorandum, 'Cuba' by Godber, 27 Sept. 1962, TNA FO371/162347 AK1051/1.
7. Philip Hanson, *Western Economic Statecraft in East–West Relations: Embargoes, Sanctions, Linkage, Economic Warfare, and Détente* (London: Royal Institute of International Affairs; New York: Routledge & Kegan Paul, 1988), pp. 26–7; Gunnar Adler-Karlsson, *Western Economic Warfare 1947–1967: A Case Study in Foreign Economic Policy* (Stockholm: Almqvist & Wiksell, 1968), pp. 49–71.
8. 'Draft Personal Message from the Foreign Secretary [Lord Home] to Mr. Dean Rusk', enclosure within Home to Prime Minister, PM/62/107, 1 Aug. 1962, TNA PREM11/4542.
9. Hull, 'Going to War in Buses', p. 797.

10. Memorandum, 'Cuba and N.A.T.O.' by Hankey, 13 April 1962; minutes by Cheetham and Reilly, 16 April 1964: TNA FO371/162368 AK1152/37.
11. Fish (BT) to Cheetham (FO), 24 May 1962, TNA T312/876.
12. Golt (BT) to Cheetham, 29 March 1962, TNA T312/876 A1071/48. For analysis of Anglo–American differences over trade to Cuba and the CoCom issue, see Scott, *Macmillan, Kennedy and the Cuban Missile Crisis*, pp. 23–32; Ian Jackson, *The Economic Cold War: America, Britain and East–West Trade, 1948–63* (Basingstoke: Palgrave, 2001), pp. 159–217; G.R. Thomas, 'Trade and Shipping to Cuba 1961–1963: An Irritant in Anglo–American Relations', doctoral thesis, Aberystwyth, 2000, chs 2 and 3.
13. Kendrick (Ministry of Defence) to Cheetham, 4 April 1962, TNA FO371/162368 AK1152/33.
14. Lord Home to President of the Board of Trade (Erroll), 15 June 1962, TNA PREM11/3689.
15. Erroll to Foreign Secretary (Home), 22 June 1962, TNA PREM11/3689.
16. 'Record of a conversation...June 24, 1962', TNA DO182/90 f 367A.
17. TNA CAB128/36 C.C. (62) 42nd Conclusions, 26 June 1962; Cabinet Secretary's Notebooks, 26 June 1962, TNA CAB195/21 C.C.42 (62).
18. Schoultz, *That Infernal Little Cuban Republic*, p. 205; Dino A. Brugioni, *Eyeball to Eyeball: The Inside Story of the Cuban Missile Crisis* (New York: Random House, 1991), p. 162.
19. Macmillan diary entry, 3 Oct. 1962: Catterall (ed.), *The Macmillan Diaries Vol. II*, p. 502.
20. 'Cuba is discussed by Rusk and Home' by Max Frankel, *New York Times*, 24 Sept 1962, p. 1.
21. Sir P. Dean (UK Mission to UN, New York) to FO, T. no. 1397, 24 Sept. 1962, TNA FO371/162355 AK1121/59.
22. Brigstocke (Washington) to Bellamy (Ministry of Transport), 25 Sept. 1962, TNA FO371/162356 AK1121/61.
23. Sutherland (Washington) to Cromartie (FO), 21 Sept. 1962, TNA FO371/162369 AK1152/59.
24. Home to Macmillan, 1 Oct. 1962, TNA PREM11/3689; Macmillan to Home, 1 Oct. 1962, TNA PREM11/3689.
25. FO to Washington, T. no. 6952, 5 Oct. 1962, TNA FO371/162356. Negotiated after their war in 1812, when 'freedom of the seas' was the US *casus belli*, the 1815 convention restored trade between the two nations and eliminated discriminatory duties.
26. Robb (Washington) to Moore (FO), 5 Oct. 1962, TNA FO371/162357 AK1121/83.
27. 'Britain rejects call for Cuba boycott', *The Times*, 5 Oct. 1962, p. 12.
28. 'El León y Androcles' por Nuez, *Revolución* (Havana), 6 Oct. 1962 (I thank Jorge Catalá Carrasco for discovering this cartoon). According to legend, the Roman slave Androcles flees a cruel master for the African desert and extracts a thorn from the paw of a lame lion he encounters. Following his capture by Romans, Androcles confronts the lion in a gladiatorial arena, but it reciprocates the slave's earlier kindness by sparing his life.
29. 'British Vessel under Fire off Cuba', *The Times*, 12 Sept. 1962, p. 8; 'Threat of Armed Attacks on Ships Trading with Cuba', *The Times*, 12 Oct. 1962, p. 11.

30. Watson to Butler, 'Cuba: Annual Review for 1963' (compiled by Scott), 7 Jan. 1964, TNA FO371/174002 AK1011/1, par. 11. Both the Batista and Castro governments had made half-hearted requests for Britain to cede sovereignty of the Cay Sal Bank, these particular islets of the Caribbean archipelago lying 70 km north of the Cuban coast and 270 km west of the capital Nassau. See Bush-Howard, 'Coming to Terms with Castro', pp. 96–100.
31. 'Memorandum for the Record' and 'Memorandum Prepared by Director of Central Intelligence McCone', 29 March 1963, *FRUS 1961–1963, Vol. XI: Cuban Missile Crisis and Aftermath* (Washington, DC: United States Govt Printing Office, 1996), pp. 744–6.
32. This intelligence cooperation is analysed in detail in James G. Hershberg, 'Their Men in Havana: Anglo–American Intelligence Exchanges and the Cuban Crises, 1961–62', *Intelligence and National Security*, 15.2 (2000), pp. 121–76.
33. G.R. Way (JIB) to Head of Chancery (Havana), 7 May 1962, TNA FO371/ 162374 AK1201/15.
34. Sutherland (Washington) to Parsons, 17 Sept. 1962, enclosing memorandum by Sutherland on conversations held at the Pentagon on 12 Sept. 1962, TNA FO371/162374 AK1201/20/G.
35. Sutherland (Washington) to Parsons, 5 Sept. 1962, TNA FO371/162314 AK1015/90.
36. Oakeshott (Havana) to Edmonds (FO), 23 March 1962, TNA FO371/162374 AK1201/10.
37. Domingo Amuchastegui, 'Cuban Intelligence and the October Crisis', in *Intelligence and the Cuban Missile Crisis*, ed. James G. Blight and David A. Welch (London: Frank Cass, 1998), pp. 101, 116 n. 41.
38. Marchant to FO, T. no. 315, 17 Aug. 1962, AK1193/2; Marchant to FO, T. no. 319, 20 Aug. 1962, AK1193/3; Marchant to FO, T. no. 322, 21 Aug. 1962, AK1193/4; FO memorandum, 'Cuba' by Slater, 24 Aug. 1962, AK1193/7: TNA FO371/162374.
39. 'Record of a meeting held at Admiralty House [...] October 23, 1962', TNA PREM11/3689; Philip M. Williams, *Hugh Gaitskell: A Political Biography* (London: Cape, 1979), pp. 693–4. Gaitskell reportedly received much anti-American correspondence. Healey initially doubted that Washington had much evidence of missiles.
40. Michael Dobbs, *One Minute to Midnight: Kennedy, Khrushchev, and Castro on the Brink of Nuclear War* (New York: Alfred A. Knopf, 2008); Scott, *Macmillan, Kennedy and the Cuban Missile Crisis*, pp. 37–189; Ashton, *Kennedy, Macmillan and the Cold War*, pp. 72–89; P.G. Boyle, 'The British Government's View of the Cuban Missile Crisis', *Contemporary Record*, 10.3 (1996), pp. 22–38.
41. G.D. Rawnsley, 'How Special Is Special? The Anglo–American Alliance during the Cuban Missile Crisis', *Contemporary Record*, 9.3 (1995), pp. 586–601 (590).
42. Marchant to FO, T. no. 454, 24 Oct. 1962, TNA FO371/162377 AK1261/59; Marchant to Home, no. 55, 30 Nov. 1962, TNA FO371/162409 AK1261/685.
43. FO to Washington, T. no. 7488, 25 Oct. 1962, TNA FO371/162375.
44. Brugioni, *Eyeball to Eyeball*, p. 402.

45. FO to New York, T. no. 3881, 23 Oct. 1962, TNA FO371/162375 AK1261/7.
46. Lord Hailsham (Lord President of the Council and Minister for Science and Technology) to Lord Chancellor (Lord Dilhorne), 25 Oct. 1962, TNA FO371/162388 AK1261/275/G.
47. Dilhorne to Foreign Secretary (Home), 26 Oct. 1962, TNA FO371/162388 AK1261/275/G.
48. Thomas, 'Trade and Shipping to Cuba', pp. 176–97; Rawnsley, 'How Special Is Special?', pp. 593–6.
49. Home to Macmillan, 27 Oct. 1962, TNA FO371/162385 AK1261/213/G.
50. Marchant to FO, T. no. 483, 29 Oct. 1962, TNA FO371/162383 AK1261/166; Ormsby Gore (Washington) to FO, T. no. 2771, 2 Nov. 1962, TNA FO371/162383 AK1261/166(A).
51. For example, 'At about 3p.m. local time today the following convoy passed the Embassy heading west.' Marchant to FO, T. no. 463, 25 Oct. 1962, TNA FO371/162380 AK1261/110.
52. Minutes by Parsons (28 Nov. 1962) and Slater (29 Nov. 1962), TNA FO371/162407 AK1261/653.
53. Sutherland (Washington) to Slater, 5 Nov. 1962, enclosing 'Intelligence Reports from Her Majesty's Embassy, Havana' for 2–8 Nov. 1962, sent to G. Summ, Office of Caribbean Affairs, State Department, Washington DC, TNA FO371/162399 AK1261/497.
54. David Reynolds, *Britannia Overruled: British Policy and World Power in the Twentieth Century* (Harlow: Longman, 2000), pp. 200–3.
55. Marchant to Slater, 27 March 1963, TNA FO371/168169 AK1051/3. The French (also representing German interests), Swiss, Swedes, Belgians, Spaniards and the Dutch all received promises of debt repayments.
56. Using Russian archives, Aleksandr Fursenko and Timothy Naftali state that Khrushchev's objective during the visit was to 'convince Castro that too overt a dependence on Moscow would work to his disadvantage'. See *'One Hell of a Gamble': Khrushchev, Castro, Kennedy, and the Cuban Missile Crisis, 1958–1964* (London: Pimlico, 1999), p. 332; FO 'Cuba: Annual Review for 1963', par. 3.
57. Marchant to Cheetham, 23 May 1963, TNA FO371/168195 AK1152/4.
58. Alan P. Dobson, 'Anglo–American Relations and Diverging Economic Defence Policies in the 1950s and 1960s', in *Twentieth Century Anglo–American Relations*, ed. Jonathan Hollowell (Basingstoke: Palgrave, 2001), pp. 143–65 (158–9).
59. Lynch (ECGD) to Parsons (FO), 24 June 1963, TNA FO371/168197 AK1154/6.
60. Mackenzie (BT) to Parsons, 24 June 1963, enclosing 'Trade with Cuba' by C.R.E., 24 June 1963, TNA FO371/168195 AK1152/6.
61. George Lambie, 'Anglo–Cuban Commercial Relations in the 1960s: A Case Study of the Leyland Motor Company Contracts with Cuba', in *The Fractured Blockade: West European–Cuban Relations during the Revolution*, ed. Alistair Hennessy and George Lambie (London: Macmillan, 1993), pp. 163–96 (167); Morley, *Imperial State and Revolution*, p. 230.
62. 'Ventana: La "Guerra de los Autobuses"', by Flavio, *Revolución* (Havana), 10 Jan. 1964, p. 2. The buses probably received this nickname due to their white with black-striped livery, and because they had metaphorically saved the lives of long-suffering bus passengers.

63. Scott to FO, 27 July 1963, TNA FO371/168195 AK1152/8.
64. Stokes to Alan Green (Minister, Board of Trade), 1 August 1963, TNA FO371/168195 AK1152/12.
65. Lynch (ECGD) to Sharp (Treasury), 2 Aug. 1963, TNA FO371/168197 AK1154/8.
66. Mackenzie to Scott, 3 Sept. 1963, TNA FO371/168195 AK1152/11.
67. Note by the Treasury E.G.C. (63) 4 'E.C.G.D. Cover for the sale of Leyland buses to Cuba', 12 Aug. 1963, TNA FO371/168197 AK1154/10.
68. Minutes of Export Guarantee Committee, 13 Aug. 1963, TNA FO371/168197 AK1154/18.
69. Note by the Secretary of Export Guarantee Committee 'E.C.G.D. Cover for the sale of Leyland buses to Cuba: Draft Submission to Ministers', 22 Aug. 1963, TNA FO371/168197 AK1154/12.
70. Smithers to Maudling, 26 Aug. 1963, TNA FO371/168197 AK1154/7.
71. Erroll to Maudling, 26 Aug. 1963, TNA FO371/168198 AK1154/26.
72. Du Cann to Smithers, 30 Aug. 1963, TNA FO371/168198 AK1154/24.
73. FO memorandum, 'Export of Leyland Buses to Cuba' by West, 30 Aug. 1963, TNA FO371/168198 AK1154/27.
74. Minute by Douglas-Home, 1 Sept. 1963, TNA FO371/168198 AK1154/27.
75. Hull, 'Going to War in Buses', p. 804.
76. Douglas-Home to du Cann, 2 Sept. 1963, TNA FO371/168198 AK1154/28.
77. Internal minute, 'Leyland Buses for Cuba' by Slater, 19 Sept. 1963, TNA FO371/168198 AK1154/32.
78. Internal minute, 'Leyland Buses for Cuba' by Slater, 20 Sept. 1963, TNA FO371/168198 AK1154/33.
79. Hull, 'Going to War in Buses', p. 806.
80. Minute by Caccia, 20 Sept. 1963, TNA FO371/168198 AK1154/34.
81. Trend to Macmillan, 'Buses for Cuba', 24 Sept. 1963, TNA PREM11/4697.
82. TNA CAB129 (114) C.C. (63) 57th conclusions, 24 Sept. 1964; Cabinet Secretary's notebooks, 24 Sept. 1963, TNA CAB195/23 C.C.57 (63).
83. Carey (BT) to Bridges (assistant private secretary to foreign secretary), 25 Sept. 1963; minute by Slater, 25 Sept. 1963: TNA FO371/168195 AK1152/18.
84. Record of conversation between US president and foreign secretary at the White House, 4 Oct. 1963, TNA FO371/168198 AK1154/37.
85. Ormsby Gore to FO, 8 Oct. 1963, TNA FO371/168196 AK1152/23.
86. Parsons to Sutherland, 25 Oct. 1963, TNA FO371/168195 AK1152/17.
87. Slater to Killick (Washington), 20 Dec. 1963, TNA FO371/168196 AK1152/40.
88. Watson to FO, 2 and 4 Dec. 1963, TNA FO371/168196 AK1152/43 and AK1152/45.
89. 'Blackmail at the Bus Stop', *Guardian*, 9 Jan. 1964, p. 8.
90. Ormsby Gore to FO, 10 Jan. 1964, TNA FO371/174072 AK1153/11.
91. Ormsby Gore to FO, 9 Jan. 1964, TNA FO371/174072 AK1153/8.
92. 'Lord Stokes: chairman of British Leyland', *The Times*, 22 July 2008; 'British to Train Cubans', *New York Times*, 9 Jan. 1964, p. 6. During the First Battle of the Marne (Sept. 1914), French troops rapidly mobilized to the warfront in requisitioned buses and taxicabs in order to fend off a German advance on Paris.
93. There is detail on the buses' involvement in Pedro Luis Padrón, 'Este es un pueblo', in idem, *Playa Girón: Derrota del imperialismo. Tomo I: La invasión y*

los Héroes (La Habana, 1961), pp. 242–9. A photo of a burning bus following attack by a B-26 bomber is found on p. 530.

94. Ormsby Gore to FO, T. no. 89, 9 Jan. 1964, TNA PREM11/4697.
95. 'Cuba Deal "unfriendly act" to U.S.', *Daily Telegraph*, 9 Jan. 1964, p. 26; 'Briton Defends Bus Sale', *New York Times*, 20 Feb. 1964, p. 3.
96. Bundy told Johnson, 'They would maintain that Cuba is no worse than the Soviet Union and that we greatly exaggerate this, and in their public, they'd be right. I mean that's their politics. The British man on the street thinks we've got a neurosis on Cuba.' 'Editorial note', citing telephone conversation between Bundy and Johnson, 7 Jan. 1964, *FRUS 1964–1968, Vol. XXXII: Dominican Republic; Cuba; Haiti; Guyana* (Washington, DC: United States Govt Printing Office, 2005), p. 546.
97. Sutherland to Hutchinson, 11 Jan. 1964, TNA FO371/174072 AK1153/21.
98. 'The Bus Sale to Cuba', *New York Times*, 12 Jan. 1964, p. 1.
99. 'Trading with Cuba: Trade or Aid?', *Economist*, 11 Jan. 1964, p. 94.
100. Watson to FO, T. no. 2, 11 Jan. 1964, TNA PREM11/4697. Wright annotated to Macmillan, 'I'm afraid you have got a good chit from Castro. This won't help with the President!'
101. Watson to Hutchinson, 22 Jan. 1964, TNA FO371/174073 AK1153/43.
102. 'Paper Prepared in the Department of State', n.d., *FRUS 1964–68, Vol. XXXII*, p. 598.
103. See summary of George Ball speech on 'United States Policy toward Cuba' to North Atlantic Council, Paris, 23 March 1964, within 'editorial note', *FRUS 1964–68, Vol. XXXII*, pp. 620–1.
104. Minutes by Hutchinson and Slater, 1 and 4 Feb. 1964, TNA FO371/174049 AK1123/3.
105. 'Memorandum of a Conversation' (British Ambassador Ormsby Gore and Under Secretary George Ball), 7 Feb. 1964, *FRUS 1964–68, Vol. XXXII*, p. 577. Ball attempted to highlight Britain's isolation in a secret session of NATO two months later when he asked if it was the intention of members that 'a single nation should be able to frustrate a serious policy affecting the defense of free world interests in a vital area of the world'. Philip Geyelin, *Lyndon B. Johnson and the World* (London: Pall Mall Press, 1966), p. 92.
106. Internal minute, 'Details of Contracts Concluded or Under Negotiation and Enquiries from the Cuban Government' by Sutherland, 11 Feb. 1964, TNA FO371/174075 AK1153/81.
107. 'Brief for the Prime Minister's Visit to the United States' on 'Anglo–Cuban Trade' by Board of Trade, 29 Jan. 1964, TNA FO371/174073 AK1153/49.
108. Internal minute 'Anglo–Cuban Trade' by American Dept., 10 Feb. 1964, TNA FO371/174074 AK1153/75.
109. Greenhill to Cheetham, 17 Jan. 1964, TNA FO371/174073 AK1153/34.
110. Greenhill to Slater, 4 Feb. 1964, TNA FO371/174074 AK1153/68.
111. Ormsby Gore to FO, 4 Feb. 1964, TNA FO371/174069 AK1151/10.
112. Morris H. Morley, 'The United States and the Global Economic Blockade of Cuba: A Study in Political Pressures on America's Allies', *Canadian Journal of Political Science*, 17.1 (1984), pp. 25–48 (34); Michael Mastanduno, *Economic Containment: CoCom and the Politics of East-West Trade* (Ithaca, NY: Cornell University Press, 1992), p. 126.

113. 'Cuba Will Buy 1000 More Buses, British Suppliers of 400 Reveal', *Washington Post*, 4 Feb. 1964, p. A13; Ormsby Gore to FO, T. no. 434, 3 Feb. 1964, TNA FO371/174069 AK1151/8.
114. Sutherland to Slater, 5 Feb. 1964, TNA FO371/174069 AK1151/13.
115. 'Sir Alec refuses to rule out March 19: Election not "top of pops" ', *Guardian*, 18 February 1964, p. 5; John Dickie, *'Special' No More: Anglo–American Relation: Rhetoric and Reality* (London: Weidenfeld & Nicolson, 1994), p. 134; Geyelin, *Lyndon B. Johnson*, p. 90.
116. Wright (Private Secretary) to Douglas-Home, 11 Feb. 1964, TNA PREM 11/4695 ff 40–1.
117. 'U.S. Calmer on Cuba "Crisis" ', *Daily Telegraph*, 10 Feb. 1964, p. 24.
118. Report of meeting 'Trade with Cuba – E.C.G.D. Cover' between FO, ECGD and Board of Trade by Mackenzie, 2 March 1964, TNA FO371/174069 AK1151/21.
119. TNA CAB C.M. (64) 16th conclusions, 3 March 1964.
120. TNA CAB C.P. (64) 20th conclusions, 24 March 1964; Cabinet memorandum, 'Export Credit Cover for Cuba' by Edward Heath, 19 March 1964, TNA CAB129 (117 Pt. 2) C.P. (64) 76.
121. Lord Harlech to FO, T. no. 1554, 25 April 1964; Greenhill to Rennie, 2 May 1964: TNA FO371/174049 AK1122/11 and AK1122/12.
122. Anthony Howard, *Rab: The Life of R.A. Butler* (London: Cape, 1987), p. 329; R.A. Butler, *The Art of the Possible: The Memoirs of Lord Butler* (London: Hamilton, 1971), pp. 256–7.
123. Lord Harlech to FO (containing personal message from US Secretary of State to Prime Minister), 29 April 1964, TNA T312/1644.
124. 'Britain Weighs Curb on Cuban Credit', *New York Times*, 11 May 1964, p. 10; 'Cuban Horse-Trading', *New Statesman*, 15 May 1964, p. 749.
125. *Hansard Vol. 689, Parliamentary Debates – House of Commons*, 10 Feb. 1964, pp. 19–20; *Hansard Vol. 690*, 25 Feb. 1964, p. 238; *Hansard Vol. 695*, 12 May 1964, p. 218.
126. 'Memorandum from Rusk to LBJ with schedule of appointments for Wilson', 28 Feb. 1964; 'Memorandum from Bundy to LBJ', 2 March 1964: Country File: United Kingdom vol. 15, March 2, 1964, Lyndon B. Johnson National Security Files, 1963–69: Liddell Hart Centre for Military Archives, King's College, London, UK, microfilm reel 9 (hereafter LBJ: LHC followed by microfilm reel number).
127. 'Memorandum of a Conversation', 2 March 1964, *FRUS, 1964–68: Volume XII Western Europe* (Washington, DC: United States Govt Printing Office, 2001), pp. 458–61.
128. 'Telegram from the [US] Embassy in France to the Department of State', 12 Feb. 1964, *FRUS 1964–68, Vol. XII*, p. 39.
129. FO official M. Brown annotated on 9 June 1964: 'Our hopes that the Cuban requirements for locomotives would have been satisfied by their recent purchases from France and the Soviet Union have proved over-optimistic': TNA FO371/174077 AK1153/150.
130. 'Ship Beached with Cuba Bus Cargo: Collision in Thames', *The Times*, 28 Oct. 1964, p. 6.
131. See Morley, *Imperial State and Revolution*, p. 236; 'CIA "waged four-year war against Cuba" ', *The Times*, 18 July 1975, p. 5; 'Was Magdeburg sunk to halt

buses for Cuba?', *Lloyd's List*, 2 June 2001, p. 6; 'Leyland Buses, Cuba and the CIA', an episode in *Document*, BBC Radio 4, 30 March 2009; E. John McGarry, *The Cuban Bus Crisis: Tales of CIA Sabotage* (self-published Kindle book, June 2011).
132. Lambie, 'Anglo–Cuban Commercial Relations', p. 183.
133. Thomas B. Allen, 'Remember the Maine?', *National Geographic*, 193.2 (Feb. 1998), pp. 92–109.
134. 'Background paper: Cuba', 6 Feb. 1964, Country File: United Kingdom vol. 15, 12 Feb. 1964 to 13 Feb. 1964, LBJ: LHC Microfilm Reel 9.
135. 'Discurso Pronunciado por el Comandante Fidel Castro Ruz…1° de mayo de 1964', www.cuba.cu/gobierno/discursos/1964/esp/f010564e.html (accessed 24 June 2010).
136. Hull, 'Going to War in Buses', pp. 821–2.
137. 'Cuban Horse-Trading', *New Statesman*, 15 May 1964, p. 749.

Conclusion

1. FO memorandum, 'An Anglo–American Balance Sheet' by Planning Staff, 21 Aug. 1964, TNA FO371/177830 PLA24/7A.
2. Harlech to Nicholls (FO), 30 June 1964, TNA FO371/177830 PLA24/2B. David Ormsby Gore assumed this title in February 1964.
3. John W. Young, 'Great Britain's Latin American Dilemma: The Foreign Office and the Overthrow of "Communist" Guatemala, June 1954', *The International History Review*, 8.4 (1986), pp. 573–92; Sharon I. Meers, 'The British Connection: How the United States Covered Its Tracks in the 1954 Coup in Guatemala', *Diplomatic History*, 16.3 (1992), pp. 409–28.
4. Robert H. Ferrell (ed.), *The Diary of James C. Hagerty: Eisenhower in Mid-Course, 1954–1955* (Bloomington: Indiana University Press, 1983), p. 75.
5. In 1965, when the Foreign Office was considering US and British disagreements over Cuba, one Planning Section official wrote, 'Our Cuban policy must to a large extent be a policy vis-à-vis the U.S. We should always therefore bear in mind how it fits in with other parts of the Anglo–American dialogue.' Minute by Thomas (FO Planning Section), 9 Feb. 1965, TNA FO371/179458 AK1072/7.
6. Watson to Slater, 4 March 1964, TNA FO371/174076 AK1153/109. Castro reportedly told the Swiss ambassador he was 'at a loss to know what to do next in his relations with Her Majesty's Government'. Watson to FO, T. no. 156, 31 March 1964, TNA FO371/174076 AK1153/123.
7. FO memorandum, 'Shell and Cuba' by Slater, 9 April 1964, TNA FO371/174076 AK1153/126.
8. 'Cuba pays £9,000 to shot Briton', *Guardian*, 16 July 1964, p. 1.
9. On 'collaborating elites' and a British–Egyptian/US–Cuban parallel, see Alan Knight, 'Rethinking British Informal Empire in Latin America (Especially Argentina)', in *Informal Empire in Latin America: Culture, Commerce and Capital*, ed. Matthew Brown (Malden, MA and Oxford: Blackwell, 2008), pp. 23–38 (35).
10. Watson to Butler, no. 28, 16 June 1963, TNA FO371/174122 AK1941/2.

11. FO memorandum, 'Trade with Cuba' by Slater, 16 June 1964, TNA FO371/174078 AK1153/157.

12. Slater to Watson, 29 June 1964, TNA FO371/174078 AK1153/157.

13. The difficult task of being a British envoy in Havana was not helped by the remoteness of US ministers/ambassadors, and their reluctance to fraternize with other foreign diplomats.

14. Fidel Castro, *My Life*, ed. by Ignacio Ramonet (London: Allen Lane, 2007), p. 499. According to Castro, the underhand 'pact' related to an Anglo–American agreement over limited application of the 1996 Helms–Burton Act and permission to make oil investments in the Middle East.

15. Wolf Grabendorff, 'The United States and Western Europe: Competition or Cooperation in Latin America?', in *Latin America Western Europe and the U.S.: Reevaluating the Atlantic Triangle*, ed. Wolf Grabendorff and Riordan Roett (New York and Eastbourne: Praeger, 1985), pp. 257–73 (266).

16. Nicholas J. White, *Decolonisation: The British Experience since 1945* (Harlow: Longman, 1999), p. 54. Jason C. Parker analyses the subject in detail in *Brother's Keeper: The United States, Race, and Empire in the British Caribbean, 1927–1962* (Oxford: Oxford University Press, 2008), pp. 161–70.

17. A long-running trade dispute between the United States and the European Union over preferential treatment did erupt in the 1990s, the so-called 'Banana War'.

18. Minute by Hankey, 5 July 1961, TNA FO371/156218 AK1192/11.

19. Cabinet secretary's notebooks, 29 Jan. 1959, TNA CAB195/18 C.C.3 (59).

20. Macmillan diary entry, 25 Sept. 1963: Catterall (ed.), *The Macmillan Diaries Vol. II*, p. 598.

21. See Table 4 in this conclusion for Board of Trade statistics for Anglo–Cuban imports/exports in the years 1959 to 1964, and Table 3 at the beginning of Chapter 8 for Cuban Treasury statistics for 1902 to 1957.

Bibliography

Primary Sources: Archival

Great Britain: National Archives of the United Kingdom, Public Record Office, Kew Gardens, London

Foreign Office Files

FO 5 Political and other departments: general correspondence before 1906, USA, Series II.

FO 72 Political and other departments: general correspondence before 1906, Spain.

FO 108 Political and other departments: general correspondence before 1906, Cuba.

FO 368 Commercial and Sanitary Department: general correspondence from 1906.

FO 371 general correspondence from 1906–66.

FO 414 Confidential print North America.

FO 461 Confidential print America.

FO 533 Confidential print Central America and the Caribbean.

FO 800/144 Private office and private papers of the Marquess of Lansdowne.

FO 881 Confidential print (numerical series).

Board of Trade Files

BT 11 Commercial Relations and Exports Department.

Colonial Office Files

CO 852 Economic General Department.

Treasury Files

T 312 Finance Overseas and Co-ordination Division.

Prime Minister's Office

PREM 11 Correspondence and Papers, 1951–64.

Cabinet Office Files

CAB 128 Cabinet Meeting Minutes (CM and CC Series).

CAB 129 Cabinet: Memoranda (CP and C Series).

CAB 195 Cabinet Secretary's Notebooks.

Ministry of Defence and Cabinet Office Files
CAB 158 Central Intelligence Machinery: Joint Intelligence Sub-Committee Later Committee: Memoranda (JIC Series).

Archival Sources: United States of America

National Archives at College Park, Maryland
Record Group 84 (NARA).

Franklin D. Roosevelt Presidential Library, Hyde Park, New York
Sumner Welles Papers (SWP).

Archival Sources: Universities

Cambridge University, Churchill Archives Centre
The Papers of Selwyn Lloyd, Personal 'confidential' diary, 1959 (SELO).

King's College, Liddell Hart Centre for Military Archives, London
Lyndon B. Johnson National Security Files (on microfilm), 1963–69 (LBJ: LHC).

Archival Sources: Regional Archives

Birmingham Libraries and Archives, Records of the Birmingham Chamber of Commerce and Industry, MS 2299.
Liverpool Record Office, Records of the Liverpool Chamber of Commerce, 380 COM.

Published Primary Sources

Great Britain

C.K. Webster (ed.), *Britain and the Independence of Latin America, 1812–1830: Select Documents from the Foreign Office Archives, Volume II* (New York: Oregon Books, 1970).

British Documents on Foreign Affairs: Reports and Papers from the Foreign Office Confidential Print (Bethesda, MD: University Publications of America, c.1986–96):
Part II: From the First to the Second World War; Series D, Latin America, 1914–1939 (editor: D.K. Adams):
Vol. 1: South America, 1914–1922.
Vol. 2: Central America and Mexico, 1914–1922.
Vol. 8: Mexico, Central and South America, August 1931–July 1932.
Vol. 9: Mexico, Central and South America, August 1932–May 1933.
Vol. 10: Mexico, Central and South America, May 1933–March 1934.
Vol. 11: Mexico, Central and South America, March 1934–June 1934.

Part II: From the First to the Second World War; Series C: North America, 1919–1939 (editor: D.K. Adams):
Vol. 17: Latin America and the Philippines, 1919–1939.
Vol. 20: Annual Reports, 1928–1932.

Part II: From the First to the Second World War; Series F: Europe, 1919–1939 (editor:
Christopher Seton-Watson):
Vol. 24: Portugal 1919–39.

United States

Papers Relating to the Foreign Relations of the United States [...] 1911 (Washington, DC: US Govt Printing Office, 1918).
Papers Relating to the Foreign Relations of the United States [...] 1912 (1919).
Papers Relating to the Foreign Relations of the United States [...] 1913 (1920).
Papers Relating to the Foreign Relations of the United States [...] 1917 (1926).
Papers Relating to the Foreign Relations of the United States [...] 1932: The American Republics Volume V (1948).
Papers Relating to the Foreign Relations of the United States [...] 1933: The American Republics Volume IV (1950).
Papers Relating to the Foreign Relations of the United States [...] 1933: The American Republics Volume V (1952).
Papers Relating to the Foreign Relations of the United States [...] 1942: The American Republics Volume VI (1963).
Foreign Relations of the United States, 1958–60: Volume VI Cuba (1991).
Foreign Relations of the United States, 1961–63: Volume XII American Republics (1996).
Foreign Relations of the United States, 1961–63: Volume XI Cuban Missile Crisis and Aftermath (1996).
Foreign Relations of the United States, 1964–68: Volume XII Western Europe (2001).
Foreign Relations of the United States, 1964–1968, Volume XXXII Dominican Republic; Cuba; Haiti; Guyana (2005).

Collected Letters, Diaries, Screenplay, Writings

Great Britain

The Letters of Queen Victoria: Volume III, 1896–1901, ed. George Earl Buckle (London: John Murray, 1932).
Churchill, Winston S. *The Second World War: Closing the Ring* (Boston, MA: Houghton Mufflin, 1951).
Our Man in Havana, screenplay by Graham Greene, directed by Carol Reed (Columbia Pictures, 1959).
The Collected Writings of John Maynard Keynes, Vol. 12: Economic Articles and Corre-spondence; Investment and Editorial, ed. Donald Moggridge (London: Macmillan for the Royal Economic Society, 1983).
Graham Greene: A Life in Letters, ed. Richard Greene (London: Little Brown, 2007).

The Macmillan Diaries Vol. II: Prime Minister and After: 1957–1966, ed. Peter Catterall (London: Macmillan, 2011).

United States

The Letters of Theodore Roosevelt: Volume 5, The Big Stick, 1905–1907, ed. Elting E. Morison (Cambridge, MA: Harvard University Press, 1951).

Franklin D. Roosevelt and Foreign Affairs: Volume I, ed. Edgar B. Nixon (Cambridge, MA: Harvard University Press, 1969).

The Diary of James C. Hagerty: Eisenhower in Mid-Course, 1954–1955, ed. Robert H. Ferrell (Bloomington: Indiana University Press, 1983).

Official Government Documents

Great Britain

Hansard, Parliamentary Debates – House of Commons.

'Report on the Trade and Commerce of the Island of Cuba for the Year ended June 30, 1913', by Vice-Consul Denys Cowan.

'Report on the Trade and Commerce of the Island of Cuba for the Year ended June 30, 1914', by Vice-Consul Denys Cowan, p. 185: doc. no. 176, *Confidential Print Vol. 2: Central America and Mexico, 1914–1922*.

'British Diplomatic and Commercial Mission to South America, 1918': report by Follett Holt (London: HMSO, May 1919).

'Second Report of the Royal Commission on the Sugar Supply, 1921', *Parliamentary Papers* cmd. 1300 (London: HMSO, 1921).

'Department of Overseas Trade: Report on the Economic Conditions in Cuba', September 1922, by Godfrey Haggard (Consul-General, Havana) (London: HMSO, 1922).

'Department of Overseas Trade: Report on the Economic Conditions in Cuba', November 1925, by M.H.C. Kelham (Acting British Consul General, Havana) (London: HMSO, 1925).

'Correspondence between His Majesty's Government and the Cuban Government Respecting the Ill-Treatment of British West Indian Labourers in Cuba', cmd. 2158 (London: HMSO, 1924).

'Further Correspondence between His Majesty's Government and the Cuban Government Respecting the Ill-Treatment of British West Indian Labourers in Cuba', cmd. 2245 (London: HMSO, 1924).

'Agreement between [HMG] and the Cuban government regarding parcel post with Cuba...., December 1, 1927', cmd. 3212 (London: HMSO, 1928).

'Department of Overseas Trade: Economic Conditions in Cuba', November 1929, by L.C. Hughes-Hallett (Acting British Consul General, Havana) (London: HMSO, 1929).

'Department of Overseas Trade: Economic Conditions in Cuba', no. 518, April 1932, by J.J. Broderick (Consul General, Havana) (London: HMSO, 1932).

'Report of the United Kingdom Sugar Industry Inquiry Committee', cmd. 4871 (London: HMSO, April 1935).

'Commercial Agreement between... the United Kingdom and Cuba... Havana, February 19, 1937', *Parliamentary Papers* cmd. 5383 (London: HMSO, 1937).

'Report to the President of the Board of Trade by the United Kingdom Trade Mission to Venezuela, Colombia, the Dominican Republic, Cuba and Mexico: November–December, 1952' (London: HMSO, 1953).

'Second Report from the Select Committee on Estimates: Sale of Military Equipment Abroad', session 1958–59, 11 March 1959 (London: HMSO, 5 Aug. 1959).

Cuba

Diario de Sesiones del Congreso de la República de Cuba, Novena Legislatura, Habana: Senado, XVIII Sesión – Mayo 30 de 1906 (1906, vol. 9).

Switzerland

League of Nations: *International Sugar Conference held in London from 5 April to 6 May 1937. I: Text of the Agreement; II: Proceedings and Documents of the Conference* (Geneva, 1937).

Online Resources

V.W. Baddeley, 'Lee, Arthur Hamilton, Viscount Lee of Fareham (1868–1947)', rev. Marc Brodie, *Oxford Dictionary of National Biography* (Oxford University Press, 2004), www.oxforddnb.com (accessed 28 Nov 2008).

'Churchill and the birth of the special relationship', www.bbc.co.uk/news/magazine-17272610, 9 March 2012.

Transcripts of Speeches

Discursos de Fidel Castro (Speeches of Fidel Castro), www.cuba.cu/gobierno/discursos.

Radio Programme

'Leyland Buses, Cuba and the CIA' (30 March 2009), an episode in *Document*, BBC Radio 4.

Secondary Sources

Newspapers and Periodicals

Great Britain

The Times
Manchester Guardian (–1959), *Guardian* (1959–)
Observer
Daily Telegraph
Daily Mail

Daily Mirror
Daily News
Daily Graphic
Pall Mall Gazette
Journal of Commerce (Liverpool)
Liverpool Courier
The Economist
New Statesman
South American Journal
Lloyd's List

Cuba

Diario de la Marina
Avance
Mediodía
Cuba Importadora e Industrial
Revolución

United States

New York Times
Washington Post
McClure's Magazine
North American Review
Time
National Geographic

Jamaica

Herald

Books, Articles, Essays and Theses

Adler-Karlsson, Gunnar. *Western Economic Warfare 1947–1967: A Case Study in Foreign Economic Policy* (Stockholm: Almqvist & Wiksell, 1968).

Aguilar, Luis E. 'Cuba, c. 1860–c. 1930', in *Cuba: A Short History*, ed. Leslie Bethell (Cambridge: Cambridge University Press, 1993), pp. 21–56.

Aguilar, Luis E. *Cuba 1933: Prologue to Revolution* (Ithaca, NY and London: Cornell University Press, 1972).

Albert, Bill. *South America and the First World War* (Cambridge: Cambridge University Press, 1988).

Albert, Bill. *South America and the World Economy from Independence to 1930* (London: Macmillan, 1983).

Albert, Bill. 'Sugar and Anglo–Peruvian Trade Negotiations in the 1930s', *Journal of Latin American Studies*, 14.1 (1982), pp. 121–42.

Albert, Bill, and Adrian Graves (eds). *The World Sugar Economy in War and Depression, 1914–40* (London: Routledge, 1988).

Amuchastegui, Domingo. 'Cuban Intelligence and the October Crisis', in *Intelligence and the Cuban Missile Crisis*, ed. James G. Blight and David A. Welch (London: Frank Cass, 1998), pp. 88–119.

Ashton, Nigel J. *Kennedy, Macmillan and the Cold War: The Irony of Interdependence* (Basingstoke: Houndmills; New York: Palgrave, 2002).

Balfour, Sebastian. 'Spain and the Great Powers in the Aftermath of the Disaster of 1898', in *Spain and the Great Powers in the Twentieth Century*, ed. Sebastian Balfour and Paul Preston (London; New York: Routledge, 1999), pp. 13–31.

Ball, S.J. 'The Macmillan Government, British Arms Exports and Indonesia', *Contemporary British History*, 16.2 (2002), pp. 77–98.

Bannock, Graham, R.E. Baxter, Evan Davis. *The Penguin Dictionary of Economics* (London: Penguin, 1992).

Barnett, Correlli. *The Collapse of British Power* (London: Eyre Methuen, 1972).

Bartlett, Christopher J. 'British Reaction to the Cuban Insurrection of 1868–1878', *Hispanic American Historical Review*, 37.3 (1957), pp. 296–312.

Benjamin, Jules R. *The United States & Cuba: Hegemony and Dependent Development, 1880–1934* (Pittsburgh, PA: University of Pittsburgh Press; London: Feffer and Simons, 1977).

Benjamin, Jules R. *The United States and the Origins of the Cuban Revolution: An Empire of Liberty in an Age of National Liberation* (Princeton, NJ: Princeton University Press, 1990).

Bethell, Leslie 'Britain and Latin America in Historical Perspective', in *Britain and Latin America: A Changing Relationship*, ed. Victor Bulmer-Thomas (Cambridge: Cambridge University Press, 1989), pp. 1–24.

Beveridge, William H. *British Food Control* (London: Oxford University Press, 1928).

Boyle, P.G. 'The British Government's View of the Cuban Missile Crisis', *Contemporary Record*, 10.3 (1996), pp. 22–38.

Braden, Spruille. *Diplomats and Demagogues: The Memoirs of Spruille Braden* (New Rochelle, NY: Arlington House, 1971).

Bradford, Richard H. *The Virginius Affair* (Boulder: Colorado Associated University Press, 1980).

Brands, Hal. *Latin America's Cold War* (Cambridge, MA: Harvard University Press, 2010).

Brugioni, Dino A. *Eyeball to Eyeball: The Inside Story of the Cuban Missile Crisis* (New York: Random House, 1991).

Buell, Raymond L. et al. *Problems of the New Cuba: Report of the Commission on Cuban Affairs* (New York: Foreign Policy Association, 1935).

Bulmer-Thomas, Victor. *The Economic History of Latin America since Independence* (Cambridge: Cambridge University Press, 2003).

Bush-Howard, Harold. 'Coming to Terms with Castro: Britain and the Cuban Revolution, 1958–1965', doctoral thesis, London School of Economics and Political Science, 1997.

Butler, R.A. *The Art of the Possible: The Memoirs of Lord Butler* (London: Hamilton, 1971).

Cain, P.J., and A.G. Hopkins. *British Imperialism, 1688–2000* (Harlow: Longman, 2002).

Cairncross, Sir Alexander. 'Economic Policy and Performance, 1945–1964', in *The Economic History of Britain since 1700, Volume 3: 1939–1992*, ed. Roderick

Floud and Donald McCloskey (Cambridge: Cambridge University Press, 1994), pp. 32–66.

Calvert, Peter. 'Great Britain and the New World, 1905–1914', in *British Foreign Policy under Sir Edward Grey*, ed. F.H. Hinsley (Cambridge: Cambridge University Press, 1977), pp. 382–94.

Calvert, Peter. *The Mexican Revolution, 1910–1914: The Diplomacy of Anglo–American Conflict* (Cambridge: Cambridge University Press, 1968).

Campbell Jr, Charles S. *Anglo–American Understanding, 1898–1903* (Baltimore, MD: Johns Hopkins Press, 1957).

Campbell Jr, Charles S. *From Revolution to Rapprochement: The United States and Great Britain, 1783–1900* (New York: Wiley, 1974).

Campbell Jr, Charles S. *Special Business Interests and the Open Door Policy* (New Haven, CT: Yale University Press, 1951).

Carr, Barry. 'Identity, Class, and Nation: Black Immigrant Workers, Cuban Communism, and the Sugar Insurgency, 1925–1934', *Hispanic-American Historical Review*, 78.1 (1998), pp. 83–116.

Castro, Fidel. *My Life*, ed. Ignacio Ramonet (London: Allen Lane, 2007).

Cecil, Robert. *A Divided Life: A Biography of Donald Maclean* (London: Bodley Head, 1988).

Chailloux Laffita, Graciela, and Robert Whitney. 'British Subjects y Pichones en Cuba', in *De dónde son los cubanos*, ed. Graciela Chailloux Laffita (La Habana: Editorial de Ciencias Sociales, 2007), pp. 55–91.

Chalmin, Philippe. *The Making of a Sugar Giant: Tate and Lyle, 1859–1989* (New York: Harwood Academic Publishers, 1990).

Chapman, Charles E. *A History of the Cuban Republic: A Study in Hispanic American Politics* (New York: Macmillan, 1927).

Churchill, Winston S. *My Early Life: A Roving Commission* (London: Thornton Butterworth, 1930).

Cluster, Dick, and Rafael Hernández. *The History of Havana* (New York: Palgrave Macmillan, 2006).

Cobiellas, Michael. 'British Economic Presence in Havana, 1900–1930', *International Journal of Cuban Studies*, 2.1 (2009), pp. 46–53.

Collingham, Lizzie. *The Taste of War: World War Two and the Battle for Food* (London: Allen Lane, 2011).

Dallek, Robert. *Franklin D. Roosevelt and American Foreign Policy, 1932–1945* (New York and Oxford: Oxford University Press, 1979).

Davis, Lance E., and Robert A. Huttenback. *Mammon and the Pursuit of Empire: The Political Economy of British Imperialism, 1860–1912* (Cambridge: Cambridge University Press, 1986).

Dear, I.C.B., and M.R.D. Foot (eds). *The Oxford Companion to the Second World War* (Oxford and New York: Oxford University Press, 1995).

Dickie, John. *'Special' No More: Anglo–American Relation: Rhetoric and Reality* (London: Weidenfeld & Nicolson, 1994).

Dobbs, Michael. *One Minute to Midnight: Kennedy, Khrushchev, and Castro on the Brink of Nuclear War* (New York: Alfred A. Knopf, 2008).

Dobson, Alan P. 'Anglo–American Relations and Diverging Economic Defence Policies in the 1950s and 1960s', in *Twentieth Century Anglo–American Relations*, ed. Jonathan Hollowell (Basingstoke: Palgrave, 2001), pp. 143–65.

Dobson, Alan P. 'The Kennedy Administration and Economic Warfare against Communism', *International Affairs*, 64.4 (1988), pp. 599–616.

Domínguez, Jorge I. 'The Batista Regime in Cuba', in *Sultanistic Regimes*, ed. H.E. Chehabi and Juan J. Linz (Baltimore and London: Johns Hopkins University Press, 1998), pp. 113–31.

Domínguez, Jorge I. *Cuba: Order and Revolution* (Cambridge, MA and London: Belknap Press of Harvard University Press, 1978).

Doyle, Michael W. *Empires* (Ithaca, NY and London: Cornell University Press, 1986).

Du Cann, Edward. *Two Lives: The Political and Business Careers of Edward Du Cann* (Upton upon Severn: Images, 1995).

Dur, Philip, and Christopher Gilcrease. 'US Diplomacy and the Downfall of a Cuban Dictator: Machado in 1933', *Journal of Latin American Studies*, 34.2 (2002), pp. 255–82.

Farber, Samuel. *Revolution and Reaction in Cuba, 1933–1960: A Political Sociology from Machado to Castro* (Middletown, CT: Wesleyan University Press, 1976).

Fitzgibbon, Russell H. *Cuba and the United States, 1900–1935* (New York: Russell & Russell, 1964).

Freeman Smith, Robert. 'Latin America, the United States and the European Powers, 1830–1930', in *The Cambridge History of Latin America: Volume IV c. 1870 to 1930*, ed. Leslie Bethell (Cambridge: Cambridge University Press, 1986), pp. 83–119.

Fry, Michael Graham, Erik Goldstein and Richard Langhorne (eds). *Guide to International Relations and Diplomacy* (London and New York, Continuum, 2002).

Fursenko, Aleksandr, and Timothy Naftali. *'One Hell of a Gamble': Khrushchev, Castro, Kennedy, and the Cuban Missile Crisis, 1958–1964* (London: Pimlico, 1999).

Galeano, Eduardo. *Open Veins of Latin America: Five Centuries of the Pillage of a Continent* (London: Serpent's Tail, 2009; first pub. in Spanish, 1973).

Gamble, Andrew. *Britain in Decline: Economic Policy, Political Strategy and the British State* (London and Basingstoke: St Martin's Press, 1994).

Gellman, Irwin F. *Roosevelt and Batista: Good Neighbor Diplomacy in Cuba, 1933–1945* (Albuquerque: University of New Mexico Press, 1973).

Gellman, Irwin F. *Secret Affairs: Franklin Roosevelt, Cordell Hull, and Sumner Welles* (Baltimore and London: Johns Hopkins University Press, 1995).

Geyelin, Philip. *Lyndon B. Johnson and the World* (London: Pall Mall Press, 1966).

Gilbert, Martin. *Churchill: A Life* (London: Pimlico, 2000).

Gleijeses, Piero. '1898: The Opposition to the Spanish–American War', *Journal of Latin American Studies*, 35.4 (2003), pp. 681–719.

Gorst, Anthony, and Lewis Johnman. *The Suez Crisis* (London: Routledge, 1997).

Gott, Richard. *Cuba: A New History* (New Haven, CT and London: Yale University Press, 2004).

Grabendorff, Wolf. 'The United States and Western Europe: Competition or Cooperation in Latin America?', in *Latin America Western Europe and the U.S.: Reevaluating the Atlantic Triangle*, ed. Wolf Grabendorff and Riordan Roett (New York and Eastbourne: Praeger, 1985), pp. 257–73.

Graff, Frank Warren. *Strategy of Involvement: A Diplomatic Biography of Sumner Welles* (New York and London: Garland, 1988).

Greene, Graham. *Our Man in Havana* (London: Heinemann, 1958).

Greene, Graham. *Ways of Escape* (London: Bodley Head, 1980).

Guerra, Ramiro. *Manual de Historia de Cuba: desde su descubrimiento hasta 1868* (La Habana: Editorial de Ciencias Sociales, 1973).

Haggerty, Sheryllynne, Anthony Webster and Nicholas J. White (eds). *The Empire in One City? Liverpool's Inconvenient Imperial Past* (Manchester: Manchester University Press, 2008).

Hanson, Philip. *Western Economic Statecraft in East–West Relations: Embargoes, Sanctions, Linkage, Economic Warfare, and Détente* (London: Royal Institute of International Affairs; New York: Routledge & Kegan Paul, 1988).

Hart Phillips, Ruby. *Cuba: Island of Paradox* (New York: McDowell/Obolensky, 1959).

Hassall, Christopher. *The Timeless Quest: Stephen Haggard* (London: Arthur Barker, 1946).

Healy, David. *Drive to Hegemony: The United States in the Caribbean 1898–1917* (Madison, WI: University of Wisconsin Press, 1988).

Healy, David. *The United States in Cuba, 1898–1902: Generals, Politicians, and the Search for Policy* (Madison: University of Wisconsin Press, 1963).

Henderson, Peter V.N. 'Woodrow Wilson, Victoriano Huerta, and the Recognition Issue in Mexico', *The Americas*, 41.2 (1984), pp. 151–76.

Hennessy, Alistair. 'Cuba, Western Europe and the US: An Historical Overview', in *The Fractured Blockade: West European–Cuban Relations during the Revolution*, ed. Alistair Hennessy and George Lambie (London: Macmillan, 1993), pp. 11–63.

Hennessy, Alistair, and George Lambie (eds). *The Fractured Blockade: West European–Cuban Relations during the Revolution* (London: Macmillan, 1993).

Hennessy, Peter. *The Prime Minister: The Office and Its Holders since 1945* (London: Allen Lane, 2000).

Hershberg, James G. 'Their Men in Havana: Anglo–American Intelligence Exchanges and the Cuban Crises, 1961–62', *Intelligence and National Security*, 15.2 (2000), pp. 121–76.

Hilton, Sylvia L., and Steve J.S. Ickringill (eds). *European Perceptions of the Spanish–American War of 1898* (Berne: Peter Lang, 1999).

Holman, Betty. *Memoirs of a Diplomat's Wife* (York: Wilton 65, 1998).

Howard, Anthony. *Rab: The Life of R.A. Butler* (London: Cape, 1987).

Howlett, Peter. 'The Wartime Economy, 1939–1945', in *The Economic History of Britain Since 1700, Volume 3: 1939–1992*, ed. Roderick Floud and Donald McCloskey (Cambridge: Cambridge University Press, 1994), pp. 1–31.

Hull, Christopher. 'British Diplomacy in Havana from the Second World War to the Revolution', *International Journal of Cuban Studies*, 2.1 (2009), pp. 54–63.

Hull, Christopher. '"Going to War in Buses": The Anglo–American Clash over Leyland Sales to Cuba, 1963–64', *Diplomatic History*, 34.5 (2010), pp. 793–822.

Hull, Christopher. 'Our Arms in Havana: British Military Sales to Batista and Castro, 1958–59', *Diplomacy and Statecraft*, 18.3 (2007), pp. 593–616.

Hull, Christopher. 'Parallel Spheres: Anglo–American Cooperation over Cuba, 1959–61', *Cold War History*, 12.1 (2012), pp. 51–68.

Hull, Christopher. 'Prophecy and Comedy in Havana: Graham Greene's Spy Novel and Cold War Reality', in Dermot Gilvary and Darren J.N. Middleton (eds), *Dangerous Edges of Graham Greene: Paradoxical Journeys with Saints and Sinners* (New York and London: Continuum, 2011), pp. 149–65.

Humphreys, R.A. *Latin America and the Second World War: Volume One 1939–1942* (London: Athlone/ ILAS, 1981).

Humphreys, R.A. *Latin America and the Second World War: Volume Two 1942–1945* (London: Athlone/ ILAS, 1982).

Humphreys, R.A. *Tradition and Revolt in Latin America and Other Essays* (London: Weidenfeld & Nicolson, 1969).

Ibarra Guitart, Jorge Renato. *El Tratado Anglo–Cubano de 1905: Estados Unidos Contra Europa* (La Habana: Editorial de Ciencias Sociales, 2006).

Jackson, Ian. *The Economic Cold War: America, Britain and East–West Trade, 1948–63* (Basingstoke: Palgrave, 2001).

Jacobs, Charles C. 'The Diplomatic History of the Cuban Ten Years' War, 1868–1878', doctoral thesis, Birmingham University, 1973.

Jenks, Leland Hamilton. *Our Cuban Colony: A Study in Sugar* (New York: Vanguard Press, 1928).

Jessup, Philip Caryl. *Elihu Root: Volume I, 1845–1909* (New York: Dodd, Mead & Co., 1938).

Jiménez, Guillermo. *Las empresas de Cuba 1958* (La Habana: Editorial de Ciencias Sociales, 2004).

Jones, Charles. 'Insurance Companies', in *Business Imperialism 1840–1930: An Inquiry Based on British Experience in Latin America*, ed. D.C.M. Platt (Oxford: Clarendon Press, 1977), pp. 53–74.

Jones, Howard. *The Bay of Pigs* (Oxford and New York: Oxford University Press, 2010).

Kapcia, Antoni. 'Fulgencio Batista, 1933–44: From Revolutionary to Populist', in *Authoritarianism in Latin America since Independence*, ed. Will Fowler (Westport, CT and London: Greenwood Press, 1996), pp. 73–92.

Kapcia, Antoni. 'The Siege of the Hotel Nacional, Cuba, 1933: A Reassessment', *Journal of Latin American Studies*, 34.2 (2002), pp. 283–310.

Kindleberger, Charles P. *The World in Depression, 1929–1939* (Berkeley, CA and London: University of California Press, 1986).

Kirk, John M., and Peter McKenna. *Canada–Cuba Relations: The Other Good Neighbor Policy* (Gainesville: University Press of Florida, 1997).

Kneer, W.G. *Great Britain and the Caribbean, 1901–1913* (East Lansing, MI: Michigan State University Press, 1975).

Knight, Alan. 'Rethinking British Informal Empire in Latin America (Especially Argentina)', in *Informal Empire in Latin America: Culture, Commerce, and Capital*, ed. Matthew Brown (Oxford: Blackwell, 2008), pp. 23–48.

LaFeber, Walter. *The Cambridge History of American Foreign Relations: The American Search for Opportunity, 1865–1913, Vol. 2* (Cambridge: Cambridge University Press, 1993).

Lambie, George. 'Anglo–Cuban Commercial Relations in the 1960s: A Case Study of the Leyland Motor Company Contracts with Cuba', in *The Fractured Blockade: West European–Cuban Relations during the Revolution*, ed. Alistair Hennessy and George Lambie (London: Macmillan, 1993), pp. 163–96.

Lewis, Colin. 'The Financing of Railway Development in Latin America, 1850–1914', *Ibero-Amerikanisches Archiv*, 9 (1983), pp. 255–78.

Lewis, Peter. *The Fifties* (London: Heinemann, 1978).

Machado y Morales, Gerardo. *Ocho años de lucha* (Miami: Ediciones Históricas Cubanas, 1982).

Mahan, Alfred Thayer. *The Interest of America in Sea Power: Present and Future* (London: Sampson Low, Marston & Co., 1897).

Mastanduno, Michael. *Economic Containment: CoCom and the Politics of East–West Trade* (Ithaca, NY: Cornell University Press, 1992).

McAvoy, Muriel. *Sugar Baron: Manuel Rionda and the Fortunes of Pre-Castro Cuba* (Gainesville: University Press of Florida, 2003).

McGarry, E. John. *The Cuban Bus Crisis: Tales of CIA Sabotage* (self-published Kindle book, June 2011).

McGinty, Stephen. *Churchill's Cigar* (London: Macmillan, 2007).

McKercher, B.J.C., and S. Enjamio. ' "Brighter Futures, Better Times": Britain, the Empire, and Anglo–American Economic Competition in Cuba, 1898–1920', *Diplomacy & Statecraft*, 18.4 (2007), pp. 663–87.

McLeod, M.C. 'Undesirable Aliens: Race, Ethnicity, and Nationalism in the Comparison of Haitian and British West Indian Immigrant Workers in Cuba, 1912–1939', *Journal of Social History*, 31.3 (1998), pp. 599–623.

Meers, Sharon I. 'The British Connection: How the United States Covered Its Tracks in the 1954 Coup in Guatemala', *Diplomatic History*, 16.3 (1992), pp. 409–28.

Miller, Rory. *Britain and Latin America in the Nineteenth and Twentieth Centuries* (London: Longman, 1993).

Millward, William. 'Life in and out of Hut 3', in *Codebreakers: The Inside Story of Bletchley Park*, ed. F.H. Hinsley and Alan Stripp (Oxford and New York: Oxford University Press, 1994), pp. 17–29.

Monger, George. *The End of Isolation: British Foreign Policy 1900–1907* (London: Nelson, 1963).

Morgan, Ted. *Churchill 1874–1915* (London: Cape, 1983).

Morley, Morris H. *Imperial State and Revolution: The United States and Cuba, 1952–1986* (Cambridge: Cambridge University Press, 1987).

Morley, Morris H. 'The United States and the Global Economic Blockade of Cuba: A Study in Political Pressures on America's Allies', *Canadian Journal of Political Science*, 17.1 (1984), pp. 25–48.

Munro, Dana G. *Intervention and Dollar Diplomacy in the Caribbean, 1900–1921* (Princeton, NJ: Princeton University Press, 1964).

Murray, David R. *Odious Commerce: Britain, Spain, and the Abolition of the Cuban Slave Trade* (Cambridge: Cambridge University Press, 1980).

Neale, R.G. *Britain and American Imperialism, 1898–1900* (Brisbane: University of Queensland Press, 1965).

Northedge, F.S. *Descent from Power: British Foreign Policy, 1945–1973* (London: Allen and Unwin, 1974).

Offer, Avner. *The First World War: An Agrarian Interpretation* (Oxford: Clarendon Press, 1989).

Offner, John L. *An Unwanted War: The Diplomacy of the United States and Spain over Cuba, 1895–1898* (Chapel Hill: University of North Carolina Press, 1992).

Ovendale, Ritchie. *Anglo–American Relations in the Twentieth Century* (Basingstoke: Macmillan, 1998).

Padrón, Pedro Luis. 'Este es un pueblo', in idem, *Playa Girón: Derrota del imperialismo. Tomo I: La invasión y los Héroes* (La Habana, 1961).

Pakenham, Thomas. *The Boer War* (London: Weidenfeld & Nicolson, 1997).

Paquette, Robert L. *Sugar Is Made with Blood: The Conspiracy of La Escalera and the Conflict between Empires over Slavery in Cuba* (Middletown, CN: Wesleyan University Press, 1988).

Parker, Jason C. *Brother's Keeper: The United States, Race, and Empire in the British Caribbean, 1927–1962* (Oxford: Oxford University Press, 2008).

Paterson, Thomas G. *Contesting Castro: The United States and the Triumph of the Cuban Revolution* (New York and Oxford: Oxford University Press, 1994).

Paterson, Thomas G., J. Garry Clifford and Kenneth J. Hagan. *American Foreign Relations Vol. 2. A History: Since 1895* (Boston, MA: Houghton Mifflin, 2000).

Pearce, Adrian J. *British Trade with Spanish America, 1763–1808* (Liverpool: Liverpool University Press, 2007).

Pearson Hobson, Richmond. *The Sinking of the 'Merrimac': A Personal Narrative of the Adventure in the Harbor of Santiago de Cuba, June 3, 1898…* (London and New York: T.F. Unwin, 1899).

Peraza Sarausa, Fermín. *Diccionario biográfico cubano: Tomo I* (La Habana, n.d.).

Pérez Jr, Louis A. *Cuba between Empires, 1878–1902* (Pittsburgh, PA: University of Pittsburgh Press, 1983).

Pérez Jr, Louis A. *Cuba: Between Reform and Revolution* (New York: Oxford University Press, 1988).

Pérez Jr, Louis A. *Cuba in the American Imagination: Metaphor and the Imperial Ethos* (Chapel Hill, NC: University of North Carolina Press, 2008).

Pérez Jr, Louis A. *Cuba under the Platt Amendment, 1902–1934* (Pittsburgh, PA: University of Pittsburgh Press, 1986).

Pérez Jr, Louis A. 'Fear and Loathing of Fidel Castro: Sources of US Policy Toward Cuba', *Journal of Latin American Studies*, 34.2 (2002), pp. 227–54.

Pérez Jr, Louis A. *Intervention, Revolution, and Politics in Cuba, 1913–1921* (Pittsburgh, PA: University of Pittsburgh Press, 1978).

Pérez Jr, Louis A. *The War of 1898: The United States and Cuba in History and Historiography* (Chapel Hill, NC and London: University of North Carolina Press, 1998).

Perkins, Dexter. *A History of the Monroe Doctrine* (London: Longmans, 1960).

Philip, George D.E. *Oil and Politics in Latin America: Nationalist Movements and State Companies* (Cambridge: Cambridge University Press, 1982).

Phillips, William. *Ventures in Diplomacy* (London: John Murray, 1955).

Phythian, Mark, and Jonathan Jardine. 'Hunters in the Backyard? The UK, the US and the Question of Arms Sales to Castro's Cuba, 1959', *Contemporary British History*, 13.1 (1999), pp. 32–61.

Pino Santos, Oscar. *El asalto a Cuba por la oligarquía financiera yanqui* (La Habana: Casa de las Américas, 1973).

Placer Cervera, Gustavo. *Inglaterra y La Habana: 1762* (La Habana: Editorial de Ciencias Sociales, 2007).

Platt, D.C.M. 'Economic Imperialism and the Businessman: Britain and Latin America before 1914', in *Studies in the Theory of Imperialism*, ed. Roger Owen and Bob Sutcliffe (Harlow: Longman, 1972), pp. 295–311.

Platt, D.C.M. *Finance, Trade, and Politics in British Foreign Policy 1815–1914* (Oxford and London: Clarendon Press, 1968).

Pletcher, David M. *The Awkward Years: American Foreign Relations under Garfield and Arthur* (Columbia: University of Missouri Press, 1962).

Pollitt, Brian. 'The Cuban Sugar Economy in the 1930s', in *The World Sugar Economy in War and Depression 1914–40*, ed. Bill Albert and Adrian Graves (London and New York: Routledge, 1988), pp. 97–108.

Rabe, Stephen G. *The Most Dangerous Area in the World: John F. Kennedy Confronts Communist Revolution in Latin America* (Chapel Hill and London: University of North Carolina Press, 1999).

Rabe, Stephen G. *U.S. Intervention in British Guiana: A Cold War Story* (Chapel Hill: University of North Carolina Press, 2005).

Rathbone, John Paul. *The Sugar King of Havana: The Rise and Fall of Julio Lobo, Cuba's Last Tycoon* (New York: Penguin, 2010).

Rawnsley, G.D. 'How Special Is Special? The Anglo–American Alliance during the Cuban Missile Crisis', *Contemporary Record*, 9.3 (1995), pp. 586–601.

Reuter, Bertha Ann. *Anglo–American Relations during the Spanish–American War* (New York: Macmillan Co., 1924).

Reynolds, David. *Britannia Overruled: British Policy and World Power in the Twentieth Century* (Harlow: Longman, 2000).

Roberts, Richard. *Schroders: Merchants and Bankers* (Basingstoke: Macmillan Press, 1992).

Ronaldshay, Earl of. *The Life of Lord Curzon: Being the Authorized Biography of George Nathaniel, Marquess Curzon of Kedleston: Vol. I* (London: Ernest Benn, 1928).

Russell, Nelson Vance. 'The Reaction in England and America to the Capture of Havana, 1762', *The Hispanic American Historical Review*, 9.3 (1929), pp. 303–16.

Sampson, Anthony. *The Arms Bazaar* (London: Hodder and Stoughton, 1977).

Sarracino, Rodolfo. *El Grupo Rockefeller actúa: entreguismo e injerencia anglo–yanqui en la década del treinta* (La Habana: Editorial de Ciencias Sociales, 1987).

Sarracino, Rodolfo. *Inglaterra: sus dos caras en la lucha cubana por la abolición* (La Habana: Editorial Letras Cubanas, 1989).

Schlesinger, Stephen, and Stephen Kinzer. *Bitter Fruit: The Story of the American Coup in Guatemala* (Cambridge, MA and London: Harvard University Press, 2005).

Schoonover, Thomas D. *Hitler's Man in Havana: Heinz Lüning and Nazi Espionage in Latin America* (Lexington: University Press of Kentucky, 2008).

Schoultz, Lars. *National Security and United States Policy toward Latin America* (Princeton, NJ and Guildford: Princeton University Press, 1987).

Schoultz, Lars. *That Infernal Little Cuban Republic: The United States and the Cuban Revolution* (Chapel Hill, NC: University of North Carolina Press, 2009).

Schumacher, Frank. 'The American Way of Empire: National Tradition and Transatlantic Adaptation in America's Search for Imperial Identity, 1898–1910', *Bulletin of the German Historical Institute*, 31 (2002), pp. 35–50.

Scott, L.V. *Macmillan, Kennedy and the Cuban Missile Crisis: Political, Military and Intelligence Aspects* (Basingstoke: Macmillan; New York: St Martin's Press, 1999).

Sherry, Norman. *The Life of Graham Greene: Volume Three, 1955–1991* (London: Cape, 2004).

Simpson, J.A, and E.S.C. Weiner (eds). *The Oxford English Dictionary: Volume I, A–Bazouki* (Oxford: Clarendon Press, 1989).

Sked, Alan, and Chris Cook. *Post-War Britain: A Political History* (London: Penguin, 1993).

Smith, Joseph. *Illusions of Conflict: Anglo–American Diplomacy toward Latin America, 1865–1896* (Pittsburgh: University of Pittsburgh Press; London: Feffer & Simons, 1979).

Smith, Joseph. *The Spanish–American War: Conflict in the Caribbean and the Pacific, 1895–1902* (London: Longman, 1995).

Smith, Peter H. *Talons of the Eagle: Dynamics of U.S.–Latin American Relations* (New York: Oxford University Press, 2000).

Smith, Tony. *The Pattern of Imperialism: The United States, Great Britain and the Late-Industrializing World since 1815* (Cambridge: Cambridge University Press, 1981).

Stafford, David. *Churchill and Secret Service* (London: John Murray, 1997).

Steiner, Zara S. *The Foreign Office and Foreign Policy, 1898–1914* (London: Cambridge University Press, 1969).

Stone, Irving. 'British Direct and Portfolio Investment in Latin America before 1914', *Journal of Economic History*, 37.3 (1977), pp. 690–722.

Swerling, B.C. *International Control of Sugar, 1918–41* (Commodity Policy Studies, 7; Stanford, CA: Food Research Institute, 1949).

Syrett, David (ed.). *The Siege and Capture of Havana 1762* (London: Navy Records Society, 1970).

Temperley, Howard. *Britain and America since Independence* (Basingstoke: Palgrave, 2002).

Thomas, G.R. 'Trade and Shipping to Cuba 1961–1963: An Irritant in Anglo–American Relations', doctoral thesis, University of Aberystwyth, 2000.

Thomas, Hugh. *Cuba, or the Pursuit of Freedom* (London: Eyre & Spottiswoode, 1971).

Thompson, Sir Geoffrey. *Front-line Diplomat* (London: Hutchinson, 1959).

Thorpe, D.R. *Supermac: The Life of Harold Macmillan* (London: Chatto & Windus, 2010).

Tilley, Sir John, and Stephen Gaselee. *The Foreign Office* (London: G.P. Putnam's Sons, 1933).

Trask, David F. *The War with Spain in 1898* (New York; London: Macmillan, 1981).

Turnbull, David. *Travels in the West: Cuba; with Notices of Porto Rico, and the Slave Trade* (London: Longman, 1840).

Villaverde, Cirilo. *Cecilia Valdés or El Angel Hill* (Oxford and New York: Oxford University Press, 2005) (Translation from the Spanish by Helen Lane. Novel first published in 1882.)

Ward, J.R. 'The British West Indies in the Age of Abolition, 1748–1815', in *The Oxford History of the British Empire, Volume II: The Eighteenth Century*, ed. P.J. Marshall and Alaine Low (Oxford and New York: Oxford University Press, 1998), pp. 415–39.

Watt, D.C. 'American Strategic Interests and Anxieties in the West Indies', *Journal of the Royal United Service Institution*, 108 (1963), pp. 224–32.

Watt, D.C. 'Demythologising the Eisenhower Era', in *The 'Special Relationship': Anglo–American Relations since 1945*, ed. Roger Louis and Hedley Bull (Oxford: Clarendon Press, 1986), pp. 65–85.

Watt, D.C. *Personalities and Policies: Studies in the Formulation of British Foreign Policy in the Twentieth Century* (London: Longmans, 1965).

Watt, D.C. *Succeeding John Bull: America in Britain's Place, 1900–1975: A Study of the Anglo–American Relationship and World Politics in the Context of British and American Foreign-policy-making in the Twentieth Century* (Cambridge: Cambridge University Press, 1984).

Wells Jr, Samuel F. 'British Strategic Withdrawal from the Western Hemisphere, 1904–1906', *Canadian Historical Journal*, 49 (1968), pp. 335–56.

Wheeler, L.A. 'War and Postwar Agricultural Problems of Latin America', in *Economic Problems of Latin America*, ed. Seymour E. Harris (New York; London: McGraw-Hill, 1944), pp. 69–91.

White, Nicholas J. *Decolonisation: The British Experience since 1945* (Harlow: Longman, 1999).

Whitney, Robert. *State and Revolution in Cuba: Mass Mobilization and Political Change, 1920–1940* (Chapel Hill, NC and London: University of North Carolina Press, 2001).

Wilkinson, Steve. 'Just How Special Is "Special"': Britain, Cuba, and US Relations 1958–2008: An Overview', *Diplomacy & Statecraft*, 20.2 (2009), pp. 291–308.

Williams, Philip M. *Hugh Gaitskell: A Political Biography* (London: Cape, 1979).

Wood, Bryce. *The Making of the Good Neighbor Policy* (New York: Norton, 1961).

Wyden, Peter. *Bay of Pigs: The Untold Story* (London: Cape, 1979).

Young, John W. 'Great Britain's Latin American Dilemma: The Foreign Office and the Overthrow of "Communist" Guatemala, June 1954', *The International History Review*, 8.4 (1986), pp. 573–92.

Zanetti, Oscar, and Alejandro García. *Sugar & Railroads: A Cuban History, 1837–1959* (Chapel Hill and London: University of North Carolina Press, 1998).

Zweiniger-Bargielowska, Ina. *Austerity in Britain: Rationing, Controls, and Consumption, 1939–1955* (Oxford: Oxford University Press, 2000).

Index

blockade, 181; pressures Britain to join blockade, 182; and Cuban missile crisis, 186, 204; commitment not to invade Cuba, 187; agrees to British request for Polaris, 188; on Leyland buses exports, 191, 193

Keynes, John Maynard; as commodities speculator, 71; negotiates for US aid in Second World War, 121

Khrushchev, Nikita; offers to locate missiles in Cuba, 179; agrees to withdraw missiles, 187; objectives when meeting Castro, 258 (n. 56)

Lansdowne, Lord; warnings to Carden from, 37, 40; and German threat, 38; wary of antagonizing Washington, 41

Lee, Arthur; British military attaché during War of Independence (1895–98), 31, 220 (n. 83); friendship with T.R. Roosevelt, 31

Leech, Stephen; judges Cuban views of First World War, 56–7; visit to Washington of, 57; background of, 63

Leyland Motor Company; Thames bus sinking 'accident', 1, 198–9, 212; 1950 bus contract of, 137–8; 1959 bus contract of, 158; negotiations of with Cuban govt, 189; UK inter-departmental views on extending credit to, 189–93; 1964 bus contract signed, 193–4; US–UK reactions to deal of, 194–5

Lindsay, Robert; opinion on British recognition, 90–1; wary of antagonizing US govt, 92, 114

Liverpool; port development of, 20; Chamber of Commerce's actions, 40–1, 44, 46, 47, 48, 223 (nn. 58, 61)

Lloyd, Selwyn, 146; *see also* arms sales (British)

Machado, Gerardo; govt of, 12, 68–9, 76; Capitolio building inaugurated by, 69; flees Cuba, 81–2

Macmillan, Harold; on US hegemony in Latin America, 13, 165; chancellor of exchequer during Suez Crisis, 145; re-establishes amicable UK–US relations, 146; re-elected in 1959, 159; favours arms sales, 160–1; criticizes US hypocrisy on 'colonialism', 165; discusses Cuba with Eisenhower, 166–7; announces new export drive, 168; relationship with Kennedy, 172; informed about Bay of Pigs plan, 174; *see also* CoCom; supporting role of during missile crisis, 186; distrust of Washington, 204

Mahan, Alfred Thayer; naval doctrine of, 24–5; on strategic importance of Cuba, 28–9

Maine, USS; disaster in Havana harbour, 1, 29

Malaysia; UK policy in Cuba linked with, 192, 195, 204

Marchant, Herbert ('Bill'); background of, 170; on burgeoning Cuban–Soviet relations, 172; describes 'Year of Education', 175; involvement during missile crisis, 185, 187; urges rethink of UK trade strategy in Cuba, 188

Mariano Gómez, Miguel; meets Guggenheim, 79; as likely successor to Barnet, 107

Martí, José; writes to British foreign secretary, 2; dies in first combat, 3; invoked by post-1933 generation, 133; centenary of birth, 144

Maudling, Reginald; on US and British Guiana, 165; criticizes FO policy, 176; calls Cuba a US 'problem', 182; supports trade with Soviet Bloc, 190, 191

McKinley, William; and US military intervention in Cuba, 30; assassination of, 38

101; losses in Cuba of, 106;
Cuban govt debts to, 114, 137;
benefitting from wartime
prosperity, 125–6; encroachment
onto property of, 134–5, 137;
efforts by to sell, 137; Cuban govt
nationalization of, 141
United States; twentieth-century
ascendency of, 14, 201;
supervision of Cuba by, 34;
diplomatic appointments to Cuba
of, 70; recognition of Latin
American regimes by, 76–7;
participation in Pan-American
Conference (1928), 69;
participation in Pan-American
Conference (1933), 80, 86–7, 94;
Department of Defense vs State
Department arms sales
disagreement, 147; British views
on US–Latin American relations,
150, 176–7; Wheat to
Soviet Union deal, 193, 194
US–Cuban relations; British views on,
5, 50, 71–4, 82, 85–6, 89, 96, 120,
123–4, 135, 156–7, 162, 167–8,
174, 208; US right of
intervention, 10; ambiguous US
foreign policy, 13–14; US attempts
to purchase Cuba, 21–22; *see also*
Reciprocity Treaty; US military
occupation of island, 32, 36; 1906
military intervention, 49–50;
Cubans' anticipation of US
intervention, 80, 86; US navy
destroyers surround Cuba, 85;
Military Assistance Program
(MAP), 147; US suspends arms
licenses to Cuba, 147–8; Castro's
anti-American rhetoric, 156;
tit-for-tat reprisals, 163, 167;
severing of diplomatic relations,
171–2

Vansittart, Robert, 67; on Cuba-Egypt
parallel, 13; on US intervention,
73; criticizes US recognition

diplomacy, 93–4; criticizes British
embassy in Washington, 96
Veterans' and Patriots' Association, *see*
Carlos García Vélez
Victoria, Queen; death of, 4, 38; *see
also* War of Independence
(1895–98)

Wall Street Crash, 69, 71, 99
War of Independence (Ten Years' War,
1868–78), 22; *Virginius* incident,
22–3, 217 (n. 36)
War of Independence (1895–98),
25–31; Winston Churchill as war
correspondent, 2, 26–7, 212, 218
(n. 56); Queen Victoria's attitude
toward, 25; policy of Prime
Minister Salisbury toward, 25–6;
see also USS *Maine; see also*
concentration camps; US military
intervention, 30–1
Welles, Benjamin Sumner; as F.D.
Roosevelt's adviser on Latin
America, 76; 1933 Pan-American
Conference involvement of, 80,
91; mission in Cuba of, 80;
mediation between Machado and
opposition of, 81; bête noire of
British diplomats, 84; *see also*
Hotel Nacional; meets Batista, 89;
criticism by colleagues
of, 97
Wellesley, Victor; British mission in
Havana inspection of, 62;
reluctant to annoy Washington,
95; criticizes US diplomacy, 96
Wilson, Harold; on US naval blockade
during missile crisis, 186; visits
President Johnson, 197–8;
comments on 'memories of Suez',
198
Wood, Leonard; US military
governor of Cuba, 35–6
Woolf, Sir Henry Drummond;
sympathy with Spain, 27, 30

Zayas, Alfredo, 60, 63, 64;